CRISIS INTERVENTION

THE CRIMINAL JUSTICE RESPONSE TO CHAOS, MAYHEM, AND DISORDER

William M. Harmening

Roosevelt University

Benedictine University

Boston   Columbus   Indianapolis   New York   San Francisco   Upper Saddle River
Amsterdam   Cape Town   Dubai   London   Madrid   Milan   Munich   Paris   Montréal   Toronto
Delhi   Mexico City   São Paulo   Sydney   Hong Kong   Seoul   Singapore   Taipei   Tokyo

Editor in Chief: Vernon Anthony
Acquisitions Editor: Sara Eilert
Assistant Editor: Megan Moffo
Editorial Assistant: Lynda Cramer
Director of Marketing: David Gesell
Marketing Manager: Mary Salzman
Senior Marketing Coordinator: Alicia Wozniak
Project Manager: Holly Shufeldt
Cover Art: Shutterstock
Full-Service Project Management/Composition: PreMediaGlobal
Printer/Binder: Courier/Westford
Cover Printer: Moore Langen

Credits and acknowledgments borrowed from other sources and reproduced, with permission, in this textbook appear on the appropriate page within the text.

Many of the designations by manufacturers and seller to distinguish their products are claimed as trademarks. Where those designations appear in this book, and the publisher was aware of a trademark claim, the designations have been printed in initial caps or all caps.

Library of Congress Cataloging-in-Publication Data
Harmening, William M.
  Crisis intervention: the criminal justice response to chaos, mayhem, and disorder /
  William M. Harmening.
    p. cm.
  Includes bibliographical references and index.
  ISBN-13: 978-0-13-215503-8 (alk. paper)
  ISBN-10: 0-13-215503-6 (alk. paper)
1. Police—United States.   2. Police training—United States.   3. Crisis
management—United States.   I. Title.
  HV8141.H2966 2014
  363.2'3—dc23
                                                        2012038161

10 9 8 7 6 5 4 3 2 1

ISBN 10: 0-13-215503-6
ISBN 13: 978-0-13-215503-8

Dedicated to the Memory and Sacrifice of
Patrolman Robert S. Hester
Memphis Police Department

Final Roll Call: January 12, 1983

BRIEF CONTENTS

TABLE OF CONTENTS

PREFACE

Someone once described police work as 90 percent boredom and 10 percent sheer terror. Although these percentages are open to debate, one thing is certain; the amount of heightened tension experienced by a police officer on the job is proportionate to the amount of *crisis* they are forced to confront. Crisis results when control is lost, either by a single person, a group of people, or in some cases by entire segments of society. It is the primary mission of the police in America, and to a lesser degree its correctional officers, to proactively guard against this loss of control, and to intervene quickly when it's lost or threatened to a significant degree. This type of intervention is indeed a dangerous endeavor. Upwards of 150 U.S. police officers each year die in the line of duty, many while responding to some type of crisis. Invariably they encounter people who have temporarily lost their ability to reason in a rational manner. Some are scared and emotionally drained, others excited to the point of frenzy, and still others agitated and overly aggressive. For the criminal justice professionals who respond, the need for effective training and proven response protocols is critical. Their very lives may depend on either or both.

Crisis is a daily occurrence in every corner of American society. At any given time police officers are responding to domestic violence calls, negotiating the release of hostages, talking down suicidal individuals, and restoring public order following natural disasters. In our prisons, correctional officers are engaged daily in the de-escalation of violent outbursts, ranging from prison yard fights involving only a few inmates to large-scale riots involving the entire prison population. The costs associated with these occurrences are extremely high, both economically and in terms of human capital. It is thus imperative that we continue to explore and study the phenomenon of crisis, in all its varied forms, with the goal of developing programs and strategies that will more effectively promote prevention, self-deterrence, and effective de-escalation. It is neither easy nor ethically acceptable to replicate crisis in a laboratory setting, so to further our understanding we will turn to the very professionals who respond daily to contain and de-escalate every type of crisis one can imagine. The methods and techniques they employ are based on decades of experience and proven success. Some are clearly promulgated in the form of written procedures and protocols, whereas others are general guideline to be followed when an officer is faced with such a unique crisis that some level of improvised response is necessary.

In the chapters to follow we will explore many of these methods and techniques. We will look behind the curtain of police protocol to get a detailed look at the criminal justice response to crisis in its many forms. Some of the issues addressed have seldom found their way onto the pages of a college textbook. They are more the substance of police and correctional training manuals. We will look at the issue of crisis primarily from the perspective of those charged with minimizing its effects, and in the process develop a fuller understanding of the nature and extent of crisis in America, as well as a greater appreciation for the men and women who daily risk their lives maintaining public order and safeguarding the free and open society we all enjoy.

GOALS OF THIS BOOK

The primary goal of this text is to introduce the reader to the phenomenon of crisis, and the various methods and techniques employed by our criminal justice professionals in their efforts to respond to, contain, and de-escalate the various forms of chaos, mayhem, and disorder occurring in America. The major types of crisis will be explored, including causative factors related to each, the various typologies of those involved, and psychosocial factors influencing their onset and escalation. A secondary goal will be to introduce the reader to the psychological effects of crisis on the criminal justice professionals who respond. We will discuss the effects of long-term exposure to trauma, including the diagnostic criteria and treatment of stress-related disorders such as PTSD. A final goal of the text will be to introduce the reader to the various ethical considerations related to crisis response.

INSTRUCTOR SUPPLEMENTS

The following instructor supplements are available for download at the Instructor Resource Center:

- PowerPoint Presentation
- Test Bank with Answer Key

To access supplementary materials online, instructors need to request an instructor access code. Go to www.pearsonhighered.com/irc to register for an instructor access code. Within 48 hours of registering, you will receive a confirming e-mail including an instructor access code. Once you have received your code, go to the site and log on for full instructions on downloading the materials you wish to use.

ALTERNATE VERSION

CourseSmart is an exciting new choice for students looking to save money. As an alternative to purchasing the printed textbook, students can purchase an electronic version of the same content. With a *CourseSmart* eTextbook, students can search the text, make notes online, print out reading assignments that incorporate lecture notes, and bookmark important passages for later review. For more information or to purchase access to the *CourseSmart* eTextbook, visit www.coursesmart.com.

ACKNOWLEDGMENTS

Thank you to the instructors who reviewed this book and provided feedback during the writing process:

- Holly Branthoover, Indiana University of Pennsylvania
- Jeffrey Freiden, the University of Memphis
- Lourdes Smith, Scottsdale Community College
- Constantine Souris, North Shore Community College
- John Schafer, Western Illinois University
- Debbie Skousen, Treasure Valley Community College

ABOUT THE AUTHOR

William Harmening is an adjunct professor of criminal justice at Roosevelt University in Chicago, Illinois, and an adjunct professor of psychology at Benedictine University in Springfield, Illinois. He is also a 30-year police officer who began his career as a deputy sheriff in a rural Illinois county. For the past 20 years he has held various state-level law enforcement positions. In 1998, as a deputy chief of investigations for the Office of the Illinois Attorney General, he founded and commanded Illinois' first statewide high-tech crimes task force and computer forensics lab. Since 2001 he has served as chief special agent for the Illinois Securities Department, where he commands a cadre of special agents tasked with investigating allegations of investment fraud. He is a recognized expert in the area of criminal behavior, and is the author of a widely used textbook on that subject. This is his seventh book. He resides in Springfield, Illinois, and is a graduate of the University of Illinois at Springfield.

1

The Problem of Crisis

LEARNING OUTCOMES

Upon completion of this chapter the student should be able to:

1. Define the phenomenon of crisis.

2. Explain the four-level scheme for classifying crisis.

3. Summarize the history of crisis intervention in America.

4. List the five steps in crisis intervention and summarize the importance of each.

Chapter Outline

INTRODUCTION

THE KATRINA CRISIS: A PERFECT STORM

On August 29, 2005, the levees protecting the city of New Orleans from the rising waters of the Mississippi River and Lake Pontchartrain began to fail under the weight of the storm surge created by Hurricane Katrina's sustained winds. Within hours, 80 percent of the city was under water, and over 400,000 desperate people found themselves homeless and in need of rescue. What followed was one of the saddest episodes in the history of American disaster response, as a crisis of cataclysmic proportion spiraled out of control with seemingly no way to stop it. As the New Orleans Police Department mobilized for its response, scores of officers abandoned their posts and simply quit, some of them trying instead to rescue their own loved ones. The Louisiana National Guard, what should have been the primary agent of social order in the face of such a calamitous event, was in large part deployed to fight two wars in Iraq and Afghanistan, leaving few contingency plans for their primary mission at home. In hospitals and nursing homes, terminally ill patients were left to die for lack of an effective action plan. Some well-intentioned medical personnel even resorted to euthanasia to prevent non-ambulatory patients from suffering a painful death. And outside on the flooded streets, looting, rape, and even murder continued unabated as the city succumbed to mass fear and panic. Even the federal government's response to the crisis seemed paralyzed by its own bureaucracy. With nowhere else to go, people moved either to their rooftops to await rescue, or they trudged through the toxic flood waters toward the perceived refuge of the Superdome. There the conditions became so deplorable and unsanitary that the trauma to those amassed under the wide expanse of its damaged roof only worsened with each passing hour.

When the immediate crisis finally ended a few days later, with over 1800 people dead and well over $80 billion in property damages, this was the costliest disaster in U.S. history (Westlaw News & Insight, 2010). In other parts of the hurricane's destructive path the response was quick and effective. But in New Orleans essentially everything that could have gone wrong, in fact did. Notwithstanding the significant pre-disaster failures in terms of preparedness and planning, the response to the crisis that followed was chaotic and ineffective. In its final report on the matter (H.R. Rep. No. 109-377, 2006), a bipartisan congressional committee concluded that those agencies responding to the crisis were significantly hindered by a lack of training, ineffective command and control, and a lack of situational awareness. Regarding specifically the New Orleans Police Department, the committee concluded that because it lacked any significant plans or protocols for continuity of operations in the event of a major crisis, it quickly lost all effectiveness. Once their command and control apparatus failed, even the police panicked. The result was a complete breakdown in social order and control. Many officers, worried about their own families, simply left their posts and went home. Others stood by while looting and other crimes took place in front of them. The populace, in the midst of its panic, had lost all fear of the police, especially when it became apparent that they, too, were operating in a chaotic fog. With essentially no effective crisis response being made by the police, Katrina had truly become the perfect storm. The quality of the response by local, state, and federal authorities in the days following the disaster was best summed up in the public testimony of one evacuee:

> We were abandoned. City officials did nothing to protect us. We were told to go to the Superdome, the Convention Center, the Interstate Bridge for safety. We did this more than once. In fact, we tried them all every day for over a week. We saw buses, helicopters, and FEMA trucks, but no one stopped to help us. We never felt so cut off in all our lives. When you feel like this you do one of two things, you either give up or go into survival mode. We chose the latter. This is how we made it. We slept next to dead bodies, we slept on streets at least four times next to human feces and urine. There was garbage everywhere in the city. Panic and fear had taken over.

> Patricia Thompson
> *New Orleans Citizen and Evacuee*
> *Select Committee Hearing*
> *December 6, 2005*

The Katrina disaster provides a perfect, albeit sad, example of the absolute necessity for systems, plans, and protocols to be in place and ready to implement following a major crisis in order for responding agencies to maintain control and get the needed help and resources to those affected. When a crisis erupts, those who respond are tasked with *containing* and *de-escalating* the crisis in order to avoid its spread and aggravation. Whether it is a police officer intervening in a spousal dispute, a fireman standing between a brush fire and a line of houses, or a school principal directing the evacuation of her students following a bomb threat, the goal of each is to contain and de-escalate the immediate crisis as quickly as possible.

To facilitate this endeavor, agencies and individuals who respond to a crisis follow predetermined plans and protocols for the type of situation to which they are responding. Effective crisis intervention demands crisis anticipation. By learning from the past, we hope to avoid similar problems when a similar crisis arises in the future. In the case of the police officer, experience tells them that when a husband strikes his wife during a dispute, there is a much greater likelihood of physical violence occurring again in the future. Therefore, the typical protocol for the police in this situation is to first contain the crisis by their physical presence, and then de-escalate the crisis by placing the husband in custody if there are any signs of physical injury to the wife. The same is true when the roles are reversed. Although the judicial system ultimately will be responsible for determining liability and dispensing justice, it is solely the responsibility of the police officer to respond to, contain, and de-escalate the immediate situation.

WHAT IS A CRISIS?

Many academic disciplines study the phenomenon of crisis. It is an issue of interest in the study of sociology, psychology, political science, and criminal justice, to name a few. Unfortunately however, there is no widely accepted definition of crisis. The definitions are as diverse as the disciplines endeavoring to understand its nature and precursory conditions. Most define it in a way that is specific to their field of study. The arborist might define crisis as anything that disrupts the natural growth of trees, such as a disease or a particularly devastating insect. For the political scientist it may be defined in terms of a legislative impasse or a geopolitical conflict. The sociologist may view crisis as a set of deteriorating social conditions that could potentially disrupt the lives of entire groups of people. For the criminologist it could be many things, ranging from civil unrest and rioting to a single individual threatening to kill a spouse or hostages. And for the behavioral scientist, a crisis may be a schizophrenic or depressed patient's particularly bad episode. In each of these definitions there are two common themes; a loss of **equilibrium**, or the balance of opposing forces within a system, and the need for some type of **intervention** to restore the system to a state of equilibrium.

We live in a world of order. Nature itself is ordered in a particular way to preserve its various ecosystems. The animal kingdom is ordered to preserve the necessary food chains to ensure the survival of the strongest species. And people exist within the restrictions of a particular social order for the purpose of avoiding chaos and preserving their very existence. The survival of any one of these systems is dependent on maintaining a state of equilibrium, or a balance of opposing forces within the system. For example, any free society is forced to balance what is best for the individual with what is best for society as a whole. Equilibrium is maintained when individual rights are allowed expression to the fullest extent possible without disrupting the existing social order. When it reaches a point where the exercise of individual rights begins to disrupt the social order, then equilibrium is maintained by restricting those rights. In American society nothing is held more sacred than the right to the free exercise of speech. The ability to say what is on our collective minds helps to maintain the social order by allowing the citizenry the opportunity to openly criticize and question our government officials, and by disseminating information critical to maintaining an open and free society. However, if that speech were to become focused on inciting riots and the overthrow of the government by use of force, then the right to free speech must be regulated or even restricted in order to maintain a state of social equilibrium.

For the individual, equilibrium is also maintained. All of us endeavor to balance our lives in order to avoid stress. We attempt to maintain a situation where the positives in our lives equal or outweigh the negatives. When we can get through the day without feeling a lasting and uncomfortable stress, then we can say we have successfully maintained a sense of equilibrium. We attempt to do this economically, physically, psychologically, and emotionally. If a circumstance disrupts our sense of equilibrium, then stress and anxiety will result. When an intoxicated husband comes home and gets verbally abusive toward his wife, her sense of equilibrium is disrupted. In most cases, the wife is able on her own to return to a state of equilibrium by various means, including just going to bed and ignoring her intoxicated husband. But in the more extreme cases, especially where physical violence erupts, equilibrium cannot be regained without intervention by a third party, which in this case would be the police. So for purposes of this text, we will define crisis as

> any event in which our systems of control, both internal and external, become stressed to the point of dysfunction, requiring third-party intervention to regain control and return those systems to a state of equilibrium.

Internal systems of control include primarily our cognitive and emotional coping mechanisms. When an individual experiencing extreme stress or depression threatens suicide, it is an acute crisis that must be de-escalated immediately. It represents a breakdown in the internal systems of control that allow us to maintain a state of emotional equilibrium. In contrast, the looting and rampant crime that oftentimes follows a natural disaster represents a breakdown in the **external systems of control** designed to maintain public order. Both situations can be described as a **crisis**, and certainly both require containment and de-escalation by third-party responders. In the more extreme occurrences, containment is necessary in order to prevent the crisis from spreading quickly to other systems of control and populations of people. For instance, a riot must be contained to prevent it from spreading not only to other geographic areas, but also to the impressionable sentiments of other people who may decide to join in and exacerbate the situation.

It can be said that a civilized society is one in which crisis is controlled. Nearly all societies intervene in crisis for the good of the social order or the ruling class; however, free and progressive societies also intervene in individual crisis for the good of the individual, and thus preserve the moral obligation a free and open society has to its citizens. The good of the social order is viewed as being preserved by insuring the good of the individual. To this desired end, our system is replete with **crisis responders**, or those who are tasked with containing and de-escalating a crisis at the earliest stage possible. We have police officers, firemen, paramedics, suicide hotline workers, disaster agencies, and a host of volunteer networks such as the Red Cross, all tasked with responding to a particular type of crisis for the purpose of preserving the social order and ensuring the welfare of its citizens.

As our definition implies, crisis can occur on many different levels, each necessitating a different mix of resources and response methodologies in order to contain and de-escalate the emergency. Some crises can effectively be dealt with by a single police officer, while others may require significantly more resources, up to and including military intervention. The level of resources needed depends on the level of crisis being responded to, and the extent to which the crisis may spread to and affect other systems within the larger social framework. This is why public policy and preparedness is so critical, especially in the event of a larger catastrophic crisis such as Hurricane Katrina. The resources needed for a crisis must be anticipated before the onset of the crisis; otherwise, chaos follows. In New Orleans entire parking lots full of buses, critical resources that could have been used to evacuate thousands of people, remained parked and unused for lack of an effective plan that anticipated their need.

Classification of Crisis

The first step in effective crisis planning is to classify crisis in a way that will facilitate an effective response by guiding the anticipation, commitment, and positioning of resources. A classification system provides a conceptual framework within which crisis can be understood in relative terms. We classify hurricanes for this very purpose. If a category 4 hurricane is approaching landfall, it gives us a clear indication of its potential destructive power, and guides our decisions regarding the evacuation of people in its path. A classification system further guides our development of public policy and protocols, and may even serve as a funding guide. And finally, a classification system facilitates the study of crisis by allowing us to focus our research efforts on a few predominant types, each with similar variables that distinguish it from the others, rather than attempting to sort through the literally thousands of specific crises that may occur at any given time in our collective field of experience.

BRONFENBRENNER'S ECOLOGICAL SYSTEMS THEORY   To classify crisis, we can turn to the Ecological Systems Theory of **Urie Bronfenbrenner** (1980). A professor of psychology at Cornell University, and a co-founder of the *Head Start* Program under President Lyndon Johnson, Bronfenbrenner looked at child development as occurring through the collective influence of multiple different systems on the child's experience. Bronfenbrenner proposed four such systems, and later a fifth, to account for psychosocial development.

The **microsystem** is the confluence of factors in a child's immediate environment, primarily the parents and siblings that influence the child's psychosocial development. This system also includes the child's peers, and the influences of both church and school. Each is considered a microsystem because of its direct contact with the child, and thus its direct influence on the child's development. It is the most important system to a child's development, and thus when a crisis occurs in any part of this system it can be particularly devastating to a developing child.

Bronfenbrenner's second system is the **mesosystem**, or the interaction of various microsystems that together shape a child's development. For example, the negative dynamics of a child's home environment, a microsystem, can potentially have a negative influence on the child's academic performance at school, another microsystem. So the mesosystem represents a confluence of microsystems in the child's life, and the developmental influences and pressures that result from the interaction of these microsystems. Whereas a microsystem influences directly, a mesosystem is a more abstract connection where microsystems are allowed to influence indirectly another part of the person's development or life. Even as adults we experience such influences in our daily lives. If we have an especially heated argument with our spouse before going off to work, there is little doubt that our job performance will be negatively impacted by the lingering emotion of the argument. In this case one microsystem (the spouse) indirectly influences another microsystem (the job). If the result then is that we are disciplined for poor job performance, an especially stressful event, we can say that the underlying cause of this new stress is a mesosystem dynamic.

Bronfenbrenner's third system is the **exosystem**, or those influences beyond the child's immediate environment that impact their development indirectly. Unlike the mesosystem, where each component of the system is a separate microsystem with a direct connection to the child, an exosystem is one step removed from the child. An example might be the workplace of one of the parents. If circumstances are such that the parent comes home each night frustrated and demoralized, then that in turn will impact the quality of that parent's interaction with the child. So even though the child has no connection to the parent's workplace, it still impacts the child's life in an indirect way. Another example might be the local school board. Although in most cases a school board has little contact with the students, it does set policy for the school, which in turn serves as a microsystem in the child's development due to its direct contact with the child. So if the school board adopts a zero-tolerance policy for inappropriate behavior, and we have a child who displays inappropriate acting-out behaviors due to a dysfunctional home environment, then indirectly the school board is impacting the child's life by causing the child to be subjected to a harsher and more immediate system of discipline. The school board then becomes an exosystem that applies its own influence and pressure on the child's development.

And finally, according to Bronfenbrenner's original formulation, there is a **macrosystem**, which represents the outer layer of influences on a child's development. The macrosystem is composed of cultural values and customs, and also the laws and social expectations which guide our lives. A macrosystem impacts the child's development by flowing downward and influencing all other systems within the child's experience. In a diverse society, ethnicity is a macrosystem that can greatly impact the child. For example, minority populations tend to have lower levels of income and education in America. They tend to populate the urban areas, where educational resources are more significantly stressed. Consequently, minority schools have less qualified teachers, less technology, less parental involvement, and greater levels of fear and anxiety in students who are forced to live and attend school in neighborhoods where crime is ever present. In this case, the child's ethnicity is a macrosystem that impacts their opportunity for a quality education, and thus it has a significant impact on their psychosocial development, a circumstance with lifelong implications.

A FOUR-LEVEL CLASSIFICATION SCHEME   We can adapt Bronfenbrenner's model to the study of crisis. One major difference concerns directionality. Bronfenbrenner looked at the ability of systems to influence a child's development. In his model, developmental influences that are external to the child move *inward* to intersect with the child's experience. In looking at crisis, however, we look at the ability of an isolated crisis event to move *outward* and impact other previously unaffected systems if not contained. We can begin by categorizing crisis as follows:

• *Microcrisis:* A crisis event that at the outset is limited to a single individual or family and their immediate environment. The person threatening suicide, the domestic dispute between husband and wife, and the destruction of a family's home by fire are all examples of a **microcrisis**. The potential for the crisis to spread is minimal. Few other systems are impacted, and those that are tend to be other systems in the immediate experience of the person or persons involved in the crisis (i.e., family and friends). Containment and de-escalation are typically carried out with relative ease by those trained to respond to the particular type of crisis, preventing it from spreading to previously unaffected parties or systems.

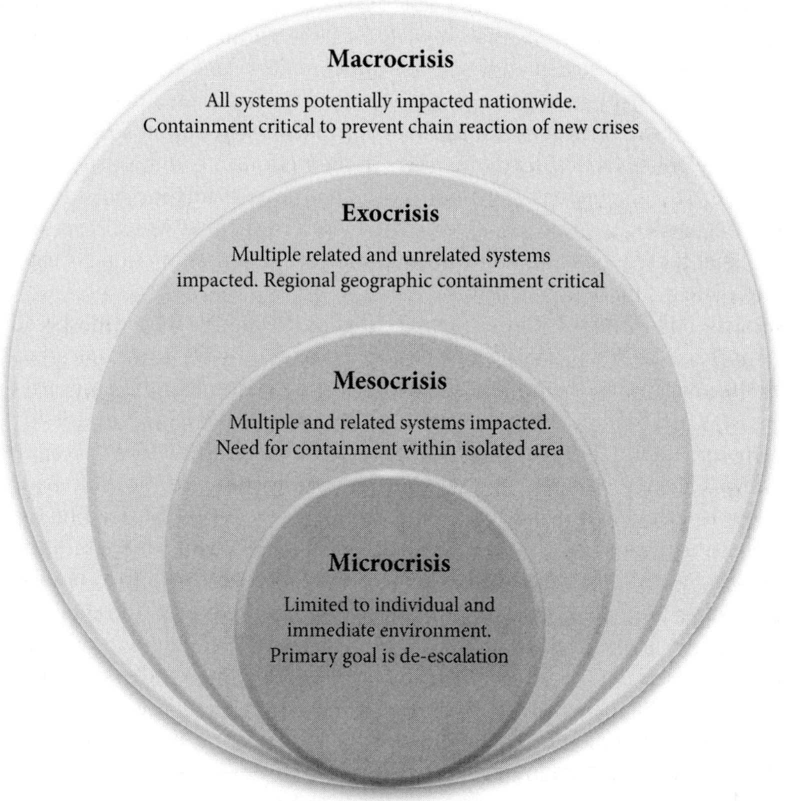

Macrocrisis

All systems potentially impacted nationwide.
Containment critical to prevent chain reaction of new crises

Exocrisis

Multiple related and unrelated systems
impacted. Regional geographic containment critical

Mesocrisis

Multiple and related systems impacted.
Need for containment within isolated area

Microcrisis

Limited to individual and
immediate environment.
Primary goal is de-escalation

FIGURE 1.1 Four-Level Crisis Classification Scheme.

We can return to the example of a domestic dispute to illustrate how a crisis may be elevated if not contained. In most cases a domestic dispute is a microcrisis. Only the participants are parties to the crisis, including family and friends who may be present, and there is very little chance of the crisis spreading beyond this group. Containment in this case is directed at preventing the crisis to worsen within this same group. If the domestic dispute were to take place in a bar, then the potential exists, especially with the presence of alcohol, for the crisis to spread, as previously unaffected individuals suddenly become participants. Other women, as well as men, may come to the aid of the woman in the dispute. Friends of the bar's owner may become aggressive toward both of the participants, and when they do friends of the participants may reciprocate. Suddenly, what began as a microcrisis now begins to spread to others, and containment becomes critically more important when the police arrive.

• *Mesocrisis:* This type of crisis carries with it the potential to spread and impact others unless contained. In our previous example of the domestic dispute inside a bar, it is hoped that the police will arrive in time to prevent this microcrisis from spreading. If it hasn't, then containment is relatively easy. If the worst has happened and previously unaffected people are now taking sides and becoming aggressive toward each other, our microcrisis has suddenly become a **mesocrisis**, and containment by the police becomes increasingly more difficult and necessary.

Another example of a mesocrisis is a school shooting, such as the one at Columbine High School in April 1999. It was a crisis that impacted a large number of people, but it had the potential for impacting many more had the police not contained and de-escalated the situation. It can be argued that this happened quite naturally with the self-inflicted deaths of the two young assailants; however, it was later determined that the two chose to commit suicide only after being surrounded by the police tactical team members in their effort to contain the crisis. A microcrisis such as a domestic dispute between spouses seldom impacts anyone outside the immediate experience of the parties involved; however, a mesocrisis is one that will spread unless stopped. It is necessary that those who respond do so with the goal of containment before any efforts are made to de-escalate the matter.

- *Exocrisis:* Following the Rodney King verdict in 1990, there were widespread riots in the city of Los Angeles. This is an example of an **exocrisis**. Not only were multiple people, families, and institutions impacted in the immediate area, but the disaster had the potential to spread to other areas had it not been contained. What distinguishes it from a mesocrisis is its ability to impact systems and interactions between systems that are far removed from the actual crisis. For example, the riots had the potential to exacerbate the already tense relationship between the Los Angeles Police Department and the city's minority populations, possibly leading to a new crisis. It had the potential for causing a crisis to erupt between the residents of the minority neighborhoods affected in East L.A. and the Korean shop owners who were willing to use deadly force to protect their properties. And it certainly had the ability to affect even those far removed from the crisis by causing city officials to reallocate resources and tax dollars to rebuild the affected areas. Whereas a mesocrisis has the ability to spread to other people and systems within its path, an exocrisis has the ability to spread even to people and systems that have no direct contact with the immediate crisis. Thus, containment and de-escalation become more far-reaching, and may extend well beyond the crisis at hand.

- *Macrocrisis:* Even though an exocrisis tends to be limited to a particular region, when the impact of the crisis has the potential to spread to other regions, or even around the world, then it can be described as a **macrocrisis**. Certainly the events of September 11, 2001, represent such a crisis. The fallout from those events impacted the entire world to varying degrees, and caused a chain reaction of crises that required the concerted efforts of many different agencies to contain. Airports were shut down, communication became difficult, and the emotional trauma that resulted consumed people all over the world. A macrocrisis invariably causes a chain reaction of events, and without containment the situation will only worsen significantly in a short period of time. The impact of a worsening macrocrisis will be felt politically, economically, and logistically. It will spiral out of control without a major containment effort on a number of different fronts. Certainly the Hurricane Katrina disaster was a macrocrisis. Gas prices shot up, there were shortages of building materials, the price of many commodities began to rise, there was political fallout that only widened the ideological chasm that exists between America's political parties, and hundreds of thousands of refugees suddenly appeared in cities around the South and the Midwest in need of housing and sustenance.

Our scheme for categorizing crisis allows us to look at any specific crisis in terms of the degree to which containment and de-escalation are needed. At the low end of the spectrum, the microcrisis, these activities are typically limited to the event itself, and may be carried out at times even by a single responder, such as a police officer responding to a domestic dispute or juvenile problem. At the high end is the macrocrisis, where containment and de-escalation extend far beyond the crisis itself, and may include the need to intervene proactively in systems with no connection at all to the actual crisis. The response is multimodal and, on many different fronts, in order to keep the crisis from spiraling out of control and causing a domino effect to occur. In the case of the September 11th terrorist attacks, essentially every major institution in American society responded in some manner. The stock markets, some of which were mere blocks from Ground Zero, closed to prevent a financial catastrophe. The banking system initiated emergency procedures to protect itself from a panic-driven run on deposits. And the entirety of our transportation infrastructure and power grid went on high alert to prevent additional attacks. The psychology of that day posed perhaps the greatest danger to American society, and many steps were taken across the country to contain, and then de-escalate the panic. Short of warfare, it was the most dangerous type of macrocrisis because unlike a hurricane, for example, the aftermath was unpredictable. We barely knew the source of the attack or if more attacks were imminent. The collective fear of the unknown that day caused an anxiety in the American people the likes of which had not been experienced since the attack on Pearl Harbor in December of 1941.

To get a clear sense of the modern structure of America's crisis response apparatus, which includes both public and private components, we will look at the historical development of crisis response in America, from the time of our nation's birth forward.

A HISTORY OF CRISIS INTERVENTION

The Whiskey Rebellion of 1794

Crisis intervention in America began shortly after the end of the Revolutionary War when President George Washington mobilized a force of militia to quell an uprising in western Pennsylvania by farmers upset with a newly imposed tariff on whiskey that all but eliminated their profits from farming. Because of the logistical difficulties of getting their crops to market, the distance and poor roads chief among them, many of these farmers took to fermenting and distilling their excess grain into whiskey to be sold or bartered for needed supplies. For most it was a profitable venture that more than made up for the heavy cost of transporting their grain to markets east of the Alleghenies. The distilled spirits could more easily be transported to the eastern population centers, and good whiskey was always in high demand. It was an ideal situation that allowed the farmers to maximize their profits with little grain going to waste.

Following the imposition of the whiskey tax in 1791, groups of protestors from western Pennsylvania began to riot and attack tax collectors throughout the territory. Those east of the Allegheny Mountains were more open to the idea of the federal government's primacy over the states, including its taxing authority; however, those west of the mountains took a more separatist view. Additionally, the tax was seen as terribly unfair, and skewed against the smaller farmers in the west. Although the larger whiskey producers, including Washington, could enjoy a flat-fee tax on their whiskey production, the smaller producers were taxed by the gallon, resulting in a much larger tax burden. This outraged the smaller producers and sparked the revolt that followed. Eventually civil protests turned to armed rebellion, with the protestors even threatening an assault on Pittsburg. As the insurgency grew in numbers, mail carriers were robbed, judges threatened, and tax collectors attacked and beaten.

The problems reached a crescendo in July 1794 when insurgents attacked a federal marshal, and a group of several hundred others burned down a regional inspector's home in Allegheny County. The increase in violence prompted President Washington to issue a proclamation mobilizing nearly 13,000 militiamen into action. It was the first use of the Militia Law of 1792, which asserted the federal government's right to suppress insurrections with federalized troops, regardless of which states those troops were from. The mobilized force, under the command of General Harry Lee, father of Robert E. Lee, marched into western Pennsylvania in October of 1794 with Washington himself riding at the head, and quickly ended the revolt without firing a shot.

The Whiskey Rebellion of 1794 represented the first time America had used military force against its own citizens for the purpose of containing and de-escalating a crisis. Washington recognized the danger to the young nation if the rebellion were allowed to spread, especially to other anti-federalist regions. It became imperative to contain the crisis, and then to de-escalate it by arresting the insurgent leaders and forcing the farmers to return to their homes. In the interest of national unity, and to further de-escalate the tension, Washington handed out presidential pardons to the convicted insurgents. The move marked a peaceful resolution to what could have been a deadly and protracted macrocrisis for the young republic. Containment and de-escalation had worked.

Throughout the early years of the nineteenth century a number of crises erupted that necessitated the involvement of the militia. Most were the result of a volatile confluence of social circumstances, particularly in the population centers along the eastern seaboard. As the population grew in numbers and diversity, and with the nation's obsession with wealth accumulation motivating people to achieve financial independence at whatever price, the social stratification of the populace began to take shape. These new tensions were only exacerbated by the political and religious anxieties of the day. In places like Boston, New York, Philadelphia, and Charleston, disorder was commonplace as people resorted to violence as a means of resolving differences. Crisis would invariably lead to more crisis until eventually the militia would be called in to suppress the violence. It was containment and de-escalation by force.

Perhaps no city suffered more from this unchecked violence than Baltimore, Maryland. A relatively new city, Baltimore's political leaders faced a constant struggle in keeping its diverse and fast-growing populace under control. By the beginning of the eighteenth century its population had ballooned to 63,000, trailing only New York and Philadelphia in size. It had gained the reputation of a city where public disorder was the rule, and where riots were commonplace as a preferred means of registering grievances or settling disputes. One of the city's worst outbreaks of rioting occurred in 1812 when a group of citizens attacked a newspaper editor who had expressed in his paper his opposition to the War of 1812. Friends of the editor came to his aid, and before it was over, one of America's worst outbreaks of violence up to that point had taken place. People were shot, others burned alive, and one friend of the editor, none other than General Harry Lee, the very commander of the militia force sent to quell the Whiskey Rebellion, was beaten and left for dead. Once again the militia was called to duty to contain and de-escalate the growing crisis.

Sir Robert Peel and the Birth of Modern Policing in 1829

The need for a new way of dealing with the problem of crisis was not unique to America in the early part of the nineteenth century. England, too, especially in the city of London, was suffering the effects of overcrowding, social stratification, and rampant crime. Although a military force could effectively suppress public disorder, it was ineffective as a means of dealing with the problem of crime or the individual crises of the citizenry. What was needed was a new type of proactive force that could quickly respond to contain and de-escalate a crisis, and in many cases by its very presence actually deter a crisis from ever occurring. The militia, and its English equivalent, which many times was a private army tasked with protecting only the interests of the person paying its wages, carried out their duties in larger units under a centralized command structure. What was needed was a smaller unit, even individual members acting alone who could respond to a crisis quickly, and who would have the authority to contain and de-escalate a crisis through the power of arrest and detention if needed.

The idea of establishing a separate *police force* to maintain public order began in 1829 when **Sir Robert Peel** introduced legislation to establish the London Metropolitan Police Department, the world's first modern police force. The major goal of Peel's force was to have a mechanism in place for responding to crime and disorder without resorting to military intervention. Additionally, by having police officers routinely patrol the streets of London, always diligent in their efforts to spot the ne'er-do-wells or a burgeoning crisis, a secondary but no less important goal became proactive intervention before either caused innocent people to be victimized. For the first time, crisis intervention had moved from the domain of the military to that of a civilian authority.

In America, the establishment of police departments in Boston (1838), New York (1844), and Philadelphia (1854) soon followed. The age of modern policing was in full bloom. Crisis intervention, at least in terms of public disorder and crime, had progressed to a new level. It was no longer enough to simply contain and de-escalate a crisis, as the militia had effectively done. With such a growing and diverse population, it became necessary for the government to take steps to prevent crisis. The combination of newly codified criminal statutes, and police departments with the authority to actively enforce those statutes, were the tools government would now use to maintain public order. By violating the codified rules, people ran the risk of receiving some type of punishment that commensurate with their crimes, up to and including the loss of their freedom for a significant number of years, or even the loss of their lives.

Establishment of the Red Cross in 1881

Although this new type of crisis intervention was effective as a means of dealing with the problem of crime, it was not necessarily designed to address the mass public disorder that invariably follows a disaster without quick intervention. With cities becoming overcrowded and compacted with people living atop one another, natural disasters, fires, and endemic disease had the effect of causing widespread panic. And the more people panicked, the more they resorted to violence to secure needed sustenance. The police were neither trained nor equipped to deal with such a crisis. Once again, the only viable means of containing and de-escalating mass disorder was through military intervention.

In 1881, **Clara Barton** and her associates turned the page on a new chapter in crisis intervention when they established the **American Red Cross**. For the first time, an organization responded to crisis not for the purpose of containment and de-escalation, not even to take steps to prevent a similar crisis from happening in the future. The goal of the Red Cross was to remediate a crisis by offering services to alleviate the hardships of those suffering the effects of the crisis. Whether it was war, natural or man-made disasters, or public disorder, the Red Cross responded quickly to provide food, shelter, and medical treatment for those in need. The Red Cross was not equipped to contain or de-escalate a major crisis, but what they were in a position to do was to help avoid further crisis by addressing the needs of those who potentially could riot or perpetrate disorder out of panic or personal need.

The Red Cross responded to its first disaster in September 1881 by assisting in relief efforts for victims of a series of deadly Michigan forest fires. In May 1889, the Red Cross responded to floods in Johnstown, Pennsylvania, that took the lives of nearly two thousand individuals. And in February 1896, they took on an international mission when they arrived in Constantinople to bring relief to Armenian victims of Turkish oppression. With chapters springing up across the country, crisis intervention was moving into the domain of volunteerism and a mission of remediation. As America took giant leaps into the modern world, leaving in its wake many thousands stranded hopelessly in poverty and deplorable living conditions, a social conscience began to take root, as non-governmental agencies like the Red Cross carried out their critical missions and contributed significantly to maintaining social order in the aftermath of catastrophic events.

The Federal Emergency Management Agency (FEMA), 1979

In the 1960s and '70s America suffered a number of major catastrophes. There were Hurricanes Carla, Betsy, and Camille, all between 1962 and 1969, and major earthquakes in Alaska and California. Additionally, there were a number of major fires. In all, nearly 100 different federal agencies had a hand in responding to the major crises of that time. Many states had similar agencies, causing extreme redundancy and a lack of efficiency. In 1979, President Jimmy Carter signed Executive Order 12127, which merged many of the federal agencies tasked with disaster response into the newly formed **Federal Emergency Management Agency (FEMA)**. This new agency placed much emphasis not only on response and remediation, but also on preparedness for major disasters. Thus another important component of the crisis intervention continuum was now in place, that of *prevention*. FEMA took steps to warn people when an impending disaster was on the horizon. In addition to working alongside the Red Cross to remediate a crisis, FEMA endeavored to respond even before the event happened in order to put needed supplies and protocols in place. As a government agency, FEMA is able to work side by side with law enforcement and the military to help maintain public order in the least intrusive way possible.

MODERN CRISIS INTERVENTION

One of the outcomes of a professional law enforcement apparatus was an expanding prison population. As prisons became overpopulated with predominantly minority inmates, many of whom were sent there by a skewed justice system, a new type of crisis emerged, the prison riot. This type of crisis called for a new type of intervention. Containment was not the issue, but de-escalation became critical because there were usually hostages taken. Following the deadly response at Attica State Prison in New York in 1971, a crisis in which 39 people were killed, 10 of them guards, new intervention techniques and methods were developed inside the prison walls to de-escalate a crisis without the loss of life. New methods for housing and moving prison populations were developed to avoid having prisoners congregate in sufficient numbers to carry out a riot. New prisons were designed with the safety of prison personnel in mind. And in the event of hostages being taken, new techniques were developed to negotiate their safe release, or, in the event that their physical safety became jeopardized, to carry out a tactical response in an effort to save them.

Today, with the progress of modern technology, police departments are able to respond to crisis in a number of effective ways, depending on the nature of the crisis. They have established new ways of containing and de-escalating a crisis with as little loss of life as possible. They have received training in mental health issues, suicide prevention, hostage negotiation, and riot control, all designed with the dual goals of containment and de-escalation in mind. They receive regular training in the use of force, and routinely employ new non-lethal methods of responding to and containing a crisis without resorting to the use of deadly force. They have established protocols with volunteer and other governmental agencies to work together when a crisis erupts. The days of the stereotypic beat cop wielding his nightstick and de-escalating crisis through force, with little interest in remediation, are long over in America. With the move toward professionalization that occurred during the latter part of the 1970s, America's law enforcement apparatus has become more attuned to the need for a seamless partnership with the communities they police. They have learned that proactive measures and those geared toward remediation ultimately will reduce crime and crisis, and increase the level of safety for both the police and the public.

Since the days of the Whiskey Rebellion, America has always endeavored to limit the effects of crisis on its citizens. To get to where we are now, with our modern techniques and systems, was not an especially smooth journey. Along the way we have had many examples where our efforts to contain and de-escalate a crisis failed, not the least of which was the response to Hurricane Katrina. And to that we can add the riot at Attica Prison in 1971, the shootings at Kent State University in 1970, the Democratic National Convention in Chicago in 1968, the L.A. riots of 1992, and many others; all examples of a lack of effective intervention, and all examples of how a crisis not properly contained and de-escalated can quickly spiral out of control and lead to an unnecessary loss of life.

The Crisis Intervention Continuum

When we speak of crisis intervention we are referring to the process of returning individuals, entities, and systems affected by crisis to a state of equilibrium. In our modern society a secondary but equally important goal is to remediate the damage caused by crisis. And finally, a third important goal is to conserve and maximize the efficient allocation of resources by preventing a similar crisis from happening again in the future. Regardless of who maintains responsibility for responding to any particular crisis, or at what point in the intervention their efforts begin, the underlying goals are the same: response, containment, de-escalation, remediation, and prevention. It is at various points along this crisis intervention continuum where resources are allocated in a coordinated effort to successfully complete each of these critical tasks.

FIGURE 1.2 **The Five Steps of Crisis Intervention.**

The combined goals of response, containment, and de-escalation rest with those individuals and entities whose primary duty is to respond to crisis as soon as possible after its reported onset. These are among the most critical, and at times most dangerous tasks associated with crisis intervention because invariably first responders enter the scene while the crisis is still in progress, and perhaps still gaining in intensity. First responders include the police, firemen, and emergency medical personnel. Their primary role is to first contain and then de-escalate the emergency, with the former being necessary in most cases in order for the latter to be successfully accomplished.

Containment of a crisis involves stopping the immediate emergency from worsening, and preventing it from spreading to other people, entities, or systems. The classic example of this dynamic is the police response to a domestic disturbance between spouses. Every police officer knows that the most critical first step in such a response is to contain the crisis, in this case a microcrisis, by separating the parties involved. Once they are separated, then the task is to de-escalate the crisis by calming the parties down, or by affecting an arrest if there is evidence of physical violence. The danger for the police officer is when an attempt is made to de-escalate without first containing the disturbance, typically the result of the officer attempting to handle the situation without sufficient backup. In this case the crisis may spread rapidly to involve even the officer, causing the officer to suddenly find themselves in a physical struggle with one or both of the combatants. Sadly, many police officers have lost their lives in this manner. To attempt to de-escalate a crisis without first containing it is tantamount to jumping into a moving vehicle. Firemen know there is no way to de-escalate a wildfire without first containing it in some manner, typically with fire lines and counter-fires. The fire is then de-escalated by dropping tons of water from airplanes and helicopters, or by simply allowing it to burn itself out.

Effective containment therefore prevents the crisis from spreading and allows the first responder to then **de-escalate** the matter, thus bringing it to an end and returning the parties involved to a state of equilibrium. One is of little value without the other. There have been well-publicized cases of containment without de-escalation. The L.A. riots following the Rodney King verdict are a good example. The LAPD made the decision to simply contain the crisis by setting up a perimeter beyond which they would not allow the crisis to spread. Unfortunately, inside the perimeter they made little effort to de-escalate the crisis for a period of time. In the end, unchecked violence in the impacted area resulted in 54 deaths and hundreds of millions of dollars in property damage. Although the lack of containment and de-escalation in New Orleans following Hurricane Katrina was unavoidable due to the chaotic conditions and lack of planning, the LAPD made the purposeful decision not to de-escalate the riots when they arguably could have. The result was unnecessary death and destruction, and allegations of institutional racism as the mostly minority neighborhoods impacted by the riot succumbed to their self-immolation while the police stood by and watched.

We previously mentioned the shootings at Columbine High School. Although the police were criticized for what some perceived as a slow response, in fact they were doing what they were trained to do in order to effectively contain and de-escalate the situation. Had the patrol officers who arrived on the scene simply stormed the premises without first containing the crisis by establishing a perimeter, then the shooters could potentially have escaped and killed even more people, or they could have killed the ill-prepared police officers who would have been attempting to de-escalate without sufficient tactical knowledge of the situation. Instead, the police established an immediate perimeter and began to quickly develop a tactical response plan based on the intelligence they were able to gather from multiple sources. The perimeter they established effectively eliminated the possibility of escape. And by returning fire at every opportunity, it greatly reduced the ability of the assailants to shoot from the windows at students and school personnel running from the building.

Had the police officers at Columbine simply set up a perimeter to contain the situation without an effort to de-escalate, the two no doubt would have killed many more inside. It was later reported by survivors that the two boys were considering using their knives to start stabbing kids. In an effort to de-escalate the situation as quickly as possible, tactical officers entered the premises once a plan was developed and began seeking out the shooters in a controlled and methodical manner. When the two young offenders saw the tactical team approaching they killed themselves, thus ending the immediate crisis. It wasn't a perfect plan perhaps, but given the police training and methods of the day, and the fact that there simply is not a more dangerous and difficult situation than an "active shooter" with an arsenal of bombs and weapons—at the time, the police believed there to be as many as eight shooters in the school—it was at worst an imperfect plan that was executed to the best of their ability. Ultimately the actions of the police that day saved lives. In the chapters to follow we will discuss in more detail the changes in police training and methods that have taken place since the tragedy at Columbine High School, specifically those relating to active shooters and the need in some instances to de-escalate a crisis in a particular manner without first containing it.

Perhaps no situation in recent memory better illustrates the containment/de-escalation dynamic than America's response to the events on September 11, 2001. On that day literally thousands of individuals moved quickly to contain the crisis. Before the public even knew for sure what was happening, government personnel were already on the move. Many public officials, primarily legislators, were quickly moved underground to safer locations. The president and his advisors were flown to an undisclosed location far away from Washington D.C. Jet fighters took to the air to intercept and, if necessary, shoot down other planes that had been hijacked. Our embassies around the world were put on high alert. Airports and transportation hubs were shut down. And on the ground in Washington D.C. and New York City thousands of police, firefighters, and emergency medical personnel moved quickly to establish perimeters and command centers in an effort to contain a crisis of catastrophic proportions. In the initial hours following the attacks, containment was all that could be attempted. Preventing the situation from getting worse was the goal; keeping more people from getting injured or killed, keeping more buildings from catching fire and collapsing, preventing looting and violence, and protecting the water, power, and transportation systems from being caught up in a domino effect. It was a catastrophe that could easily have spread its way clear across the country had it not been contained.

Once it became apparent that the attacks were in fact over and the crisis contained, de-escalation became the goal. Fires had to be extinguished and people rescued, thousands had to be evacuated in an orderly manner from the affected areas, the police had to restrict access to significant portions of both cities, and communication systems were established for people to track down their loved ones. The president, in a commendable act, attempted to de-escalate the collective fear of the American people by personally going to Ground Zero of the attacks and vowing to retaliate against those responsible. And from one end of the country to the other private individuals, volunteer organizations, corporations, and government agencies took the necessary steps to de-escalate the crisis, in this case a macrocrisis, and return the country to a much-needed state of equilibrium.

Once a crisis is sufficiently contained and de-escalated, then those activities related to remediating the crisis can occur. In the case of the individual threatening suicide, **remediation** may involve an involuntary commitment for psychiatric evaluation and services. At Columbine High School remediation involved bringing in counselors to assist traumatized students and teachers. In the case of the L.A. riots it included rebuilding the buildings that had been damaged or destroyed, and bringing to justice those responsible for the crisis. When those who respond to crisis suffer the effects of emotional trauma, remediation occurs in the form of critical incident debriefings and follow-up services. Some agencies, such as the Red Cross and the Salvation Army, are specifically tasked with crisis remediation. They are there to alleviate pain and suffering once the crisis has been sufficiently de-escalated. They may provide food and shelter, medical services, transportation, or even job training to begin life anew.

Why is remediation a necessary component of the crisis intervention continuum? There is both a philosophical and practical reason. Philosophically, remediation is the moral obligation of any free society that espouses such foundational principles as life, liberty, and the pursuit of happiness. We endeavor not only to stop the harmful effects of crisis and return those affected to a state of equilibrium, but out of an altruistic concern for our fellow citizens we take steps to ease their pain and suffering in an effort to return them to their pre-crisis condition, at least to the extent possible. Practically speaking however, we endeavor to remediate crisis in order to avoid further crisis. The lack of remediation after the Katrina disaster only prolonged the crisis. Even today, nearly half a decade later, people in New Orleans who were most impacted by the crisis are still fighting to get acceptable housing and assistance to rebuild their lives. Without acceptable remediation the resulting frustration can easily boil over and lead to a new crisis in need of containment and de-escalation. It may be violent protests or riots born out of the frustration of disaffection or alienation, or perhaps a completed suicide by someone for whom no remediation was made available, but eventually the lingering effects of the crisis will become manifest unless steps are taken to remediate them.

The final stop on the crisis continuum is **prevention**. After 9/11 the Department of Homeland Security was established for the sole purpose of protecting the homeland from outside attacks. Additionally, the U.S. military invaded Afghanistan, a haven for terrorist groups such as al-Qaeda and their training camps. The singular goal of this military action was to prevent another terrorist attack on America, and to avert another disaster like the one experienced on 9/11. In New Orleans, where unfortunately the levy system remains vulnerable, new response protocols have been established in the event of another destructive hurricane. These protocols are aimed at evacuating people more efficiently in advance of a hurricane's landfall and greatly improving the emergency response to contain and de-escalate the crisis before it becomes a disaster. Since the Rodney King riots the LAPD has made great strides in improving relations between the police department and the public. Those efforts have included hiring a new reform-minded police chief, establishing new community policing standards, instituting new disciplinary procedures for officers who violate policy, and increasing minority hiring so the makeup of the department more closely mirrors that of the city they are charged with policing.

Prevention is the product of what we learn from crisis. Our goal is to head off crisis before it reaches the point where intervention becomes necessary. We have crisis centers, suicide prevention hotlines, anger management classes, support groups, and on a grander scale, public policy designed to alleviate the strain of poverty. In our prisons we have skills training and counseling designed to reduce recidivism. Our legal system issues restraining orders and orders of protection in an effort to reduce the possibility of spousal abuse and interpersonal violence. In our schools we have anti-drug programs, anti-bullying programs, zero-tolerance policies, and various types of values training designed to increase self-esteem and reduce delinquency. All are designed as preventative measures.

It can be said that prevention is the most important component of the crisis intervention continuum. It is where the majority of our resources should be directed. Unfortunately,

ISSUES & ETHICS IN CRISIS INTERVENTION
When Duty Calls

Paul Schubert was a 30-year police officer for the New Orleans Police Department. He was also the husband of a woman disabled by rheumatoid arthritis, a debilitating disease that can leave a person unable to move without experiencing severe pain in their joints. His duty as a police officer and his obligation as a husband would find themselves in conflict in the days following Hurricane Katrina.

In 2006, Schubert and other officers were fired for leaving their jobs in the midst of the Hurricane Katrina disaster. More than 200 officers were ultimately investigated. Many of them, including Schubert, were eventually fired. In Schubert's case, a police panel hearing the cases ruled that Schubert should keep his job; however, Police Superintendent Warren Riley overruled the decision.

Schubert's case was unique. Some officers simply quit or walked away from their posts. Others were later convicted of crimes up to and including murder. Officer Schubert, however, left after getting permission from a supervisor to leave to evacuate his disabled wife to Texas. Although he advised his supervisor that he would return the next day, it took over four weeks to make his way back to New Orleans, as he and his wife searched for housing and medical care. When he reported back to duty he was met with a 30-day suspension without pay, pending an administrative hearing to determine his future with the department. The reason given for his eventual termination was "an unforgiveable neglect of duty."

In all, 76 officers were fired for abandoning their jobs. Another 11 officers were fired for neglecting their duties. Forty-one were reassigned for various acts of misconduct. Numerous others were suspended for various reasons connected to the Katrina aftermath. And in 2011, two former officers were sentenced to 17 and 25 years in prison for killing an innocent man, and then attempting to conceal the death by burning the body in a vehicle.

Discussion Questions

1. Is there a difference between ethics and morality? Did Officer Schubert face a legitimate conflict between his ethical duty and his moral obligation? Did he make the right decision, or should he have placed duty above his obligation as a husband?
2. Should police officers be held to a higher ethical standard than other members of society?
3. What would you have done in Officer Schubert's situation? Have you ever been faced with a similar situation, where you knew that to help a friend or family member would violate a rule or expectation? How did you handle it?

however, that is often not the case. When government budgets are cut, it is typically the preventative programs that get cut first because the success of such programs is difficult to measure. It is an inexact science to calculate how many people would have committed a crime, would have committed suicide, or would have engaged in drug or alcohol abuse without some proactive measures taken to prevent such occurrences. We live in a society that tends to be more reactive than proactive. Money is spent in areas where people feel the most threatened. The fact is, few of us feel threatened by a third-grader who may or may not become a problem at some point in the future. Consequently there are limits to the amount of public dollars we are willing to spend on that third-grader in order to prevent a negative outcome. The collective fear created by the terrorist attacks on 9/11, however, is a different story. It doesn't matter that statistically speaking the at-risk third-grader has a greater chance of growing up and impacting our lives in a negative way than does a foreign terrorist. We feel a much greater threat from the latter, and thus we are open not only to the idea of spending unlimited public dollars in support of homeland security, but we are willing even to limit our own civil rights in support of that particular mission.

Chapter Summary

Intervening in the lives of those suffering the stress and trauma of crisis is a necessary obligation of any modern and free society. In America, our police and emergency response agencies are charged with containing and de-escalating crisis, and then taking the necessary steps to remediate and prevent further crisis. These crises may be human-driven, such as riots, hostage situations, and other types of criminal offenses, or they may be the result of natural disasters such as floods, earthquakes, and hurricanes. Regardless of the type, people are invariably left in its wake in need of services and assistance.

From the time of the Whiskey Rebellion of 1794 to the establishment of the Department of Homeland Security following the tragic events of September 11, 2001, America has steadily improved and professionalized its ability to respond to crisis. Today it has the most advanced technological resources and, more importantly, the most dedicated and proficient human resources, anywhere in the world for carrying out this critical mission.

Key Terms

Crisis
Crisis responders
Intervention
Urie Bronfenbrenner
Equilibrium
Internal/External systems of
    control
Microcrisis

Microsystem
Mesocrisis
Mesosystem
Exocrisis
Exosystem
Macrocrisis
Macrosystem
The Whiskey Rebellion of 1794

Sir Robert Peel
Clara Barton
American Red Cross
FEMA
Containment
De-escalation
Remediation
Prevention

Discussion Questions

1. Select any recent national or international crisis and discuss the response to that event in terms of the crisis intervention continuum. Was the response successful? Was it criticized?

2. Many times large amounts of resources are spent de-escalating a microcrisis involving a single individual. For example, a large number of police and other emergency personnel may be deployed to intervene in the case of an individual threatening to jump from a building or bridge. Should we as a society weigh the decision to intervene in such a crisis against the potential cost to the taxpayer? Why or why not?

3. In the event of a macrocrisis, like the events of September 11, 2001, is it an acceptable measure at times to limit the rights and freedoms of American citizens in order to contain and de-escalate the crisis?

2

Fight, Flight, or Freeze: The Psychophysiology of Crisis

LEARNING OUTCOMES

Upon completion of this chapter the student should be able to:

1. Summarize the psychophysiological response to stress.

2. Explain the relationship between crisis and stress.

3. Explain how the stress response is mediated, and to list the factors that buffer a person against the negative effects of stress.

4. Describe potential patterns of behavior by an offender when confronted by police.

Chapter Outline

Introduction
    Fight, Flight, or Freeze
The Crisis-stress Dynamic
    Homeostasis
    General Adaptation Syndrome
    Cox and MacKay's Transactional
        Model of Stress

The Stress Response
    The Physical Response
    The Psychological Response
        Control and Predictability
    Response Modes
Chapter Summary

INTRODUCTION

FIGHT, FLIGHT, OR FREEZE

On November 16, 1996, two rural Illinois sheriff's deputies, both only twenty minutes into their midnight shift, found themselves face to face with a suicidal man pointing a loaded shotgun directly at them. In a few short but chaotic moments the suicidal man was dead. The deputies had acted appropriately. They attempted to get the man to drop his weapon, but when it became apparent that he was becoming increasingly more emotional and preparing to pull the trigger, one of the deputies fired his service weapon, bringing the crisis to a quick end. Following the episode there was a critical incident debriefing, and neither reported any type of post-event stress, nor did either have any apprehensions about returning to duty. One of the deputies was relatively new to police work, having graduated from the police academy only two months prior to the shooting. He had yet to find himself in a situation requiring the potential use of deadly force. And while he was not the deputy who pulled the trigger that night, he did respond appropriately, and in a manner consistent with his training.

Three nights following the shooting, and again at the beginning of their shift, the two deputies received a call that a man with a shotgun was threatening to shoot his wife. As the more experienced deputy switched on his lights and siren to respond, he noticed his partner quietly staring out the window with his face turned away. Within seconds the inexperienced deputy was shaking uncontrollably, and seemed almost paralyzed by fear. When they arrived, the visibly shaken deputy exited his vehicle with gun drawn, but it was obvious he was in no condition to respond effectively to such a dangerous situation. Fortunately another unit had responded to back them up, and the situation was brought to a quick and peaceful resolution. The deputy later confided in his partner that he had no idea what had come over him. He described when the call came across the radio how he immediately began to think about the chaotic events from a few nights earlier. The next thing he knew he was shaking uncontrollably.

What happened to the deputy that night was an inability to properly mediate a common physiological reaction to stress. With the introduction of a significant stressor, in this case the radio call, the deputy's body began a complex chain of physiological events designed to prepare him to deal with the immediate stressor. His heart began to beat faster and his breathing quickened, both processes having evolved over time to facilitate the rapid production of energy. It is this energy that makes us stronger, faster, and able to jump higher in a moment of crisis. We have all heard stories of people demonstrating superhuman strength in a moment of extreme stress, such as the man who single-handedly lifts a vehicle off a person trapped underneath. It is the physiological changes that take place in response to stress that allow for such feats. It is this same process that leads a soldier in the heat of intense battle to carry out heroic deeds without noticing the pain of his own wounds, or an Olympic runner to complete a race with a fractured bone in her leg.

But what about the deputy's reaction that night when confronted with the stress of a man threatening to shoot his wife? There was no superhuman strength in his case. In fact, the result was just the opposite. The answer lies in the regulatory systems that tell the body when enough energy has been produced to meet the demands of the situation, and how effectively the body can utilize that energy rather than allowing it to build up to a point of critical mass. The primary means for mediating this process in humans is through our cognitive processing capabilities. For example, if we were to awaken in the night to the sight and smell of smoke filling our house, these physiological changes will rapidly occur as we jump from bed, immediately wide awake, and run to grab our children and escape the crisis. It may require a great deal of strength to carry our children and navigate quickly through the darkened house, but our body has prepared us to meet the challenge. Once safely outside then, we begin to calm down as our body returns to its normal state. It does this because we have the ability to regulate the process by how we think. We process the information in our sensory field, and once we conclude that we are safely away from the danger, the physiological systems that initially prepared us to react quickly to the crisis are signaled to stand down and return to a normal state. If the body does not stand down, and the stress of this heightened physiological activity continues, then what has evolved in humans to be an effective adaptation mechanism can begin to have negative consequences. In the case of the deputy, he was overwhelmed by the physiological response to the stressor, the radio call, because he was unable to effectively mediate it. He became immediately focused on the chaotic events from a few nights earlier, and suddenly a perceived lack of control and predictability, two variables that are crucial for mediating the stress of crisis (Sapolsky, 2004), caused his physiological response to increase unabated until it overwhelmed his ability to manage it, and thus his uncontrollable shaking and inability to think coherently. The deputy was experiencing one potential outcome of the **fight, flight, or freeze response**, or the increased stimulation of the body's energy-producing systems to meet the demands of a stress-producing situation.

As the disciplines of criminal justice and psychology continue to merge and build upon each other's body of knowledge, our understanding of the psychology of crisis has continued to evolve in many unique and varied ways. As previously discussed, the response to crisis involves a complex dynamic of physiological and psychological mechanisms that together can lead to a number of varied behavioral outcomes. By understanding and anticipating these mechanisms, those who respond to crisis can take steps to facilitate their own optimal performance and buffer themselves against the negative effects of stress. Additionally, those who respond to and attempt to contain and de-escalate crisis can be in a better position to anticipate the actions of those causing the crisis. This capability will increase safety and allow the responder to more effectively intervene in the least intrusive manner possible, and in a manner that will maximize remediation and prevention. Predictability is a powerful tool for a first responder to have in their arsenal of weapons. By being able to predict a person's behavior, the police officer can adjust their own methods and behavior to maximize cooperation and de-escalation. For the correctional officer, they can more effectively manage a prison population and minimize violent outbursts against prison staff and other inmates. For these and other reasons, it is critical that criminal justice professionals understand the psychology of crisis, and the behavioral dynamics that occur when those who intervene in crisis interact with those in the midst of crisis.

THE CRISIS-STRESS DYNAMIC

Acting in the capacity of a first responder, whether a police officer, firefighter, or correctional officer, requires an extraordinarily demanding effort. In most cases the stakes are high. Someone's life could literally hinge on the quickness and quality of the response. Many times the first responder is running toward a crisis while everyone else is frantically running away from it. Regardless of how well an individual is trained, any crisis response involves some amount of **stress**. Many times it involves such a high degree that a responder's effectiveness, and perhaps even their personal safety, can be placed in jeopardy, as in the case of the deputy sheriff in our opening example. It is the stress present in a situation that can distort a first responder's sensation, perception, and ultimately their judgment. At its extreme it can render the responder helpless for purposes of containing and de-escalating the crisis at hand.

We all know stress when we feel it. It is an uncomfortable condition, both physically and emotionally, which we try to avoid if possible. An adolescent may feel stress on exam day, or when trying to build up the courage to ask another student out on a date. A young adult with a new family may feel stress related to finances, or perhaps in applying for a new job or purchasing a new home. We feel stress in traffic jams, waiting in line at the DMV, at the dentist's office, and even in something as simple as trying to connect to the Internet. Robert Sapolsky (2004), a professor of biology at Stanford University, calls these stress-producing cognitions **speciocentric** in nature. Humans are unique because we have the ability to perform mental operations, and to anticipate events well in advance of their actual occurrence. Unfortunately this uniqueness brings with it the capacity to produce significant amounts of stress based solely on our cognition. When something is bothering us, the more we think about it the more stress we feel. Many serial offenders are caught in a cycle of violence that includes a period of time between their crimes when the stress related to simply thinking about their behavior builds to the point of leading them to commit new crimes to relieve the pressure caused by the stress.

To draw a comparison, imagine a zebra on the African flatlands. For animals the most distressing things tend to be acute physical stressors. Sapolsky uses the example of a zebra that has been attacked and critically injured by a lion, but manages to momentarily escape. The situation produces stress for both animals, but their stress differs. For the zebra, it is the stress of being killed and eaten by the lion now snapping at its heels. For the lion, it is the stress of possible starvation if it doesn't prevail in the hunt. Both situations demand their immediate physiological adaptation. For the lion, an extraordinary burst of speed and strength is required to bring down its prey. And for the zebra, an explosive burst of speed in spite of its pain is needed to escape its attacker.

The combined physiological response of the lion and zebra is what we commonly refer to as the *fight-or-flight response*, a term first used by Walter Cannon (1915), a professor of physiology at Harvard University. He found that animals react to threats in their immediate sensory field with a discharge of the sympathetic nervous system. He later came to recognize this response as the first stage in a complex adaptation syndrome that regulates stress in the organism. The fight-or-flight response is the *physiological* component of this adaptation mechanism that prepares a person to effectively cope both physically and psychologically with an actual or perceived threat. It is what allows us to run faster, feel less pain, and demonstrate a greater amount of physical strength when confronted by crisis. Although the fight-or-flight response first evolved to handle short-term physical stressors, as our cognitive abilities evolved to allow for mental operations and anticipatory thinking, psychological stressors began to activate the same physiological response. It is this latter ability that sets us apart from other animals.

Homeostasis

Stress tends to knock us off balance, or "out of sorts," to use an aged colloquialism. In neurological terms, that is exactly what stress does. The brain has evolved to maintain a state of physiological and psychological equilibrium, or **homeostasis**. Any threat to such balance can be described as a stressor. If the internal homeostatic system has been disrupted, the stress response (i.e., fight or flight) is the body's effort to reestablish homeostasis. Stress can be both good and bad. In a crisis situation some degree of stress and arousal is necessary to respond effectively. Stress becomes problematic when it reaches an extreme level, or when it becomes chronic at any level. For those who respond to crisis, extreme or chronic stress can be physically and psychologically compromising unless compensatory action is taken to return to a state of optimal arousal. When stress completely breaks down the person's ability to compensate, then **tonic immobility**, or the freeze response, becomes a real possibility (Bracha et al., 2004).

General Adaptation Syndrome

Dr. Hans Selye (1956), a Canadian endocrinologist and pioneer in the area of stress research, defined the stress response as the physiological adaptation to any nonspecific demand on the body. Although the origins of stress may be dynamic and diverse, the manner in which the body responds to that stress remains relatively constant. He proposed a three-stage model of the stress response to illustrate the body's reaction to the introduction of a stressor. During the first stage of Selye's **General Adaptation Syndrome**, the **alarm stage**, the fight-or-flight response is activated by the hypothalamus in the brain to prepare the individual to effectively confront the stressor. The stressor can be real, irrational, physical, or psychological. The alarm is sounded and the fight-or-flight mechanism is activated just the same. For an individual who remains stressed for any length of time, the body will attempt to adapt to the prolonged stress in an effort to resist its negative effects and return to a state of homeostasis, even in the face of the ongoing stress. In this second stage, the **resistance stage**, the individual remains in a state of heightened sensitivity to the stress, but the initial surge of the fight-or-flight response is absent. In short, the body is attempting to adapt to the stressor, even while energy is rapidly being depleted.

In the final stage of Selye's model, the **exhaustion stage**, the stress response begins to become more harmful than helpful, as the body's stress-resisting capacity is slowly diminished and then eventually exhausted. We see this progression in the battle-weary soldiers of any particular war. In their first skirmish the fight-or-flight mechanism is activated, and they enter the battle barely able to think in a coherent manner, but still able to push themselves in nearly superhuman ways to get on the beach, up the mountain, or across the rice paddy in a sprint that would never have been possible during routine training exercises. As the battle wages on, sometimes for many days, they remain in a state of heightened sensitivity to the dangers around them. Their bodies continue to respond to the stress by keeping them awake, alert, and buffered against the pain of their wounds and exhaustion. Eventually though, when the body's ability to respond is exhausted, or when available energy is depleted, battle fatigue is almost immediate. Suddenly the afflicted lose all ability to respond to the present situation. They become physically weakened, and psychologically spent. During WWII, someone coined the phrase "thousand-yard-stare," to describe those suffering from extreme battle fatigue. These soldiers would sit almost catatonically in their trenches and stare into space. Their stress-resisting systems had completely shut down, and the fight-or-flight response had given way to the freeze response. In its most extreme form, this final stage of the stress response can result in severe psychosis. Even in its less extreme form, the ongoing effects of stress can lead to depression, impaired immunity, atherosclerosis, obesity, bone demineralization, and atrophy of the nerve cells in the brain (McEwen, 2006).

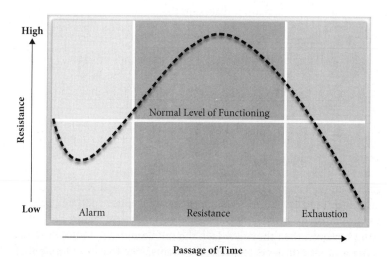

FIGURE 2.1   Selye's General Adaptation Syndrome.

One criticism that has been leveled against Selye's formulation is its lack of specificity regarding the stressors that signal the General Adaptation Syndrome into action. Lazarus and Folkman (1984) argued that it is not the stressor that causes the stress response, as Selye had suggested, but rather the person's perception of the stressor. They concluded that the physiological, emotional, and behavioral changes that take place during the stress response depend on the person's appraisal of the stressor. Tomaka et al. (1993) found that when a person appraises the stressor as challenging, better performance and positive emotions take place. In contrast however, when the stressor is appraised as threatening, their performance is decreased and they experience negative emotions.

Cox and Mackay's Transactional Model of Stress

Cox and Mackay (1976) proposed a psychological model of the stress response in which the amount of stress experienced varies as a result of the individual's perception of the demand the stressor places on them and the extent to which they believe they can cope with that demand. Stress occurs when the individual begins to doubt their ability to cope with the situation. When the stressor is introduced there is an increase in physical and cognitive performance to handle the demand the stressor places on the individual. There is a point however where the individual reaches their optimal performance level. If the stressor remains, then their performance will begin to decrease. A simple example of this dynamic can be seen in the video game *Pac-Man*. When the game begins, our confidence level is high, and thus we are quite able to carry out various strategies and anticipate events with little stress. But very quickly, as anyone who has played the game knows, the events begin to speed up. Those experienced in playing the game will experience little change in their ability to respond to the increased demand. But for the novice, as things speed up, suddenly there is a physiological reaction. The person's heart begins to beat faster, their breathing increases, they begin to lose their peripheral vision and the ability to attend to unrelated auditory stimuli. If their confidence in their ability to meet the demands of the game remains strong, then they haven't yet reached their **level of optimal performance**. The physiological changes taking place have a positive effect on their performance. But even the experienced Pac-Man player reaches a point where the speed of the game begins to overpower their ability to respond to the demand it places on the person's sensory and motor skills. When their confidence begins to wane, then it can be said that they have surpassed their level of optimal performance. Now their ability to think in the same manner and anticipate events begins to fade as their stress level rapidly rises. In a short time, any semblance of strategy is gone as the player shifts into a defensive mode in an effort to escape the inevitable. And finally, when the person has lost all confidence in their ability to handle the demand, they may simply give up and await the inevitable.

Cox and MacKay's formulation has many important implications for crisis intervention. From the perspective of the police, prison guards, and firemen, it supports the idea of realistic training. A police officer, for example, routinely faces situations a civilian never will. A well-trained officer responds to situations they have trained for over and again. Thus, when faced with a real situation, their perception is that they are quite capable of handling the stressors, making the ascent to their level of optimal performance slower, perhaps even never reaching it at all during the course of their response. If they have not enjoyed the benefit of ongoing and realistic training however, then they may lack the self-confidence to get through a crisis without experiencing a significant level of stress, a circumstance that could potentially leave them dangerously exposed.

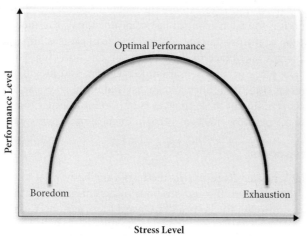

FIGURE 2.2   Cox and Mackay's Transactional Model of Stress.

Cox and MacKay's model also tells us something about the criminal offender. Police officers are acutely aware of what they like to call "survival mode" in a certain kind of criminal offender, especially one they need to disarm or apprehend. Another way of describing this survival instinct is to say that the criminal offender who demonstrates it has a high degree of confidence in their ability to cope with the situation. Let's use the example of a career criminal who has been arrested many times, and who is quite confident in his physical prowess. The individual is wanted by the police, and has stated that he will never go back to prison. In his mind he has nothing to lose by putting up a fight. When he is finally confronted by the police, his confidence level is high. He is instantly in *fight* mode, and because his perception is that he has absolutely nothing to lose, he has a long way to go to reach his level of optimal performance. In fact, he may feel little or no stress in this situation, and thus he is able to think clearly and evaluate his available options. And because he is in fight mode, and still not close to his level of optimal performance, he may even be buffered against pain, including a shot from a Taser, a canister of pepper spray, or even an officer's service weapon. The police are well aware of the dangers posed by this type of individual. An officer with little training, and perhaps even less physical conditioning, coming face to face with such an offender is at a disadvantage physically and psychologically. Only their arsenal of weapons puts them on an equal footing with the offender. If a physical confrontation ensues, and the officer is poorly trained to handle such a situation, then very quickly the officer begins to react from a defensive mode while the offender continues to do so from a superior offensive mode. The end result is an officer who may very well be disarmed and wounded or even killed with their own service weapon, a sad circumstance that has been repeated many times in America.

THE STRESS RESPONSE

Now that we have explored the relationship between crisis and stress, the former being any real or imagined set of variables that gives rise to the internal experience of the latter, we will next look at the actual physiological and psychological changes that take place in response to crisis.

These are themes we will continue to explore throughout the course of this text as we look at the various types of crises to which criminal justice professionals routinely respond. For now, a foundational discussion of the psychophysiological effects of crisis is important.

Qualitative changes take place in the body when an individual is confronted by crisis. Similarly, changes take place in their sensation, perception, and judgment, as the physiological effects of the stressor begin to influence their psychological response. For a criminal justice professional, an understanding of these changes is important in order to be in the best position possible to minimize the negative effects of stress in the heat of a crisis situation.

The Physical Response

The brain is the body's master gland. It tells the rest of the body what to do and when to do it. It does this by sending messages through millions of neural pathways that begin in the brain and branch downward through the body and outward to its periphery. One branch of this vast communication system is a set of nerve projections that are activated automatically in response to stimuli from the individual's sensory field. This system, referred to as the **autonomic nervous system (ANS)**, controls the body's visceral functions. When activated, it affects heart rate, the intake of oxygen, digestion, the size of the pupils, perspiration, and salivation, among other things. The ANS stimulates the stress response in some situations, and suppresses it in others. It

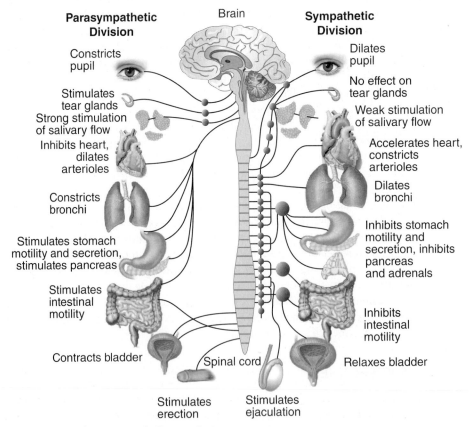

FIGURE 2.3 The Autonomic Nervous System.

does this through the influence of two subsystems, the *sympathetic* and *parasympathetic* nervous systems, each working in opposition to the other.

The actions of the two ANS subsystems, one excitatory and the other inhibitory, are similar to those of a light switch. In the presence of a stressor the switch, the **sympathetic nervous system**, is turned on to rapidly produce and deliver energy throughout the body. It is this subsystem that is responsible for the fight-or-flight response. When activated, it allows the body to prepare itself to meet the demands of the particular stressor that has caused the switch to be turned on. Some of the physiological changes that automatically take place to maximize the body's response include:

- Increased heart rate to deliver more blood to the skeletal muscles, leading to increased strength, speed, and dexterity.
- Pupils dilate to allow more light to enter the eye, thus increasing visual acuity.
- Bronchioles in the lungs dilate to maximize oxygen intake for greater enrichment of blood supply, leading to improvements in strength and endurance.
- Blood vessels in skin and gastrointestinal tract constrict to divert blood to skeletal muscles, leading to enhanced physical performance.

Whenever the body prepares itself in this manner it creates a significant amount of stress on the various physiological systems involved. It is a level of stress that cannot be sustained for prolonged periods of time without negative consequences. It therefore becomes necessary for the body to return itself to a normal state once the crisis has passed and the stressor is no longer present. Although the sympathetic nervous system is responsible for the fight-or-flight response, the **parasympathetic nervous system**, once activated, is said to cause the "rest-and-digest" response. Through its inhibitory influence, the parasympathetic system causes the following changes in the body:

- Decreased heart rate as the body shifts from energy production to energy storage.
- Bronchioles constrict to return to normal oxygen intake.
- Sweat and salivary glands return to normal functioning.
- Blood vessels leading to the GI tract dilate to stimulate digestion.

This interchange between sympathetic and parasympathetic systems is analogous to the idle mechanism on an automobile. When a stressor is introduced, such as the heat of a summer day, the vehicle increases its idle in order to more effectively run the fan to cool the engine. When the engine has cooled, and the crisis passed, then the idle is reduced. We see the same dynamic when we first start our car in the morning. This is perhaps the most stress an engine will experience, and thus the car idles high to compensate for the engine's inability to run efficiently just yet. In a short amount of time however the engine is warmed up and running smoothly, allowing the idle to lower itself. The idle mechanism thus regulates the flow of energy, providing the engine more when needed, and then providing less when the need has passed. The result is that the engine does not malfunction when confronted by a mechanical crisis, such as starting it on a cold morning, nor is it overpowered by too much energy when the need for energy has diminished. Regardless of the conditions, the engine maintains a degree of equilibrium through the actions of the idle mechanism.

So what is it exactly that causes the body to react as it does? After all, there isn't a switch we can consciously turn on and off as circumstances warrant. Rather, the physiological changes that take place in response to crisis and its aftermath happen quite automatically and without conscious effort on the part of the individual. To understand exactly how this process takes place, and how the "switch" is turned on and off, we must look to another of the body's physiological components, the **endocrine system**. This system is composed of a series of glands located throughout the body that secrete a particular type of hormone involved in the regulation of bodily functions. These glands include the hypothalamus, pituitary, thyroid, and adrenal glands, among others. Like the nervous and circulatory systems, the primary purpose of the endocrine system is homeostatic maintenance.

When a stressor is experienced by the individual, the information is processed primarily in an area of the brain called the **amygdala**. A danger signal is sent out, and the **hypothalamus**, the primary interface between the nervous and endocrine systems, releases a chemical messenger called **"CRH" (corticotrophin-releasing hormone)**. The release of this hormone signals the **pituitary glands** to in turn direct the **adrenal glands** to release the stress hormones **epinephrine and norepinephrine**, which in turn activate the sympathetic nervous system to initiate the physiological changes previously discussed. This coordinated activity occurs along the **hypothalamus-pituitary-adrenal axis**, or simply the HPA Axis. Figure 2.4 provides a visual representation of this process, as well as the sympathetic and parasympathetic effects on bodily functions.

So when a stressor is introduced into the sensory experience of the individual, a chain reaction of events takes place. First the person processes the information cognitively, and thus perceives the threat. This perception causes the release of hormones along the HPA axis, which in turn activates the sympathetic nervous system and causes the fight-or-flight response to take place. But, as previously mentioned, there is a third possibility. At extreme levels of stress the individual may actually become overwhelmed by the mind and body's efforts to adapt to the stressor. In this case the individual may experience the third leg of the fight, flight, or freeze response. In the animal kingdom, when an animal is threatened its first reaction is to run and escape the present danger (flight). When it becomes apparent that escape is not possible the animal will

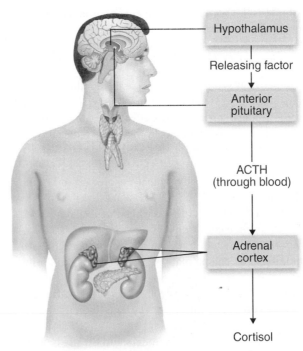

FIGURE 2.4   The Hypothalamus-Pituitary-Adrenal Axis.

aggress in an effort to ward off the attacker (fight). At some point, when it becomes instinctively hopeless for the animal, they may as a last resort play dead (freeze). This is not a cognitive operation on the part of the animal, but an instinctive physiological response. Some animals, such as opossums, have even evolved to very quickly enter a state of *tonic immobility* when threatened with attack. In their case, the body is very quickly overwhelmed by the stress response, a successful adaptation that has evolved over time.

In humans, the freeze response occurs when the stress response so overwhelms the body that cognitive mediation is no longer possible. The interaction of the two processes can be thought of as a perfectly balanced scale. On one side are the individual's physiological systems. On the other, their ability to think, analyze, and anticipate. When the weight of a stressor is added, the body reacts, and the scale is tipped. In order to maintain some balance the individual must become hypervigilant and acutely aware of their sensory field. Their cognitive processing must speed up dramatically in order to analyze and anticipate the threat. For most people, certainly those not accustomed to dealing with stressful situations, this becomes extremely difficult as they fall victim eventually to tunnel vision, an inability to attend to their sensory field, and an increasing difficulty with their ability to think clearly. Their efforts to do so, however, add weight to the opposing side of the scale. Although the scale is never perfectly balanced during the crisis event, it is balanced enough to allow them to adapt to some degree to the stressor, albeit inefficiently and imperfectly. In the most extreme cases however, cognitive processing shuts down, and the scale bottoms out on the side of physiology. When this happens, adaptation is impossible. The individual freezes, begins to shake uncontrollably, and may even pass out from the effects of the physiological changes taking place in response to the extreme stress.

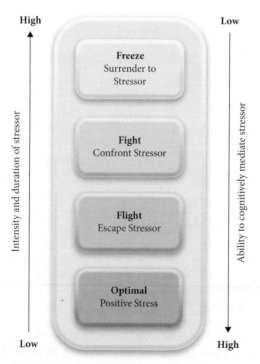

FIGURE 2.5 The Stress Response Continuum.

The Psychological Response

As previously noted, a stressor can be physical or psychological in nature. What sets us apart from other animals is our ability to imagine or anticipate a crisis absent any stressors in our sensory field. This type of cognitive processing has the ability to elicit a physiological reaction as if the crisis were real and present. In fact, the body's stress response mechanisms are quite blind to whether a crisis is real or imagined, present or anticipated. The body simply reacts to signals sent by the brain. Anyone knows that when they sit alone in a room and ruminate on a significant problem in their life, their breathing quickens, their heart races, and they may even experience a panic-like attack. Understanding the psychological influences on the stress experience, therefore, is critical to comprehending the complex and dynamic nature of crisis.

Many times psychological variables have an equal or greater influence on the stress response than the stressor itself. For example, how many times have we witnessed on television or in person a vacant building being brought down by explosives in a controlled manner? No stress is involved in witnessing such an event. In fact, for most it is an exhilarating experience. But what did most of us experience as we watched the World Trade Center come down in a strangely similar controlled manner on September 11, 2001? There was no excitement at all in watching that tragedy, but a profound sense of crisis. As we watched it we thought about the possibility of other terrorist strikes around the country, perhaps even in our own city. We analyzed, we anticipated, and we imagined the worst. And the more we processed the information cognitively, the more stress we experienced physically. For those on the ground that day, the fight, flight, or freeze response was in full activation. People either ran toward Ground Zero in an effort to help the injured, away from it out of extreme fear, or they just stood frozen in place in a state of near-shock at the happenings around them.

CONTROL AND PREDICTABILITY   How one perceives an event is unique to each individual, and thus everyone experiences crisis in a slightly different way. We all come from different backgrounds, have different life experiences, and our physical capabilities are highly diverse. All of these factors, as well as many others, play into our perception of a crisis, and thus will influence the level of stress the crisis produces. For example, someone walking alone down a dimly lit city street will have a much different reaction if they see two men in business attire approaching as opposed to two adolescents in gang clothing. The latter will undoubtedly cause more stress. And if the person walking alone is a woman, then the level of stress will likely be significantly higher than for a man. Sapolsky (2004) has argued that several psychological factors together determine to what degree the stress response will be experienced during a crisis, among them *control* and *predictability*.

Control plays an important role in how we experience and perceive crisis. The perception that one is in control acts to buffer the individual against the negative effects of the stressor. A simple example is the stress we almost always feel when driving in a new location, especially a large urban setting. Even if we are accustomed to driving in such a setting, likely with little or no stress, in this new unfamiliar location we are immediately on edge, we're hypervigilant, and we are so focused on our directions that we see very little of what is happening on the sidewalk next to us. This is precisely why police officers, firemen, and correctional officers feel less stress in a crisis situation than the average citizen. Their extensive training and equipment, including their weapons, allows them to maintain a great deal of control. When this control is diminished however, such as in the midst of a riot or other chaotic situation, then the stress level of the officers involved will rise rapidly.

Control can be either internal or external (Rotter, 1954, 1990). An internal **locus of control** refers to a person's belief that they are in control of their own destiny, regardless of the circumstances. Success is attributed to personal skills, and failure to their own shortcomings. In a crisis situation an individual with an internal orientation relies on their own resources and problem-solving skills to address the situation. Their confidence in their own ability to adequately control the crisis acts as a buffer against the adverse and potentially overwhelming effects of the stress response. For this confidence to be present, the individual must possess a degree of **self-efficacy** (Bandura, 1977), or the belief that they are capable of succeeding and achieving a desired goal. Self-efficacy results from a developmental process involving the degree to which a child is afforded the autonomy at an early age to begin making their own decisions and, more importantly, the degree to which the parents reinforce appropriate and successful decision making by the child in a positive and responsive manner. Simply put, when a child experiences and internalizes success, then self-efficacy develops. And with self-efficacy comes the level of confidence necessary for an individual to meet the demands of any given situation that is within the realm of their capabilities.

In contrast, an *external* locus of control, or an external orientation, refers to the belief that one's fate is determined largely by external forces, and that the individual has little choice in what happens to them. In a crisis situation, an external orientation translates into a lack of perceived control, which in turn only accelerates the stress response and its effects on the person's ability to respond in an appropriate manner. Typically a person has an external orientation because they lack a sufficient degree of self-efficacy. These two dimensions, orientation and self-efficacy, interact as shown in Figure 2.6. At the high end of the spectrum we have assertiveness as a response type. At the low end, helplessness.

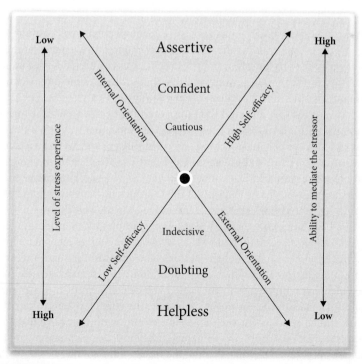

FIGURE 2.6 Interaction of orientation and self-efficacy.

Obviously for those who routinely run into the path of danger, the assertive response type is the most effective. This type of individual has an internal orientation plus a high degree of self-efficacy. They feel in control, and they are confident they can meet the demands of the situation in order to contain and de-escalate the crisis. With this increased perception of control, the effects of the stress response are lessened. The individual is able to process what is happening in their sensory field with less disruptive effect. This is why when most police officers enter a crisis situation, especially one that may pose some degree of danger, they are still able to keep the area around them under observation for any potential threats, and are able to react to multiple threats simultaneously. Although the physiological response to stress naturally leads to tunnel vision and an inability to perceive multiple and simultaneous auditory stimuli, most emergency personnel, especially police officers, are able to buffer themselves against these negative effects with their perceived control of the situation.

At the opposite end of the spectrum is the helpless response type. These individuals, with an external orientation and low self-efficacy, feel they have no control over circumstances, and further, have little confidence in their ability to meet the demands of any particular crisis. It is hoped that few who fall at this extreme end of the spectrum ever make their way into the ranks of law enforcement, corrections, or other emergency professions. At this extreme is where we find many victims of crime who immediately succumb to the effects of stress in the midst of their crisis, such as the abused spouse who cowers in a darkened bedroom shaking uncontrollably at the sound of her intoxicated husband coming home. In this case the effects of the stress response are quite pronounced and debilitating, as the *freeze* response sets in and the individual loses all ability to mediate the stress of the situation.

The middle ground of the spectrum is where most people fall in terms of their response to crisis. Part of the goal of testing applicants for potential employment in law enforcement, corrections, and other emergency services is to identify those who are above the center point rather than below. These individuals are naturally more resistant to the effects of stress. With the proper training it is hoped they will increase this resistance through enhanced cognitive mediation. Put another way, with the proper training these individuals will feel an even greater degree of control and self-confidence in the face of crisis, and thus become less impacted by the stress it produces.

Predictability is a second important variable that influences the intensity of the stress response during a crisis situation. In an often-cited study with rats, Weiss (1972) administered electric shock to two groups of rats, and then measured the degree to which stomach ulceration had taken place as a result of the associated stress. He found that those rats that were signaled beforehand that a shock was coming experienced less ulceration than those shocked with no advanced warning. Both groups experienced significantly more ulceration than a control group receiving no shocks. The results indicate that the degree to which a crisis can be predicted lessens the effects of the stress it produces. Sapolsky (2004) argues further, in support of Weiss's findings, that when a stressor is predictable, the individual has the ability to prepare for the event and anticipate its beginning and ending points. For example, when a prison tactical team has to enter a hostile inmate's cell and remove him by force, the stress level is relatively low, even given the potentially violent nature of the action. Not only are the team members in control of the situation, but it is something they have done many times, and trained for even more. It is very predictable what will happen as they enter the cell. In contrast, if the team is forced to enter a section of the prison where a riot is underway, the stress level rises dramatically, even in spite of their continued training for such an event. Not only do they have less control in a riot situation, but it is a great deal more unpredictable. They must determine how many inmates are involved, whether weapons are involved, and if the inmates are holding hostages. As the number of unknown variables increases, so too does the stress level.

Returning to the events of September 11, 2001, it didn't matter if you were in New York City; Washington, D.C.; or Peoria, Illinois, that day. People were panicked and severely stressed. There simply was no degree of predictability. People were unsure whether more terrorist attacks were imminent, or if the terrorists themselves were lurking somewhere in their midst. It was mass hysteria brought on by a collective inability to anticipate events. Only after a few days of media saturation of the government's efforts to protect the homeland did the public begin to de-compress and think rationally again. As we came to the realization that controls were once again in place, making the predictability of events easier, the stress levels associated with the macrocri-sis finally began to subside and level off.

The dual ideas of control and predictability have many implications for the training of emergency personnel. By engaging in realistic training that anticipates and prepares personnel for a wide range of possibilities, the level of predictability in an actual situation increases dramat-ically. Additionally, training and preparation will only increase a person's confidence that they can in fact handle a similar situation when it arises. Confidence translates into control, and as we have discussed, the combination of control and predictability buffers the emergency responder against many of the adverse cognitive and physiological effects associated with crisis, and thus allows them to respond at or near their level of optimal performance.

Response Modes

Thus far we have said a great deal about those who place themselves in harm's way in an effort to contain and de-escalate crisis. In large part, how they respond to any particular crisis is pre-determined by their level of training and preparation. But what about those on the other side of a crisis event, those who help to create a crisis by their actions? We have previously talked about functioning at one's level of optimal performance, and how some offenders shift into survival mode under stress. But that is just one response mode to crisis. When we look again at the dual dimensions of control and predictability, we see four distinct **response modes** begin to emerge: *offense, defense, escape,* and *panic*. Those who respond to crisis are well advised to understand these response types. They provide an indication of the level of force or engagement that may be necessary in order to contain and de-escalate a crisis. And as we have discussed, this ability to anticipate a crisis only increases the emergency responder's perception of control and their abil-ity to predict events.

The **offense mode** is a pattern of behavior typically demonstrated by an offender who perceives themselves as being in control, and the circumstances, predictable. Their stress level is comparatively low, and they are able to think clearly as they consider their possible options. What we previously described as "survival mode" would fall in this category. These individuals take offensive measures. An example might be the abusive husband whose wife has called the po-lice. The man is quite confident in his physical prowess. He is on his own turf, and he has no in-tention of going to jail. He feels in complete control of the situation, albeit foolishly so. Also, he is well aware that the police, once they arrive, will make every effort to place him under arrest once they see his wife's bloody face, and he knows exactly the methods they will use. The situation is quite predictable. As the police pull up, the man's heart begins to beat faster as his sympathetic nervous system is activated. His stress response is elevated, but still low when measured against the typical stress response. He is ready for a fight.

Offenders on the street aren't the only ones who function from this mode. Certainly prison inmates almost always respond to crisis in this manner, thus making them an extremely dangerous population. They live in a culture of crisis inside the prison walls where control and

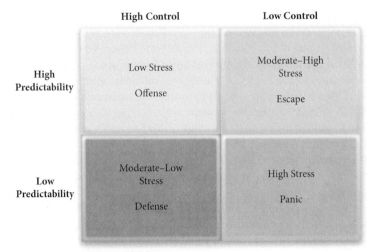

FIGURE 2.7   Offender response modes.

predictability are important components of staying alive. Those incarcerated for extended periods, especially those sentenced to life behind bars, may take on a "nothing to lose" demeanor. These inmates can be extremely dangerous, and in a confrontation may have the upper hand, especially against a correctional officer, because of their lack of a disruptive stress response and their ability to think clearly even in the heat of confrontation.

The second response type, the **defense mode**, is typically demonstrated by an offender who feels some degree of control over the situation, but perceives the variables as somewhat unpredictable. For example, a hostage taker in a failed bank robbery may be well armed, and thus feel quite in control of the situation, but they cannot predict what is happening outside the bank. Is the tactical response team preparing for an assault? Will a police sniper attempt to take him out if he steps close to a window? In the defense mode the individual feels low to moderate stress even given the unpredictability of the situation, because they still feel somewhat in control and are confident in their ability to adapt to a changing situation. Rather than attack and fight, they choose to sit back and wait for the fight to come to them.

If we return to our example of the abusive husband, one who responds from a defensive mode feels confident in his control over the situation, but he is not quite sure what to expect when the police arrive. Rather than attack and put up a fight from the beginning, as our first husband did, this one sits back and waits to see what transpires. His stress level is higher because of the unpredictability of things; however, if circumstances move against him, this individual will likely react aggressively because his confidence level remains high.

As we have already discussed, when an individual perceives a lack or loss of control in a crisis situation their stress level increases significantly. When such an individual can predict events and circumstances, then they respond from an **escape mode** in order to avoid the circumstances they anticipate. On September 11, 2001, people on the street in New York City tended to respond from this mode. They obviously felt no control whatsoever over the circumstances that were unfolding, and given the devastation all around, it was easy to predict more danger, whether from additional terrorist attacks, or from fire, explosions, and falling debris. Consequently, people ran from Ground Zero in an effort to escape the danger. The emergency personnel on the scene however ran toward the crisis. They felt in control because of their experience and training, and for them the looming dangers were more predictable. Thus, their stress levels were initially lower than those fleeing the area.

ISSUES & ETHICS IN CRISIS INTERVENTION
The Fog of Crisis

In the early morning hours of January 1, 2009, a San Francisco area BART train arrived at the Fruitvale Station with as many as 12 intoxicated passengers engaged in a physical altercation. One of those involved was 22-year-old Oscar Grant III of Oakland. When the train arrived, two BART police officers were waiting, with five others responding. The situation quickly became chaotic. Grant and another individual attempted to flee by jumping back on the train, but when the other individual was quickly subdued by one of the officers, Grant voluntarily stepped back off the train.

With a sufficient number of officers now on the scene, those involved in the disturbance were placed against a wall to contain and de-escalate the situation. Officer Johannes Mehserle, who had been with the BART Police Dept less than two years, was present. He was instructed by another officer to arrest Grant. When Grant attempted to stand up in protest, he was taken to the ground. A struggle then ensued as the officers attempted to gain control of Grant's wrists to place him in handcuffs. Grant resisted by struggling to keep his hands beneath his prone body.

What happened next was caught on multiple cell phone cameras. As the situation became even more chaotic, with the crowd becoming more aggressive in their verbal assault on the officers, Mehserle yelled at Grant that he was going to shoot him with his Taser gun if he did not stop resisting. As Grant continued to struggle, Mehserle stood up, pulled his service weapon, and to everyone's shock, including his own, fired one shot into Grant's back, mortally wounding him. Witnesses stated that Mehserle immediately said "Oh my God!" and then put his hands to his head (Mehserle motion for bail, 2009).

There was no doubt what had happened. In the stress of the moment, Mehserle had reached for his Taser, a weapon he had only recently begun to carry, and mistakenly grabbed his service weapon. In the days to follow, protests would erupt in the area, some violent, and Officer Mehserle would be charged with the murder of Oscar Grant. On July 8, 2010, 18 months after the incident, a jury found Mehserle guilty of involuntary manslaughter, a lesser offense. His attorneys had successfully proven that he had no intention of shooting Grant, and that the shooting was a terrible accident. Mehserle was sentenced to just two years in prison, and given credit for time served.

The incident was a stark reminder not only of the effects of stress on a person's judgment, even a police officer's, but also of the absolute necessity for the police to train extensively with the weapons they carry on duty. In Mehserle's case, he had simply become unable to properly mediate the stress of the moment and think clearly about what he was doing. The type of unconscious, automatic response that comes with training and experience, in Mehserle's case simply did not happen.

Discussion Questions

1. Should Officer Mehserle have been found guilty of any crime, given the accidental nature of his actions?
2. Did Oscar Grant contribute to his own death by not obeying the officer's instructions to free his hands and allow himself to be handcuffed? Should there be an expectation that police officers are properly trained with their weapons, and that human error should never be an acceptable excuse when something like this incident happens?

In the case of our abusive husband, he may feel like he is in complete control of his wife, but he knows he is no match for the police, and therefore when he hears the sirens getting close, his stress level shoots through the ceiling. The situation is quite predictable. He knows when they see his wife's injuries they will place him in handcuffs and transport him to jail. His stress level continues to rise until he shifts into escape mode and runs out the back door. Unlike the offense mode, which compels our abusive husband to seek confrontation, or the defense mode, which leads him to sit back and wait for confrontation to come to him, those who respond from the escape mode run from confrontation. With no perceived control over the situation, the *flight* response takes hold.

The final response type, and the one associated with the highest level of stress, is the **panic mode**. In this mode the individual is overwhelmed by the stress response due to a perceived lack of control and an inability to predict circumstances and outcomes. Many who are victimized respond from this mode, such as a woman being held in her apartment at gunpoint by an intruder. When there is neither control nor predictability, the stress level is so high that the woman simply submits in fear. In contrast, a man who is robbed on the street by a perpetrator with a knife may feel some control over the situation. He can predict the offender's physical capabilities by his size and body type. Rather than panic, his stress level may remain low, so that when the opportunity presents itself he reacts offensively and attacks the attacker in an effort to disarm him.

When someone responds from the panic mode, they have lost their ability to effectively mediate the stress response. The sympathetic nervous system, once activated, increases its effect unabated until the individual is overwhelmed by the situation. With no ability to regulate the pressure through a perceived sense of control and predictability, the individual quickly loses the ability to even put forward a viable response. An individual responding from the panic mode can be extremely dangerous to emergency personnel, especially police and correctional officers. They may respond with violence, not as a calculated offensive act, or a perceived defensive measure, but rather as an irrational and conditioned response to the panic.

Our response to crisis is highly influenced by our cognitive appraisal of the levels of control and predictability associated with the situation. And this response will impact, as well as be impacted by, the extent to which we are able to communicate effectively during and after the crisis. In Chapter 3 we will explore the problems associated with attempting to communicate in the heat of a crisis, along with techniques designed to facilitate containment and de-escalation.

Chapter Summary

When we talk about the psychology of crisis, we are referring to the body's physiological response to real or imagined stressors, and the extent to which the individual can control the effects of that physiological response through some type of cognitive mediation. Simply put, when a crisis occurs, those involved will experience a sudden increase in the secretion of a particular type of hormone that acts to prepare the body for fight or flight. Which is chosen will depend on the degree to which the individual feels control over the situation, along with the predictability of the circumstances. When this cognitive mediation fails, and the physiological stress produced by the crisis continues to rise, eventually the individual can be completely overwhelmed, and the fight-or-flight instinct gives way to the freeze response.

In addition to the physiological changes that occur in response to crisis, there is also a psychological response. This response consists of an immediate appraisal of the degree of control the individual perceives themselves as having over the situation, as well as the level of predictability regarding the potential outcomes. The higher the level of perceived control and predictability, the better able the individual is to effectively mediate the physiological response. In contrast, if the individual under stress perceives themselves as having little control, and the circumstances as unpredictable, then the elevated autonomic response is not so easily mediated, and the individual is at risk of being overwhelmed, physically and psychologically, by its effects.

Key Terms

Fight, flight, or freeze response
Stress
Speciocentric
Homeostasis
Tonic immobility
General Adaptation Syndrome
Level of optimal
    performance

Autonomic nervous system
Sympathetic nervous system
Parasympathetic nervous system
Endocrine system
Amygdala
Hypothalamus
CRH
HPA axis

Locus of control
Self-efficacy
Predictability
Response modes
Offense mode
Defense mode
Escape mode
Panic mode

Discussion Questions

1. How does training benefit a police officer in a stressful situation? How does a nothing-to-lose mentality benefit an offender? Answer both in psychophysiological terms.
2. Consider a bank robber trapped inside a bank by responding police officers. Employees are inside and the robber is armed. Describe how the robber might respond under each of the four response modes described in the chapter.
3. Describe the type of orientation (locus of control) the child of an abusive, authoritarian parent might demonstrate during adolescence and into adulthood, and why.

3

Crisis Communication

LEARNING OUTCOMES

Upon completion of this chapter the student should be able to:

1. Summarize the importance of communication to crisis intervention.

2. Define the basic tenants of Transactional Analysis as a model for crisis communication.

3. List and explain the typical communication patterns of those in crisis.

4. Summarize the communication skills necessary to effectively de-escalate a person in crisis.

Chapter Outline

Introduction
An Officer's Most Effective Weapon

Goals of Crisis Communication
Containment and De-escalation
Reducing Liability

Transactional Analysis
Ego States
The Parent Ego State
The Adult Ego State

The Child Ego State
Contamination

Transactions
The Parallel Transaction
The Crossed Transaction
The Ulterior Transaction

The Crisis Transaction

Active Listening Skills

Chapter Summary

INTRODUCTION

AN OFFICER'S MOST EFFECTIVE WEAPON

It has been said that a police officer's most powerful weapon is their ability to communicate effectively. Certainly in the heat of a crisis that ability is critically important. Done properly, communication is the key to de-escalation. Done improperly, it can have the opposite effect, and oftentimes does. How many times have we watched on television or in the movies as some cynical police officer convinces a "leaper" to come down off the ledge of a building by telling them to go ahead and jump? Or how about the officer who tells the failed bank robber to go ahead and shoot the hostages if he wants, and how he will then shoot the robber? And, of course, any discussion of such methods must include the single line of dialogue that has become permanently etched in our pop lexicon: "Go ahead punk, make my day!" Such unconventional methods always seem to elicit the desired response. But in reality such methods, especially when employed in a crisis situation, can have deadly results. They are better left to the creative talents of those who entertain, rather than those who routinely risk their lives to contain and de-escalate crisis.

In this chapter we will explore some of the critically important skills that are relevant to crisis intervention. We will focus on the role of communication in the containment and de-escalation of the types of crises that police and correctional officers face each and every day while on the job. We will look specifically at Transactional Analysis (TA), one of the first theories of interpersonal communications to find its way into police training and still considered the gold standard. It is a model grounded in the psychoanalytic theory of Sigmund Freud and, thus, it is solidly connected to longstanding and widely accepted theory. Although a number of other programs have since been developed and delivered throughout the criminal justice system, programs such as *Verbal Judo* and *Neuro-linguistic Programming*, most are simply reformulations of the foundational concepts first proposed by the developers and practitioners of Transactional Analysis. For this reason we will focus our Learning efforts on the TA model.

GOALS OF CRISIS COMMUNICATION

Containment and De-escalation

The goals of crisis communication are twofold: containment and de-escalation. As any police officer knows, you must contain an unruly crowd before attempting to calm the individuals down. A paramedic must stop the bleeding before attempting to treat the patient. And a firefighter must stop the spread of a fire before attempting to extinguish it. Containment is an absolute necessity before attempting to de-escalate a crisis. Sometimes the two require completely different communication styles. Containment may require an authoritarian voice, for example, to get two combatants on the street to stop their brawl. De-escalation may then require a softer, more engaging voice in order to make a connection with the person, which in turn will facilitate their compliance. Much of the law enforcement mission involves confronting and reducing conflict. Communication is the primary means of accomplishing this. It is the first step in the use of force and, if done effectively, it is hoped that no increase in the level of force will be required to resolve the issue. For the officer, communication is a juggling act. They must know not only what style works best in any particular situation, but they must also be able to adjust their style depending on the person to whom they are communicating. To a large degree, crisis communication is manipulative. Neither a police officer nor a correctional officer intends to build a lasting friendship with the people they come in contact with. Their goal is to resolve conflict and control behavior. Effective communication includes the ability to facilitate both with words alone. An officer may talk down an aggressive offender, gain the cooperation of a hostile witness, or reshape a person's perception of events entirely through the use of a communication style aimed at achieving any of those specific goals.

Reducing Liability

In this day of out-of-control litigation, a secondary goal of crisis communication is to reduce the amount of liability to the officer and their department, the latter of course being funded in almost every case by the taxpaying public. A lot is expected of police and correctional officers. Unlike other jobs, there is essentially no room for error. The presumption on the part of the public is that police and correctional officers know perfectly well how to do their jobs, and when something goes wrong, both the public and the legal system can be terribly unforgiving. For this reason law enforcement administrators are investing more time and dollars in training programs designed to enhance their officers' ability to communicate effectively while on the job. It has become a staple component of academy training for new officers, as well as the subject of advanced training for experienced personnel.

TRANSACTIONAL ANALYSIS

Ego States

Transactional Analysis was first introduced by Dr. Eric Berne (1958), a Canadian psychiatrist who studied the communication patterns of his patients in their verbal and non-verbal exchanges with other people. He referred to these exchanges as **transactions**. He found that people tend to shift between various styles of communication during transactions, depending on their stated and ulterior motives for the exchange. He developed a model in which a person is shown to communicate from one of three ego states: the parent, adult, and child. From the parent ego state the individual can communicate both as a critical parent or a nurturing parent, and from the child ego state, either as an adapted child or a natural child. These ego states are components of our personality. In other words, they are reflective of who we are. It is important that a police or correctional officer be able to identify not only the ego state of the person with whom they are interacting, but also their own ego state. As we shall see, there are times when two individuals engage in a crossed transaction. When this happens the two individuals are no longer effectively communicating, and may not be communicating at all. In the heat of a crisis this can create a dangerous or deadly situation. Before we look at the various types of good and bad transactions, and how they apply to police and correctional officers, we will first describe each ego state in more detail.

The Parent Ego State

When we communicate from our **parent ego state**, we are communicating in ways that are similar to how our parents communicated with us when we were young children. This part of our personality serves as a storehouse for all the rules, imperatives, and values we were taught as children, primarily by our parents. During the course of our early development we internalize

FIGURE 3.1   The three ego states of Transactional Analysis.

these parental norms and they become part of us. They influence us both consciously and unconsciously and, although we may make every effort to break free of their hold, it is quite difficult to do so entirely. Even those who believe they are free of their influence may still, in a moment of stress, find themselves reacting in ways similar to how their father or mother reacted in a similar situation.

In terms of communication, the parent, and more specifically the **critical parent**, is the part of us that demands, directs, orders, and seeks compliance. The critical parent lectures, moralizes, scolds, and judges others. The message embedded in this type of communication is "I'm OK; you're not OK." Examples include the police officer who confronts a group of adolescents by placing them against a wall and threatening to arrest them for loitering; or the correctional officer who privately threatens an inmate with negative consequences if he refuses to snitch on his fellow inmates; or the police officer who approaches a stopped vehicle and lectures the driver on the dangers of driving over the speed limit. Each is an example of communicating from the critical parent ego state.

The parent ego state also serves as a storehouse for the good values we are taught as children; things such as compassion, fairness, and honesty. We tap into these values when we respond from our **nurturing parent**. Just as our parents could be both nurturing and critical toward us, we react similarly toward the people with whom we come in contact. The police officer who provides comfort to an abused spouse, or attempts to help a troubled adolescent, or talk down a suicidal person is said to be responding from their nurturing parent. From this ego state we also send the message "I'm OK; you're not OK," but rather than being demanding, we are instead sending the message that we intend to help make better their condition or circumstances.

Sometimes a police officer may communicate from both ego states with the same person. For example, a police officer may communicate from their critical parent to gain the compliance of an unruly person in an effort to contain the immediate crisis, and then shift to their nurturing parent to de-escalate the matter. The message shifts from a forceful "comply or suffer the consequences!"

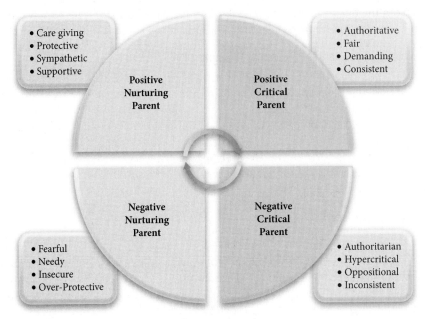

FIGURE 3.2   Parent ego state and functional modes.

to an engaging "I just want to help." The most effective police and correctional officers understand when to use both. To communicate entirely from one or the other will likely create problems for an officer. The natural inclination of an offender or inmate is to take advantage of a nurturing parent, and to fight back and become hostile toward a critical parent. An officer must know when to shift from one to the other, or to avoid communicating from their parent ego state at all. As we will see further on in the chapter, they may also respond from either their adult or child ego states.

Offenders will also respond from their critical parent when interacting with the police. The message they send, too, is "I'm OK; you're not OK." They may be overbearing and intimidating, and they view themselves as being dominant over the police, rather than the other way around. The critical parent is demonstrated in statements such as "You better call for more backup if you think you're going to take me in!" Or the one every officer hears at some point in their career: "Take that badge off and we'll see how tough you are." This personality type is quite common among those with whom the police come in contact. And certainly it is common in a prison setting, where a demeanor of toughness and intimidation is a survival mechanism among inmates.

Every parent, in talking to their children, may respond at times from their critical parent. When they do, they typically respond from their **positive critical parent**. From this ego state parents are authoritative and demanding, but also fair and consistent in their demands. The positive critical parent is an effective ego state for parents. It allows them to set necessary boundaries for their children, and then consistently reinforce those boundaries with positive outcomes. When an offender responds to a police officer in the way just described, however, or when a parent is overly harsh, inconsistent, and critical of their children, or even when a police officer is verbally abusive on a traffic stop, it can be said that all are responding from their **negative critical parent**. Rather than being authoritative, from this ego state they tend to be authoritarian, a much different demeanor that typically has negative outcomes. Susannah Temple (1999) looks at these response patterns as *functional modes* rather than ego states, and illustrates the parent as follows:

It is from the two negative modes we find problematic behavior. The negative nurturing parent might be overprotective to the point of emotionally smothering their child or loved one. And while this may certainly cause problems in a relationship, it tends not to lead often to a crisis of the sort the police would respond to. A negative critical parent however may lead to police intervention. The individual responding from this mode may be a physically abusive father or husband. And as previously described, they may become very overbearing or even hostile toward the police. Although the negative nurturing parent is overly protective, the negative critical parent is overly harsh and reactive. As we will see in a moment, when communicating with a person who is responding from their negative critical parent, the goal is to get the individual to switch to a mode that allows for a more effective interchange. This desired goal is at the heart of TA, and one of the main objectives of crisis communication. The techniques for doing this will be described later in the chapter.

The Adult Ego State

When we communicate from our **adult ego state**, we are communicating on a cognitive level rather than an emotional one. The adult ego state is the rational problem-solving component of our personality. When we communicate from this ego state we are analyzing the data that is being received during the transaction and responding to it in a rational and objective manner. The message of this ego state is "only the facts please." It is the adult in us that measures the transaction against known reality to make sense of it. The message it sends is "I'm OK; you're OK."

The police or correctional officer who responds from their adult is maintaining a professional demeanor. They are showing little or no emotion, are not being judgmental, and they show little or no sympathetic arousal. They portray themselves like Agent Joe Friday from the hit 1960s television show, *The FBI*, a man interested only in the facts of the case, and who had little emotional connection with anyone he came in contact with. Many times a police or correctional officer may start out a transaction by communicating from their adult ego state, but when tempers begin to escalate they shift to their critical parent to gain control of the situation. In the same sense, they may shift from their adult to their nurturing parent when circumstances require it. For example, while interviewing the victim of a violent offense, the officer may put their interview notes aside and attempt to console a victim after they become emotional while re-telling their story. They begin the interview from their adult ego state, maintaining a professional demeanor and gathering the facts of the case without influencing the victim's answers with their own emotional reactions. When the situation becomes overly stressful for the victim, however, a common occurrence in this type of interview, and one the officer must respond to immediately to avoid further trauma to the victim, they shift into their nurturing parent to console the victim and de-escalate their stress.

Because it is unemotional, and because at the heart of almost every crisis is a problematic pattern of emotional functioning, the adult ego state tends not to be an ego state or functional mode demonstrated by the person in crisis. It is, however, an important factor in de-escalating a crisis, as we shall see.

The Child Ego State

Whereas the parent ego state includes all of our learned rules and values, and the adult ego state our ability to rationalize and analyze, the **child ego state** includes all of our felt emotions. Another way of saying this is that our child ego state includes all the feelings we developed during childhood through our interactions with our parents, whether they were being critical or nurturing toward us. People in crisis respond mostly from their child ego state. Intoxicated people respond mostly from this position. It is irrational, emotional, and selfish. Communicating from this ego state is typically not very effective. Even police and correctional officers can respond from their child. Examples include the overly macho cop who views every woman as a conquest; the playful cop who seems always on the lookout for an opportunity to play a practical joke on another cop; and the correctional officer who endeavors to fit in with the inmates by slapping hands and talking their talk, or perhaps even by smuggling contraband into the prison for them. Responding from the child ego state is anything but professional for the police or correctional officer. It seldom has a place or purpose in either profession.

Like the parent, there are two sub-components to the child ego state: the natural child and the adapted child. The **natural child** is the raw emotional part of our personality, or the patterns of behavior we developed and demonstrated in childhood when our parents were mostly not present. It is how we *naturally* acted in situations. This is the part of us that is spontaneous and selfish, with little concern for others. The natural child in us seeks gratification. It wants what it wants, and when it wants it! There is little concern for rules and boundaries. The natural child is egocentric and focused on its own desires and pleasure seeking. At one end of the emotional spectrum the natural child seeks intimacy. At the other it seeks pleasure. It is the cognitive-oriented *adult* that must mediate these two extremes without violating the rules and expectations of the *parent*. The influence of the child can lead to a crisis in either case. For example, the craving for intimacy can potentially lead to abusive behavior by an individual when that craving is thwarted in some manner, such as when a spouse attempts to end a marriage. The craving for sexual pleasure on the other hand can potentially lead to sexual assault or multiple assaults, depending on the strength of the craving and the ability of the individual's *adult* ego state to mediate such cravings. The message of the natural child is either "I'm OK; you're OK," or "I'm OK; you're not OK," depending on the influence of the person's *adult* and *parent* ego states.

Among the police we can also see the influence of the natural child at work. An example can be seen in the social activities of many cops. They drink together, play together, and many times get in trouble together while participating in *choir practice*, a term coined by author Joseph Wambaugh to describe the off-duty activities of cops (*The Choir Boys*, 1977, 1987). Their playfulness and their need for camaraderie are both symptoms of the child ego state. Although such activities do have a positive purpose, it is when an officer is unable to regulate his or her natural child that the problems begin. Almost daily in America we see news reports of police officers arrested for driving while intoxicated, fighting, or even stealing money from street-level drug dealers while on duty. All are behavioral manifestations of the natural child.

In contrast, the **adapted child** is that part of us that seeks acceptance, and is manipulative in its efforts to gain it. The person responding from their adapted child complains, nags, and protests in an effort to protect their sense of self. Here we find all the strategies we employed as children when dealing with our parents, now being used as adults. The adapted child does not act as children naturally do, but rather with calculated intentions or with over-adapted behaviors such as anxiety, fear, and depression. The message of the adapted child is either "I'm not OK; you're OK," or "I'm not OK; you're not OK." At its worst, the adapted child is defensive, paranoid, depressed, or even schizophrenic. In a police officer, it is the adapted child that compels them to plant evidence in order to earn the accolades that come with a high-profile arrest. It is the adapted child in a police officer that constantly complains about the job, their supervisors, and the court system, and blames their own shortcomings and poor job performance on everyone but themselves.

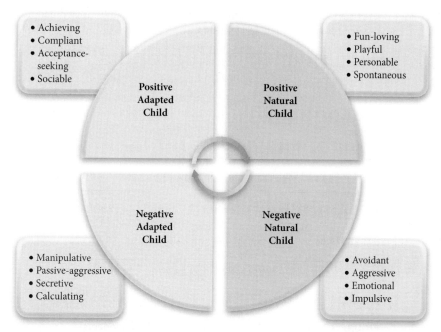

FIGURE 3.3   Child ego states and functional modes.

Like the parent ego state, the child has both positive and negative functional modes. The negative child modes are at the heart of most crises. The prison riot, for example, is typically the manifestation of a collective negative natural child. Although the positive natural child is fun-loving and pleasure-seeking, the negative natural child demands gratification, and is willing to seek it even at the physical and emotional expense of others. The uncontrolled looting that followed Hurricane Katrina in New Orleans was an example of the negative natural child. With the negative adapted child we find crisis behavior directed at protecting an individual's sense of self. Here we find suicide, which is the ultimate protective measure. When the two young men went on their murderous rampage at Columbine High School in 1999, they were acting out their frustrations, their hatred, and their insecurities by killing innocent people; again, a negative adapted child response.

Another way of drawing the distinction between the natural and adapted child ego states is to return to the parent-child interaction. The natural child is how we behaved when our parents were not around. We were not restricted by their rules or expectations. As children, our primary objective was to do those things that maximized the amount of pleasure we experienced, even if it meant doing things our parents would disapprove of. Those things were either positive, meaning they were pleasure-directed and affected no one in a negative way, or negative, meaning we selfishly intruded on someone else's rights, privacy, or well-being in order to achieve an object of gratification. In contrast, the adapted child is how we behaved when under the control of our parents. These were the behaviors and patterns of behavior we developed to maximize the amount of attention and acceptance we received from them. These behaviors could be positive, meaning they were sincere and honest, or negative, meaning they were deceptive and dishonest.

FIGURE 3.4   The three ego states and their sub-components.

The three ego states and their various sub-components and functional modes can be illustrated as follows in Figure 3.4:

It is from the negative natural or adapted child, along with the negative critical parent that crisis erupts. In the case of the former, uncontrolled, emotional, and irrational behavior is demonstrated, and in the latter, abusive and punitive behavior. To de-escalate a crisis requires the participants to be influenced to communicate from a different ego state or functional mode. This influence is the result of an officer's own communication style. As we shall see, crisis communication involves the ability on the part of the officer to influence the person in crisis in this manner. It involves the ability to move the person away from emotionality and toward rationality by communicating in a way that allows the officer to control the exchange in subtle but effective ways.

Contamination

Before we proceed further it is important to point out that although the three ego states look like clearly demarcated aspects of a single personality, in reality they are not always so. Many people have developed an adult ego state that is contaminated by either the parent or child. In a normally functioning individual, one who is pressured by their parent ego state to conform to rules and expectations, and by their child ego state to shirk off the limitations imposed by the parent in order to maximize pleasure and gratification, "there is a well-developed adult capable of mediating the two . We all experience this from time to time. The analogy that has been used frequently throughout our pop culture is the little devil on one shoulder and the little angel on the other, each trying to convince us to pursue a different course of action. In between we have our ability to think rationally and mediate the conflict in a way that benefits us the most. For example, how many times while dieting has the little devil (child) whispered in your ear,

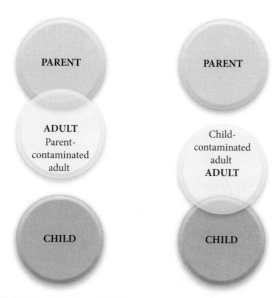

FIGURE 3.5 Parent and child contaminated adult ego state.

"Go ahead and eat that piece of pie! You can start your diet again tomorrow!" while the little angel (parent) whispers in your other ear, "You can't eat that piece of pie! If you do you will be fat and no one will like you!" One seeks gratification while the other seeks compliance and conformity. It is hoped that the adult will be able to find an acceptable alternative that gratifies the child without violating the parent, such as substituting the piece of pie with a healthy snack of fresh fruit.

When a person experiences **contamination** however, their adult ego state has lost its ability to mediate internal conflict due to the disproportionate influence of either the parent or child. When a person has a parent-contaminated adult, they have a personality that is either demanding and critical, or overprotective and needy as a normal mode of functioning. Police officers come across the parent-contaminated adult all the time, at least those contaminated by their negative critical parent. These are the "tough guys" who try to intimidate, bully, and control others, including the police, for their own benefit. Many people will react from their negative critical parent in certain situations, but the contaminated personality seldom veers from this pattern of behavior. The abusive husband or father is a good example of this personality type. Additionally, many prison inmates develop a critical parent-contaminated personality. For them, such a personality is a survival mechanism. To be intimidated in a prison setting is to mark yourself as vulnerable, a situation that can have negative consequences. Thus, those who enter the prison system must adapt to the potential danger by taking on a new demeanor, a circumstance that over time reshapes their personality.

In contrast, the child-contaminated adult is one who routinely acts either impulsively and without caution, or they're deceptive and manipulative. Neither of these personality types are strangers to the police either. Habitual criminals such as burglars, bank robbers, and petty thieves can be described as having a child-contaminated personality or more specifically, an adult contaminated by their negative adapted child. The police also deal with individuals who routinely drink, fight, and destroy property. These are people who have no boundaries to their behavior. They can be described as contaminated by their negative natural child.

As previously discussed, it is imperative for those who respond to crisis to recognize and understand the various ego states in order to respond in a way that maximizes their efforts to contain and de-escalate the crisis. This response, which is done from one of the officer's own ego states, is the other half of the transaction as a unit of communication between two or more people consisting of verbal, nonverbal, and ulterior inputs.

TRANSACTIONS

Understanding the three ego states and their various components and functional modes is only half the battle. On their own, they have little relevance to anything. After all, a person doesn't choose a particular ego state to communicate with themselves. What must be understood is the dynamic that happens when two or more people, possibly each operating from a different ego state, attempt to communicate with each other. This is at the heart of Transactional Analysis. This exchange between two or more people is what Eric Berne referred to as a *transaction*. It is a basic unit of communication consisting of a stimulus and a response (Romano, 1981). One person says something to the other, and that person interprets what has been said and then responds. Both parties to the transaction pursue their own stated or ulterior goals.

In her book *Transactional Analysis for Police Personnel* (1981), Anne T. Romano, who at the time served as an instructor at the NYPD training academy, describes the types of transactions police officers routinely enter into. For the first responder to any particular type of crisis, the transaction that ensues may mean the difference between someone's life and death. It is therefore critically important, according to Romano, that the responding officer be able to understand and answer four important questions about the transaction:

1. From which ego state is the other person communicating?
2. From which ego state are they communicating?
3. Which ego state would be most effective with this particular individual and situation?
4. How can they influence the other person's ego state in order to get them to a place where effective communication can take place?

The Parallel Transaction

Three types of transactions can take place between two people. The first is the **parallel transaction**. A common way of describing this exchange in our popular culture is by saying "we're on the same wavelength." In a parallel transaction, both parties clearly understand the words and intentions of the other. They are effectively communicating, though the substance of such communication is not always best for the given situation. Consider the following exchange between an officer and a person stopped for speeding:

OFFICER: "Is there a reason you're driving like a maniac?"

SPEEDER: "I'm sorry, Officer. Please give me a break. It'll be my third ticket."

OFFICER: "Your problems are not my fault. Now give me your license. You're getting a ticket!"

SPEEDER: "Please, Officer, I'm begging you. I'll lose my job!"

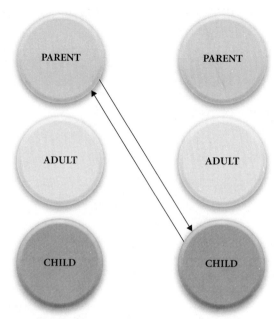

FIGURE 3.6 Parent-Child parallel transaction.

In this short exchange there is little to be misunderstood or misinterpreted. The officer is responding from their negative critical parent, and the speeder from their negative adapted child. A parent-child transaction, though not a desirable one, especially for the officer, is still a parallel transaction. The response of each to the other's words is predictable and anticipated, and in fact, because it is parallel they reinforce each other's chosen ego state and functional mode. This short exchange can be diagrammed as shown in Figure 3.6.

Now consider an example of both the officer and the speeder communicating from their child ego state.

OFFICER: "It looks like this just isn't your day, pal!"

SPEEDER: "Why don't you find some real criminals to harass!"

OFFICER: "Why should I when I have jerks like you to mess with?"

SPEEDER: "You're a big tough guy when you can hide behind that badge."

OFFICER: "Well why don't I just take this badge off and you can find out how tough I am!"

Truly both are acting like children. They are communicating with emotion, and neither would be considered totally rational in this case. It is highly unlikely that the officer would ever take off his badge and engage in a physical altercation with a person whose only violation is speeding. It is irrational to assume that taking off the badge would even make a difference. But the two are communicating nonetheless. They are clearly getting their message across to the other about how they feel, and their intentions. Their transaction is predictable and anticipated, thus making it parallel. And again, because it is parallel, each reinforces the other's ego state, in this case their child. We can diagram this transaction, as shown in Figure 3.7.

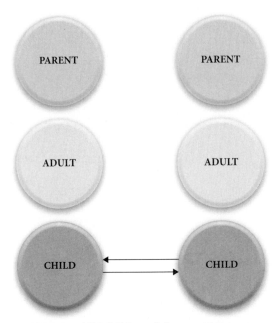

FIGURE 3.7   Child-Child parallel transaction.

The Crossed Transaction

The second type of transaction is the **crossed transaction**. This type of transaction too has been colorfully described in our popular culture. It is common for people to say things like "we're not on the same wavelength," or "we really have our wires crossed!" when trying to describe the inability of two or more people to effectively communicate. A crossed transaction is one in which the exchange is neither predictable nor anticipated because one of the participants is communicating from an ego state other than the one to whom the other participants are directing their words. In our previous example of the officer responding from their critical parent to the speeder, there is little doubt the officer is directing their communication to the other person's child. The officer is speaking down to the speeder in the same way as a critical parent would speak to their child. And because the speeder responds from their child, the transaction is parallel. But what happens when the officer directs their communication to the speeder's child, but then the speeder responds back from their critical parent? Consider the following exchange:

OFFICER: "Is there a reason you're driving like a maniac?"

SPEEDER: "Look, pal, you don't know who I am! You better get back in that squad car and forget you ever stopped me!"

OFFICER: "I need to see your driver's license, and NOW!"

SPEEDER: "Who do you think you are talking to me like that?"

In this transaction we have both the officer and the speeder communicating from their critical parent to the other's child, a crossed transaction. Another way of saying it is that both

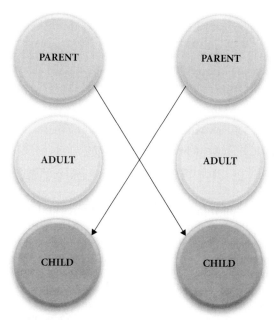

FIGURE 3.8 Parent-Parent crossed transaction.

are talking *down* to the other. We can diagram this transaction as shown in Figure 3.8. In a crossed transaction, effective communication is no longer happening, and there will be no good resolution until this situation corrects itself by becoming either an adult-adult or parent-child parallel transaction. Consider the same transaction above, only now it has progressed as follows:

OFFICER: "I'm the law, that's who I am!"

SPEEDER: "Yeah, you're right, Officer. I guess I'm just having a bad day."

OFFICER: "Your license, please."

SPEEDER: "I guess I blew my chances for a break?"

OFFICER: "I would have written the ticket anyway. You really need to slow down in this part of town. There's a school right around the corner."

Here you can see the transaction has become a little more effective. The officer continues to communicate from their critical parent, but now from a positive functional mode. In contrast, the speeder has now switched to communicating from their child ego state, specifically their positive adapted child. We now have a parallel transaction, and the two are able to move toward a resolution. Had they both continued from their critical parent, then the officer may have resolved the matter by dropping a ticket in the window and leaving, but the situation would not have been resolved to anyone's benefit. Of course, a crisis situation is not as simple as a speeding violation. The officer handling a crisis does not have the luxury of dropping a ticket in the window and leaving. The situation must be resolved through de-escalation.

The Ulterior Transaction

The final type of transaction is the **ulterior transaction**. We all encounter times when we know for certain that what someone is saying to us and what they really mean are two different things. The ulterior transaction is one in which there is an apparent message on one level, but a hidden message on another. Consider the following exchange:

OFFICER: "Ma'am, I stopped you for speeding. May I see your license, please?"

SPEEDER: "I'm sorry, Officer, I didn't realize I was going that fast."

OFFICER: "I'm afraid I'll have to issue you a citation."

SPEEDER: "But that'll be my third ticket, Officer. Is there some other way we can handle this?"

This is a common ulterior transaction that many officers find themselves in at some point in their career. In this case the officer maintains a professional demeanor while responding from his adult ego state to the speeder's adult. On the surface the female speeder appears to be responding in the same manner; however, below the surface she is attempting to engage the officer's natural child. Her *apparent* meaning is that she would like to find some acceptable alternative to the officer writing a ticket. Her *hidden* message, however, is that she may be willing to trade sexual favors for the officer not writing her the ticket.

Ulterior transactions are a common occurrence in our daily lives, and also in the professional lives of police and correctional officers, although they tend not to be the dominant communication style in the heat of a crisis. People tend to respond in a way that communicates exactly what they want to communicate when under stress. The goal of the responding officer is to ensure that the critical transactions that follow do not become crossed, thus making a successful resolution more difficult due to a breakdown in communication.

THE CRISIS TRANSACTION

People in crisis will tend to respond from a negative functional mode, either from their natural or adapted child. There are times, such as during the negotiating stage of a prison crisis, when a person at the heart of a crisis will respond from their adult, but these situations are rare. There are two goals during a crisis exchange; first, to maintain a positive parallel transaction, and second, to attempt to *hook* the person into an adult-adult transaction. When a person responds from their adult, they respond with reason and rationality, and without the emotion of the child ego state. Consider the following exchange:

SUBJECT: "I'm tired of living! Just leave me alone and let me shoot myself."

OFFICER: "Sir, you're in violation of the law by having that weapon. I'm going to ask you to put it down and put your hands against the wall."

Obviously the officer's response will not go very far toward resolving the matter. In this case we have the subject responding from their child to the officer's parent ("I'm not OK; you're OK"), and the officer responding from their adult to the subject's adult ("I'm OK; you're OK"). We have a crossed transaction, as shown in Figure 3.9. The individual wanting to kill themselves is in fact not OK, so to respond to them as if they are (adult-adult) does little to de-escalate the matter. The person in crisis will interpret such a demeanor as unresponsive and uncaring, a circumstance that could potentially exacerbate the situation.

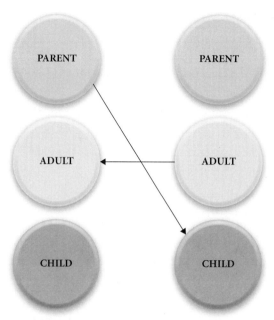

FIGURE 3.9   Crossed Adult-Child transaction.

Now let's look at this same situation from two other perspectives:

SUBJECT: "Go ahead, pig, shoot me! You think I care? I want to die!"

OFFICER: "Why should I waste a bullet on you? You want to die, do it yourself!"

In this case the subject is responding from their child to the officer's parent, and the officer is responding back in like manner, parent to child. So here we do have a parallel transaction, but it's originating from the negative functional mode of both individuals. This is seldom an effective strategy in a crisis situation, which is true of almost all negative transactions on the part of the police or other crisis responders.

SUBJECT: "My life sucks! I lost my job, my wife is leaving me, and my kids won't even talk to me! I'm just going to end it now and make everyone's life better!"

OFFICER: "Man, do I ever know how you feel. If my life gets anymore screwed up, they may find me holding a gun to my head."

Here we have a rather unique transaction that is neither crossed nor parallel. The subject responds from their child to the officer's nurturing parent; however, the officer then responds back from their natural child. Both are communicating from a positive functional mode, so the two are no doubt communicating. The subject could not anticipate this response from the officer, but because the response is neither oppositional nor crossed, it still allows for some degree of communication. Its purpose is to hook the person into a parallel transaction. Another way of saying this is that its intended purpose is to build quick rapport by connecting with the individual. This type of transaction can be effective, but must be used with caution. If an officer attempts to bluff the subject with such an exchange, and the subject senses it, then any rapport will be lost. Also, this exchange takes the focus off the subject momentarily and places it on the

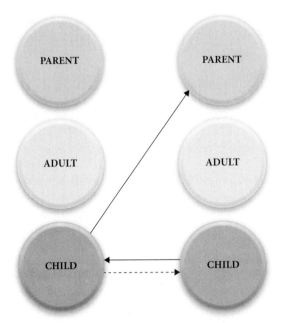

FIGURE 3.10   Child-Child hooking transaction.

officer. This is not a preferable communication pattern. It may send the message that the officer is more concerned about their own problems rather than the persons in crisis.

Finally, let's look at this scenario from a child-parent perspective:

Subject: "I don't want to live anymore. No one loves me, or cares if I live or die!"

Officer: "I'm here to help. And I care if you live or die."

In this exchange the subject responds from their adapted child to the officer's parent, and the officer responds back from their positive nurturing parent to the subject's child, an ideal strategy for building rapport and trust with a person in crisis. It is a parallel transaction, and from here effective communication is possible and likely. It is not always the case, however, that responding from the officer's nurturing parent is the most effective strategy. Consider the crisis following Katrina, or a riot inside a prison. To contain and de-escalate such a crisis requires a clear, quick, and consistent message of authority. Thus in these cases, communication is best from the responding officer's critical parent. Responding from the nurturing parent will potentially be seen as weakness, and may even result in causing the crisis to worsen.

So what is the officer to do when a crossed transaction is apparent? As in our previous example, this is when the experienced officer will hook the subject into a parallel transaction. Most people have known someone, perhaps a sibling or friend, who always seems intent on picking an argument over the most trivial of matters. Those who know such people usually develop a strategy for dealing with them that involves not responding to their invitation to argue. They may change the subject, or they may even agree with them in order to take the steam out of their confrontational demeanor. In this case you have one person directing their communication to the other's child in order to start an argument, and that person in turn attempting to hook the other's adult in order to avoid the confrontation.

So **hooking** is an effort by one person to control an exchange with another by leading them to respond in a rational way and move away from negative or ulterior messaging. In crisis communication, the goal is to hook an individual into responding from their adult. To do this requires that rapport be established. There are situations when rapport is less necessary, such as the prison riot; however, if the rioters are holding hostages, then rapport is critical. In any situation that cannot be resolved by force alone, rapport is critical. And rapport is built through positive parallel transactions, either child-child or child-parent, with the latter the more common and effective.

Noesner and Webster (1997) have outlined a number of skills that are necessary to the task of building rapport. First, the officer must remove themselves as an immediate threat in the eyes of the person in crisis, at least in those situations that cannot be resolved by force alone. This involves responding from the adult or nurturing parent ego state, and by avoiding threatening and authoritarian language (critical parent). Depending on the situation, it is appropriate and necessary for the officer to have their gun drawn, and perhaps even have it aimed at the person in crisis, but if the use of deadly force is not immediately warranted, then the officer's verbal commands and body language can signal to the subject that the situation is stable, and that the officer is not going to use deadly force at that moment. The officer responds in a professional and authoritative way, as opposed to authoritarian and, depending on the situation, may even show some amount of empathy (nurturing parent). They must avoid any demeaning, lecturing, or critical comments. These are critical parent or child responses, and more than likely will lead either to a crossed or negative parallel transaction once the subject responds. Neither will be beneficial in the early stages of the exchange before rapport has been established.

ACTIVE LISTENING SKILLS

Once the officer sends the message that they are not an immediate threat, then rapport is built through a series of techniques that are each part of what we refer to as the process of **active listening**. These techniques are at the heart of crisis negotiations, and are now taught to hostage and crisis negotiators throughout the American criminal justice system. As Noesner and Webster describe it, these techniques allow officers to respond to the emotional needs of those in crisis, clearing the way for the necessary behavioral changes that must take place in order to bring about a successful resolution. Active listening techniques include the following:

- **Minimal Encouragements**: These are simply short verbal replies that demonstrate the officer's concern for what the person in crisis is saying. Responses such as "I understand" or "I see" communicate the message that the officer is listening. People in crisis want to be heard, and they want people to understand their situation. By providing these simple responses, the officer can keep the person talking. And the more they talk, the more the officer can take control of the exchange through effective adult or nurturing-parent transactions. They can also facilitate this desired goal with their body language. Maintaining eye contact and nodding the head to acknowledge what the person is saying are simple, but effective measures.
- **Paraphrasing**: Paraphrasing involves the officer repeating the person's words back to them to demonstrate that they are listening, and that they understand what the person has said. This conveys a sense of empathy on the part of the officer. For example, if the person says something like, "I don't want to live anymore. No one wants me around," the officer might respond by saying, "I understand, you believe no one wants you around." Or in the midst

of prison riot one of the leaders of the uprising says, "Get those guards away from that door or else I'll start cutting these hostages!" The negotiator might respond with something like, "I understand, you want the guards to back away from the door." Paraphrasing validates the person's concern or position, and can momentarily ease the tension. It also can hook a person responding from a negative functional mode to a more positive one. Consider the following exchange:

HOSTAGE TAKER: "Get those officers back or I'll shoot this woman!"

NEGOTIator: "I understand, you want the officers to move back."

HOSTAGE TAKER: "It's making me nervous seeing all those guns pointed at me."

NEGOTIATOR: "I can see you're nervous. Anyone would be nervous with guns pointed at them."

HOSTAGE TAKER: "I don't want to hurt anyone. I just want to be treated with a little respect for once."

NEGOTIATOR: "I know you don't want to hurt anyone. Everyone wants to be respected. I understand that."

In this short exchange you can see how paraphrasing is already hooking the individual to move from a negative child response to a more positive child response directed at the negotiator's nurturing-parent. This parallel transaction will foster rapport-building. Many people in crisis have little desire to see their situations end badly. Through some complex mix of circumstances they find themselves unable to change the course of events, and before they know it the events are spiraling out of control. By paraphrasing and demonstrating empathy, the officer sends the message that perhaps there is a way out of their predicament without the need for a violent and tragic ending.

- **Emotion-Labeling:** As previously stated, people in crisis respond for the most part from their negative child ego state, and thus they are highly emotional. The officer cannot avoid this dimension of their behavior, and must respond to it, at least until they can effectively hook the subject into responding from their adult ego state. Until then, they must respond to their child. To interact with an emotional person by responding to their adult ego state will not be effective. It will instantly send the message that the officer does not understand or care about the person's situation. The officer must respond to the person's child, and they must understand the person's emotional state as the person understands it. For example, it would be ineffective to tell a person complaining of being depressed that they're only confused.

A person knows what depression feels like, at least in their own experience, so it is important that the officer respond to it accordingly. Emotion-labeling allows the officer to attach a label to what the person is feeling, and to demonstrate their understanding. Once again, this sends a message of empathy, a very powerful technique for building rapport. For example, an officer confronting a domestic hostage-taker might say something like, "It sounds as though something happened between you and your wife today that made you very angry." By labeling the emotion, the officer hopes to get the person to validate the assessment by saying something like, "Yes, I'm angry! No man should have to put up with this." By labeling the emotion, the officer has sent the message that they understand what the hostage-taker is going through. And with this connection, indeed a parallel transaction, comes the potential for rapport-building.

Active listening skills

- Minimal Encouragements
- Paraphrasing
- Emotion-labeling
- Open-ended Questions
- Effective Pauses

FIGURE 3.11   Active listening skills.

- **Open-Ended Questions:** The use of open-ended questions allows the officer to gather important information about the person's feelings and intent without giving the appearance that they are conducting an interrogation. Open-ended questions invite the person to continue talking, which is almost always preferable in a crisis situation. When the officer dominates the exchange there is less of an opportunity to gather important information about the person. Consider the following transaction:

SUICIDAL PERSON: "I don't want to live anymore! There's nothing left for me in this world."

OFFICER: "Can you help me understand why you feel that way?"

Suicidal person: "There's nothing to understand. Life sucks!"

OFFICER: "Please, tell me more about what got you to this point."

As long as the officer keeps the individual talking, the more they will find out about the person's situation and why they are suicidal. Open-ended questions send the message that the officer is interested, and that alone will usually lead a person to share with the officer more of their feelings, and the reasons for their present circumstances. Once again, when the person responds to an open-ended question it is typically a parallel transaction, and the officer has a greater opportunity to hook the individual into an adult-adult transaction, assuming they are not already communicating at that level.

- **"I" Messages:** When a person in crisis sees another human being across from them rather than simply a police uniform with a body in it, there is a much greater chance for effective communication. The use of "I" messages tends to personalize the officer by allowing them to express their own feelings and connect with the person in crisis on an emotional level.

The use of "I" messages can also allow the officer to redirect an argumentative or combative person without provoking them. Compare the following two responses:

OFFICER RESPONSE 1: "Stop arguing and listen to what I'm saying!"

OFFICER RESPONSE 2: "I'm having a difficult time communicating when you argue like that."

The difference is obvious. In the first case, the officer's words may only provoke more argument. It comes across as a command (i.e., critical-parent) directed at the person in crisis. Commanding and authoritarian language on the part of the officer is usually unproductive. If a person is led to their current situation by an overly critical spouse or boss, then such language by the officer may only reinforce the person's crisis behavior.

ISSUES & ETHICS IN CRISIS INTERVENTION

When the Police Lie

One communication technique that is seldom included in a police training program, but one that is often employed, is for an officer to simply lie to achieve a desired goal. For example, consider the officer who tells a potential combative suspect that he needs to place him in handcuffs only temporarily while completing some necessary paperwork, and that he will release him when he's finished. Once the cuffs are secure however, the officer advises the suspect he is in fact under arrest. He lies to avoid a potentially dangerous situation. Another example is the officer who advises an abusive husband that his wife does not wish to file a complaint, a lie, and then attempts to get him to admit that he struck her. Of course, once he does, then the husband is placed under arrest. And finally, consider the hostage-taker who gives up after he is informed by the responding officers that the prosecuting attorney has agreed to charge him only with a minor infraction, again, a lie intended to de-escalate the crisis and effect the safe release of the hostage.

The idea of the police lying seems repulsive to some, but to others, especially the police, it is a legitimate method for containing and de-escalating a crisis at times. Is it legal? Absolutely; however, there are limitations on the extent to which the police can lie. The courts have essentially ruled that *intrinsic* lies, or those lies that misrepresent a person's connection to a crime in order to gain a confession, are acceptable. For example, telling a suspect that his car was observed by a witness at the scene of the crime, even if not true, is an acceptable intrinsic lie. *Extrinsic* lies, or those lies that may potentially distort a person's ability to make a rational choice about confessing to a crime, are mostly not acceptable. For example, threatening to take a mother's children from her unless she confesses to a crime would likely render the confession inadmissible due to its coercive nature. Some of the relevant court cases on police lying are as follows:

Frazier v. Cupp, 394 U.S. 731 (1969).

Holland v. McGinnis, 963 F.2d 1044, 1050-51 (7th Cir. 1992).

Lynumn v. Illinois, 372 U.S. 528 (1963).

Spano v. New York, 360 U.S. 315 (1959).

State v. Kelekolio, 849 P.2d 58, 73 (Haw. 1993).

United States v. Flemmi, 225 F.3d 78, 84 (1st Cir. 2000).

United States v. Rodman, 519 F.2d 1058; 1975 U.S. App. LEXIS 13204 (1st Cir. 1975).

Discussion Questions

1. Should the police ever resort to the use of lies, even if legal and used for the purpose of saving lives?
2. Discuss some ways in which the use of lies by the police could potentially be misused.
3. Do some basic internet research on the concept of police "entrapment," and discuss the differences between entrapment and the legitimate use of lies by the police.

The second response is much different. No commands are being directed at the person. It also personalizes the officer, and sends the message that they are in fact trying to communicate. It is not provoking in any way, and may in fact cause the person to accept some responsibility for the transaction and begin to respond in a more effective way. It is difficult, if not impossible to argue with a person who focuses only on themselves rather than the other person. In a crisis situation arguing is never productive. Using "I" messages can help an officer avoid being hooked into responding from their critical-parent or negative-child and arguing with the person they are trying to help.

- **Effective Pauses:** There are times in a crisis situation when the best strategy is to simply remain quiet. Silence can be uncomfortable, even for a person in crisis. It may encourage them to keep talking and provide additional information about their situation. Additionally, silence can be used to disrupt argumentative or emotional outbursts by simply not responding to them. Many times people in crisis expect the police to respond from their critical parent or negative child, and thus attack them in an authoritarian or argumentative way. By maintaining strategically placed periods of silence, the officer can quell this expectation. The emotional energy that powers an argument comes from the interaction of two people responding to each person's negativity. By remaining silent, the officer can control the direction of the exchange, and perhaps even hook the person into an adult-adult transaction.

The active listening skills just discussed have a twofold purpose. They help the officer establish rapport with the person, and by actively listening they learn a great deal about what brought the person to this point. If they are successful in hooking the person into an adult-adult transaction, or even a nurturing parent-child transaction, then they are in a position to begin offering the person alternatives and a way out of their predicament. Many people in crisis really just want a way out of their crisis, but in a way that preserves their sense of self, however distorted it may be at that point. If the officer has established rapport, then the person will likely be open to at least considering the available options. It is then when the officer can seek the person's commitment to take the necessary action that will bring the event to a safe and peaceful conclusion.

Chapter Summary

The ability of a criminal justice professional to effectively communicate in the heat of a crisis is a skill that can mean the difference between life and death. As stated at the outset of this chapter, the days of the authoritarian officer attempting to scare a hostage-taker into submission with little regard for the hostages, or the cavalier officer telling a "leaper" to go ahead and leap, are long over, and thankfully so. In today's criminal justice system, communication skills are critically necessary, and a great deal of basic, intermediate, and advanced training is provided at nearly every level of the various professions within the criminal justice system. These training programs, including Transactional Analysis, all boil down to some simple skills that facilitate effective communication. First, we immediately set about the task of building rapport. As we do, we listen both to what the person is saying and what they are not saying, and we demonstrate our concern for their situation through active-listening skills. We avoid responding with too much or too little emotion. And once rapport is established, we attempt to get the person to respond in a rational way with the goal of gaining their commitment to de-escalate the crisis in a safe and peaceful manner.

Key Terms

Transactional analysis	Adult	Crossed transaction
Transaction	Child	Ulterior transaction
Ego state	Contamination	Hooking
Parent	Parallel transaction	Active listening

Discussion Questions

1. Consider a male police officer responding to a domestic dispute involving a verbally abusive husband. How might the officer respond, and what types of things might he say, if he were to respond from his critical parent ego state? From his adult? From his natural child?

2. Think of someone in your life who is routinely argumentative, perhaps a friend or family member. Describe the tactic you typically employ to thwart their efforts to suck you into the argument, and then relate that tactic to "hooking."

3. Should male and female criminal justice professionals use the same communication style and tactics in any given situation, or are there gender differences in terms of what communication style works best?

4

The Use of Force

LEARNING OUTCOMES

Upon completion of this chapter the student should be able to:

1. Summarize the concept of force, and to define the force continuum that guides its use.
2. Explain the legal constraints on the use of force by police and correctional officers.
3. Explain the phenomenon of "contagious shooting."
4. Summarize the psychology of force, and to define the phenomenon of "perceptual distortion."
5. Explain the potential role race plays in the use of force.

Chapter Outline

INTRODUCTION

THE CASE OF AMADOU DIALLO

On a cold New York City night in early February, 1999, a young African immigrant named Amadou Diallo was ordered by four NYPD plainclothes officers to stop as he entered the hallway of his Bronx apartment building. Diallo matched the description of a rape suspect the officers had been looking for in the hours preceding the incident. Doing what he believed to be appropriate, Diallo slowly reached into his pocket to retrieve his identification. In the chaotic seconds that followed, the officers pulled their service weapons and shot a total of 41 times in Diallo's direction, striking him 19 times and killing him (New York Times, Feb. 5, 1999). The shooting immediately set off a series of protests, and further inflamed the already tense relationship between the NYPD and the city's minority communities. To the passive observer, the incident appeared nothing more nor less than four white police officers brutally murdering an unarmed and defenseless Black man. People simply could not fathom how the four police officers could justify firing their weapons so many times at someone who was not firing back.

The four officers—Kenneth Boss, Sean Carroll, Edward McMellon, and Richard Murphy—maintained throughout that they thought Diallo had pulled a gun from his pocket when they ordered him to stop, thus justifying their use of deadly force. They also made the case that when they clearly identified themselves as NYPD officers and ordered him to stop, Diallo instead ran up the steps to the doorway of his building. From there things quickly escalated. One of the officers yelled "GUN!" and, as the first shot rang out, one of the other officers tripped and fell. In the chaotic seconds that followed, the unarmed Diallo was killed in a hail of gunfire. The three officers left standing later reported that they thought the fourth officer had been shot when he fell to the ground.

The shooting only intensified public debate over the NYPD and its practices. Charges of police brutality and racial profiling were commonplace, some of the former actually involving the use of torture on suspected offenders (Delattre, 2002). The case also brought to the public's attention a phenomenon called contagious shooting (Wilson, 2006), a circumstance in which one officer firing their service weapon induces other officers to follow suit even before the others are consciously aware of the reasons for their use of deadly force. Following an investigation of the Diallo shooting, the four officers were indicted by a grand jury on charges of second-degree murder and reckless homicide, charges that carried with them the possibility of the four officers being sentenced to 25 years to life in prison (New York Times, April 1, 1999). To the shock of many, all four of the officers were eventually acquitted by a mixed-race jury.

During the trial the attorneys representing the four officers successfully made the case that tragic though the shooting was, their guilt or innocence boiled down to their state of mind at the time of the shooting, and that they fully believed Diallo had pulled a gun from his pocket and was preparing to shoot, or had in fact shot. It is an argument that has been made many times in cases where police officers are prosecuted for wrongful shooting deaths. Very few are ever convicted because a state of mind is so difficult to disprove, as the prosecution is required to do in these cases. In the Diallo case they attempted to do so by the number of shots that were fired, which they argued showed a premeditated desire to kill Diallo when their own lives were not in jeopardy. The defense successfully countered that argument by suggesting that most of the shots were the result of **contagious shooting**, and that though it does reflect some degree of panic on the part of the officers, it also supports a purported state of mind that Diallo was a threat to their safety. In the end, psychology was on the side of the officers, and they walked away from the courthouse acquitted of their alleged crimes. The city eventually settled a civil suit brought by Diallo's family, awarding them $3 million.

On the positive side, a number of reforms were put in place following the Diallo case. For starters, the NYPD disbanded its street crime unit. Not only were the four officers members of this aggressive unit, but many of the allegations of brutality and misconduct that had been leveled in recent years were directed at members of the unit. The case also caused the NYPD to revisit the issue of deadly force, and to look for ways to better train its officers in the decision-making skills related to its use. The case also heightened public awareness of issues on both sides of the use of force argument, and caused a flurry of new research on the psychology of deadly force, along with new techniques for accomplishing the same outcome by less lethal means.

THE USE OF FORCE

The **use of force**, or a police officer's use of weapons and techniques designed to control, incapacitate, or kill a suspect threatening or perpetrating violence against the officer or other people, is one method by which the police contain and de-escalate crisis. If trained properly, a police officer will use elevated levels of force as a last resort, but will not hesitate to do so when circumstances dictate its use. It is hoped that just the general knowledge and belief on the part of the public that the police will in fact resort to force when necessary will in many cases prevent a crisis from ever erupting. The police wear the instruments of force in plain view: firearms, Tasers, pepper spray, and expandable batons, to name a few. The deterrent effect of a fully equipped uniformed officer can be quite powerful for those who wisely see the futility of being confrontational. As we shall see, the lowest level of force employed by an officer is their mere presence and verbal commands. But that presence is much more than simply being in close proximity to the crisis. It includes the presence of the threat of force, as demonstrated by the visible tools of their trade.

The use of force as a crisis intervention strategy is not limited to just the police. It is routinely used in correctional settings to contain and de-escalate riots and unruly inmates by threatening or actually using force against them. No situation is more dangerous than an unarmed correctional officer getting caught up in a prison riot with inmates armed with shanks and other improvised weapons. It typically begins with an attack by one inmate on another, perhaps from a rival gang, or to settle a score. If steps are not immediately taken to contain the crisis through the threat of force, then group behavior can overtake the situation and lead to a riot. If a correctional officer happens to be caught in the middle, their safety, and possibly their life, is immediately jeopardized. Deadly force will be used without hesitation, if necessary, to contain and de-escalate the situation.

Perhaps no other aspect of the criminal justice mission has been questioned, criticized, and defended more than the use of force. Much of the criticism results from the misuse of force, especially in the days prior to the Supreme Court's decision to better define exactly when deadly force can be employed. Even today, however, the use of force by the police invariably leads to allegations of brutality and racism by a general public that has a limited understanding of the concept of force, and the legal parameters for its use. Unfortunately Hollywood has not helped the cause of law enforcement in this regard. Movies and television shows leave the impression in the public mind that police officers shoot first for the legs, or perhaps at a hand holding a weapon, and that they shoot only after being fired upon first, or when they successfully beat the bad guy to the draw. Of course nothing could be further from the truth. Police officers are trained to shoot for one area of the body, "center mass," and to shoot to kill. It is this gap between public perception and reality that leads to the criticism that oftentimes follows a police shooting.

In this chapter we will explore the use of force as a means to contain and de-escalate crisis. We will look at the **force continuum** that dictates exactly what level of force a law enforcement or correctional officer may legally use in a given situation. We will look at the psychology of force, and the impact of stress on the perception of the officer. We will try to understand why at least one of the officers in the Diallo case was sure he saw a gun in Diallo's hand, and why so many shots were fired when Diallo obviously was not shooting back. And finally we will look at the role race and ethnicity may play in an officer's decision to use deadly force. But first we will look at the history of the use of force in America, and how the current legal constraints on its use came to be.

THE HISTORY OF FORCE IN AMERICA

Tennessee v. Garner: The Fleeing Felon Rule

Prior to the Supreme Court's decision in the case of *Tennessee v. Garner* (1984), police departments across the country allowed for the use of deadly force by their officers in one of two situations. The first obviously was to protect their own life, or the lives of others. But the second reason was more controversial. The **fleeing felon rule** allowed officers to shoot to kill a felony suspect as a last resort to prevent their escape. This rule essentially made the act of killing discretionary on the part of the officer(s) involved. There was no requirement that the officer or anyone else be placed in jeopardy of death or bodily harm by the suspect. It was simply enough that they were attempting to escape arrest.

For decades police departments operated under this standard. New police officers were trained in the use of deadly force with the fleeing felon rule being one of their foundational training principles. A staple of police training in Illinois for example was the acronym "MARK V. BART," which delineated the various felonies for which a fleeing suspect could be shot and killed (murder, arson, robbery, kidnapping, vehicle theft, burglary, aggravated assault, rape, and treason). The result of this standard was a high number of unarmed suspects over the years literally shot in the back as they attempted to avoid capture.

The use of deadly force by the police was finally restricted in 1985 when the U.S. Supreme Court heard the case of *Tennessee v. Garner* (471 U.S. 1). The case was a civil suit brought by the father of Edward Garner against the City of Memphis and one of its police officers, patrolman Elton Hymon, and alleging violations of the Civil Rights Act of 1871. The case would test the constitutionality of the fleeing felon rule, and ultimately restrict the use of deadly force by law enforcement all across America.

The incident that gave rise to the Supreme Court's review of the deadly force issue took place on October 3, 1974. On that night, at approximately 10:45 P.M., two Memphis patrolmen, Elton Hymon and Leslie Wright, were dispatched to a possible burglary in progress. As Officer Hymon went to the rear of the house, he spotted 15-year-old Edward Garner running across the yard and eventually stopping at a 6 ft. high chain fence. Hymon had a clear view of Garner's hands in his flashlight beam, and could see he was not armed. He ordered the teenager to halt, but Garner disregarded his command and began climbing the fence. Without hesitation Hymon fired his service revolver and struck Garner in the back of the head, killing him. Ten dollars and a purse from the burglarized house were found in his possession.

Hymon was cleared by his department of any wrongdoing since his actions were allowed under Tennessee State law, and also the policies of the Memphis Police Department, which allowed for the use of all necessary force to affect the arrest of a felony suspect. In Garner's case, he was a suspect in a residential burglary, which was and still is a felony offense. In the civil case that ensued, the original court of jurisdiction, the U.S. District Court for the Western District of Tennessee, found in favor of the officer by ruling that the fleeing felon rule was in fact constitutional. Garner's father appealed the decision, and the U.S. Court of Appeals reversed the lower court's ruling. The Appeals Court held that the killing of a suspect is a "seizure" for purposes of the Fourth Amendment, and thus a **reasonableness** requirement applies. In other words, the killing of a suspect is constitutional only if it is reasonable. Based on the facts of the case, the Appeals Court ruled that it was unreasonable to use deadly force against a teenager for a suspected burglary. At the same time, the Appeals Court ruled that the State of Tennessee had failed to restrict the use of deadly force by reference to the severity of the crime. In the end the Supreme Court upheld the Appellate Court's ruling, and with its decision forever changed the requirements for the use of deadly force by law enforcement.

THE FORCE CONTINUUM

Following the Supreme Court's decision in *Tennessee v. Garner*, police departments around the country adjusted their training and policies relating to the use of deadly force. The change wasn't limited to just the police. Correctional officers, parole officers, and even armed security officers would now be held to the same standard. No longer could a fleeing felon be shot while escaping, unless his or her escape posed an immediate threat to the officer or others. Now the situation would dictate the amount of force that could be used rather than a listing of acceptable crimes. Deadly force was always justified in the case of an officer protecting themselves or others, not unlike the circumstances under which a private citizen can use such force. But now that would become the only legal standard governing the use of deadly force.

What the Supreme Court's decision did was make the use of force a state of mind issue. In other words, it was now up to the subjective evaluation of the officer to determine when deadly force is necessary in order to protect themselves or others. Whereas the use of force is found in three separate types of scenarios, as seen in Figure 4.1, the most extreme form of force could now be used only in two of them. It was no longer acceptable to use deadly force simply to gain compliance, except when attempting to do so results in the officer having to defend themselves or others. The use of force now sat squarely in the domain of psychology, and the criminal justice system quickly learned that it was not a black-and-white issue by any measure. Although the Supreme Court now required the officer to perceive imminent threat before resorting to deadly force, it did not require an untainted, or even a correct perception of the threat on the part of the officer. The case of Amadou Diallo provides a perfect example of the subjectivity of this evaluation. The officers were found justified in their use of force because their perception of the event was that Diallo had a gun. The fact that he did not have a weapon in his possession was secondary to what the officers perceived, imperfect though it was.

As the criminal justice system adjusted their training and procedures, it quickly became apparent that by injecting a reasonableness standard into the use of force, the Supreme Court was necessarily saying that the level of force that would be considered reasonable in any situation would be based on the severity of the situation itself. With police officers facing situations of varying levels of severity each and every day, it now became necessary to train officers to use force at varying levels. The force continuum, or the varying levels of force used by the police, from verbal commands to deadly measures, that are employed and progressively elevated depending on the amount of force the officer perceives as necessary to de-escalate the situation,

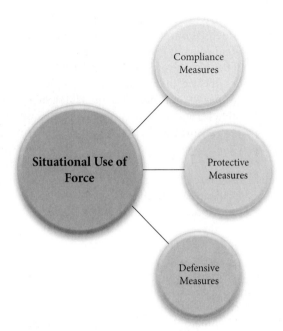

FIGURE 4.1   Situational Use of Force.

became the standard and remains so to this day. Unfortunately though, the formulation of the continuum is not standardized. There are many different variations, all beginning with a mild form of force and ending with the use of deadly force. In between are various levels, all representing a progressive escalation in the amount of force that will be deemed reasonable under the circumstances.

The force continuum, as presented in the current text, is a guide for the use of force that spells out five different levels, from something as unobtrusive as the officer's verbal commands, to force of a lethal nature. Police officers are trained to use the least amount of force necessary in a given situation, and to elevate their level of force as the severity of the situation rises. For example, when an officer responds to a domestic disturbance, if an arrest is warranted, then the officer attempts to affect the arrest with nothing more than verbal commands, the lowest level of force on the continuum. If the suspect pulls away from the officer, then the severity of the situation has risen, and the officer responds by elevating his level of force to physically restrain the suspect. If the suspect pulls a gun from his pocket at any point in the confrontation, then the officer justifiably increases his level of force to lethal, and may shoot the suspect before he or an innocent party is harmed. In this case the officer is justified in skipping over all levels of force in between once the threat of the gun is presented. It is not uncommon for a situation to be so fluid that the amount of force reasonably necessary shifts between a number of levels, either up or down, in a matter of seconds before the crisis is de-escalated.

To better understand the force continuum, we will look at each level separately.

Level One: Verbal Commands

The lowest level of force is simply the officer's **verbal commands**. It is hoped that when the officer arrives on the scene, or when the correctional officer comes in close proximity to a crisis

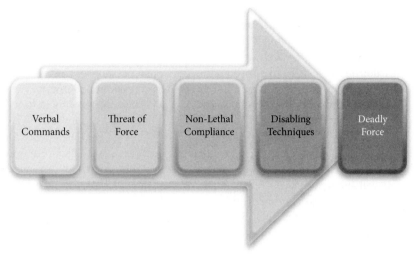

FIGURE 4.2 The Force Continuum.

among the prison population, just their visible presence and verbal commands will be sufficient to contain and de-escalate the crisis. This, of course, is always the desired level of force to resolve any situation. The officer is effective at this level by maintaining a professional and assertive demeanor without appearing or sounding aggressive or abusive. If the officer's body language appears aggressive and confrontational, or if their verbal commands are intended to intimidate or belittle, then the crisis may be escalated out of the suspect's anger or their expectation of the officer's own physical aggression. This will cause the officer to escalate their level of force in response. An officer can also be ineffective at this level of force if their demeanor is timid, or if they appear nervous or scared. A suspect may escalate their level of confrontation if they suspect this is so. In either case, if the officer's demeanor is overbearing or timid, it may become necessary to increase the level of force when perhaps it could have been avoided. This is precisely why police and correctional officers receive training in interpersonal communication strategies during their initial training phase.

It is important to point out that many times officers do not intervene at this lowest level of force just for the sake of trying the least intrusive level first, and then working their way up, nor are they expected to in every situation. For example, if an officer arrives at a domestic disturbance to find a man attempting to stab his wife, to waste time with verbal commands could mean the difference between life and death. In this case, the officer may very well resort immediately to deadly force and shoot the attacker, something the officer would be completely justified in doing. If, however, the man was only holding a knife, and perhaps had some distance between he and his wife, then it might be considered reasonable to verbally command the man to drop the knife without immediately resorting to deadly force. It is up to the subjective evaluation of the officer to determine what is reasonable in each situation.

Level Two: Threat of Force

The second level of force involves the **threat of force**, or a level of force in which the officer attempts to gain the compliance of a suspect by overtly threatening the use of physical force or a weapon against them in response to continued non-compliance. If the situation warrants, the officer may threaten any number of possible consequences if the individual does not comply with their verbal commands. The officer may point a canister of pepper spray at the suspect, or they may verbally advise the individual that if they do not comply with their verbal commands, then physical force will be used. The officer may draw their weapon and point it at the suspect. Or they may threaten to release a police dog on the suspect. In a prison setting, emergency response teams will clearly advise an inmate what is about to happen if they do not comply with the commands they have been given. If they refuse, an overwhelming amount of physical force typically follows, without delay.

In most cases the threat of force is sufficient to gain the individual's compliance. It is important to point out though that not just any threat can be leveled by the officer. The level of force that is threatened is the amount of force considered reasonable given the circumstances. For example, let's assume the officer is investigating a case of vandalism, and has detained a couple juveniles who were in the area. He will attempt, through verbal commands, to gain their compliance in sitting quietly on the ground while he calls the property owner. If one of them refuses to sit down, however, the officer may escalate to the threat of force, but the force threatened cannot exceed what is reasonable in this situation. For example, the officer may threaten to place the boy in handcuffs. What they can't threaten is the use of disabling or deadly force, because neither would be considered reasonable under the circumstances. If, however, the officer notices the juvenile fidgeting back and forth to hide what appears to be a bulge in his pocket, then the officer will be justified in threatening deadly force by drawing their weapon if they can articulate that it was their state of mind at the time that they thought the youth may have had a gun in his pocket. Perception dictates the level of force that is reasonable, and the level of force considered reasonable dictates the level of force that can be threatened.

Level Three: Non-lethal Compliance Techniques

The third level of force is the use of **non-lethal compliance techniques**, or a level of force in which the officer attempts to gain physical control of a suspect without causing disabling injury. The goal is to gain physical control of the individual in order to force their compliance. The most common form of level three force is physical force. The officer may begin with a "soft hand" approach, intended to move the individual into position to be handcuffed. If this doesn't work then the officer may be forced to use control tactics such as pressure points and physical take-down techniques to gain immediate control. When ERT members enter the prison cell of an inmate refusing to comply, they are trained to gain quick control over the individual through the use of body shields, shackles, and overwhelming physical force. Once again, the goal is not to disable, but to gain compliance through physical control.

With this level of force the possibility of injury is greatly increased. Defensive tactics continue to be a mainstay of police training. The goal is to teach officers the quickest and most effective methods for gaining physical control of a suspect or inmate without harming them. And to further offset the potential for injury, a number of new weapons have been developed—things such as body nets and a type of foam spray that encases a suspect, making it difficult, if not impossible to maneuver— that are designed to gain control in a non-lethal and even non-disabling manner. Although these new weapons are not yet in widespread use, with the liability costs related to policing ever-increasing the financial strain on municipalities, their deployment will inevitably become standard protocol.

Level Four: Disabling Techniques

Level four involves the use of **disabling techniques**. These are techniques designed to physically incapacitate the individual, rendering them incapable of resisting further the officer's commands. Using our prison example, if ERT members are simply unable to gain control of an inmate, then chances are they will escalate their level of force to the use of pepper spray, baton strikes, or possibly a Taser. It may also involve physically striking the individual. If an officer takes down a suspect in an effort to handcuff and control them, and the individual is at risk of getting up and fighting back with only one handcuff secured, then the officer will be justified in escalating their level of force to level four. At this point they may remove their Taser or pepper spray and use it against the individual. The goal is not to control, but to render the individual incapable of further non-compliance.

Certainly at this stage the risk of physical injury to the suspect is greatly increased. In fact, there is a real danger of death. A number of deaths have been reported following the use of a Taser or pepper spray on a suspect. Most have resulted not from the use of the weapon necessarily, but rather from other medical conditions that were aggravated by the use of the weapon. As previously stated, many new non-lethal weapons have been developed—such high pitched sound devices and bean bags fired from shotguns—that are designed to disable an individual without causing lasting harm. Again, the goal at level four is to deliver sufficient force to prevent the suspect or inmate's continued non-compliance, or to remove an immediate threat by meeting force with a commensurate amount of counterforce.

Level Five: Lethal Force

Of course the final level of force is **lethal force**. When an officer resorts to this level, they are either attempting to kill the individual, or they are taking an action that could reasonably be expected to result in death. Shooting an individual, striking them in the head with a baton, or using a squad car to force another vehicle off the road in an effort to terminate a high speed chase are all forms of deadly force. When an officer resorts to this level of force, they have determined that no lesser amount of force will be effective, and that someone's life will be in jeopardy if the individual in not brought under immediate control. The standard is simply that: someone will be killed or seriously harmed if the suspect is not stopped, and the officer has determined in their mind that no lesser amount of force will be effective in accomplishing this. Examples include the following:

- An officer comes upon another officer struggling with an individual pulled over in a routine traffic stop. Anytime an officer is being physically accosted, there is the possibility of the assailant gaining control of the officer's weapon. In this case the second officer strikes the assailant with his squad car, killing him. Could he have pulled up, exited his vehicle, and used the threat of force to stop the attack? Absolutely, but if the officer articulates that it was their state of mind at the time that had they done so it would have given the attacker time to disarm and possibly kill the officer, then deadly force becomes justified.
- A prison guard posted in the guard tower suddenly observes a riot in the prison yard. Immediately a command is given for all inmates to drop to the ground. Rather than doing so, they continue to riot and the guard spots an inmate with a knife in his hand approaching another inmate in an aggressive manner with his knife raised. The guard shoots and kills the inmate. Again, deadly force is justified.
- A very large and muscular police officer is approached on the street by a much smaller intoxicated man who threatens to beat the officer up. The officer is not overly concerned about the man's ability to follow through on his threat. Is deadly force justified? Likely not. In this case the officer might begin with a verbal command, followed by a threat of force if the man does not comply. If that doesn't work, then the force used will likely be a non-lethal compliance technique. But now let's assume the officer spots a knife in the man's hand as he approaches with his threat. In this case deadly force may be justified, assuming there

is no time for verbal commands or a threat of force, as the officer confronts threatened force with a commensurate amount of counterforce. Finally, let's assume the intoxicated man has a very large muscular build, and the police officer is a female. In this case there is little doubt that the man can easily overpower the officer physically. There is little chance that a non-lethal compliance technique will ensure the officer's safety, and even a disabling technique such as a Taser or pepper spray is not guaranteed. In this case, given the officer's state of mind, there is a good chance that deadly force will be justified if verbal commands and threat of force have failed, or even if the officer can articulate that there was no time to even attempt reduced levels of force.

In just about every crisis in which a police officer or correctional officer intervenes, there is at least the possibility that force will need to be used in order to contain and de-escalate the matter. In the case of the correctional officer, some level of force is probable. It is critical that criminal justice professionals understand the force continuum and its role in crisis intervention. It is designed not only to protect the officer, but to limit the unnecessary killing of people with whom they come in contact.

THE PSYCHOLOGY OF FORCE

As previously stated, by adding the reasonableness standard, the Supreme Court left responsibility for the use of force to the psychology of the officer using it. It became a state of mind issue, and thus the perception of the officer became the mediating factor. But by doing this they made the use of force reliant upon an imperfect decision-making process, because a person's perception can so easily be skewed, especially when excited. It is this reality that can lead an officer to use deadly force perhaps when not justified, as in the case of Amadou Diallo, but it is the science of perception that will so often lead a jury to acquit those officers charged with the excessive use of force.

The Role of Perception

Perception, or the process by which we interpret and understand stimuli in our sensory field, is one of those aspects of human behavior that is highly influenced by a person's emotions. What we see, hear, taste, smell, and touch, are highly influenced by the degree to which our neurological system is either excited or inhibited at the time our senses are stimulated. A person who suffers from bipolar disorder for example, will report the color of the sky being less vivid in their depressive state than when they are at the manic end of their disease, even when the color is exactly the same (Barrick et al., 2000). Anyone who has been through a traumatic event will report phenomena such as events happening in slow motion or tunnel vision constricting their visual field. Unfortunately police officers are not immune to these perceptual distortions in times of high stress. Many times these distortions will contribute to their use, and in some cases misuse of force. They may see a gun in a person's hand when in reality it is only a wallet. They may see a person on the street who perfectly matches a wanted poster in their squad room, only to find out after placing the individual under arrest that there really was no likeness. They may see a furtive movement by an individual in a vehicle they have stopped which turns out to be nothing more than the driver turning down the radio. All of these situations could easily lead to the officer's use of force.

To look at how a police officer's perception is influenced by situational factors, Dr. Alexis Artwohl (2002) surveyed 157 officers involved in duty-related shootings between 1994 and 1999. Officers were administered a written survey from two to four weeks following the shooting, and after an internal investigation of the event had been completed. The survey revealed some startling findings about the officers' perception during the actual event. Sixty-two percent of the officers reported viewing the incident in slow motion. Eighty-four percent reported that the sounds around them seemed subdued. Seventy-nine percent of the officers had tunnel vision, and 74 percent reported responding to their crisis on "automatic pilot," with very little conscious thought given to options and alternatives. Twenty-one percent of the officers, after undergoing a debriefing and being advised of the facts of the case, admitted to memory distortion. These officers saw, heard, or experienced something that did not really happen, or it happened much differently than they remembered.

Other researchers have found similar perceptual distortions. Solomon and Horn (1986), in a survey of 86 officers involved in duty-related shootings, found that 67 percent of the officers observed the event in slow motion. Fifty-one percent of the officers reported diminished sounds, with 37 percent experiencing tunnel vision. Hoenig and Roland (1998) found similar reports in a survey of 348 officers involved in shootings. It is important to point that although many officers report seeing the events unfold in slow motion, a smaller percentage in each sample reported actually seeing events speed up. Also, a smaller percentage reported hearing the sounds around them intensify rather than diminish. In each of these cases, regardless of the effect, there was perceptual distortion in some form. For most, their perceptual functioning became inhibited in various ways, whereas a lesser number became hypersensitive to their sensory field.

Cognitive Modes

So what happens to our cognitive functioning in the heat of crisis? Epstein (1994) found that people oftentimes shift to an entirely different type of thinking when faced with an immediate crisis, such as when a police officer must make the decision to resort to deadly force. He found that people have two distinctly different modes of processing information. The first is the **rational-thinking mode**. This is how we tend to think as we go about our day. We take in new information, and then we process it in order to make it meaningful. Sometimes we may have to analyze the information from various perspectives or reference points before we can make it meaningful. This type of thinking is conscious, deliberate, and analytical.

Sometimes we shift to what Epstein refers to as **experiential-thinking mode**. Epstein says that in those times when immediate action is required, we simply do not have the luxury of the time needed to analyze the situation before we act. Thus our thinking becomes automatic, rapid, and effortless. Our interpretation of the events unfolding before us takes place below the level of conscious awareness, and is based as much on our experience as it is on the actual event itself. We simply react without consciously directing our actions. Many times people involved in acute emergency situations describe themselves as having been on "autopilot." They are using a metaphor to describe experiential thinking.

The problem of course is that our perception is not always accurate when we are thinking in experiential-thinking mode. Almost always our memory of the event will be fragmented because we have not consciously processed it. Consider the following real-life examples presented by Artwohl (2002):

- "If it hadn't been for the recoil, I wouldn't have known my gun was working. Not only didn't I hear the shots, but afterwards my ears weren't even ringing."
- "I saw the suspect suddenly point his gun at my partner. As I shot him, I saw my partner go down in a spray of blood. I ran over to help my partner, and he was standing there unharmed. The suspect never even got off a shot."

- "When I got home after the shooting, my wife told me that I had called her on my cell phone during the pursuit of the violent suspect just before the shooting. I have no memory of making that phone call."
- "I told the SWAT team that the suspect was firing at me from down a long dark hallway about 40 feet long. When I went back to the scene the next day, I was shocked to discover that he had actually been only about 5 feet in front of me in an open room. There was no dark hallway."

The above examples illustrate just how distorted our perception can become in the heat of an acute crisis. The secret to why we do this may be found in our nightly dreams. There have been many different theories that attempt to account for our dream material. The most plausible is simply that while we sleep our brains are still actively working. As we reach a particular level of sleep, the stem of our brain becomes active and begins to elicit fragmented memories. These are random memories, and so they may be images or sounds from years earlier. As the memories are elicited our brain attempts to put them in a storyline to make sense of them. This is why dreams almost always tell a story. But as we consciously process the story after we awaken, we oftentimes quickly realize that the story made no sense at all. Or we realize that although the story we created in our dream was about a particular person who is known to us, as we think about it the next morning we realize the image was of a completely different person, or perhaps the person actually changed throughout the dream.

The fact is, without our rational, analytical thinking, which is shut down during sleep, our thinking shifts to something akin to Epstein's experiential thinking. It becomes automatic and below the level of conscious awareness. It is highly affected by our experience, which is why our dreams are memory-based. But seldom are they true to the actual memory, and seldom do we remember a dream in its entirety for any length of time. Many times a person's memory of an emergency event is entirely different than what investigators later determine to be the actual sequence of events. And almost always parts of the event are not recalled. Our rational thinking is shut down to varying degrees, and our brain attempts to fill in the gaps of our fragmented memories to construct a storyline. So if a police officer responds to a report of a man with a gun, and then is confronted by that man, it is not unrealistic that the officer may see a gun where none is present, as his thinking becomes automatic and experientially based. In this case his brain is simply filling in the gaps without his conscious direction. With the experiences of a police officer as they are, and with those experiences underlying their automatic thinking, it is little wonder as they shift into autopilot that they see a gun and respond with deadly force.

CONTAGIOUS SHOOTING

Certainly it is possible that at least one of the officers in the Amadou Diallo shooting thought he saw a gun in Diallo's hand. But what is it that so often compels police officers to literally empty their weapons on a suspect who may not even be returning fire? Time and again we have seen news accounts of this phenomenon. An officer fires their weapon, and then suddenly other officers around them follow suit. One survey of Los Angeles County police officer shootings (Aveni, 2006) revealed the following data:

- Shots fired per officer with only 1 officer involved   3.59
- Shots fired per officer with 2 officers involved   4.98
- Shots fired per officer with more than 2 officers involved   6.48

Obviously there is something at work here that leads an officer to shoot more times when more officers are present. The phenomenon has been referred to as *contagious shooting, bunch*

ISSUES & ETHICS IN CRISIS INTERVENTION
When Children Get Tased

On November 11, 2009, Ozark Arkansas police officer Dustin Bradshaw was dispatched to a domestic disturbance between a mother and her 10-year-old daughter. When he arrived the girl was curled up on the floor screaming and kicking. Her mother told the officer the crisis began when the girl refused to take a shower. Officer Bradshaw attempted to take the young girl into custody, but she continued to violently kick at him. It was then that the girl's mother gave officer Bradshaw permission to use a Taser gun in an effort to gain control of the girl. According to his report he delivered a very brief stun to her back. It was enough to disable her, and after placing handcuffs on the child, officer Bradshaw carried the 65-pound girl to his squad car. His actions were later determined to be in compliance with department policy, and ultimately he received a short suspension with pay only for not engaging his video camera during the incident.

A growing number of children in America are finding themselves on the receiving end of a police officer's Taser. A 14-year-old in Chicago went into cardiac arrest after being Tased in 2005. In that same year a 6-year-old Florida boy threatening to cut himself with a piece of glass was Tased by police, as well as a 12-year-old girl guilty only of skipping school. And in 2010 two federal lawsuits were filed in Illinois, each seeking $10 million, after a Kankakee police officer Tased two 12-year-olds in their school classroom just to demonstrate how the weapon works. These are just a few of the many reported incidents.

The idea of using such a weapon on a child continues to be hotly debated. Most police departments allow for its use with children in certain situations, and the makers of the Taser gun argue that it is a safe and effective weapon for gaining control of an unmanageable person, even a child. They argue that although it is painful and disabling, it has no lasting effects, and its use may even prevent the child from harming themselves much more seriously by continuing to struggle.

Discussion Questions

1. Should there be limits placed on the types of weapons a police officer may use against a child?
2. Is there an even greater risk of harm or civil liability related to a police officer physically subduing a child with their hands?
3. Should a child's parents have the right to give a police officer permission to use a Taser on their uncontrollable child?

shooting, *synchronous fire*, and the more scientifically sounding *mass reflexive response*. Most choose to call it something that has the connotations that fit their particular perspective. For example, few police departments will refer to it as contagious shooting because that terminology connotes a reason for the shooting other than the threat posed by the suspect. Most police departments prefer to use the term *synchronous fire*, and they argue that all officers involved in such events shoot when they deem it appropriate, and the number of times they determine to be necessary. And further, they stop when they decide independently of the other officers' actions that no further force is needed. But the evidence and data do not support this notion. It is also interesting to note that in the survey referenced above it was found that accuracy was greatly reduced as more officers fired. When only a single officer was involved, the hit ratio was 51 percent. When two officers were involved the hit ratio was reduced to 23 percent. And when more than two officers were involved in the shooting the hit ratio dropped all the way down to 9 percent (Aveni, 2006). So as more officers fired their weapons, individual officers shot more times and with less accuracy.

One possible explanation for contagious shooting comes from the discipline of neurology and the study of social conformity. Dr. Vasily Klucharev (2009) has suggested that humans have an innate neural mechanism that triggers an alert signal when the individual's behavior diverges from that of the crowd. It is this signal that compels the individual to adjust their behavior in order to feel included. If such a mechanism exists, then it likely is the result of the evolutionary process. In other words, those individuals in prehistory who were more inclined to follow the behavior of the group were more likely to survive the perils of the day, and thus they more successfully passed on their genetic code until the mechanism became an innate characteristic of all humans.

Klucharev conducted his research by looking at the brain activity of people who were asked to judge the attractiveness of a particular face. He specifically was interested in those individuals whose initial judgment was in conflict with that of the group's. By employing functional magnetic resonance imaging, Klucharev was able to monitor the neural activity of those individuals who ultimately changed their evaluation to conform to the group's. In these individuals it was found that the conflict led to an increase in activity in the part of the brain that signals a **prediction error**. This signal is released by the brain when the individual's expected outcomes are in conflict with actual outcomes, thus compelling the individual to change their behavior. In this particular study, the prediction error signal was released when individuals discovered that their initial evaluation of the face was in conflict with how the rest of the group evaluated it. We see similar examples of this phenomenon in everyday life. People oftentimes choose to conform to the group, even when doing so compromises their own beliefs and value system.

Klucharev's research, when combined with Epstein's theory, provides a plausible explanation for the phenomenon of contagious shooting. When multiple police officers engage a deadly force situation, it is likely that they are already thinking in experiential mode, and thus they are not analyzing the situation, but simply responding in an automatic manner based on their training and experience. But it may also be that in this mode of thinking they are responding with certain genetic predispositions, such as Klucharev's neural alert signal. Training and experience compels them to use deadly force, and without the ability to fully analyze the situation in a rational way, neurology compels them to follow the lead of the other officer(s) and shoot. It would seem an easy thing to argue that with one or more officers already shooting, others in close proximity should simply stand by and wait for the situation to de-escalate. But this would require an evaluation of the situation, which may be difficult at best while thinking in experiential mode.

RACE AS A FACTOR IN THE USE OF FORCE

One additional factor must be discussed in relation to the use of force, and that is the influence of race in a police officer's decision to elevate their use of force. Without a doubt, police officers have shot and killed African Americans at a higher rate than whites before and after the Supreme Court's decision in *Tennessee v. Garner*. The Bureau of Justice Statistics (2001) reports that in 1978 the rate (per one million of population) at which police officers justifiably killed African Americans was 8 times that of whites. In 1998, long after the Garner decision, the rate for African Americans was still 4 times that of whites. Geller and Scott (1992) point out the following:

- Chicago police officers shot at Blacks 3.8 times more than at whites during the 1970s.
- New York City police officers shot at Blacks 6 times more than at whites during the 1970s.

- Dallas police officers shot at Blacks 4.5 times more than at whites during the 1970s and 1980s.
- St. Louis police officers shot at Blacks 7.7 times more than at whites from 1987 to 1991.
- Memphis police officers fatally shot at Blacks 5.1 times more than at whites from 1969 to 1974; 2.6 times more from 1980 to 1984; and 1.6 times more from 1985 to 1989; they were 9.4 times more likely to shoot at Blacks than at whites in relation to suspected property crimes from 1969 to 1974 and 13 times more from 1980 to 1984; and Blacks were the only property crimes suspects shot at from 1985 to 1989.

One might argue that it is simply demographics at play, and that African Americans live in high-crime neighborhoods, and are thus more inclined to be in places where a police shooting might take place. But a very telling bit of data comes from Memphis, the very city where young Edward Garner was shot and killed. Sparger and Giacopassi (1992) looked at the police shootings in that city both before and after the Garner decision. They found that there was a wide disparity in the use of deadly force when the fleeing felon rule was still standard police practice. From 1969 to 1974, of 14 police killings of individuals classified as "unarmed and not assaultive," 13 of them were African American. In other words, when the use of force was discretionary on the part of the police officer to stop a fleeing felon, the police were much more inclined to shoot to kill when the suspect was Black. In contrast, from 1985 to 1989, after the Supreme Court's decision, there were 0 police killings in Memphis of unarmed and non-assaultive suspects.

A number of studies have been carried out to look further at this issue. Keith Payne (2001) looked at the role of race in causing an individual to misperceive the presence of a weapon. In his study Payne flashed a face on a screen just before flashing an object, either a weapon or a hand tool. The participants, all non-police officers, were directed to disregard the face and respond only to the object. The faces that were flashed were either African American or Caucasian. Payne carried out two trials. In the first, participants could take their time to process the information and respond whether the object was a weapon or a hand tool. In the second trial, participants were given only a second and a half to respond.

The results of the study suggested a definite race factor in the participants' perception of a weapon. In the first trial, when participants were given time to process the information, their accuracy was high regardless of race; however, it was found that on average participants perceived the weapon faster when preceded by an African American face. According to Payne this suggests that the Black face readied people to detect a weapon, but it did not distort their perception. In the second trial however, when participants were given less than two seconds to respond, participants falsely reported seeing a gun more often when preceded by a Black face.

According to Payne, the reason for this type of perceptual distortion is that the unintentional aspects of our behavior are influenced by our stereotypical associations. People more often associate Black people with violence and crime, and thus when we act without the benefit of processing the information our perception becomes distorted by those associations. It is not dissimilar from Epstein's (1994) formulation of "experiential thinking," as we previously discussed.

Another study (Correll, Judd, and Wittenbrink, 2002) set up an experimental design in which participants had to make a split-second decision whether to shoot an armed suspect shown on a video screen. The video shown to participants approximated the experience of a police officer confronted with an ambiguous but potentially hostile individual. In each case then, the participant had to make a shoot/don't shoot decision based on the presence of a weapon in the individual's hand. Individuals shown on the video were either African American or Caucasian in a number of different scenarios, with some carrying objects other than a weapon (i.e., cans, cell phones, etc.). All participants in the study were undergraduate college students.

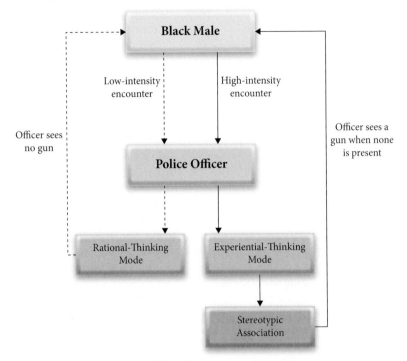

FIGURE 4.3 An Example of Cognitive-Perceptual Distortion.

The results of the study reflected a definite racial influence over the participants' decision to shoot. Like the previous study, the researchers concluded that stereotypical traits associated with African Americans, that they are violent and dangerous, can influence perceptions of an ambiguously threatening target. In the study participants fired on armed targets more quickly when the individual was African American rather than white. They also decided not to shoot an unarmed target quicker when the target was white. When the researchers increased the error rate by requiring a quicker reaction time, participants failed to shoot an armed target more often when the target was white, and had a higher incidence of shooting unarmed African American targets than unarmed white targets.

One final study worth noting (Correll, Judd, Wittenbrink, Sadler, and Keesee, 2007) used actual Denver area police officers in their shoot/don't shoot scenario. As expected, the police officers made fewer mistakes than non-police officers in their decision to shoot, but the results indicated that their response time with targets congruent with prevalent stereotypes (armed Blacks, unarmed whites) was significantly shorter than with stereotype-incongruent targets (unarmed Blacks, armed whites), again indicating a racial bias in the speed with which they decide to use deadly force.

There is little doubt that police and correctional officers are influenced to some degree by personal bias. Some bring this to the job with them, whereas others develop it only after being on the job for a period of time. Most criminal justice professionals are able to keep their personal feeling in abeyance. They quickly learn that it is advantageous to do so. But in the heat of confrontation and crisis, in those moments when we shift into "autopilot," it is then when personal bias can cause a police officer to see a gun that isn't there and react accordingly. It is a sad reality of policing that innocent people die due to perceptual distortions. Does it mean the police in those situations are guilty of a crime? No, because a crime requires the element of *mens rea*, or a guilty mind. Put another way, it requires intent. Whether the suspect actually has a gun, or the police officer mistakenly sees one during a high-intensity encounter, the intent of the officer in resorting to deadly force is to protect themselves or others, not to kill an innocent individual.

Chapter Summary

How we respond to a crisis can be highly influenced by emotion, race, and even the actions of those responding at our side. In the majority of crises responded to by police and correctional officers, containment and de-escalation may ultimately require the use of force, up to and including the use of deadly force. Much of the training armed criminal justice professionals go through relates to the use of force. It is an issue that can inflame a community quicker than just about anything. Part of the reason is because the public has little understanding of the issue of force, and is heavily influenced by the media. We are conditioned to believe that the police should shoot the gun out of the suspect's hand rather than kill them, or perhaps fire a couple warning shots in the air, or even take them out with a shot to the leg. What they don't realize is that for the most part the use of a handgun, even by a police officer, is effective only at a relatively short distance. Furthermore, police are trained only to kill with their guns, not to disable. If they have reached a point in an exchange where they have unholstered their weapon, then deadly force, at least in theory, is justified.

One of the goals of the criminal justice system is to properly train its officers in the use of force with as much life-like training as possible, so that in those times when their thinking does shift into experiential mode the automatic behaviors that are elicited are guided not by personal experience and bias, but by the training that has been encoded in their memory in such a way that the officer resorts to it as a first course of action. Special units such as police and prison tactical response teams do a tremendous amount of training. Their actions are finely choreographed, and seldom are they criticized for violating the force continuum. More often than not, when there are criticisms it typically involves a uniformed officer on the street who may or may not be required to participate in regular training beyond their initial police academy training. What ultimately becomes encoded in their memory are the stereotypic associations that are acquired by working the streets each day. And without significant and intense training to back them up, they are more prone to see guns where there aren't any, and to succumb to the contagion of group conformity by joining in on the shooting when no further force is necessary to contain and de-escalate the situation.

Key Terms

Contagious shooting
Use of force
Force continuum
Fleeing felon rule
Reasonableness
Verbal commands

Threat of force
Non-lethal compliance
   techniques
Disabling techniques
Lethal force
Perception

Cognitive Modes
Rational-thinking mode
Experiential-thinking mode
Prediction error

Discussion Questions

1. Do you believe the use of force by the police should be more heavily regulated by the courts and legislative bodies, or should its use be entirely dictated by the state of mind of the individual police officer?

2. Should the police be held accountable for a misuse of force, such as in the case of Amadou Diallo, even when it was their perception at the time that such force was necessary to protect lives, including possibly their own?

3. Think of a time when you got caught up in the moment and found yourself doing something just because everyone else was doing it, such as running down the aisle of a department store to grab the latest toy craze without even considering why you would want it. Now relate that to the phenomenon of "contagious shooting." Are there similarities?

5

The Tactical Response

LEARNING OUTCOMES

Upon completion of this chapter the student should be able to:

1. Explain the role of tactical teams in the containment and de-escalation of crisis.

2. Summarize the historical development of police S.W.A.T.

3. Explain the techniques for de-escalating an "active shooter" crisis.

4. List and define police rapid deployment tactics.

5. List and define the various types of tactical entry.

Chapter Outline

INTRODUCTION

THE ADVENT OF S.W.A.T.

When we think of the concept of a tactical response in law enforcement, we typically think of **S.W.A.T.** (Special Weapons and Tactics). The idea of such a team was first developed by the LAPD in the 1960s and 1970s in response to civil unrest and the emergence of well-armed militant groups who were not afraid to battle the police. The idea was to develop a team of specially trained officers who were equipped with the weaponry and tactics to meet these new challenges, and to do so in a way that reduced the risk to the officers involved as much as possible. It was a quasi-military unit in all respects, and once its existence became public knowledge it didn't take long for the media to contribute to its mystique and reputation. A popular 1970s television show (*S.W.A.T.*) was aired using the tagline, "When people need help they call the police. When the police need help they call S.W.A.T.!" It helped to create a new image of the police that was much different from the traditional representations of the day. They were well-trained and battle-hardened officers who were not afraid to engage their targets head-on. With the creation of these teams, the police in America, perhaps for the first time, gained the upper hand in tactical situations of any size or threat level.

Today there is a **tactical team** in essentially every medium to large police department in America. Some still identify themselves by the original acronym. Others have chosen a different moniker, one they feel best describes their unit's mission and purpose, including ERT (Emergency Response Team), ESU (Emergency Services Unit), and TRT (Tactical Response Team), among others. Regardless of the acronyms used, the types of duties carried out by these teams are essentially the same. They include:

- Hostage rescues
- High-risk arrest and search warrants
- Active shooter situations
- Resolving situations involving barricaded subjects with minimal loss of life
- Dealing with high-risk mentally ill or suicidal subjects
- Terrorist threats

A number of things define a tactical situation. They are situations in which the use of force is likely to be met with force. They are high-risk operations that require special weapons and tactics, as the name suggests. Tactical situations tend to go beyond the capabilities of patrol officers, although most tactical officers are, in fact, patrol officers when not deployed. The tactical response, whether by police or correctional personnel, is barely distinguishable from a military operation. Tactical officers transform themselves on a moment's notice to nameless, and in many cases faceless soldiers dressed in black Kevlar suits and carrying weapons seldom seen in the hands of uniformed police officers. They are trained to work in teams, and to move quickly, with each member knowing exactly what to do and when to do it. Tactical teams are not trained to take up a defensive position and wait out a situation. They are trained to contain and de-escalate a situation by force when other measures have failed.

Prior to the development of S.W.A.T. by the LAPD, many of the trappings of present-day tactical teams, namely automatic weapons and uniforms designed to hide the identities of the officers wearing them, were considered by many to be counterproductive to the police mission. At the time, community engagement was becoming a major goal of law enforcement. The quasi-military approach to policing was being replaced by the community policing model still prevalent to this day. Consequently, S.W.A.T. went against the grain of respected opinion; however, social circumstances were such that the development of a highly trained and heavily armed tactical unit was necessary for the safety of the uniformed officers who would otherwise be required to handle such situations. Even with the advent of S.W.A.T., however, with the great increase in violence and weaponry that accompanied the explosion in illicit drug activity during the 1980s, especially the cocaine trade, it became apparent that even uniformed officers on routine patrol needed to be prepared for a tactical response when circumstances demanded immediate action.

THE NORTH HOLLYWOOD BANK ROBBERY: 44 MINUTES THAT REDEFINED POLICE TACTICS

Incident Overview

On February 28, 1997, two heavily armed men, Larry Eugene Phillips Jr. and Emil Matasareanu, entered a branch of Bank of America in the North Hollywood district of Los Angeles intent upon robbing it and making their getaway without incident. When the incident ended 44 minutes later, both men were dead and 11 LAPD officers and 7 civilians were injured. In all, over 2000 rounds were fired during the confrontation, most of them from high-powered assault rifles carried by the two perpetrators (Nally, 2007).

The North Hollywood incident was unique in that it was broadcast live on television nearly from beginning to end by a news helicopter. The confrontation began at approximately 9:30 A.M. when the two robbers entered the bank. They had spent weeks preparing for the robbery, and anticipated that it would take 8 minutes for police to respond. Unfortunately for the robbers, an LAPD patrol car observed them entering the bank and called for backup. By the time Phillips and Matasareanu exited with a bag of cash the bank was surrounded by police, and all possible exits were blocked. At this point, the shooting began.

The two men had prepared for this possibility. They were both dressed in bullet-proof clothing reinforced with armor plating and, together, they had over 3000 rounds of ammunition with them. The responding officers on the other hand were armed only with 9-mm semi-automatic handguns, in some cases .38 caliber revolvers, and a number of 12-gauge shotguns. The police officers discovered very quickly that their weapons had little effect. Most of the bullets were simply bouncing off the heavily reinforced clothing. Phillips and Matasareanu on the other hand were having a devastating effect, quickly wounding a number of the officers. Although S.W.A.T. had been deployed almost immediately, most of the officers and civilians who were wounded were shot prior to their arrival.

Within minutes the two robbers were separated, one attempting to escape in a vehicle and the other walking away from the area with the news helicopter above still broadcasting. By this time nearly 300 police officers were responding at various levels, and S.W.A.T. had arrived. Phillips was the first to go down. After being shot in the hand and dropping his handgun, he is seen on video picking it up, placing it under his chin, and shooting himself. At the same time, a bullet from a S.W.A.T. member's AR15 severed his spine. Blocks away, Matasareanu continued his escape but his car was disabled by police. After an unsuccessful carjacking attempt, he fired one last volley of bullets before giving up and lying down. He died before an ambulance could arrive to render medical aid. It was later determined that he had been shot 29 times in the shins and feet.

The Aftermath and a Change in Tactics

The North Hollywood bank robbery incident has been called the longest and bloodiest event in U.S. police history (Fuchs, 2003). Although this may be subject to debate, it cannot be denied that the police were terribly out-gunned that day. More than anything the incident demonstrated the devastating effects of military-style assault rifles, and how ineffective traditional police weaponry is against them. It clearly showed the need for patrol officers, not just S.W.A.T., to be prepared for a tactical situation with the necessary weapons and tactics to quickly contain a crisis. The North Hollywood incident was simply uncontainable for a long enough period of time and allowed the two perpetrators to leave the immediate area and continue to wound people.

In the aftermath, police departments around the country began arming their officers with high-velocity assault rifles to carry in their squad cars. Some have issued heavier Kevlar tactical vests to be worn when necessary, while others have added reinforced plating to the doors of their squad cars. With this increase in firepower has also come new tactics for containing and de-escalating high-risk confrontations. Although S.W.A.T. is still a valuable component of the police mission, patrol officers are now being trained to act immediately in situations where lives are in jeopardy. As we move forward we will look at some of these high-risk situations.

THE ACTIVE SHOOTER

From Columbine to Ft. Hood

One of the tactical situations in which a patrol officer, as well as tactical team members, may have to act quickly in order to save innocent lives is one involving an **active shooter**. There are many definitions, but a simple and straightforward one is offered by the El Paso County, Colorado Sheriff's procedure manual (2003). In it they define an active shooter as "… an armed person who has used deadly physical force on other persons and continues to do so while having unrestricted access to additional victims." As the definition suggests, an active shooter crisis is one that is uncontained and deadly. It is typically one in which the perpetrator intends to kill, and in many cases has no thought of escape or capture. This reality gives the perpetrator a tactical advantage against police or correctional officers not adequately prepared or trained for such a confrontation.

In recent years we have witnessed a number of active shooter situations, including the following highly publicized cases:

- *Columbine High School:* April 20, 1999. Twelve students and one teacher were murdered when two senior students, Eric Harris and Dylan Klebold, entered the school heavily armed and began shooting indiscriminately. Both committed suicide as police entered the building. It was reported that the two had a history of legal issues and emotional problems, and that they had indicated in journals their desire to kill those they hated (Cullen, 2004).
- *Goleta, California, Postal Sorting Facility:* January 30, 2006. Six employees of the facility are shot and killed by a former employee, Jennifer San Marco, age 44. She commits suicide at the facility following her deadly rampage. It was believed that her actions were motivated by the Postal Service who forced her to retire due to her worsening mental condition (BBC News, 2006).
- *Virginia Tech:* April 16, 2007. Seung-Hui Cho, an English student who had been previously diagnosed with a severe anxiety disorder, killed 32 students and wounded many more, in a campus residence hall and a number of classrooms. Between two separate attacks he

managed to send a package to NBC News containing, among other things, a manifesto in which he described his hatred of the wealthy. The shooting became the deadliest by a single attacker in U.S. history (*New York Times*, April 16, 2007).

- *Northern Illinois University:* February 14, 2008. Steven Kazmierczak, a graduate student at the University of Illinois Champaign-Urbana, and a graduate of Northern Illinois University in DeKalb, Illinois, returned to NIU, entered a lecture hall where approximately 150 students were attending an oceanography class, and opened fire from the stage. He shot 24 people, killed 5 of them, and then committed suicide as police arrived. It is reported that he was a model student; however, he had recently discontinued taking prescribed medication for depression and anxiety, and his behavior had reportedly become erratic (CNN, February 18, 2008).

- *Fort Hood, Texas:* November 5, 2009. Army Major Nidal Malik Hasan, a military psychiatrist, killed 13 soldiers and wounded 30 others waiting to be deployed. He was eventually gunned down by civilian police officers stationed at Fort Hood. Hasan survived the shooting and is now paralyzed from the chest down. It is reported that Hasan carried out his attack out of anger over being deployed to Afghanistan (CNN, November 12, 2009).

Each of the above cases has a common denominator: the attacker went to the location of the attack with one objective in mind, to kill as many people as possible. It is a type of crisis that must be contained and de-escalated immediately. Containment will not suffice if the shooter is actively engaged in killing. Nor will attempting to establish communication and negotiating with the attacker. There is only one viable option in this type of scenario: find the attacker as quickly as possible and stop their attack by using an equal or greater level of force against them. This is now the standard in essentially all police training related to this type of situation.

A Change in Thinking

There was a time when the preferred tactic followed by the police in an active shooter situation was to set up a containment perimeter and wait for S.W.A.T. to arrive to enter the location and seek out the shooter. That all changed following the situation at Columbine High School in 1999. The police training apparatus in America began to develop new tactics and methods for rapid deployment by officers arriving on the scene of an active shooter. The old doctrine of containment was no longer acceptable. It only allowed the shooter additional time to kill more innocent people, and to better prepare for the inevitable battle that would take place once the tactical team made entry to the premises.

In a study conducted by the commercial law enforcement training company Hard Tactics (Barchers, 2010), researchers concluded that the faster a shooter is confronted by police, the higher the probability of de-escalating the situation with no further loss of life. They reviewed over 40 active shooter situations and the police response to each. They found that in those cases where police followed the traditional model of setting up a containment perimeter and attempting contact with the shooter, the outcomes were less successful than in those cases where the responding officers immediately made contact with the shooter and attempted to de-escalate the situation through the use of force. This doctrine of immediate contact is now the standard in American law enforcement. It represents a paradigm shift in how the police respond to high-risk situations involving an active shooter. This shift is rather succinctly summarized by Officer James Scanlon (2001) of the Columbus Ohio Police Department:

> What is the primary duty of every law enforcement officer in the country? Without a doubt it is to preserve life. In one form or another it is incorporated into every officer's oath. Simplified, we agree to put ourselves between the good guys and the bad guys, even when it

is unsafe to do so. There are no qualifiers, such as "when it's safe," "when we have a larger gun," or "when we have adequate backup." Therefore we cannot permit people to seriously hurt or kill other people once police officers arrive on the scene. The traditional practice of containing the situation and waiting for S.W.A.T. to respond has served us well over the past 27–30 years. It continues to be the right thing to do in most situations. However, if a person is seriously injuring or killing people, once officers arrive at the scene, those officers are required to make entry and stop the suspect. We believe it is an officer's professional, legal, and moral obligation to do so. While we recognize the fact that some officers may refuse to enter into such a dangerous situation, we believe they are in the minority. Those law enforcement officers who can't put themselves into such a situation should consider a different career path!

For most dedicated police officers confronted by an active shooter situation, the issue is no longer *if* they will enter the premises in an effort to save innocent lives, but *how* they will enter. By following accepted best practices, those officers responding to an active shooter can significantly reduce the risks that await them when they arrive and move in to confront the shooter.

Rapid Deployment Tactics

New tactics have been developed to facilitate immediate contact with an active shooter while limiting to the extent possible the danger to the responding officers. Many departments have committed this rapid deployment strategy to their policies and procedures. The El Paso County Sheriff's Department in Colorado (2004) has adopted an active shooter response protocol that includes seven tenets to guide their response. These tenets include the following:

1. **Goal:** The overall purpose of these tactics is to save lives and prevent serious injuries. The goal for police response at an active shooter event is neutralization by denying access to additional victims, rescuing injured victims, and/or rescuing potential victims.
2. **Assume tactical responsibility:** One initial deputy must take charge of the active shooter incident. Assumption of tactical responsibility may be based on rank, expertise, or seniority. However, it must be made immediately clear to both the communications center and the other deputies who are in charge. A deputy of superior rank who is on scene and fully briefed may ultimately assume incident command. Any change in incident command will be made known to dispatch and the other deputies.
3. **Situational analysis:** The deputy taking charge must, based on all information available, make a situation analysis. The analysis will be continuous, taking into account new information from dispatch and observations from deputies and citizens. The analysis must lead to a decision as to whether the situation is an active shooter event, whether an opportunity exists for immediate intervention leading to accomplishment of one of the goals listed above, and how responding resources should be employed at the scene.
4. **Incident command:** No action will be taken that is unplanned or without controls. The first deputy arriving on the scene will initiate incident command. He/she will initiate the situation analysis and determine initial deployment of responding resources. At least one person possessing all available information on tactical plans will remain at the command post to brief arriving personnel. Command personnel en route to the incident will monitor the radio to gain information, but shall not obstruct ongoing intervention. Command personnel must be on scene and fully briefed before assuming incident command.

5. **First responder tactical intervention:** When responding to active shooter incidents, the EPSO endorses the concept of first responder tactical intervention. It is critical that all deputies, supervisors, and command personnel are familiar with the definition of an active shooter as well as the tactics deemed appropriate for active shooter response. The traditional uniform responses of contain, isolate, evacuate, and wait for S.W.A.T. and crisis negotiators may not be adequate in an active shooter incident. The first deputy on scene will need to consider the following:

    a. **Rescue/ contact team:** First responder intervention will be based on opportunity (meaning it is at least feasible to attempt to enter and seek out the active shooter). Rescue teams will be in the form of deputies with an identified element leader. Team movement will be in a controlled and disciplined tactical action under the control and direction of the element leader.

    b. **Containment:** Dedicated security elements should always be a component of intervention teams. Individual action is discouraged, as it is usually counterproductive to a coordinated, focused response to an active shooter event. Site containment will be left to the discretion to the first deputy on scene who assumes incident responsibility and initiates the situation assessment. Containment of an active shooter incident may take the form of deputies serving in an "observe and report" capacity.

6. **Active shooter site security:** No location associated with an active shooter will be considered secure until the S.W.A.T. commander declares it so. Deputies assigned to security functions will maintain positions until properly relieved.

7. **Special Weapons and Tactics (S.W.A.T.):** When S.W.A.T. units are prepared to deploy, the initial responding officers may be relieved or deployed by S.W.A.T.

As you can see from these seven tenets, the goal in an active shooter situation is immediate contact, but in a controlled and disciplined manner. Only as a last resort should a responding officer enter a building alone in search of an active shooter. This may be necessary in a jurisdiction with only a single officer however, or in a situation where additional responding officers may be many miles from the scene. The overriding concern, especially when shots are being fired, is to prevent the shooter from killing or wounding additional victims.

Response Team Structure and Duties

Assuming there are sufficient officers, then the tactics employed are those developed and first used by the LAPD. In their model, which is now the standard in police training, there are four objectives to be met in an active shooter incident; 1) make contact with the shooter, 2) rescue the injured, 3) secure the perimeter, and 4) evacuate potential victims away from the shooter. Ideally each of these objectives should be pursued by a separate team of officers, all under the command and control of a single incident commander. It is a coordinated effort designed to bring a quick end to the incident and limit the loss of life.

The first and most important component of this coordinated tactical response is the **contact team**'s entry into the building or other location where the shooter is actively killing or wounding innocent people. The ideal number of officers to enter an active shooter location is four, and they maintain a "diamond" or "T" formation as they move toward the sound of the gunfire. This allows them a 360-degree field of view as they move forward. During this maneuver the contact team does not enter rooms, nor do they stop to aid the wounded. Their only objective is to move toward the sound of the gunfire, or toward the last known location of the shooter. As they move forward, they direct people to evacuate behind them and gather as much information as possible about the shooter. The team moves swiftly, but in a manner that allows them to take advantage of available cover as they stop, listen, and observe just long enough to adjust their course and contact point. By moving in quickly before the shooter has time to prepare for the assault, and thus taking advantage of the element of surprise and by using this method of focused movement, the contact team is able to take away much of the tactical advantage enjoyed by a shooter with little thought of escape or capture.

Every active shooter situation is potentially a deadly force situation. The contact team has one goal in mind, and that is to neutralize the shooter in the quickest way possible. If this can be done by challenging the shooter from a place of cover when there are no potential victims in the shooter's proximity, then chances are the officers will attempt an arrest. But if cover is not available, or the shooter appears to be preparing to shoot either at the officers or innocent victims, then the officers will use deadly force and shoot the suspect. Once this potential outcome takes place, and if there is information indicating the presence of another shooter, as in the case of Columbine High School, then the contact team immediately disarms the downed suspect and continues their tactical movement toward the second shooter. If there is no indication of additional shooters, then the contact team's mission is complete and a perimeter is established until S.W.A.T. is deployed to do a safety sweep of the entire location.

Concurrent with the contact team's movement toward the active shooter, a **rescue team** is sent in behind them to rescue the injured and remove them to a safe location for medical treatment. The rescue team moves at a safe distance behind the contact team, but still remains vigilant for the possibility of making contact with the shooter. The rescue team has a security function, which is to establish a perimeter around the rescue area while officers remove the wounded.

The **perimeter team**'s objective is to secure any potential escape routes the shooter may attempt to take. They also protect innocent bystanders from entering the shooter's field of fire. Their goal is to establish an area free of all civilians, and to check that area for such things as explosive devices, getaway vehicles, or accomplices. Once the perimeter is established, then it is maintained until the incident commander gives the all-clear signal.

Finally, an **evacuation team** helps those running from the location to a place of safety. Anyone who recalls the scene at Columbine High School will remember teenagers running from the school in a panic. Some left through doors, others through open windows. The evacuation team not only assists people from the premises, but also directs their movement to a safe location and provides cover in the event the shooter attempts to fire upon them. During the crisis at Columbine High School the two shooters did in fact attempt to fire on students being evacuated from the premises. Their shots were met with return fire by officers outside the building, and the two quickly discontinued their attack and directed their deadly efforts elsewhere.

The change in active shooter tactics that followed the incident at Columbine High School and others like it has also spurred on the development of new equipment for police use. Many departments now issue lightweight ballistic shields that a uniformed officer can deploy in the event they have to enter an active shooter location prior to the arrival of a fully equipped tactical team. These shields have been developed to provide maximum protection while allowing officers to aim and shoot a number of different types of weapons without obstruction. The *Baker Batshield* is one example of this new technology. Along with these shields, officers are being issued ballistic shin guards, helmets, and heavier ballistic vests that can be put on quickly atop their standard-issue uniform vest.

Short of a terrorist attack, the active shooter situation is perhaps the deadliest type of situation a police officer will ever encounter. It is a situation where the lives of many could hinge on the actions of even a single officer entering the location and neutralizing the shooter. Those responding become human shields for the innocent victims behind them, and provide cover for those in front of them who may still be in the shooter's field of fire. The old way of securing a perimeter and waiting for S.W.A.T. and negotiators to arrive is no longer considered adequate when a shooter is actively hunting down and killing innocent people. They can potentially kill many in the time it takes for responding uniformed officers to enter the location, and even more in the time it takes for S.W.A.T. to deploy. The police simply cannot stand back and wait, even if it means placing themselves directly in the shooter's line of fire.

THE TACTICAL ENTRY

In an active shooter situation the entry team enters a location to seek out and immobilize the shooter. But there are other times when the entry team expects to be confronted by force immediately upon entry. These situations may include hostage rescues, drug raids, barricaded suspects, and the execution of high-risk arrest and search warrants. They are extremely dangerous operations, and the teams that make these types of entry do so only after a great deal of training. Anyone who has ever watched one of these teams in action, either in real life or on television, can see that it is a finely choreographed maneuver, with each member of the team knowing exactly what to do before, during, and after the entry. As we discussed in Chapter 2, a number of physiological changes take place in response to the autonomic nervous system being hyper-activated. For the members of a tactical entry team, constant and realistic training is the key to compensating for this diminished capacity.

Tactical Options

When a tactical team responds to a crisis, the commander on the scene has a number of options available, depending on the nature of the crisis. Although high-risk arrest and search warrants certainly employ tactical entry teams on a regular basis, we really cannot apply our definition of crisis to those types of operations. For our purposes, we will focus primarily on hostage rescues and barricaded suspects; in the case of the latter, especially if the suspect is armed and taking shots at innocent people. In either case, the operational commander can attempt any of the following:

- *Ruse:* The operational commander can attempt to entice the individual out of the building or to a different location inside the building through a pretense in order to make it easier to affect an arrest. This, of course, carries with it the risk of upsetting the individual if the ruse is discovered. Additionally, people who find themselves on the other side of the police in these situations tend to be hypervigilant, distrustful, and even paranoid during the course of the crisis, which makes the ruse a dangerous option, especially with hostages involved. Additionally, a ruse may be used to attempt to reposition a hostage-taker inside the location in order for a police sniper to have a clear shot at the suspect. This has been done a number of times. Of course, the sniper option carries with it the risk of missing the target and causing the suspect to start shooting their hostages.
- *Surround and call out:* With this option, the tactical team can simply surround the area, announce their presence, and command the individual to walk out with their hands in plain view. This option may work with an individual who never intended to be in the situation they now find themselves, such as a bank robbery gone bad. If the individual intended to take hostages, however, or if they intended to barricade themselves and shoot anyone who approaches the location, then it is unlikely they will simply walk out and surrender. It is even less likely if they made the conscious decision at the outset of their criminal act to die rather than be arrested and possibly face a lengthy prison term.

- *Breach and hold:* The entry team may be directed to breach an entry point, perhaps a door, and then hold their positions without immediately entering. This option announces to the suspect that significant force is standing by and prepared to move in. It also gives the entry team time to clear the area inside the doorway that lies within their field of view. This option may be used when it is anticipated that an armed suspect is positioned to ambush the entry team. In such a case, the entry team may maintain their position and use a "flash" grenade to disorient the suspect before making entry.
- *Deliberate entry:* The deliberate and dynamic entries differ only in the speed with which the entry team moves through the target location. In a deliberate entry, the movement is slow and methodical once an entry point is breached. The team moves through and clears one area before moving on to the next. As people are encountered, they are searched and secured before moving on. The downside to the deliberate entry is that it may give the suspect ample time to arm themselves and prepare for a confrontation.
- *Dynamic entry:* Obviously, if there are hostages, then a deliberate entry may not be suitable, especially if the hostage-taker has made threats to harm the hostages in the event of a rescue attempt. In this case the element of surprise is critical, and a dynamic entry may be ordered. The critical components of a dynamic entry are speed and domination. When the entry team dominates an area, it simply means they have complete control of that area, and any suspect entering it will be quickly engaged and immobilized. The team moves rapidly toward its objective, but not so fast that they cannot effectively engage a suspect. Unlike the deliberate entry, during a dynamic entry if people are encountered who obviously are not armed, then the team may quickly move past them toward their objective while a containment team takes responsibility for securing those people. The dynamic entry is extremely focused and, once begun, it does not stop until the objective is met or the team is forced by return fire to turn back or hold their positions.

Phases of a Tactical Entry

Regardless of a deliberate or dynamic entry, the steps and techniques involved are essentially the same. James Scanlon (2005), a member of the Columbus Ohio Police Department, describes a five-phase approach to conducting a **tactical entry**. During the first phase, the **scouting phase**, members of the tactical team scout out the location to determine a number of things. Are there potential points of entry that can be breached to allow for quick access? Are there fences or other obstacles that may impede a rapid approach? Are there dogs or other animals to contend with? What kind of doors will the team have to breach? Are there any potential escape routes for the people inside? In the case of a drug raid or the execution of a high-risk warrant, the team will usually have the luxury of time to properly scout the location. In the chaos of a crisis, however, the scouting phase may be cut short out of necessity. Every effort will still be made however to gather the necessary intelligence to make the entry as safe as possible for the team members.

The second phase is the **planning phase**. Now the team takes the intelligence they have gathered and they develop a plan for the entry. How many officers will be needed? What types of weapons? How will they breach an entry point? Will it be a deliberate or dynamic entry? If the latter, will they "flashbang" the room using flash grenades? It is also critical that they determine how best to approach the location, and identify points of cover if they come under fire during their approach. These are all issues that must be planned in advance of the actual entry.

The next phase is the **briefing phase**. Now the plan is shared with all the team members, and the assignments are made. The briefing includes the entry team, the containment team, K9 units, and any other officers detailed to assist. Because of the extensive training tactical teams go through, no assignment or component of the plan should be foreign to any of the team members. If there is confusion, it must be dealt with quickly. Each member of the team must signal their understanding and know exactly what's expected of them.

The **execution phase** is next. Now the plan is implemented and the entry made. With the proper intelligence gathered during the scouting phase, and the most effective plan developed during the planning phase, and finally with all team members properly briefed, then the entry should be a well-choreographed operation that reduces or eliminates as much risk to the team members as possible. We will discuss the tactics employed during the actual entry in the next section.

The final phase of the operation, and one that is critically important and not to be overlooked, is the **debriefing phase**. There is no better training than real-life experience. It is absolutely critical that the team learn from each and every experience. If things go right, then proper tactics are reinforced. If things go wrong, then the team moves immediately to adjust their training and correct them. The debriefing occurs immediately after the actual operation. It is mandatory that all team members attend. The debriefing is a time when rank is set aside and the team members are free to discuss the operation openly and honestly. Team members critique the action, not the persons involved.

Tactics and Techniques

THE BREACH   We turn now to the actual tactics employed during a tactical entry. We will discuss the breach, clearing before the entry, the actual entry, and movement through the location being entered. The tactics and techniques described are standard among tactical teams throughout the United States. They are designed to maximize both the effectiveness of the mission and the safety of the officers making the entry.

Before any entry is attempted, there typically must be a **breach** made in the structure. Breaching is simply the act of creating an opening for the team to enter the structure through. This is typically done by knocking in a door with a battering ram. Sometimes other tools may be required, such as bolt cutters, a sledge hammer, or a hydraulic spreader. If the door opens outward, then a "hooligan tool" may be used, which is a tool carried by most fire departments and used for prying open doors. The person assigned as the breacher is typically someone with the body size and strength to affect the breach quickly.

As the team reaches the doorway, they take up positions in a "stack" formation on either or both sides of the door. If the door opens inward, then the first officer on the side of the door opposite the door knob has a clear view of at least a portion of the interior of the structure, and is the first to enter. If the door opens outward, then the first officer on the same side as the door knob is the first to **clear and enter**.

Once the door is fully breached, then the team has three options. They can 1) breach and hold, 2) clear and enter, or 3) make a blind entry. When they breach and hold, they do not make an immediate entry. Instead, they hold their positions, call out their presence, and command the suspect to follow their directives. If they have chosen to clear and enter, then their first objective is to clear the immediate area of the entry of any threats and then enter the structure. They do this with a method referred to as **slicing the pie**. When officers execute this tactic, they simply move slowly to the side with their weapon aimed and ready to carefully expose more of the room to their field of view with each shuffle of their feet. Done properly, they will likely see a suspect before the suspect sees them.

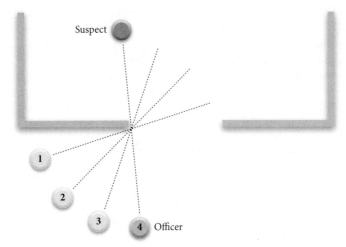

FIGURE 5.1   "Slicing the Pie".

With the final option, the **blind entry**, the team simply breaches and enters immediately, clearing the room as they move inside. This is obviously the most dangerous type of entry, but it also maximizes the element of surprise. It might be used in the case of a hostage situation where there is credible intelligence that the hostage-takers intend to kill the hostages if an assault is attempted.

TYPES OF ENTRY   Once the structure is breached and cleared from the outside, then the actual entry is made. A number of techniques are employed for entering the structure. With a **crisscross entry**, team members stack on both sides of the door, and then enter by crossing each other's path and moving to the opposite side of the room. When the officer in the first position enters, the goal is to move quickly to a position that will provide maximum domination of the area. The officer in the second position enters quickly and immediately scans the room for threats. This allows for triangulation of any threat inside the room, or targeting a threat from two different locations, making it impossible for a suspect inside the room to attack both officers simultaneously. An armed suspect will be focused on targeting the first officer, who will use speed to make targeting more difficult. The second officer will then immediately take advantage of the suspect's inability to target two officers simultaneously.

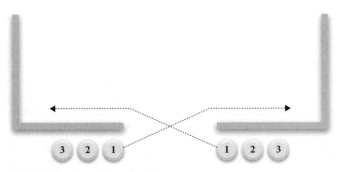

FIGURE 5.2   The "Crisscross" Entry.

ISSUES & ETHICS IN CRISIS INTERVENTION

The Siege at Waco

On February 28, 1993, a tactical team from the U.S. Bureau of Alcohol, Tobacco, and Firearms (ATF) attempted entry of a compound outside Waco, Texas, to serve a search warrant for suspected illegal weapons. Inside the building were approximately 80 members of a religious sect called the Branch Davidians, including their leader, David Koresh. As the agents attempted entry from different breach points, an intense gun battle erupted. Four ATF agents were killed, as well as six of the sect members. A siege began which would last for the next 50 days, as the FBI attempted to negotiate the sect's surrender. On April 19th a second assault was carried out by federal agents, this time involving military-style track vehicles that knocked holes in the side of the building and introduced tear gas in an effort to get those inside to exit and surrender. At some point during the assault the wooden structure caught fire and quickly burned to the ground. Seventy-six members of the Branch Davidians, including at least 20 children, died in the blaze.

In the aftermath of the incident the federal law enforcement agencies involved, especially the ATF and FBI, were criticized for how they handled the matter. One of the most pressing questions was whether the FBI had used pyrotechnic tear gas rounds in the second assault on the compound, thus causing the deadly fire. There were also questions about whether FBI agents were indiscriminately firing into the compound at a time when they were not under fire. Finally, there were many questions about the attempted entry itself, such as whether it was even necessary. It was discovered that the sect members knew of the impending assault after being tipped off by a mail carrier who had learned of the plan from a reporter to whom the ATF had given advance notice.

In September 1999, Attorney General Janet Reno appointed former Senator John C. Danforth (R-MO) as special counsel to head up an independent investigation into the Waco tragedy. In his "Final Report to the Deputy Attorney General Concerning the 1993 Confrontation at the Mt. Carmel Complex" (November 8, 2000), Danforth essentially exonerated the federal agents of any wrongdoing; however, it did little to reassure the public that the ATF and FBI had acted appropriately. To this day the questions remain, and evidence exists that seems to contradict some of the conclusions in the Danforth Report.

Do some basic Internet research on the Waco siege and then answer the following questions.

Discussion Questions

1. Should ATF ever have attempted a tactical entry knowing there were children inside, especially with no evidence that anyone was being held against their will?
2. Discuss the potential alternatives for resolving the Waco siege. Was a second assault on the compound necessary? Do you believe the ATF was motivated less by the possibility of illegal weapons at the compound, and more by the belief that the Branch Davidians were a religious "cult"? Discuss the reaction of most Americans, including law enforcement, toward a suspected cult.

With a **buttonhook entry**, team members again stack on both sides of the doorway but, rather than crossing each other's paths as they enter, they instead enter by rounding the door jam and moving quickly to a point of domination on the same side of the room as they entered. Again, the same triangulation method is used to quickly immobilize any threat that may be present.

The team may also execute a **combination entry**. Here, team members stack on the same side of the door and alternate their entry between buttonhook and crisscross. This places half the team on one side of the structure, and half on the other. In any of these techniques, an officer in the third spot can also take a position in the middle. The corners allow for maximum domination of the area. When two officers are positioned in opposing corners, they have the entire area in

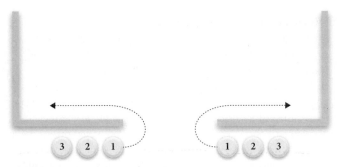

FIGURE 5.3 The "Buttonhook" Entry.

their combined field of view. If an armed suspect attempts to position themselves to take a shot at one team member, it is likely they will expose themselves to the other.

The final element of the tactical entry is the team's movement through the structure. To some extent how they do this will be determined by the type of crisis they are responding to. If it is a hostage rescue, they will move immediately toward the location of the hostage, if known. If not known, then it is likely that two separate teams will move in opposite directions, clearing each room as they go until the hostage is located. The same is true if they have a barricaded suspect they must locate and immobilize.

The goal of a tactical entry is to dominate one area of a structure at a time until the target is reached. This may be done slow and methodically, or it may be accomplished with very little pause on the part of the team members. The speed with which the team executes the entry is determined by the objective. Done correctly, each team member can almost immediately reduce their threat area from 360 degrees to 180 degrees, and possibly even 90 degrees, depending on the configuration of the structure's walls. When an officer has only one quarter of their visual field to focus on, with the other three quarters covered by other team members, this creates a very dominating position for the team, especially against a suspect who is still attempting to focus on a 360-degree threat area.

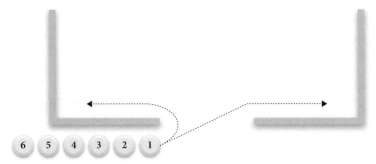

FIGURE 5.4 The "Combination" Entry.

Chapter Summary

Anytime a police officer responds to a situation, there is a chance that it could turn into a crisis, regardless of how routine the initial call may be. In the case of tactical officers, the crisis has typically already begun by the time they get there. Tactical situations are among the most dangerous for the police. Almost always weapons are involved and innocent people stand in harm's way. The tactical crisis demands that action be taken immediately once circumstances allow it, especially in the case of an active shooter. Officers are now trained to immediately move in and seek out a shooter in a steady and methodical way, confronting them before they have sufficient time to adjust their own tactics to defend against an inevitable assault by police.

In those cases where there is sufficient time to allow a tactical entry team to respond, a number of options are available to the commander on the scene. The option selected will be determined by a number of factors, including the presence of weapons, hostages being held, the aggression level of the person inside, and the physical structure itself. If it is determined that an entry is necessary, then team members will gather as much intelligence on the structure being breached as they can in the amount of time allotted. They will brief all participants in the operation—perimeter officers, K9 units, emergency medical personnel—on the tactical plan and any contingencies. And then they will execute their entry according to their predetermined plan. Those officers who execute a tactical entry are highly trained to enter a physical structure in a way that maximizes their ability to quickly immobilize any threats they confront inside, and then to move quickly through the structure to carry out their desired objective of seizing evidence, arresting suspects, or freeing hostages.

Key Terms

S.W.A.T.
Tactical team
Active shooter
Contact team
Rescue team
Perimeter team
Evacuation team
Tactical entry
Ruse

Surround and call out
Breach and hold
Deliberate entry
Dynamic entry
Scouting phase
Planning phase
Briefing phase
Execution phase
Debriefing phase

Breach
Slicing the pie
Clear and enter
Blind entry
Crisscross entry
Buttonhook entry
Combination entry

Discussion Questions

1. The tactical mission of the police could perhaps be better carried out by military units. Do you believe there is a downside in allowing the U.S. military to participate in police tactical operations?
2. The image portrayed by police tactical units is much different than a typical officer on the beat. Do you believe this image has been helpful to the police mission in America in terms of police-community relations, or has it hindered that goal?
3. Discuss the differences in the psychological state of most active shooters, such as those at Columbine High School, and the tactical team members who confront them. How does training impact the psychological state of the tactical officers?

6

Suicide and the Psychology of Self-destruction

LEARNING OUTCOMES

Upon completion of this chapter the student should be able to:

1. Summarize the social impact of suicide in America.

2. List and explain the predominant theories of suicide.

3. Define a typology scheme for suicide, and to summarize the dangers associated with each to those who respond to this type of crisis.

4. List and summarize the techniques and protocols for responding to and de-escalating suicide.

5. Summarize the special classes of suicide.

Chapter Outline

INTRODUCTION

THE PROBLEM OF SUICIDE

Suicide is the ultimate microcrisis. It is the final act of a desperate person seeking refuge in the quiet calm of nothingness. People choose to end their lives for many reasons, but one thing they all have in common is a bleeding out so to speak of their sense of self. For most, by the time they reach the point where suicide becomes a viable option, there simply is nothing left. Their family and friends, and all of their dreams and aspirations, get sucked into the darkness of their extreme egocentrism like matter into a black hole. Some do it quietly. Others use more violent means. Most make it a solitary act. Still others use it as an opportunity to make a final statement by taking family, friends, or complete strangers with them. The social and economic costs associated with suicide are staggering. Consider the following estimates (Stone, 2001):

- In America there are an estimated 80 deaths from suicide every single day.
- Approximately 300,000 Americans survive a suicide attempt each year.
- Around 116,000 people who survive a suicide attempt each year require hospitalization, with an average cost per stay of $15,000.
- Of those who survive an attempt, an estimated 19,000 are left permanently disabled at a cost per patient of $127,000 annually for their continued care.
- About 1 percent of Americans end their lives by suicide. It is the eighth-leading cause of death in the United States.

Obviously a great many resources are committed each day to saving the lives of those who would rather die. Police officers are frequently dispatched to reports of threatened suicide, and they are a daily occurrence in our jails and prisons. For those who respond to these types of situations it can be a dangerous endeavor. Most of the time this intervention is successful in de-escalating the immediate threat of suicide, and the majority of those who are convinced not to end their lives never again attempt or threaten such an act. Sometimes it is simply a matter of getting the person to a safe place until sobriety can intervene.

But then there are those who are so desperate to end their pain that not even sobriety can deter them. For the police who respond to these situations, precautions must be taken. People in this condition tend to lose their ability to weigh the moral rightness or wrongness of their actions. If their desperation is deep enough, then any attempt to prevent them from carrying out their act may be viewed with hostility. It is an extremely dangerous situation, one in which the officer may even be provoked into using deadly force to relieve the individual from doing it themselves.

Before we discuss the methods and techniques of suicide intervention, and the various typologies of those who choose to end their lives, we must address a few of the theories that have attempted to account for this type of behavior. None have been entirely successful in doing so, mostly because of the many and varied reasons why people end their lives.

THEORIES OF SUICIDE

People commit suicide for many reasons, but very few theories can account for a common etiology. Theories have originated from within the disciplines of sociology, psychology, anthropology, philosophy, and theology. All have looked at the reasons people end their lives within the context of their particular paradigms, but arguably none have successfully peeled away the biopsychosocial layers to that mysterious place in our psyche where the idea of self-destruction is born, at least not in a way that lends itself to the scientific method.

Emile Durkheim's Sociological Theory

One of the first theories offered to account for the phenomenon of suicide was by the great sociologist Emile Durkheim (1897). He looked at suicide as being primarily the result of the person's relationship to the broader social structure. Durkheim proposed four types of suicide based on an imbalance between two social forces, **social integration** and **moral regulation**. The former refers to the extent to which an individual or group of individuals feels accepted as full members of the larger society. Minority groups, especially in America, for decades lacked any degree of social integration, and thus their opportunities, both real and perceived, for jobs, education, and health care were greatly diminished. For Durkheim, at least in his day, many of the problems faced by society, such as crime, poverty, and even mental illness, were the result of people lacking a sense of social solidarity with the majority class.

Durkheim's concept of moral regulation refers to the rules and norms established by society that sets limits on what are otherwise limitless and destructive desires. For example, he would argue that the lack of moral regulation of wealth by a capitalist society only breeds social problems as people attempt to gain as much wealth as possible. The more they gain, the more they must exploit others, namely the working class, which breeds contempt for one social class by another. And for those who are not successful in gaining wealth, alternative means for doing so, such as crime, are employed.

Durkheim's four suicide types then are the result of one or both of these social forces having a negative impact on the individual. He described each as follows:

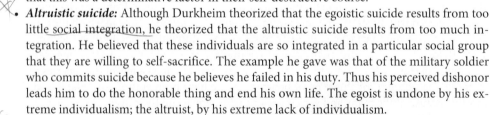

- *Egoistic suicide:* This type of suicide results from too little social integration. These individuals, according to Durkheim, lack the values, traditions, and norms of the dominant society, and therefore lack a sense of belongingness to social groups and the social supports necessary to buffer the individual against despair and a socially driven sense of hopelessness. Durkheim found that unmarried adult males had a higher prevalence of suicide than their married counterparts. From this data he surmised that because the unmarried males were less socially integrated, because marriage in his day was considered a social norm, that this was a determinative factor in their self-destructive course.
- *Altruistic suicide:* Although Durkheim theorized that the egoistic suicide results from too little social integration, he theorized that the altruistic suicide results from too much integration. He believed that these individuals are so integrated in a particular social group that they are willing to self-sacrifice. The example he gave was that of the military soldier who commits suicide because he believes he failed in his duty. Thus his perceived dishonor leads him to do the honorable thing and end his own life. The egoist is undone by his extreme individualism; the altruist, by his extreme lack of individualism.
- *Anomic suicide:* Durkheim theorized two types of suicide related to moral regulation. The first, anomic suicide, involves an imbalance of means and needs. Put another way, suicide in this case results when the individual's social means are no longer sufficient to meet their personal needs. Durkheim proposed four subtypes of anomic suicide:
  1. *Acute economic anomie* occurs when traditional institutions (i.e., church, government, trade) are no longer sufficient to meet the individual's social needs. In this case the despair that results is overwhelming. Once again, Durkheim argued that the lack of moral regulation of society during and following the industrial revolution created a situation

where the poor and despondent were no longer cared for in the same manner. The rich got richer during that time only at the expense of the poor and working classes. The hopelessness of poverty in that time caused many to take the extreme measure of suicide.

2. *Chronic economic anomie*, in contrast, occurs when wealth and prosperity themselves are insufficient to replace the lost regulators of society. Durkheim referenced data that showed a higher rate of suicide among the wealthy than the poor. In short, according to Durkheim, the industrial revolution had brought about the means to the desired end of wealth and property, but in the process it had eroded traditional social regulators. Many discovered that wealth simply could not buy happiness.

3. *Acute domestic anomie* occurs when a sudden change takes place on a personal level that leaves the individual incapable of adapting to meet their social needs. The most common example cited by Durkheim was sudden widowhood. Once again, with the industrial revolution came changes in the moral regulation on caring for widows and orphans. Where once a society regulated by the dictates of the Church required parishioners to support the widows and orphans of the congregation, the new secular society of the industrial age turned them into beggars. Many simply could not deal with the despair of poverty and, instead, ended their lives.

4. *Chronic domestic anomie*, according to Durkheim, occurs only in men. He believed that marriage played an important role in regulating the sexuality and behavior of men and women. Single men lacked this important moral regulator. As marriage became less a requirement before sex, as the Church required, more men chose singlehood, and with it a life unregulated by marriage. Durkheim noted that the rate of suicide among single men was significantly higher than among married men. He attributed this to their lack of goals and expectations. He believed that women were not subject to this type of social anomie.

• **Fatalistic suicide:** Durkheim's final suicide type occurs in social conditions where the individual experiences pervasive oppression. Unlike the under-regulation of anomie, those who commit fatalistic suicide do so as a result of excessive regulation. In Durkheim's day, this may have included those conscripted to slavery or military service. It may also have included a young man trapped in an unfulfilling and confining marriage, or a childless woman ostracized by a society that demanded of a woman little else than to procreate and carry on her husband's name and bloodline.

Durkheim's theory has not been without its critics. Kershner and Sterk (2005) have argued that Durkheim used incomplete data to support his theory. He did not look at attempted suicides for example, which are equally important for studying this phenomenon. Also, Durkheim argues that the advancement of women toward a less subjugated role in society led to lower birth rates, less integration for women, and increased fatalistic suicide. The authors contend that this position was not supported by the data of the day, but rather by the biased interpretation of that data by Durkheim and his contemporaries. Finally, they discount his use of military suicides as the only example of altruistic suicide. They argue that the available statistics do not support the idea of self-sacrificing suicide among military personnel, resulting from over-integration. Rather, it is the over-regulation of military life that seems to be the predominant factor, both in Durkheim's day and in our modern times.

Poppel and Day (1996) have also questioned Durkheim's model. They point to Durkheim's discussion of the connection between religious affiliation and social integration. To bolster his theory, Durkheim provided statistics reflecting a much higher rate of suicide among Protestants than Catholics. He argued that Protestants were in the social minority of his day because of their religion, and thus were less socially integrated. This, according to Durkheim, accounted for their higher rate of suicide. But the authors have identified a flaw in Durkheim's data. In analyzing data gathered concurrent with Durkheim's, they have concluded that the suicide rate among Catholics was not necessarily lower than that of Protestants, but that because of the more negative view of suicide held by Catholics, in reality the families of Catholic-affiliated suicide victims in Durkheim's day simply chose more often to conceal the cause of death. The authors argue that by committing this "ecological fallacy," it calls into question Durkheim's use of sociological explanations for the phenomenon of suicide.

Durkheim's theory certainly provides a comprehensive sociological model of suicide, but it still falls short of explaining what it is that compels some to commit suicide, and others in similar situations to choose alternative coping strategies. His theory also avoids the issue of mental illness, especially major depression, as a contributing factor in suicide. Finally, any theory based on social integration and moral regulation is at risk of losing its relevance when society and its moral parameters change, as they have in America since the 1960s. The excessive regulation of Durkheim's fatalistic suicide is rarely seen in our modern permissive society. And the ability to achieve an acceptable level of social integration has been removed from the control of a dominant majority intent upon oppressing the voiceless minority and placed squarely in the hands of anyone, regardless of their race or ethnicity, with the determination to work hard. Yet in America suicide rates are as high as ever. So we must conclude that something more than simply a person's relationship to the larger social order influences their decision to commit suicide.

Sigmund Freud's Psychoanalytic Theory

Sigmund Freud is considered the father of modern psychology, and many consider his psychoanalytic theory to be the only model that truly gets to the core psychological mechanism that compels an individual to take their own life rather than look for alternative coping strategies to relieve their despair. To understand this component of Freud's extensive theory, we must first understand the simple reflex demonstrated when you touch the palm of a baby's hand. Any mother knows that the baby will instinctively grasp the finger that is touching it. Evolutionists, of course, will argue that such a reflex is a leftover of the evolutionary process, and that it results from the need in our primate ancestors to grasp tree limbs at an early age in order to survive. Those babies that could do so were more successful in surviving and passing on their genetic code. Eventually the ability to grasp at an early age, perhaps even before the eyes are fully developed, became a reflex in all human babies as the inability to grasp was selected out of the human genome.

Freud, an evolutionist, endeavored to identify what the evolutionary process had left behind in terms of behavior and motivation, as opposed to physical ability. He wanted to identify what instincts we enter the world with that compel us to act in particular ways. What is it that causes us to be happy, sad, or angry? What is the source of a child's frustration when they cannot have a particular toy another child is playing with? Freud believed that the forces motivating human behavior had to be genetically determined just like the physical reflexes. His theory can be described as biological in nature, and thus he provides us biopsychosocial model to understand the phenomenon of suicide.

Ultimately Freud (1920, 1923) arrived at the conclusion that we enter the world with two instincts that motivate all behavior. The first he labeled **Eros**, or the life instinct. He believed this to be the force within us that seeks pleasure, either physical or psychological, and moves us forward in a goal-oriented manner. Freud believed that when this instinct is allowed expression then a state of psychic equilibrium, or contentment, is the result. He believed we are motivated always to maintain this equilibrium, but when circumstances prevent it, then the negative emotions of anxiety and frustration result.

The second instinct in Freud's formulation is **Thanatos**, or the death instinct. He believed we are born with a biological need to return to the quiet calm of the womb, and even to the nothingness of pre-existence. It is this instinct that seeks the calm of emotional equilibrium and compels us to act when equilibrium is lost. Put another way, whereas Eros seeks out pleasure, Thanatos seeks only to maintain a state of equilibrium by motivating the individual to intervene when equilibrium is lost. This intervention may be in the form of aggression. For example, a small child may spot a particular toy they want to play with because of the pleasurable sensory experience it provides. Eros motivates the child to seek out control of the toy. But if the toy is being held by another child, then we have a problem, especially if the other child will not hand it over. In this case equilibrium is momentarily lost because the child cannot enjoy the pleasurable activity of playing with the toy, so the child acts aggressively and grabs the toy away from the child holding it. Thanatos compels the child to act in an aggressive manner and, once the toy is secured, then a state of equilibrium returns, albeit potentially accompanied by feelings of guilt depending on the child's level of cognitive development, feelings that can result in yet another loss of equilibrium.

For Freud, the dual instincts of Eros and Thanatos work in a coordinated way to ensure psychic equilibrium. One motivates us to move through life seeking pleasure, whereas the other compels some type of intervening behavior when pleasure is not achieved, or when too much pleasure reaches a point of critical mass and begins to promote the opposite effect. It can be said that the happiest people are those who have developed the necessary coping strategies to maintain equilibrium and, when lost, to regain it a manner that does not provide a short-term fix that in the long run will only exacerbate the situation further, as in the case with most aggressive behaviors.

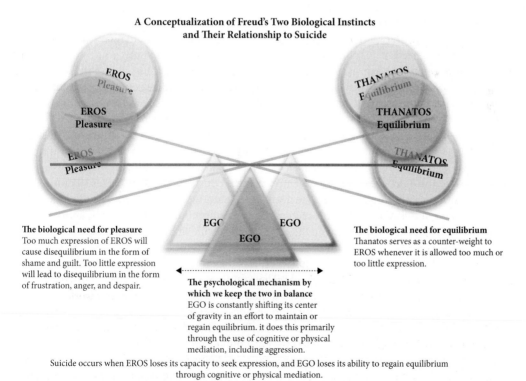

A Conceptualization of Freud's Two Biological Instincts and Their Relationship to Suicide

EROS Pleasure

THANATOS Equilibrium

The biological need for pleasure
Too much expression of EROS will cause disequilibrium in the form of shame and guilt. Too little expression will lead to disequilibrium in the form of frustration, anger, and despair.

EGO

The biological need for equilibrium
Thanatos serves as a counter-weight to EROS whenever it is allowed too much or too little expression.

The psychological mechanism by which we keep the two in balance
EGO is constantly shifting its center of gravity in an effort to maintain or regain equilibrium. it does this primarily through the use of cognitive or physical mediation, including aggression.

Suicide occurs when EROS loses its capacity to seek expression, and EGO loses its ability to regain equilibrium through cognitive or physical mediation.

FIGURE 6.1 Freud's Two Biological Instincts.

Now let's look at an example involving adult behavior. Depression is a clinical syndrome that affects every aspect of an individual's life. It can be so severe that the activities people typically find pleasurable, including interpersonal relationships, become nearly impossible. Because Eros is not allowed expression, disequilibrium results, and the individual is compelled to intervene (Thanatos). Many will try new healthier activities and routines, and even therapy to make their lives better. Others will intervene in ways that are not so healthy, such as drugs and alcohol, or sexual promiscuity. With the former, especially therapy, equilibrium is potentially regained; however, in the case of the latter examples, it becomes even more elusive, which demands even more of Thanatos and creates a dangerous cycle of destructive behavior that has the opposite effect of its intended purpose. This is the reality of alcoholism and drug dependence especially. The sense of equilibrium that results from their use is short-lived, and only contributes to their chronic disequilibrium in the long run.

So how does all this relate to the phenomenon of suicide? According to Freud, regardless of the typology, suicide occurs when equilibrium is lost, and the individual perceives it as hopeless that it can ever be regained. Does that mean Thanatos no longer compels behavior? Quite the contrary. Thanatos still has one major card up its sleeve to return the individual to the calm of nothingness, and that is the ultimate equilibrium: death. Suicide occurs when the individual has simply given up, and when the instinctive drive to regain equilibrium is so incredibly strong that such an irrational option as suicide suddenly seems viable. For someone so desperate, the usual mediator of the tug and pull of Eros and Thanatos, the individual's ego, or sense of self, is suddenly gone. In their hyperegocentric state, and without the mediation of self, the absolutes become incredibly clear. To relieve their pain they need only to escape into the calm of non-existence.

Freud's theory does an effective job of providing us a common etiological foundation for all typologies of suicide. All involve the inability of the individual to maintain a psychic equilibrium, a biological need that is common to all people. Without it we are overcome by despair, and to escape the emotional pain we escape our very existence. Freud thus places suicide squarely in the realm of psychobiology. Our sense of self (psychology) mediates our instinctive need for pleasure and emotional equilibrium (biology). The question has arisen as to why animals don't commit suicide. After all they seek pleasure in the form of nourishment, play, and sexual activity. They also aggress if those needs are not met. So what sets them apart from humans? It seems reasonable to conclude that animals are simply not aware of their own inevitable death, and therefore death is not an option. Humans have conceptualized death in many ways. It's easy for us to consider the quiet calm of non-existence. It's that consideration that makes suicide an option. Without the ability to conceptualize death, or the abstract non-existence on the other side of existence, then it is not possible for that to be a learned option. In other words, animals must be able to conceptualize and anticipate the outcome of suicide in order for that outcome to reinforce the behavior.

Freud's theory has been tested empirically. Kaslow et al. (2001) looked at hospitalized psychiatric patients who had attempted suicide. Their findings supported Freud's theory of suicide, and further found that those who had a childhood history of emotional disequilibrium related to a significant loss were more susceptible to self-destructive behavior as adults. Fowler et al. (2001), too, found support for Freud's theory, specifically the relationship of suicide to a person's inability to maintain an internal balance (i.e., "ego boundaries") necessary for equilibrium. They also studied a group of severely disturbed psychiatric patients with the goal of being able to predict suicidal behavior through the administration of various psychological tests.

SUICIDE TYPOLOGIES

For those who respond to suicide, a unified theory of its cause is probably of less value than a thorough understanding of the various typologies of suicide and the behavioral characteristics that correlate with each. Different motivations for suicide produce different levels of danger for those who respond to such crises. We can classify suicide with the use of a typology wheel based on an individual's motivation. By using a classification scheme we can begin to establish response protocols based on potential risks to the responder, family members, hostages, and the suicidal person themselves. The goal of course is to save as many lives as possible, including those of the potential victims of suicide. The scheme we will employ includes four broad categories of suicide: *anger, despair, egoistic,* and *proactive*. Within those four typologies are nine subtypes. Descriptions of each follow.

Anger Suicide

Anger suicide includes those individuals who choose to end their lives out of self-contempt, or as a way of exacting revenge on another person. In the case of the former, it may include the individual who hates himself because he cannot stop drinking or using drugs. Perhaps a pedophile whose guilt over his deviant thoughts and actions cause him to loath himself. Maybe a former soldier who killed innocent people in the heat of battle and now doesn't feel he deserves to live. There are many reasons why a person may dislike or even hate who they are. This type of suicide is an anger turned inward. Typically those who fall in this category have insufficient support systems to turn to when their self-contempt reaches its crescendo. Alcohol and drugs are also typically involved. The person who experiences severe self-contempt typically turns to these substances as a way of quieting the inner rage they feel. Eventually this short-term cure only intensifies the feelings they are trying to deaden. When it gets to the point where nothing seems to work, then the individual is at risk of carrying out the suicide.

The other subtype within this category includes those who commit suicide to exact revenge on another person or persons. Here we might find the despondent wife who kills herself and her children in order to get back at her husband following an unwanted divorce. Perhaps a juvenile who kills him- or herself to exact revenge on an authoritarian parent. Typically a revenge suicide involves a family member or intimate partner. These people are especially dangerous because they may take others with them, especially children. Every year innocent children die at the hands of a suicidal parent, usually in the midst of, or following an especially, bad divorce. People who commit a revenge suicide are trying to make a statement with their final act. Their own death is secondary in importance to making someone feel responsible for their death, or the death of others. Whereas self-contempt suicide is *self-directed*, revenge suicide is *other-directed*.

For those who respond to a threatened anger suicide, caution must be taken because that anger can be immediately projected onto those who are trying to help. The person intent upon committing a self-contempt suicide is seeking the ultimate self-persecution. Many will seek to further justify their own death by creating a situation where the responding police have no choice but to use deadly force against the individual. This **"suicide by cop"** is a common occurrence. Some resort to such a tactic because they simply do not have the courage to do it themselves. But others, perhaps the majority, cause the police to kill them as a way of further justifying their perceived need for persecution. Unfortunately though, this creates an extremely dangerous situation for the responding police officers. An effort to avoid deadly force could potentially cause the individual to shift their anger toward the officers, even to the point of leaving the officers no other option but to kill the individual.

Even if the individual has no plans to force the police to kill them, the self-contempt suicide still creates an extremely dangerous situation for the responding officers. This type of individual may hate themselves for what they are, but projecting blame onto an external source is common. The responding officers typically have very limited psychosocial history on the individual during the initial response. It may be an individual whose self-contempt developed after years of prison confinement. For such an individual, blaming the police for their problems is an easy thing. In fact, the police are oftentimes blamed for a person's problematic life. Either the police caused their problems by arresting them, or they caused them by not arresting someone else. For example, the adult male who was sexually abused as a child by his own father may blame the police for not intervening, regardless of whether or not the police had any knowledge of the abuse.

For the person committing revenge suicide, it is almost always a volatile situation for those who respond because of the person's rage. The police officers may be perceived by the individual as siding with the individual upon whom the suicidal person seeks revenge, or once again the police may be blamed for whatever situation led to the present circumstances. The very fact that the officers are attempting to dissuade the individual from killing themselves will likely be perceived as the officers not understanding how they have been victimized, and why their rage against the other person is justified. This can very easily lead the individual to suddenly group the police officers with the person upon whom they are seeking revenge. When this happens, assuming there is a gun involved in the incident, the officers can very easily be targeted.

Despair Suicide

Despair suicide includes those who choose to end their lives simply because they are tired of living. This category includes those who are so consumed by their despair that they no longer perceive any purpose in living. This type of suicide is self-directed, but not necessarily related to any feelings of self-contempt. They are people who have experienced either chronic emotional or physical suffering. The former category includes those who suffer from depression or extreme loneliness or isolation. It may include those who suffer from PTSD or the effects of long-term discrimination. Long-term poverty and financial problems may lead someone to end their life. The common variable with all chronic-emotional suicides is a sense of *hopelessness*. The individual simply cannot see the light at the end of the tunnel. They experience a sense of emptiness, a void in their sense of self that can no longer be filled with relationships, interests, or vocations. They may in fact have some very supportive family and friends, but their despair simply cannot be relieved.

Many times those who suffer from debilitating despair try various coping strategies. Many turn to alcohol and illicit drugs, which of course provide only a temporary fix, and eventually exacerbate the individual's despair. Others turn to religion and other spiritual exercises. Many times this has been found to be successful in alleviating the person's emotional despair for a time. Religion gives the individual something they lack, and that is a sense of hope. But for those who suffer a despair so extreme it would cause them to consider suicide, the positive effects of spirituality will for the most part begin to wear off without a complete and total dedication of their lives to the spiritual endeavor. Still others attempt therapeutic intervention and prescription drugs. This has been found to be perhaps the most successful course for those experiencing chronic-emotional despair. Drug therapy, coupled with some form of counseling and new and effective coping strategies can be highly effective in reducing the level of a person's despair, especially when there is no specific source for the person's emotional suffering, as is true with most cases of major depression.

The other source of despair that can lead a person to commit suicide is chronic-physical suffering. This can result from a debilitating injury or illness that causes the person to suffer chronic pain. Like its emotional counterpart, chronic physical pain can affect every aspect of a person's life and lead to feelings of hopelessness. Eventually, when it seems apparent to the individual that their pain may never subside, it can easily lead to a desire to end their suffering. We often see this in cases of assisted suicide. These individuals typically suffer from incurable and very painful neuromuscular diseases, and view it as their right to terminate their life when the pain is no longer bearable, and their quality of life has deteriorated dramatically. But among those in the medical community who choose to assist these patients, assisted suicide is reserved for the terminally ill. This, however, has not prevented many from simply committing unassisted suicide for physical conditions that would not be considered terminal by any measure. For example, people suffering the chronic pain of back problems, rheumatoid arthritis, and migraine headaches, among other conditions, have all committed suicide. All are medically treatable, and none are considered terminal.

The dangers for those who respond to these types of suicides is certainly less than that of anger suicides, but precautions must still be taken. These people tend not to project anger or cast blame on those who respond in an effort to save their lives, but they still can become very irrational, especially if they are suffering a depressive episode, or if they have failed to take prescribed medication. And of course there is always the possibility of alcohol or illicit drugs being a factor in the person's decision. In these cases the individual may not even be fully aware of their own actions, which may become very unpredictable and entirely inconsistent with their normal behavior patterns.

Egoistic Suicide

What sets the **egoistic suicide** apart is that it involves a deterioration of the person's self-identity. The person suffering self-contempt has no illusions of hanging on to some semblance of an identity. Their self-contempt is the result of long-term identity diffusion. The egoistic suicide, however, results from a more acute depreciation of a person's self-concept. There are two subcategories, the acute situational and the suicide related to abandonment issues. Both result from what is perceived by the individual to be a complete devaluation of their sense of self. From the psychoanalytic perspective this type of suicide can be thought of as *ego death,* and creates a dangerous situation where the individual loses the ability to control and mediate impulsive thoughts and actions. The egoistic suicide is one born out of panic.

The acute situational suicide is one of the most common, especially among men. Some examples might include the man who is despondent over losing a job, or the pastor caught trading child pornography over the Internet. Being arrested and having their crimes exposed in public is often the cause of jailhouse suicides. The adolescent boy labeled by his peers as being gay when he is not may lead to suicide. Or the gay adolescent being humiliated and isolated by his peers for his sexuality. Another example is the well-publicized case of Admiral Michael Boorda, the U.S. Naval Chief, who in 1996 committed suicide after it was learned he was wearing medals he did not deserve (*New York Times*, 1996). The public humiliation and attack on his honor was simply too much to bear. His military service was such a significant part of his identity that to have it called into question resulted in a sudden devaluation of that identity.

The second type of egoistic suicide involves the issue of abandonment. This is one of the most complex emotions in the human repertoire, and is the result of a long developmental process that begins in early infancy. One of the first developmental tasks of a newborn child is to establish an emotional bond with the primary caregiver, typically the mother. This emotional bond, or attachment, is primarily the result of responsive parenting (Cohn et al., 1992). When a child is securely attached they feel safe in the world, and they're able to begin the process of establishing autonomy. When they are insecurely attached they never feel safe to venture away from the parents, and their fear turns into dependence. The problem for these people is that the quality of their childhood attachment will eventually impact the quality of their intimate relationships in adulthood. Those who are insecurely attached are afraid of abandonment by their parents as children, and thus their display of separation anxiety, and as adults they fear abandonment by their significant others because they never fully establish a sense of personal autonomy.

Typically, people who choose to commit suicide as a result of abandonment do so following a divorce or break-up. It is considered an egoistic suicide because their very identity is enmeshed with their dependence on the other person (Ledgerwood, 1999). When the relationship ends they lose more than just the relationship. They lose their attachment figure, since either a secure or insecure attachment to a parent will eventually be transferred in like measure to a significant other. In such a case, even the end of a toxic relationship is devastating. With no sense of true autonomy, the loss of their attachment figure results in the loss of their sense of self. Once again, in psychoanalytic terms the individual experiences ego death. Many come through their feelings of abandonment by turning to alcohol or drugs, or even immediately entering another toxic relationship. Others are simply unable to recover and decide to end their lives.

Those who respond to a threatened egoistic suicide are dealing with a person who sees no other solution. Their emotionality is acute, and thus its intensity level will be high. Many times they will be intoxicated, having turned to alcohol or drugs either to reduce their pain or their apprehensions about carrying out the intended act. Anytime you have the combination of intense emotionality and either alcohol or drugs you have a very volatile situation that is extremely dangerous for the first responder. These people have no real sense of self to mediate their impulsive thoughts and actions. In their acute phase they lose the ability to reason on a moral level, and with the presence of alcohol or drugs may even lose sight of the line between reality and fantasy. These individuals too may seek to create a situation where the police have no choice but to resort to deadly force against them.

In comparison to the other types of suicide, the individual contemplating an egoistic suicide is the most erratic and impulsive. Those who commit anger or despair-driven suicides do so with a well-defined purpose. In the case of the former, the individual wishes to persecute themselves or others. In an effort to do so, they make a reasoned decision to commit suicide for that purpose. In the case of the despair-driven suicide, the individual simply wants to end their pain. They may have tried alternative treatments or courses of action, but now they have determined their situation to be hopeless. By contrast, the individual who threatens an egoistic suicide typically has not thought out their situation. They have no specific purpose because they can neither reclaim the lost relationship nor reverse the actions that led to their situation. They typically haven't experienced long-term despair. More than the others, they are like a cornered animal with no way out, and without the ability to look past the source of their acute emotionality, suicide looks like the only viable option.

Proactive Suicide

If positive reasons for suicide are possible, then they would fall under the category of **proactive suicide**: This type of suicide is proactive because the person intends by their final act to create some future condition or circumstance they consider positive in some way. Three subtypes are under this category: pre-emptive, altruistic, and ritualistic suicide.

Those who commit pre-emptive suicide do so to avoid a future negative consequence. Many who have participated in assisted suicide have done so to end their lives before their circumstances worsen. Certainly others have done so because of prolonged physical pain, but the pre-emptive suicide occurs in advance of the worst to come. Others have committed suicide after receiving news of a terminal disease. In the 1980s, before the medical advances that now allow AIDS patients to live a much longer life, many diagnosed with the disease ended their lives. Here we also see a number of elderly suicides, many of them following the death of their spouse. They simply pre-empt the possibility of living out their lives alone and without the spouse they may have spent decades with. Pre-emptive suicides are not always related to death and dying. Many have committed suicide in advance of a long prison sentence, or perhaps a required military deployment. During WWII, spies carried with them cyanide capsules to use in the event of their capture and inevitable torture. People who commit pre-emptive suicide do not necessarily want to die, but rather, they are motivated more by their desire to avoid an inevitable circumstance.

The second subcategory of proactive suicide is the individual who ends his or her life for altruistic reasons. The individual who commits suicide after being diagnosed with a terminal illness, not to avoid future consequences, but to prevent their family from having to bear the burden of their illness, would be considered an altruistic suicide. Another might be an individual who commits suicide in order for their family to enjoy the benefits of a life insurance policy. There have been many such cases where the suicide is disguised as a traffic accident to preclude the possibility of a "suicide clause" preventing payment of the life insurance proceeds. Like the pre-emptive suicide, the person contemplating an altruistic suicide does not necessarily want to die, but they see their death as having a positive benefit for others. A chronically depressed woman may commit suicide not because of prolonged emotional despair, but to avoid putting her family through any further hardships caused by her illness.

The final subcategory is the ritualistic suicide. This form of suicide is carried out for reasons external to the individual committing the act. They are typically motivated either by religious, spiritual, or political factors, and are seen as sacrificial acts by those who end their lives in this manner. An example would be that of Norman Morrison, a 31-year-old Quaker who, on November 2, 1965, set himself on fire under Secretary of Defense Robert McNamara's window at the Pentagon. Morrison was deeply troubled by the war in Vietnam, and decided to end his life in the manner he did to protest the war and draw attention to the atrocities that were occurring as a result of the American bombing (*Washington Post*, 1965). A less noble example would be the Heaven's Gate cult suicides in March 1997. In that case 39 members of the group committed suicide so their souls could rendezvous with a spaceship purportedly following the Hale-Bopp comet (CNN, 1997). And perhaps the most common threatened ritualistic suicide in America is the hunger strike, which almost always occurs in prisons and jails. Although the vast majority of such cases end with the individual accepting nourishment, it is a common method of protest for inmates.

Ritualistic suicide can carry with it much less or, in some cases, much more risk for those who respond than do the other types of suicide discussed previously. Certainly those like

FIGURE 6.2 Suicide Typologies.

Norman Morrison who are carrying out their final act for moral reasons will have little interest in hurting others, including those who respond and attempt to prevent them from doing so. Those participating in hunger strikes will likely fall in the same class because they do so to better the circumstances of others. To respond to intervention attempts with force or threat of force will only erode any moral advantage they may enjoy. These are not necessarily people who want to die, nor are they typically people who want others to die, because they view their actions as sacrificial in nature and for the benefit of others.

Certainly this is not the case with ritualistic suicide tied to the various types of cults, especially those viewing their suicides as a conduit to an afterlife. These are extremely dangerous situations for anyone who responds and attempts to intervene. Many times the family of cult members will contact the police with fears that their family member is going to participate in a ritualistic suicide. The police must be very careful how they respond to these situations. These cults exist as closed subcultures with their own moral codes. They feel no moral obligation to society as a whole, and in most cases the police are viewed as agents for an enemy they are attempting to escape. Those who preach a "doomsday" message can be extremely dangerous. The police attempting to intervene in some manner will only feed that message, and may intensify and speed up their plans to carry out their final act in order to enjoy the benefits of the afterlife they believe awaits them.

It is difficult to codify the dangers posed by suicidal individuals. The police and correctional officers who respond daily to such incidents view them all as dangerous. Anyone preparing to take their own life has greatly restricted their ability to reason, ranging from an inability to view their circumstances from another point of view, to being entirely irrational and displaying schizophrenic-like behaviors.

RESPONDING TO AND DE-ESCALATING A THREATENED SUICIDE: THE FIVE STEPS OF SUICIDE INTERVENTION

Hollywood has done a great disservice to the task of suicide intervention. How many times have we watched movies in which a police officer tries to talk someone out of leaping from a building or bridge by saying something like "Go ahead and jump, I don't work on commission!" Or "Come on pal, you're only going to create a lot of paperwork for me if you do this." Although such a cavalier attitude is entertaining in movies and television, it can be deadly in real life, both for the police officer and the individual whose life could potentially be saved if the officer responds in an appropriate manner.

Regardless of the type of suicide being responded to, there are common elements of an intervention that should be kept in mind when attempting to de-escalate the crisis. The officer's demeanor is absolutely critical to a successful intervention. In the case of a threatened suicide, assuming the officer arrives in time, the first step is containment if a gun, knife, explosive device, or other potentially deadly weapon is involved. The officer must take immediate steps to secure the area to prevent innocent onlookers from getting too close. In most cases the presence of onlookers will only exacerbate the person's emotional condition. They will be viewed by the suicidal person as uncaring and unsympathetic, and only interested in watching someone kill themselves. There have been reported cases of onlookers actually chanting to entice an individual to carry out their threatened act.

Once the situation is contained to the best of the first responder's ability, then the intervention must immediately begin. A plethora of textbooks and training guides detail the therapeutic process for those considering suicide, but therapy is not the goal of an immediate crisis intervention. The goal is de-escalation in order to get the individual to a safe place where the therapeutic process can begin in earnest. As we discussed in the previous chapter on crisis communication, there are five steps to the intervention process: *engage, establish rapport, listen, offer an out*, and *gain commitment*. Each is a critical component of the process, and a misstep at any of these stages can have negative consequences.

Engagement

How the officer engages the individual threatening suicide is important because the purpose of this initial engagement is to momentarily focus the person's attention away from their intended act and onto the officer. The officer's approach must not be threatening to the individual, and it certainly should not compromise the officer's own safety. The following guidelines are suggested:

- If possible without compromising their own safety, the officer should avoid approaching the individual with gun, Taser, pepper spray, or handcuffs drawn. It is best to remain in close proximity in a location providing acceptable cover. The individual must see that the officer has established acceptable boundaries that will not be violated without their permission.
- During their approach, the officer should keep their hands visible to the extent possible. The approach should be slow and steady. Also, the officer should avoid looking around or talking on their radio. The person threatening suicide must not be placed in fear of an imminent attempt to subdue them. This could have deadly results.
- It is critical that only one officer attempt the intervention. The suicide is less likely when the individual is focused on something else, namely the officer. More than one officer

FIGURE 6.3   Suicide Intervention Steps.

attempting the intervention is confusing, and an already confused individual will simply focus back on their intended suicide.

- It is important that the officer identify him or herself by name. A calm and professional demeanor is important. The introduction must not be authoritative, nor should it be overly friendly. The latter will be perceived by the person as disingenuous. The officer's introduction should be followed by a simple purpose statement, such as "I'm only here to help you," or perhaps "I'm here to help sort through what's troubling you today."

Establishing Rapport

The next task for the officer is to establish rapport. There is no better way to begin this process than to ask the individual's name. This personalizes the exchange, and for a person whose sense of self may rapidly be bleeding out, it allows them to regain a small piece of who they are, or at least who they were prior to the onset of their crisis. It also shows sincerity on the part of the officer. Some further suggestions are as follows:

- The officer should allay any fears the person may have about being subdued, especially if they are nervously looking around. The goal for the officer is to get the individual to focus their attention on them so rapport can be established. This is assuming there is a weapon involved that prevents officers from moving in quickly to subdue the person. If that possibility presents itself in a way that insures officer safety to a large degree, then the opportunity should be taken. Once again, the goal of intervention in this case is to save the individual's life and get them to a place of safety for longer-term therapeutic intervention.
- If the individual is highly emotional, the officer should attempt to de-escalate the person's emotion in a calm and non-judgmental way. The officer must be reassuring and let the individual know he is there to help. The best way to de-escalate high emotionality is to get them talking. Questions unrelated to the person's problem can work for this purpose, such as "Are you from around here (name)?" Or perhaps, "Do you mind if we talk (name)?" At this point, questions about the person's family should be avoided, because there is a very good chance the family is central to their reasons for wanting to kill themselves.

- Whatever actions the officer takes, they should be careful to inform the person before doing so, unless those actions are related to subduing the individual. For example, if the officer wants to sit down or move to a better location, they should announce their intentions, and ask the individual if it is okay to do so. It is important for the person threatening suicide to feel as though they are in control of the situation, and by asking the person if it is okay to take a particular action, the officer is furthering that goal.
- Two things must be avoided at this point. First, giving false assurances that everything will be OK, and second, trying to make the person feel guilty by causing them to think about their kids or other family members. Everything will not be okay in the short-term, and the person knows it. It may only upset them to have someone totally unfamiliar with their circumstances telling them this. It gives the intervention an air of insincerity. And to say anything that may intensify their self-guilt could potentially be deadly.
- Sometimes there are things about the individual that are apparent from their appearance. For example, he may be wearing a shirt or hat emblazoned with the logo of a particular sports team. He may have the markings of a military veteran, or the physique of a weightlifter. Anything that can be ascertained from the person's appearance that is non-threatening to the individual to talk about is worth exploring in an effort to build rapport and focus attention away from the threatened suicide. However, it must be done carefully and in a way that shows sincerity. In other words, the officer should not announce that the Chicago Cubs is their favorite baseball team in an effort to connect with the person without being able to name the team's starting players. Honesty is very important in this situation. Also, the officer must be very careful to quickly shift away from a particular subject if it becomes obvious that it is suddenly causing the individual to become more emotional.

Active Listening

The goal of the rapport phase is to create a situation where the individual feels safe talking to the officer. If they start talking there is a good chance the suicide can be averted. The officer should avoid asking the person to start talking about their problems until a degree of rapport is established. Once they are comfortable that requirement has been met, then the third phase of the intervention is to simply listen. The majority of the time this is all the person really wants, someone who will simply listen to them. During this phase the following should be considered:

- The officer should avoid ordering or directing the person to talk about their problems. Chances are if some amount of rapport has been established they will want to tell the officer about their problems. It will likely take little prompting. The officer can simply ask something like, "What can I do to help (name)?"
- Sometimes listening is not such an easy thing, especially for police officers who are accustomed to ordering and directing people. In this case it is critical that the officer listen and not interrupt. If they are in view of the person, they should acknowledge their understanding of what is being said with eye contact and head nods. The officer should avoid "why" questions, and should reassure the person with comments like, "I understand (name)," or perhaps, "I understand why you're upset (name)." The goal is to keep the person talking with promptings like, "Can you tell me about ...," or "(name), I'm interested in hearing about...." If the person believes the officer sincerely cares about their plight, then again, the chances of averting the suicide are greatly increased.

- Sometimes an individual threatening suicide will get highly emotional talking about their problems. The officer must be ready to act to de-escalate this emotional flair up when it happens. The more emotional a person is the less rational they become. It is imperative that the officer attempt to carefully guide the person's attention away from the source of their emotion. The officer should remain calm and speak in a reassuring voice. They should also watch carefully for signs that the person is about to carry out the suicide. The behavioral cues that indicate the suicide is imminent include the following:

  - The person begins to nervously scan the area around them
  - They no longer attend to the officer's words
  - An obvious quickening in their rate of breathing
  - "Cadence"-like behaviors, such as rocking their head or counting under their breath
  - Sudden laughing or extreme emotionality

The officer must be ready to act when these signs present themselves. At this point the person will likely be focused on nothing else but the act they are about to carry out. The officer must change their demeanor quickly in an effort to refocus the person's attention. At this point it is necessary for the officer to become authoritarian and loud. They should demand that the person look at them now and stop what they're doing. The officer should try not to sound panicked, but rather like an authoritarian parent. They should continue their demands until they regain the person's attention. If other forms of non-lethal force can be used safely, now is when the officer must give the signal to employ those devices.

Offering an Out

Once the officer has de-escalated any emotional flair-ups and determines that the person has gained some benefit from talking, meaning they have become less emotional or perhaps they have lowered their weapon, then it is time to offer the individual an out. Many times the person sees no way out of their predicament. They look around and see emergency personnel standing by, and maybe even television news cameras showing up. It can seem quite overwhelming. If the individual has committed no crime, then the officer should consider the following:

- First acknowledge that they understand the person's situation, thank them for sharing the information, and then calmly advise them that they would now like to help them resolve their situation. If being arrested is causing some concern, then the officer should advise the person that no one is there to arrest them, but only to help.
- If rapport has been established, then the officer should advise the person that they personally will stay with them for as long as possible. At this point the person may ask where they will be going. The officer should avoid terms like *psych ward, shrink,* or *commitment.* Instead, they should simply tell the person they will be going to see someone who can help them through their situation. As a rule, the officer should not lie to the individual at this point by telling them they can go home or to some other desired location. In most states the police have a statutory obligation to seek an involuntary psychiatric exam for anyone who is found to be a danger to themselves. Once they begin an intervention then they are responsible for that person. They cannot just simply drop them off at home and leave.

Gaining Commitment

The final phase of the intervention is to gain their commitment. It is important that the officer give the person some autonomy in this decision. If it appears the person is willing to discontinue their threatened suicide, the officer should ask them if they would be willing to put their weapon down for their own safety and come with the officer. Once they do, then as many officers as needed should approach the person and place them in handcuffs for their own safety. The officer who conducted the intervention should thank the individual for their cooperation, reassure them that they did the right thing, and accompany them as far as permissible, which is typically to a waiting ambulance for transport to the emergency room or mental health center.

The process just described is applicable to a situation where an individual is threatening to end their life with a gun, knife, or explosive device, all of which preclude the police from using immediate force. But what if they are not holding a weapon, such as a person threatening to jump from a bridge, or perhaps to strike a match after dousing themselves with gasoline? The primary goal of police intervention in a threatened suicide is not therapy, but to save the person from killing themselves so the therapeutic process can take place. If force can safely be used to bring a quick end to the episode, then it should be. Many types of non-lethal force have been employed for this purpose, including water cannons, nets, Tasers, and even weapons that direct disabling sound waves at the individual. The downside to the police taking the time to listen to the problems of someone wanting to end their life is that they may in fact do so while the police are listening. The decision to use force rather than attempt to engage the individual is one the police officer in charge at the scene must make based on their experience. They must weigh their options against any potential danger to the person threatening suicide as well as to the officers involved, and also against the likelihood of success. To attempt to use force in such a situation and fail can have disastrous results.

INVOLUNTARY COMMITMENTS

In most states the standard protocol in the case of a threatened suicide that has been successfully de-escalated is an **involuntary commitment** to a hospital or mental health center for a psychiatric evaluation, typically for a period of anywhere from 24 to 120 hours. Most states require the involvement of a physician or mental health professional in order to commit someone for evaluation against their wishes; however, it is typically the case that the police have the power to do so based on their probable cause that the individual is a physical threat to themselves or others, or that the individual because of mental illness is unable to provide for their own physical needs. There is certainly a lot of room for discretion in these criteria, and for that reason the police use this power sparingly, typically only in cases of threatened suicide or extreme schizophrenic episodes. In the case of a threatened suicide they are obligated to take the necessary steps to protect the individual.

Most states have a similar protocol for involuntary commitments. Once the officer determines that the individual meets the criteria for an involuntary evaluation, they are then authorized by law to take the person into custody and transport them to the hospital or mental health center. For reasons of liability it is typically departmental policy that the person be transported in an ambulance rather than a squad car. Once they arrive, the officer is required to sign a petition for involuntary commitment. Typically there is a state-mandated period of time within which the individual must be evaluated by a psychiatrist or other qualified person, with the most common being 24 hours, excluding holidays, and in some cases weekends. If no evaluation takes place, then the person is released.

Although this is an involuntary procedure, like all imposed legal actions in America, the individual is afforded due process. Once the initial evaluation is completed by a qualified practitioner, any further commitment for treatment will require a court order. In such a case, the evidence upon which the officer based the initial petition is submitted to the Court along with the practitioner's evaluation and evidence supporting continued commitment. It is then for the Court to rule whether the person's involuntary commitment will be allowed to continue. If it is, periodic hearings will be held to monitor the patient's progress and their need for continued commitment. In some states the Court will order that treatment take place in the least restrictive environment possible for that particular patient. The patient will also be provided the services of a lawyer who will ensure that their constitutional rights are not violated, throughout this process.

SPECIAL SITUATIONS

Unfortunately, suicide is anything but an act with common circumstances and variables in each and every case. Some situations bring with them special problems and considerations for those who attempt to intervene. This section will detail some of those situations.

Suicide by Cop

As mentioned previously, sometimes an individual decides to commit suicide by forcing a police officer into a situation where they have no choice but to use deadly force against them. Some choose this method because they simply don't have the courage to do it themselves. Others do it as a means of justifying their self-contempt and their perceived need for persecution. This type of situation can be extremely dangerous for those who respond. It should be assumed that the person will do whatever is necessary to get the intended result, up to and including firing a weapon at the officer or lunging at them with a knife. When it reaches that point the officer will react according to their training, and deadly force will be used. Never should an officer assume that because the situation is likely a suicide by cop it is safe to react differently than any other deadly force encounter.

The close examination of police shootings has found a large percentage to be suspected suicides by cop. One prominent study (Huston and Anglin et al., 1998) examined shootings by deputies from the L.A. County Sheriff's Department. The survey looked at 430 shootings that occurred between 1987 and 1997. It was determined that 11 percent of all police shootings and 13 percent of all fatal police shootings were people who intended to commit suicide. Dr. Barry Perrou (1999), a former commander of the L.A. County Sheriff's Hostage negotiation team, further analyzed the data from the above survey and found the following:

- Ninety-six percent of the perpetrators were male
- Ages ranged from 18 to 54
- Weapons used included firearms (46 percent), knives (46 percent), and firearm replicas (8 percent)
- Fifty-eight percent asked to be killed by the police
- Fifty-eight percent had a psychiatric history
- Thirty-eight percent had previously attempted suicide
- Fifty percent were intoxicated

- Forty-two percent had a history of domestic violence
- Thirty-eight percent had a criminal history

One of the most troubling statistics related to suicide by cop was revealed in a survey of police shootings in Marion County, Oregon and Dade County, Florida (Wilson and David et al., 1998). That study found that a full 60 percent of those killed by police in apparent suicides by cop actually used or attempted to use their weapons. For those who respond, it must be kept in mind that chances are good the individual will be intoxicated, mentally ill, or extremely upset during or following an intensely upsetting event. Rational thinking should not be expected.

Suicide by cop is a sad reality of crisis response and intervention. People know the police shoot to kill when they encounter a threat of deadly force. It is a quick way to die, and is especially suited to those who simply haven't the courage to pull the trigger themselves. Unfortunately, the fact that they wanted to die anyway does not make it any easier for the officers involved. In some respects it has the potential for creating even more post-incident trauma for those involved, especially when it is discovered that the person was holding an unloaded gun, or even a toy. The vast majority of police officers are dedicated public servants who take very seriously their primary mission of helping people. When an officer is forced to kill someone who is literally crying out for help, it is a heavy burden to bear.

The case of Moshe Pergament (Associated Press, 1997) illustrates the oftentimes tragic nature of suicide by cop. Pergament was a 19-year-old college student from New York who was despondent over a large gambling debt. On November 17, 1997, an officer pulled him over on the Long Island Expressway after observing him driving erratically. As the officer approached, Pergament jumped from his car and pointed a revolver at the officer. The officer ordered him to drop the weapon, but Pergament refused and continued to advance toward him. As expected, the officer opened fire and killed the young man. The weapon turned out to be a toy, and in his car were 10 envelopes addressed to various people. One was addressed "to the officer who shot me." It read:

> Officer, it was a plan. I'm sorry to get you involved. I just needed to die. Please send the letters and break the news slowly to my family and let them know I had to do this. And that I love them very much. I'm sorry for getting you involved. Please remember that this was all my doing. You had no way of knowing.

Teen Suicide

Unlike adult suicide, most teen suicides are preventable if teachers, police officers, and especially parents recognize the warning signs when they see them. Teens tend to wear their emotions on their sleeves for all to see, so those who are troubled to the point of wanting to kill themselves will invariably act out their despondency in some manner. The real danger with teens, especially younger ones, is that they may not have a true appreciation for the finality of death. The line between reality and fantasy can at times become blurred. This creates a dangerous situation for the young person who is deeply troubled by some circumstance in their personal life.

The reasons teens kill themselves are a bit less varied than for adults, mostly because of their limited life experience. Their suicides tend to be related either to *attachment* or *identity* issues. Regardless of the type, what the adolescent feels is a sense of hopelessness about their life. Suicide becomes a viable option because it will end the sense of dread they feel from the moment they awaken in the morning till the time they go to bed at night. If they turn to drugs and alcohol, eventually that sense of dread will only be intensified.

Two things are true of adolescent development. First, adolescents want to be loved, and to the extent they feel they are is a direct result of the attachment process. When we speak of attachment we are referring to the emotional bond between child and parent. Although adolescents tend to pull away from their parents emotionally, their ability to do so in an emotionally healthy manner is a result of a secure attachment. Children who do not enjoy this bond, usually the result of neglectful, authoritarian, or abusive parenting, are at high risk for emotional problems during their adolescent years and beyond. The quality of their attachment to the parents will directly impact the quality of their intimate relationships, and even their ability to form such relationships. What a secure attachment also does is give the adolescent a sense of self-efficacy, or the belief that they are capable of accomplishing things in their life and solving problems.

The second reality of adolescent development is that teens want to feel good about themselves, and they want to be comfortable with who they are. We refer to this as **identity formation**, or the process a teen goes through to figure out the type of person they wish to be. The closer they are to their ideal-self the stronger their identity. When the gap that exists between a young person's perceived-self and ideal-self is wide or insurmountable, then the young person is said to be identity-diffused (Marcia, 1966). They have neither a healthy self-image nor the self-esteem that comes with it. And these two processes are inextricably linked. A secure attachment to a parent will foster a healthy identity. Conversely, an insecure attachment will invariably create significant problems during the identity-formation stage.

Unlike adult suicide, which may or may not be precipitated by a particular event, teen suicide almost always follows a particularly stressful situation. Although an insecure attachment and diffused identity may be the underlying cause of self-destructive behavior, it is a specific event that typically causes the underlying problem to dramatically manifest itself. It may be a bad fight with a parent, an encounter with the police, the break-up of a relationship, or even a fight with another adolescent. Two problems arise. Adolescents with an insecure attachment and/or diffused identity simply do not have the security or self-confidence to keep minor problems from becoming major ones. Even stressors healthy teens tend to view as not so significant after a cooling off period can send the insecurely attached/identity-diffused teen into an emotional tailspin.

The second problem for these teens is the same for almost all teens. They simply don't have the life experience to adequately process a stressful situation in terms of available options. Much of what they measure their personal circumstances against is not real-life experience, but rather the symbolism of music, video games, movies, and other forms of media. This only contributes to blurring the line between reality and fantasy. Suddenly a teen is responding to a stressful situation not in a way that is pragmatic and goal-oriented, but in a way consistent with a particular song or entertainer. And if the song or entertainer happens to glorify suicide or other delinquent behavior, then the adolescent may act out that behavior in real life. This is especially true if they lack a secure attachment to a parent or a personal identity that does not breed self-contempt.

A good analogy for teen suicide is the building built upon a weak foundation. On the surface it may look strong and solid, but the least bit of wind has the potential to cause it to crumble upon itself. In the case of the teenager, if those stressors are attachment related, then they may include a fight with a parent, an encounter with the police or other authority figure, uncontrollable rage, or a deep sense of loneliness and an inability to form relationships. If the stressors are identity related, then they may involve being humiliated in front of other young people; being turned down for a date; being unable to express their homosexuality; or having feelings of physical, emotional, or academic inadequacy. Attachment issues influence the adolescent's relationships with others, whereas identity issues influence the degree to which they are accepting of themselves. The former will certainly influence the latter.

The other important factor in teen suicide is the presence of mental illness, especially depression. Researchers at Columbia University (Schaffer et al., 2004) found that 90 percent of teens who kill themselves suffered from a mental illness, and 63 percent of those young people experienced symptoms of their mental illness for at least one year prior to their deaths. In some cases their depression is the result of environmental factors, such as their family circumstances. In other cases it may be organic in nature. The result is the same, and the treatment is the same. Depression in young people is treatable, but so many go undiagnosed because of a young person's inability to articulate their problems to people who can help, especially their parents and other adults.

Once again, one of the things that makes teen suicide highly preventable is their tendency to demonstrate obvious signs that something is seriously wrong. In many cases these young people will have an encounter with the police prior to their suicide attempt. This may be the result of a particularly bad argument with their parents, getting caught with alcohol or drugs, or engaging in delinquent behavior. It is critical in any interactions with juveniles that police officers look for these signs. These include the following:

- Talking about death or suicide, even in the form of jokes
- Writing poetry or drawing pictures with a death or suicide orientation
- Withdrawing from friends and family
- Giving away possessions
- Significant changes in eating and sleeping habits
- Academic failure and a refusal to discuss long-term school plans
- A sudden interest in guns or other deadly weapons
- Expressing feelings of hopelessness
- Self-mutilating behaviors
- Telling friends they are planning to go away or do something "big"
- Having trouble concentrating

When an officer comes across an adolescent demonstrating some of these telltale signs, especially in the context of a crisis involving the youth, they must be very careful not to leave without further evaluation. The best course is usually to bring in a qualified juvenile officer who has been trained to assess suicide risk, and to take the appropriate steps when it is determined that the risk is real. Young people will typically answer honestly when asked if they are thinking about killing themselves. An affirmative answer to that question should be taken seriously, and an intervention should be immediately initiated.

If there is no impending crisis, then the officer must take steps to get the young person to a hospital or mental health center for an evaluation. It is always best to engage the parents and get them to agree to the commitment, but absent that, then the officer must pursue an involuntary commitment. In most states the process for involuntary commitment is essentially the same for juveniles as it is for adults. There is an emergency commitment followed by a court hearing to determine if additional commitment is necessary, assuming the young person or the parents do not consent to the treatment.

If the officer responds to a suicide in progress, then the procedures are essentially the same as for an adult. The officer must engage the teen, establish rapport, listen to what they have to say, offer alternatives, and gain commitment. It must be kept in mind that many times at the core of the young person's problems is an authoritarian or critical parent. The officer must be careful not to display those same characteristics, instead remaining calm and respectful, and assuring the young person that they are there to help them get through their problems. Young people respond well to attempts to build rapport, because many times it is an attachment-related rapport that is lacking in their lives. With the right tone and demeanor on the part of the officer, the young person may project their need for attachment onto the officer and respond to them as a surrogate parent. When this happens the officer is in a real position to de-escalate the situation and help the young person.

Elder Suicide

Most people would be surprised to know that the suicide rate in America is highest in men 85 years of age and older. According to the National Center for Injury Prevention and Control (cdc.gov, accessed 2011), in 2005 the suicide rate for this age group was 45.23 per 100,000, 2.5 times higher than the rate for men of all ages. Also, although in young people there is an estimated 1 suicide in every 100 to 200 attempts; in the elderly that number increases to 1 in every 4 attempts. An elderly person preparing for suicide often goes entirely unnoticed. They tend to live alone, have few social contacts, and have family they may see only occasionally. The elderly typically do not discuss their plans, nor are their intentions apparent in their behavior. When a younger person commits suicide, those who knew them will typically say they expected it. It usually does not come as a surprise. When an elderly person commits suicide, however, it tends to be a shock to those who knew them, and even to their own family in many cases.

Elder suicides are almost always men, and their reasons for doing so in a majority of the cases are either illness or the loss of a loved one. Thus, elder suicides tend to be pre-emptive in nature. Either they do not wish to continue their lives without the loved one they recently lost, or they are trying to avoid the inevitable pain and expense of a diagnosed illness, typically a terminal one. Suicides among the elderly are seldom impulsive acts as they are with younger people, especially juveniles and young adults. The elderly usually come to their decision after giving it considerable thought and taking the time to make final plans. For them death is a reality they are facing in the foreseeable future anyway, so the decision to shorten their life is reached in a more rational way and with less despair than in the case of a younger person.

One of the more recent innovations in law enforcement is the "elder services" officer. These specially trained officers are assigned to respond to situations in their jurisdictions involving the elderly. They may take complaints from them, check in on them at the request of family, or serve as a referral source for various social services. These officers must be prepared to recognize in the elderly people with whom they come in contact the warning signs that a suicide is being considered. These signs include the following:

- The recent death of a loved one, especially a spouse
- Physical illness, especially one involving uncontrollable pain
- Social isolation
- Talk of depression and despair
- Refusal of necessary medical care

Any police officer who comes across such an individual should follow the protocol that has hopefully been established for these situations. They should immediately call in a certified elder services officer to complete a brief assessment and make the appropriate referral. Any known family should also be called. If the department has no elder services officer, then the local senior center should be contacted. These centers typically have staff and volunteers who are especially good at dealing with these situations. Senior centers are also wonderful referral sources for needed social and medical services.

It will seldom be the case that an officer is called to an actual threatened suicide in progress involving an elderly person. Because they tend to live alone, there is typically no one around when they choose to do so. Also, the elderly make their final act less dramatic than a younger person, and it almost never is brought on by an acute stressor like a fight with a spouse or an arrest. They simply decide when the time is appropriate and quietly commit their final act. Thus, the involuntary commitment process is seldom used for the elderly. Most interventions carried out by police officers will involve identifying an at-risk person, engaging any known family members, and taking proactive steps to help the individual by referring them for necessary services.

Suicide in Prisons and Jails

Those incarcerated in our prisons and jails make up one of the most volatile populations of people in terms of their potential for crisis, including suicide. Most are in the throes of crisis when they enter the institution. They could be detoxing from drugs and alcohol, coming off a violent argument or physical confrontation, or facing the sudden reality of losing their freedom for a lengthy period of time. For some, escape is the only viable option, making them extremely dangerous. For others, especially those suffering from guilt, shame, or despair over their circumstances, suicide is seen as the quickest and most efficient way of dealing with their problems.

Bonner (1992) provides two suicide profiles that can be used to identify high-risk inmates. The first is the **pretrial inmate**. These offenders are typically in city and county jails awaiting trial. They tend to be young males, 20–25 years of age, unmarried, and first-time offenders. Those incarcerated in city and county jails may be housed in those institutions until such time that they are sentenced to the state correctional system. The process of arraignment, trial, and sentencing can take anywhere from a few weeks to a number of months to complete, depending on the severity of the crime, whether a trial takes place or a plea agreement is reached, and the extent of any pre- and post-trial motions.

There are two high-risk periods for those fitting the pretrial profile. The first is the 24-hour period following their initial lockup, especially if they were intoxicated or under the influence of drugs when they were booked in. When a person is experiencing the effects of detoxification it only magnifies any problems they are having. Suddenly a minor arrest can look like an insurmountable obstacle. A sense of extreme dread may set in when the full weight of their actions bears down on them. They may suddenly be faced with the reality of losing an intimate partner, a career, or even their freedom. On top of that, the loneliness of incarceration only aggravates the negative perception they have of their circumstances.

A second high-risk period for this individual is just before the final disposition of the case, typically a hearing to enter a guilty plea or a sentencing hearing following a conviction. Once again, this is a time when the individual is confronted by reality. They quickly become accustomed to the jail culture as they get to know the staff and other inmates. It is easy to lose sight of the ultimate consequences they may face. They may even be visited regularly by family. But eventually they are forced to confront their consequences, and in many cases this is when their despair comes screaming back and causes them to commit their final act.

The second suicide profile is the **sentenced inmate**. This individual has already been convicted of a crime and sentenced to prison. In most states, any sentence over one year requires that the individual be housed by the department of corrections in that particular state rather than in a county or city lockup. People who commit suicide in prison tend to be older (30-35), and tend to do so after being incarcerated for a number of years. They tend to be inmates with longer sentences who don't enjoy the emotional benefits of a release date in the foreseeable future. The suicide usually follows a particularly stressful event, to include the following:

- the loss of an appeal
- a fight with another inmate
- sexual assault
- altercation with prison staff
- learning of negative family events
- emotional breakdown related to isolation

One method of reducing the number of suicides in correctional faculties is to screen inmates to determine their risk level when they first enter the institution. For those detained in a county or city lockup following an arrest, the most common indicators of risk for suicide include the following:

- the individual is intoxicated
- they have a history of mental health treatment or previous suicide attempts
- they are very emotional, and express shame or guilt for their actions
- the individual has been in prison before and states that he will not return
- the individual has limited social support, and says no one cares about him
- the individual is prescribed an anti-depressant or other psychotropic drug

When any of these indicators are present, the individual should be placed on heightened observation, and perhaps even be required to meet with a mental health professional as part of their intake process. They should be placed in the general population and not isolated, and they must be observed by jail staff at least every 15 minutes. It is also absolutely critical that each shift be briefed on any new inmates with a higher-than-normal suicide risk level, and have a protocol in place to respond quickly to any threatened suicide or suicide in progress without jeopardizing the safety of the jail staff.

When an inmate is actively suicidal, then a crisis intervention must begin and continue until the threat has been de-escalated. Most jail and prison suicides occur by hanging when the individual is segregated for whatever reason from the general population. Extra caution must be taken with an inmate who is actively expressing a desire to kill themselves. Although it is typically the case that a correctional facility attempts to use the least restrictive means of protecting the inmate, the fact is, physical restraints may be necessary. The first course of action should be to remove from the inmate's cell the means by which they can potentially commit suicide. Hanging is the most common method, so any loose material, including the inmate's own clothes, must be removed. Most jails are also equipped with at least one padded cell, so if the individual appears as though they will make an attempt in any particular way they can, then the inmate should be moved to a soft cell and kept under constant video surveillance. A mental health practitioner should also be engaged to conduct a more thorough risk assessment, and to guide an involuntary commitment to a mental health center if necessary. As a last resort, the inmate must be physically restrained with restraining devices to prevent self-injury.

Because of the diverse nature of county and city jails, there are no standardized procedures for potential suicide risks. Jails range in size from holding hundreds, and in some cases thousands of inmates, down to rural jails that may hold less than 20. Some are modern high-tech facilities, whereas others may be decades old, making it more difficult to properly manage suicidal inmates. One of the biggest problems in a jail setting, especially a small rural facility, is a lack of training among the staff. Correctional officers must be trained not only to respond to an attempted suicide, but also to proactively identify and monitor those at risk of committing suicide.

Prisons, unlike jails, almost always have comprehensive procedures in place for dealing with suicide risks. They also employ mental health professionals who understand the complexities of institutional behavior. Additionally, they have special units for housing and monitoring suicide risks, and their own medical-psychiatric centers where inmates can receive the proper treatment. Unfortunately though, their best intentions and protocols cannot stop every suicide. It requires more than simple psychological assessments and self-reports. Prison officials must be attuned to what is going on both inside and outside the prison walls. Inside, they must utilize intelligence sources to know when someone has had their life threatened or been sexually assaulted, or when someone is openly telling other inmates of their plans to end their own life. Counselors must stay engaged with those who lose appeals or have parole denied, both high-risk windows for suicide. Outside the prison walls they must make it a priority to know when an inmate loses a loved one or is told by an intimate partner that they no longer wish to be involved with the inmate.

Once information is gathered indicating that an inmate is facing a particular stressor that could potentially lead to a suicide attempt, an intervention must begin. Work assignments are adjusted, privileges are restricted, perhaps special housing is ordered, and counseling begins immediately. Unfortunately one thing an inmate has more than they need is time to think. By acting immediately, and intervening in a proactive manner, prison officials cut down on the time an inmate has to sit in a darkened cell thinking the worst about a situation. The problem only festers like an open wound when that is allowed to happen.

ISSUES & ETHICS IN CRISIS INTERVENTION

Assisted Suicide: Murder or Mercy?

On February 26, 2009, four people were arrested in Georgia and Florida for assisting in the suicide of a 58-year-old Georgia man suffering from severe throat and mouth cancer, and who had endured multiple reconstructive surgeries. His mother, who denied knowledge of the assisted suicide, described her son as being in severe pain. The four were members of a group identified as the Final Exit Network, an all-volunteer group based in Marietta, Georgia. They were arrested following an undercover investigation by the Georgia Bureau of Investigation during which one of their agents sought out the services of the group following the death of the Georgia man.

What they discovered was a group that assisted in the suicides of those seeking their help by administering excess helium gas into their system. For $50, a potential client would fill out an application and then be visited by an "exit guide." This person would instruct the client to secure two tanks of helium of a particular size and type, along with a breathing hood described as an "exit hood." At the appropriate time, and always at the choosing of the client, the exit guide, along with a senior exit guide, would visit the person's home and assist them in securing the hood and inhaling the gas.

Following the arrests, GBI agents executed search warrants in multiple states, seeking evidence against the group. All four were charged with assisted suicide and violations of Georgia's Racketeer Influenced and Corrupt Organizations Act.

Discussion Questions

1. Is the act of assisted suicide a matter the criminal justice system should even concern itself with? Why or why not?
2. What is lost or gained by a society that allows assisted suicide?
3. Discuss your thoughts on the conflict between a police officer's obligation to ease the pain and suffering of those in their jurisdiction, and enforcing an assisted suicide law that prevents a person from ending their own pain and suffering.

Suicide and the Mentally Ill

Although it can certainly be argued that all people who attempt or complete a suicide are mentally ill, some simply do not have the capacity to fully understand the implications of their act. They may be schizophrenic and believe their suicide will cause them to be transported to a flying saucer. They may be extremely paranoid, and believe they are being followed by the agents of some sinister governmental agency, and that suicide is the only escape. Or they may be so severely depressed for reasons unknown even to them that they attribute their despair to no other possible source but a Biblical demon.

When the severely mentally ill threaten suicide, there is perhaps not a more dangerous situation for those who respond and attempt to de-escalate the crisis. If the person is delusional, then the police officer may very well become a cast member in the individual's delusion. Suddenly the officer is the sinister agent who has been following them, or an enemy alien disguised as a police officer. If the officer is not properly trained to deal with the severely mentally ill, their words and actions may very well escalate the situation and hasten the individual's suicide attempt.

Dealing with the mentally ill, including a threatened suicide, will be discussed in greater detail in Chapter 12 of the text. It is a type of crisis intervention that brings with it some very special considerations and conditions that must be kept in mind not only for the safety of the officer, but also for the safety of the individual experiencing the crisis. The seriously mentally ill are neither deterred by consequences nor guided by rational thinking. The unpredictability of their actions makes crisis intervention in these cases better left to those specially trained for the task.

Chapter Summary

A person chooses to end their life through suicide for many reasons. Police and correctional officers respond daily to these types of situations, and how they respond may contribute significantly to the person choosing to change their mind and accept help for the problems that plague them. Those who respond must engage the individual in a way that demonstrates sincerity and an appreciation for their circumstances. They must build rapport with the individual, and do so quickly. Then they must simply listen, always demonstrating their sincerity with their body language and words. When the officer feels that the time is right, then they offer the individual a way out of their situation and work to gain their commitment.

An officer responding to a threatened suicide never leaves once the suicide is de-escalated. They must offer the person the services they need, specifically a period of observation and evaluation in a psychiatric facility, either a community mental health center or a hospital. In those cases where the person refuses such services after the situation has been de-escalated, it is then up to the officer to determine if an involuntary commitment is necessary. These commitments are typically short-term in nature, after which the person is either released with follow-up care, or committed for a longer period of time.

The cost of suicide is high in America, and it is critically important that both police and correctional officers become well trained in the techniques of de-escalation, and also become familiar with their respective state statutes regarding involuntary commitments. Their actions can save the lives of people drowning in despair, but, if done incorrectly, can also contribute to the person's decision to actually complete the act.

Key Terms

Social integration
Moral regulation
Egoistic suicide (Durkheim)
Altruistic suicide (Durkheim)
Anomic suicide
Fatalistic suicide

Eros
Thanatos
Anger suicide
Despair suicide
Egoistic suicide
Proactive suicide

Involuntary commitment
Identity formation
Pretrial inmate
Sentenced inmate

Discussion Questions

1. Why should the criminal justice system concern itself to the extent it does with the crisis of suicide? Should people have the right to end their own lives without fear of the police intervening?
2. Discuss whether you believe suicide is primarily the result of external sociological conditions and circumstances, or more the result of internal psychological factors. Or is it a combination of both?
3. Discuss some of the major differences between teen suicide and adult suicide.

7

The Crisis of Domestic Violence

LEARNING OUTCOMES

Upon completion of this chapter the student should be able to:

1. Explain the problem and prevalence of domestic violence in America.

2. Summarize the historical police response to domestic violence.

3. List the typologies and behavioral characteristics of domestic abusers.

4. Explain battered spouse syndrome and list its symptoms.

5. Define the best practices for the police response to domestic violence cases.

Chapter Outline

Introduction
Domestic Violence in America

The Historical Response

The Cycle of Violence
The Honeymoon Phase
The Tension-building Phase
The Acute Violence Phase

The Abuser
Abuser Typologies
Domestic Abuse and Personality
Dysfunction

The Victim
Battered Spouse syndrome
Other Victim-oriented Theories

Same Sex Violence

The Effects of Domestic Violence on Children

Intervening in Domestic Violence
The Minneapolis Project
The Duluth Model
The North Carolina Model

Chapter Summary

INTRODUCTION

DOMESTIC VIOLENCE IN AMERICA

The statistics on domestic violence in America are staggering. On average, more than three women are murdered by their spouses or boyfriends in this country every single day (Bureau of Justice Statistics [BJS], 2003). A subsequent BJS study (2005) found the following:

- Of the almost 3.5 million violent crimes committed against family members, 49 percent of these were crimes against spouses.
- Eighty-four percent of spouse abuse victims were females, and 86 percent of victims of dating partner abuse were female.
- Males were 83 percent of spouse murderers and 75 percent of dating partner murderers.
- Fifty percent of offenders in state prison for spousal abuse had killed their victims. Wives were more likely than husbands to be killed by their spouses. Wives were about half of all spouses in the population in 2002, but 81 percent of all persons killed during acts of domestic violence.

From these statistics it is clear to see that the problem of domestic violence is predominantly a male problem. It is a problem that knows no cultural or economic boundaries, and is not limited to any particular age group. In a study of 724 adolescent mothers between the ages of 12 and 18, 1 of every 8 reported a physical assault by the father of her baby during the preceding 12 months (Wiemann, 2000). Of these, 40 percent also reported experiencing violence at the hands of a family member or relative. Even the elderly can be subjected to this type of violence. According to the Committee on National Statistics and Behavioral and Social Sciences and Education (2003), between 1 and 2 million Americans ages 65 or older have been injured, exploited, or otherwise mistreated by someone they depended on for protection, in many cases by a spouse.

Domestic violence is also not limited strictly to heterosexual couples. One survey (Tjaden and Thoennes, 2003) found that gay and lesbian cohabitants reported significantly more intimate partner violence than did heterosexual cohabitants. Among women, 39.2 percent of those in same-sex relationships, compared to 21.7 percent of heterosexual women, reported being raped, physically assaulted, and/or stalked by a spouse or cohabiting partner at some point in the past. Of special concern for gay and lesbian victims is the degree to which their complaints are taken seriously by a criminal justice system that traditionally has taken a dismissive demeanor toward them. As we shall see, the same likelihood of continued abuse we find in heterosexual abusers we also find in gay and lesbian abusers. The need for the same level of response by the police to their complaints is, therefore, critical.

Before we go forward it is important that we define exactly what we mean by domestic violence. It can mean more than just physical violence. **Domestic abuse** can also include psychological abuse, sexual assault, social isolation, deprivation, intimidation, or even economic coercion. For the police who respond to a domestic crisis, however, it is physical violence, or the threat of, that they must attempt to contain and de-escalate either through negotiation or arrest. We will focus our attention throughout this chapter primarily on physical abuse. We will look at the dynamics of spousal abuse, and the proper police response to domestic violence complaints. We will also look at the psychology of both the abuser and the victim; in particular, why abusers continue to abuse when they know their behavior is wrong, and why victims continue to take the abuse knowing full well the most recent assault will not be their last. It is an extremely complicated syndrome, and one that police officers recognize as one of the most volatile and dangerous situations in which they can involve themselves. Every year in America there are officers injured or killed while responding to cases of domestic abuse, sometimes by the very person they were attempting to help. And sadly, in a large number of reported cases there are children present in the home who witness the abuse. One thing we know with near certainty is that those who witness repeated abuse during their childhood years are at risk of growing into abusive adults. It is a generational cycle that must be broken, and those who respond to cases of domestic violence, especially the police, have the ability to facilitate that goal by taking the appropriate steps to contain, de-escalate, and effectively mediate the domestic crisis.

THE HISTORICAL RESPONSE

There was a time when domestic abuse was considered a family problem that should be dealt with by the family without the aid or intervention of outside parties, especially the police. It was one of those things families simply did not talk about outside the home. As a consequence, many women spent years being victimized by an abusive spouse. And the fact that divorce was looked upon unfavorably by society only added to the problem. Another sad consequence was generations of children who grew up learning to use aggression as a way of confronting problems in the home. Children model the behavior of their parents, and when aggression and violence against a spouse continues unabated, the likelihood of those behavior patterns being repeated by the children increases dramatically.

Law enforcement was of little help in the days prior to its awakening to the devastating effects of domestic violence. The police considered domestic violence a family matter, and in most cases they attempted to contain and de-escalate a domestic crisis with little thought given to mediation and prevention. If they could just get the couple to quit fighting for the night, even when there were signs of physical abuse, then they considered their mission accomplished. Many abused women no doubt received friendly advice from responding officers that if they would just quit "nagging" their husbands, then maybe the husbands would quit being abusive. Few officers understood the cycle of violence that commonly underlies an abusive relationship, or how inaction on the part of the police only perpetuates that cycle.

In those cases when an abusive husband found himself in front of a judge charged with battering his wife, there was a good chance that a short period of probation, a small fine, and a lecture from the judge would be all the punishment that would be doled out. And if the wife let it be known that she was not interested in testifying against her husband, which was often the case, then there was a very good chance the charges would simply be dropped and the case closed. This was typically followed by a terse lecture from the responding officer to never again call the police and waste their time. The end result, sadly, was that the abused woman oftentimes became the person at fault in the eyes of the justice system, whereas the abusive husband walked away free, and able to continue his abusive ways.

THE CYCLE OF VIOLENCE

When we look specifically at spousal abuse, we see a particular dynamic that is present in almost every case involving physical abuse over a period of time. It is important to understand this dynamic because so often those who intervene at various stages of spousal abuse make the mistaken judgment that things are better between the two, and that the abusing spouse has discontinued his abusive practices. Of course in most cases, nothing could be further from the truth.

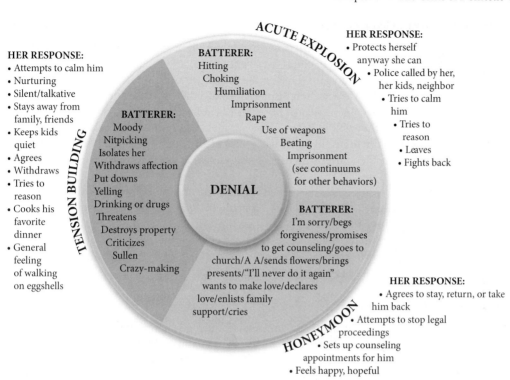

FIGURE 7.1 The Cycle of Violence.

The Honeymoon Phase

The **cycle of violence** begins immediately following a violent episode. Regardless of whether the police are called, almost immediately after the abusive episode there is a period of calm during which the abuser attempts to make things better by apologizing, agreeing to seek counseling, or promising the victim that the abuse will not happen again. Even if the abuser finds himself in jail for the night, it is so often the abused spouse who will post the necessary bond to get him released. During this **honeymoon phase**, the abuser will go out of his way to give the appearance that things are better. They may send their spouse flowers, go to church with her, and even make public declarations of his guilt to other family members, especially their kids, along with commitments to do better.

For the person stuck in this cycle of violence, the honeymoon phase is a welcomed respite from the tension and physical violence that occurred before and during the abusive episode. There is usually a euphoric feeling with the hope that the abuser will finally change. The abused partner may make the abuser's counseling appointment, speak on their behalf to the prosecuting attorney, assuming an arrest was made, and if there was previously a threat by the victim to leave the abuser, they may even commit to stay. It is also not uncommon for the abused spouse to accept blame for their own abuse and apologize to the abuser, in the process committing to change their own behavior.

The Tension-building Phase

Unfortunately, those who abuse their partner over a period of time are not changed so easily, at least not without a legal or behavioral intervention. Invariably an event will happen that will cause the tension to build again. During the **tension-building phase** the abuser will become moody and withdraw the affection displayed toward their partner during the honeymoon phase, and will start to become verbally abusive. If the abuser uses drugs or alcohol, which is typically the case, then they will begin to use again after a period of abstinence following the last abusive episode. Many times this abstinence, absent any drug or alcohol intervention, contributes significantly to the abuser's increasing moodiness as their system begins to crave the substance.

During this phase the abused partner enters a period of fear and apprehension. They may become even more nurturing in an effort to dissipate the growing tension. They will begin to isolate from family and friends, and they will try anything they can to prevent an abusive episode, which they know is imminent. They become increasingly fearful as the tension builds, and as they find that their nurturing behavior begins to make things even worse, they withdraw into silence and try to avoid doing anything to upset the abuser.

The Acute Violence Phase

The final stage of course is the **acute violence phase**, during which the increasing verbal abuse becomes physical in nature, and may even include sexual abuse. At this stage there is little the victim can do to stop the violence. Any attempts to be supportive or loving may even aggravate the situation. There is no telling what will set off the violent episode. Just about anything big or small will cause the abuser to react in a physical way. Even a victim's efforts to remain quiet and non-confrontational can provoke the abuser. Some victims will fight back or call the police. Others may take their children and leave the premises. Many times the abuser will prevent them from leaving, or if they have already left will go looking for them. Many victims have been talked into returning with the promise that things will be better, only to be physically assaulted once back in the house and under the control of the abuser.

It is important for the first responder to understand the psychology of both the abuser and the abused. To protect the victims of domestic violence, the police must understand the cycle of violence and the likelihood of repeated abuse. They must also understand the experience of the abused, and why some appear uncooperative, even when they were the ones who called the police. It is a complicated psychological dynamic, and one that can easily be misunderstood by an uninformed police officer who may be responding to a reported domestic disturbance at the same address they have been multiple times before.

THE ABUSER

Abuser Typologies

A number of studies have been carried out in an effort to identify the various typologies of those who batter their spouses or intimate partners. The benefits of doing so include the development of the most effective treatment strategies, as well as providing those on the front lines of this issue some predictive ability when dealing with potential repeat offenders. Daniel G. Saunders (1992) identified three typologies by surveying a group of 165 abusive men using such psychological measures as childhood victimization, level of conflict, anger, depression, and jealously, among others. He found that abusers can be categorized as follows:

- Type I: "Family-only" aggressors: These abusers report the highest level of satisfaction with their relationships, and the lowest levels of anger, jealousy, and depression. They tend not to have been abused as children, and their aggression is limited to conflict in the home. These abusers are good at suppressing their anger, and their overt aggression typically takes place after the introduction of alcohol or a significant stressor. These abusers are characterized by poor communication skills, especially when interacting with their victims. Outside the home they may appear quite normal, providing little evidence of their abusive behavior.

- Type II: "Generally violent" aggressors: These abusers are violent outside the home as well. Many from this group were physically abused as children, and have thus internalized aggression as a way of coping with stress. They are mostly unable to experience intimacy, and maintain very rigid attitudes about sex roles. They may display hostility toward women in general. These abusers oftentimes severely harm their victims. Their anger is explosive. For the police who respond to domestic calls involving type II abusers, the danger will increase significantly. The abuser will display as much aggression toward the police as he did toward his victim. Alcohol is oftentimes involved in their abusive episodes, and a high percentage of the time the abuser is alcohol dependent.

- Type III: "Emotionally volatile" aggressors: These abusers are those who live in fear of losing their spouse. Their abuse tends to be associated with feelings of jealousy and inadequacy. They are less aggressive than the type II abuser, but the likelihood of murder, suicide, or both increases dramatically with this group. Like the type I offender, communication patterns in the home are typically dysfunctional, and as the stress rises, so too does the abuser's fear of losing their partner. Their abusive tactics are meant to control and manipulate. Psychological abuse is highest among this group, and these abusers report higher levels of depression.

Domestic Abuse and Personality Dysfunction

A second study (White and Gondolph, 2000) looked at spousal abuse in terms of personality dysfunction. They concluded that those men who abuse are characterized by low, moderate, or severe personality dysfunction, and that their dysfunction is either narcissistic or avoidant in nature. The American Psychiatric Association's *Diagnostic and Statistical Manual of Mental Disorders*, text revision (*DSM-IV-TR*) (2000)/describes each of these personality disorders as follows:

- *Narcissistic Personality Disorder:* "Characterized by a pervasive pattern of grandiosity, need for admiration, and lack of empathy that begins by early adulthood and is present in a variety of contexts."

- *Avoidant Personality Disorder:* "Characterized by a pervasive pattern of social inhibition, feelings of inadequacy, and hypersensitivity to negative evaluation that begins by early adulthood and is present in a variety of contexts."

The narcissistic abuser is self-centered. They are insensitive to the needs and feelings of others, and any interaction that may threaten their fragile sense of security may be met with aggression. They cannot handle having their perceived dominance over their spouse confronted or questioned, and they expect submissiveness. When there is a danger of losing their spouse, they

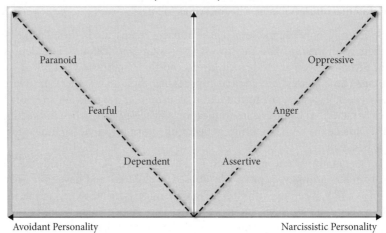

FIGURE 7.2 White & Gondolph's Model of the Relationship between Personality Disorder and Domestic Abuse.

may act disinterested or even laugh at or mock their victim. But if an effort is made by the spouse to leave, they may physically prevent it. If they have already left, their anger may increase to the point where they go looking for their spouse. The narcissistic abuser is also a manipulator, and will resort to feigned feelings of concern for their spouse in an effort to get them to return. If they refuse, and especially if alcohol is involved, this can potentially become a dangerous time for the abused spouse. When the narcissistic abuser sees that his manipulative methods are not working, his frustration may cause his aggressive tendencies to explode.

The avoidant abuser is much different from his narcissistic counterpart. The avoidant personality is extremely fragile. These individuals tend to become emotionally dependent on their spouse. They fear rejection, and thus they live with the paranoia that they might lose their spouse. They are extremely distrustful of their spouse, and may resort to following them, tapping their phones, or reading their emails. They have little ability to experience true intimacy. The relationship is more about emotional security than intimacy. If the avoidant abuser fears that their spouse is leaving them, they may become desperate. They tend not to be manipulators like the narcissistic abuser, but will instead resort to begging the spouse to stay, and in the process making promises that the abuse will cease. If their pleas fail, this can become a very dangerous situation for their victim. The avoidant abuser is unable to consider living without the spouse a viable option. Murder-suicide becomes a real possibility, a situation that happens often in America.

In both cases, whether narcissistic or avoidant, the abuser suffers from a personality disorder that typically begins early in life. Although there are many reasons for the development of a dysfunctional personality, it almost always begins with the parent-child relationship. A narcissistic personality can develop from permissive or neglectful parenting where few rules are imposed on the child, and discipline is lacking. The child becomes very egocentric and demanding because they never learn to control their impulses or to be sensitive to the needs of others. They typically engage in substance abuse and criminal conduct at an early age. Behavioral parameters and boundaries are routinely disregarded by the narcissistic abuser. Their egocentrism simply precludes them from measuring their behavior against the needs or expectations of others.

The avoidant personality also is a product of developmental problems. This type of personality can develop as a result of abusive or authoritarian parenting where positives in the parent-child relationship are conditional, inconsistent, or absent. These individuals become dependent on others because they lack a well-defined sense of self, or the personal confidence and security to maintain healthy relationships. Their lack of attachment in early childhood translates into a dysfunctional need for attachment in adulthood. As previously stated, these abusers are distrusting, fearful of rejection, and may become paranoid. For the narcissistic offender, the spouse fills a physical need and buttresses their inflated self-evaluation. For the avoidant abuser, the spouse fills an emotional need and buttresses their deficient self-evaluation. Neither can handle the loss of a spouse, and without effective intervention it is unlikely that either will discontinue their abusive tactics. The cycle of violence will continue, and with each abusive episode the use of violence as a coping strategy will be reinforced in the abuser. As this behavior pattern continues and strengthens, so too will the dysfunctional response of the victim unless the cycle is broken by some type of forced or voluntary intervention.

THE VICTIM

Battered Spouse Syndrome

In the past, the victim of domestic violence has been quite an enigma to those who intervene on their behalf, especially the police. Any officer with even minimal experience knows the feeling of responding to a domestic abuse call only to have the victim refuse to cooperate, or in some cases even become violent with the responding officers. It is difficult to understand at times why an abused spouse would want to remain in the abusive relationship. In recent years, however, our understanding of this phenomenon has been dramatically enhanced by much research and study. We better understand the psychology of the abused spouse, and the very powerful forces that compel them to remain in the relationship even when the prospect of continued abuse is real. In this section we will look at these forces, all of which we can collectively refer to as **battered spouse syndrome**. This syndrome describes the psychological effects of spousal abuse, which include the following:

- Feeling helpless to stop the abuse
- Accepting blame for the abuse
- Hyperarousal and high levels of anxiety
- Avoidance behaviors and social isolation

The term *battered woman syndrome* was first used by feminist researcher Lenore Walker (1984). She surveyed nearly 500 abused women in Colorado over a three-year period in an effort to identify key social and psychological factors that made up her proposed syndrome. From her research she was able to adapt Seligman's (1967) theory of learned helplessness to spousal abuse in an effort to explain why abused women many times refuse to leave their abusers. Seligman's research involved the repeated and non-contingent shock of laboratory animals until they were simply unable to escape the painful situation even when the route of escape was readily apparent to animals that were not being shocked. Seligman argued that in such a situation perception is distorted to the point that the correctness of a possible action (i.e., route of escape) becomes unpredictable.

Walker generalized this research to victims of domestic abuse. She hypothesized that, like the laboratory animals, women who are subjected to repeated episodes of abuse will over time develop learned helplessness, and their motivation for escaping the abuse will be diminished. Using Seligman's argument, these women simply lose their ability to predict the efficacy of their own actions. This seems to be confirmed by the self-report of many abused women who describe a sense of utter hopelessness and surrender in the face of the ongoing abuse.

Other Victim-oriented Theories

Other theories have been offered to account for why some women stay in their abusive relationships. **Traumatic bonding theory** (Dutton and Painter, 1981) attempts to make a connection between the victim's relationship with her parents and their inability to escape the abuse. This theory suggests that a woman who was abused or neglected by her own parents, thus forming an unhealthy and insecure attachments to them, will carry that dysfunctional attachment pattern into adulthood and form equally unhealthy relationships with intimate partners. These women crave the affection and positive acceptance they never experienced as children, and thus they are highly susceptible to the manipulative methods of the abuser during their remorseful phase following the abuse.

Another theory, **psychological entrapment theory** (Brockner and Rubin, 1985), argues that women remain in an abusive relationship because they simply have too much invested to let go of it. These women are willing to tolerate the abuse. They are motivated by an idealistic view of what a relationship should be, and they live in the hope that the abuser will stop. Rather than escape the abuse, they devise strategies for minimizing it as much as possible without leaving. These women will hide the abuse from family and friends, and may even accept responsibility for the abuser's actions in hopes of minimizing the violence.

The Stockholm syndrome (Ochberg, 2005) (explained in more depth in Chapter 9) has been offered as a potential explanation for a battered woman's dysfunctional behavior. Often used to describe the psychological effects experienced by hostages, the theory suggests that when a person is isolated and in that isolation is totally subjected to the will and authority of another person, then the victim will begin to form a peculiar bond with that person, and will begin to show kindness toward them, and may even support them. In an abusive relationship, this power dominance is typically present. The abused spouse isolates herself from family and friends, and in the face of their continuing pleas that she leave the relationship, may even turn against them and side with the abuser.

Multifactor ecological theory (Crowell and Burgess, 1996) suggests that women remain in their abusive relations for a number of reasons, including finances, children, societal and cultural norms, and for reasons related to their own family history. An ecological theory looks at a number of different contextual inputs that come together to create a unique situation for the individual. It does not attempt to identify a single reason why an abused spouse remains in their relationship, but rather it attempts to understand how multiple variables interact to lead to this circumstance. It looks at each victim of abuse as unique, and the reasons for their unwillingness to leave the relationship as comprehensible only in the context of their own experience.

Regardless of the reasons why a woman stays in an abusive relationship, the outcome is typically the same. Aside from the physical impact of continued abuse, the emotional costs are high. Roughly 60 percent of abused women report high levels of depression (Barnett, 2000). Additionally, there is also a significant risk of suicide among victims of abuse. Fischbach and Herbert (1997) found that 25 percent of suicide attempts among Caucasian women, and 50 percent among African-American women, were preceded by abuse. Battered spouse syndrome can be thought of as a subcategory of post-traumatic stress syndrome (PTSD), as defined by the DSM-IV-R. Its prevalence among abused women has been found to be significant. Vitanza, Vogel, and Marshall (1995) found a significant correlation between domestic abuse and PTSD, with 55.9 percent of their sample meeting the DSM-IV-R criteria. Another study, Mertin and Mohr (2000), found that 45 out of 100 abused women in their sample met the DSM-IV-R criteria. It is a debilitating existence for those women trapped in an abusive relationship. Their sense of helplessness eventually turns to one of hopelessness. In many cases when this happens, the idea of escaping the abuse no longer seems a viable option. It is imperative that those who respond to domestic violence understand this sad progression.

SAME SEX VIOLENCE

Domestic violence is not reserved for just heterosexual couples. There has been a gradual increase in reported cases among gay and lesbian couples. One survey (Tjaden, 2003) found that 11 percent of lesbians and 15 percent of gay men reported violence by their partners. Of those who sought services from New York City's Gay and Lesbian Anti-Violence Project in 2004, 38 percent had filed domestic violence reports with the police department (Dolan-Soto and Kaplan, 2005). In comparison with heterosexual couples, there are even studies that suggest domestic violence may be an even larger problem in the gay community. Tjaden and Thoennes (2000) found that gay and lesbian couples reported significantly more domestic violence than heterosexual couples. Among women, 39.2 percent of lesbians, compared to 21.7 percent of heterosexual women, reported being raped, assaulted, or stalked by an intimate partner in the past.

With more and more states taking steps to make the cohabitation of gay couples easier and more widely accepted, this trend will no doubt continue. The challenge will be to get law enforcement, traditionally a very conservative institution in America, to take the problem seriously. The perception of physical equality in gay couples can make it appear to the police that they lack the dominant-submissive dynamic of a heterosexual couple, and thus the relationship is perceived by the police as lacking a vulnerable victim unable to fend for themselves. But the truth is that dynamic is oftentimes present, with victims who experience all the same negative physical and psychological effects felt by an abused heterosexual partner. The level and intensity of response should be the same on the part of the police and other emergency personnel.

THE EFFECTS OF DOMESTIC VIOLENCE ON CHILDREN

Domestic violence is devastating for the children who are forced to witness and experience it. Whitfield et al. (2003) estimated that over 15 million children in the United States live in families where domestic abuse had occurred at least once in the prior year, with nearly half of them involving severe partner violence. The National Network to End Domestic Violence (2009) surveyed domestic violence shelters and transitional housing facilities and found that on a single day in 2008 there were 16,458 children living in these facilities as a result of domestic violence. An additional 6430 children had requested services from non-residential programs. The statistics on domestic violence in America are staggering, but when you include the secondary victims, especially the children who are forced to endure the emotional trauma, then the problem is compounded 10-fold. Sadly, it has further been found to be the case that in 60 percent to 70 percent of families in which a woman is the victim of domestic violence, children in the home are also physically abused, and the risk of sexual abuse increases dramatically (Osofsky, 1999). We will address the issue of child abuse in greater detail in the chapter to follow.

Emotionally speaking, the effects on children of witnessing domestic violence are similar to children who are abused. The scars left behind can last a lifetime and leave the child at risk of repeating the pattern and becoming an abusive adult. These children live in constant fear of the abusive parent and their violent outbursts. They isolate themselves from friends out of fear that the abuse will be discovered. What results is a toxic mix of shame, fear, and even guilt, as some children, especially the younger ones, may actually blame themselves for the problems within the family. The stress of raising children in our modern world can at times be overwhelming. Unfortunately there are no prerequisites for being a parent. When two adults engaged in a dysfunctional relationship have children, it doesn't take long for the entire family system to become dysfunctional. As the stress increases, especially with alcohol and drugs in the mix, a parent with a propensity for aggression may act out that aggression in the form of domestic battery. It doesn't take long before the child hears things like "we should never have had these kids!" Or perhaps something like, "if I didn't have these mouths to feed I could divorce you and have my life back!" It is little wonder then that when violence erupts, the child invariably accepts and internalizes the blame. Other effects may include the following:

- Academic problems
- Depression
- Feelings of not belonging
- Low self-esteem
- Low empathic awareness
- PTSD and suicidal behaviors

As teenagers, children who have witnessed domestic violence potentially experience a multitude of problems. During these important developmental years, a time when they are carving out their identity, being exposed to violence in the home can be terribly disruptive to that process. The result is an adolescent who is confused about who they are. They are frustrated by their inability to feel normal, and to establish normal relationships. Many young people in this situation will act out their frustration in aggressive ways. They may turn to unhealthy peer groups to seek the validation they don't receive from their parents. They may turn to delinquent behavior as a way of venting their aggression, and may engage in abusive dating relationships themselves, either as the abused or the abuser. And finally, drug and alcohol use may become an alternative to the negative feelings they endure. They discover after experimenting with either that the bad feelings go away for a time. They also become less inhibited and better able to engage others socially. Unfortunately though, anytime drugs and alcohol are used as a coping mechanism, especially by an adolescent, experimentation and casual use eventually turns to abuse, and the risk of addiction rises dramatically. Addiction of course will only compound the very problems they are running from.

INTERVENING IN DOMESTIC VIOLENCE

How a police officer responds to a report of domestic abuse can be a life or death matter. The officer must be able to recognize when an abusive situation is occurring, even in the absence of physical evidence. What an officer finds upon arrival at such a situation, especially when the initial call came from someone other than the victim, is anything but a clearly discernible case of domestic battery. More often than not the abuser will answer the door as if nothing has happened. When the officers enter the premises, the family may portray themselves as the perfect family. In this case the victim denies the abuse, while the children, who sadly have many times become quite proficient in this situation, remain quiet. If asked, they may deny that anything has happened.

So what is the appropriate police response to a report of domestic abuse? As previously stated, prior to the 1980s, the preferred response was to do as little as possible. If the police could get the abuser to commit to stop their abusive behavior, then it was considered to be mission accomplished. The more progressively minded cops took the extra step of requesting that the abuser leave for the night so things could settle down. Seldom were arrests made except in the most brutal of cases, and even then a warrantless arrest was left up to the discretion of the officer. Few departments had specific policies relating to the department's response to domestic violence.

The Minneapolis Project

In the early 1980s things changed dramatically. Advocacy groups began to push the criminal justice system for tougher enforcement. Domestic violence became more of a political issue than it had been in the past, and departments began to weigh the efficacy of a mandatory arrest policy in cases where there was evidence that a battery had taken place. From 1981 to 1982 the Minneapolis Police Department, acting under a grant from the National Institute of Justice, carried out the first large scale study of this issue (Sherman and Berk, 1984). In what would become known as the *Minneapolis Project*, researchers tested the efficacy of arrest in cases of domestic battery. Up to that time it was found that most police departments allowed their officers to use discretion in these cases, and most employed one of four different responses: negotiating the dispute with no arrest; threatening arrest if officers had to return; asking one of the parties to leave for the night; or making an arrest without negotiation. One major study on the frequency of arrest in Boston, Chicago, and Washington, D.C. (Black, 1980), found that in only 27 percent of the cases involving violence that rose to the level of a felony were arrests made, and in misdemeanor cases, arrests were made in only 17 percent of the cases.

The Minnesota Project was the first effort made to measure the outcomes of these various response types. During the course of the experiment the 34 officers who participated in the study were randomly given the response type they were to follow in each case of domestic violence they responded to. Only misdemeanor cases were involved in the study. When an officer responded to a domestic call they would use a specially prepared pad of report forms to document the incident. At the top of each individual report form the response type they were to follow was indicated. The three alternatives were as follows:

- The officer would attempt to mediate the problem on-scene by giving both parties advice on possible corrective actions and coping strategies. In this case no arrest was made.
- The officer would require the abuser to leave the premises for an eight-hour period in order to avoid arrest.
- The officer would arrest the abuser if probable cause for the arrest were present.

Obviously there were times when circumstances dictated an outcome different from what the study directed; however, the majority of the time the officers were able to follow the protocol. In those cases where the officers were directed to make the arrest, 98.9 percent of the time they did so. In those cases where the officers were directed to mediate the conflict, they did so 77.8 percent of the time. And in those cases where the officers were directed to make the abuser leave the premises, 72.8 percent of the time they were able to follow the study's protocol.

In addition to gathering valuable data on the efficacy of the various response types, the researchers were also able to gather from the officers' reports demographic data on the parties

The Minneapolis Project
Victim and Suspect Demographics

A. **Unemployment**
   - Victims 61%
   - Suspects 60%

B. **Relationship of Suspect to Victim**
   - Divorced or separated husband 3%
   - Unmarried male lover 45%
   - Current husband 35%
   - Wife or girlfriend 2%
   - Son, brother, roommate. Other 15%

C. **Prior Assaults and Police Involvement**
   - Victims assaulted by suspect, last six months 80%
   - Police intervention in domestic dispute, last six months 60%
   - Couple in counseling program 27%

D. **Prior Arrests of Male Suspects**
   - Ever arrested for any offense 59%
   - Ever arrested for crime against person 31%
   - Ever arrested on domestic violence statute 5%
   - Ever arrested on an alcohol offense 29%

E. **Mean Age**
   - Victims 30 years
   - Suspects 32 years

F. **Education**
   - Victim Suspect <high school 43% 42%
   - high school only 33% 36%
   - high school 24% 22%

G. **Race (Victim Suspect)**
   - White 57% 45%
   - Black 23% 36%
   - Native-American 18% 16%
   - Other 2% 3%

FIGURE 7.3 Demographic Data from the Minneapolis Project.

involved in the domestic disputes. Figure 7.3 provides a summary of that data. One of the most striking pieces of data is that in 80 percent of the cases responded to, the victim had been assaulted at least once by their abuser in the previous six months. Also telling, nearly 60 percent of the male abusers had been arrested previously for various crimes, the majority of them crimes against persons.

Following the initial police response, research assistants followed up by conducting bi-weekly interviews of the victims for a period of six months to determine if any further abuse had occurred. Of the original 330 cases handled during the study period, researchers were able to maintain contact with 205 of the victims. The results are summarized in Figure 7.4. It was found that the lowest percentage of reoffending occurred among those abusers who were initially arrested by the police, with the highest percentage being among those who were asked to leave the premises by the police with no arrest being made.

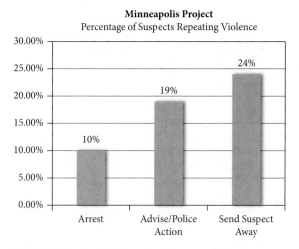

FIGURE 7.4   Results from the Minneapolis Project.

As a result of the study, the Minneapolis Police Department in 1984 adopted a more aggressive policy to guide their response to cases of domestic violence. The new policy did not make an arrest mandatory, but it required the officer to explain their reasons for not making an arrest if probable cause existed to do so. Their actions, and the results of the study, reverberated throughout the law enforcement community, and departments across the country began to follow suit. By the end of the decade many departments had adopted a mandatory arrest policy that took away any officer discretion and mandated an arrest if there were any visible signs of injury.

Mandatory arrest policies have had their critics. First of all, by taking away officer discretion, even injury to the abuser caused by a victim trying to defend themselves exposes the victim to possible arrest. Also, a mandatory arrest policy does not consider the economic hardship an arrest will cause for the family. In many, if not most cases, the family will remain intact throughout and following the judicial proceedings. The costs associated with attorneys, court fees, and lost wages can be substantial. If there are young children in the family, the economic hardship is only compounded, which in the future can potentially trigger more violence in the home.

The other criticism leveled against mandatory arrest policies is that they have no demonstrable effect on recidivism, and there are studies that support this contention. Dunford (1992) replicated the Minneapolis Project in Omaha, Nebraska. The result indicated that the Minneapolis Project may have been flawed in its design by doing only a six-month follow-up. In their study the researchers used a 12-month follow-up and found no differences in recidivism rates between the three response types. Ford (1991) found that the recidivism rate among spousal abusers was increased by the amount of anger they experienced as a result of the initial intervention. Of those abusers arrested at the scene, 40 percent battered their victims again within six months. Lower rates were found among those abusers who were brought to court via an arrest warrant or summons after the initial altercation, or diverted to an anger management program as an alternative to arrest. The findings would suggest that the most successful police response is one that attempts to contain and de-escalate the crisis in ways that serve to avoid arrest whenever possible, and then take immediate steps to mediate it. In contrast, many mandatory arrest policies simply contain and de-escalate the matter with no attempt at mediation. And finally, Swisher and Wekesser (1994), in replicating the Minneapolis Project in the city of Milwaukee,

ISSUES & ETHICS IS CRISIS INTERVENTION

The Police Response to LGBT Violence

On March 29, 1998, 28-year-old Marc Kajs, a gay man from Houston, Texas, was fatally shot by his former lover at the restaurant where he worked. His assailant then turned the gun on himself. Kajs had complained to the police a number of times about being stalked by his former partner, and on one occasion even sought refuge inside a police station where the man threatened him in view of a police officer. Two years after his death his mother filed a lawsuit against the Houston Police Department for failing to protect her son. The lawsuit alleged that just hours before her son's death he filed a report at Houston's Montrose police station after receiving more threats from the man. The police turned him away, advising him that the domestic violence unit was closed on weekends. Hours later he was dead.

In a survey conducted by Amnesty International (2006) it was found that the case of Marc Kajs was not unique. They obtained reports from a number of American cities detailing an inadequate police response to LGBT domestic violence. Their survey found instances of the police responding to such cases in an inappropriate, racist, or homophobic manner, or failing to respond at all. The result, according to Amnesty International, is that many in the LGBT communities surveyed have developed a mistrust of the police and refuse to contact them in domestic violence situations.

In a study involving new police cadets in Illinois (Harmening, 1992), a series of videotaped scenarios were created in which the cadets, as observers, were asked to use their discretion in deciding whether to issue minor speeding tickets to the subjects depicted. The cadets were initially advised that their feedback was needed to assist in the development of training videos. In reality, the focus of the study was to measure the amount of bias new police cadets enter the profession with. Scenarios were created involving ethnic minorities, as well as stereotypically gay men. The results were striking. Although a stereotypically heterosexual male received the least number of tickets, when the scenario was repeated eight weeks later with the same individual now acting stereotypically gay, he received the highest number of speeding tickets. As many as 25 percent of the 210 cadets surveyed changed their decision, to the detriment of the stereotypically gay man. The author concluded that a definite bias exists within the law enforcement profession against members of the LGBT community, a bias that may even be reinforced over time by the sentiments and expectations of the police personality.

Discussion Questions

1. What are some of the reasons why the police may be less responsive to the LGBT community?
2. Should cases of domestic violence among LGBT individuals be treated the same by the courts as those involving heterosexual individuals? Why or why not?
3. Discuss the impact legalizing gay marriage may have on the issue of domestic violence within the LGBT community.

Wisconsin, found that arresting domestic abusers actually increased recidivism rates overall, although they admit that that outcome cannot be generalized to all offenders.

The Duluth Model

So what is the most effective police response to domestic violence? Today most law enforcement and women's advocacy groups agree that quick, consistent, and tough enforcement of domestic violence laws is important. One of the most emulated models is one developed in Duluth, Minnesota, at approximately the same time that the Minneapolis study was conducted. The

Duluth Model is a collaborative initiative involving law enforcement, the courts, the local prosecutor's office, mental health agencies, and domestic violence shelters and advocacy programs. It is a holistic victim-oriented approach, unlike the cold offender-oriented approach implicit in the early mandatory arrest policies of many departments.

The Duluth model is guided by four strategic principles. First, that all agencies involved in the issue of domestic violence must be coordinated in their response, and they must have sufficient interagency agreements in place to support this objective and allow for effective communication between the agencies involved. The model requires that agencies provide cross-training to the other member agencies in order to facilitate the full integration of their missions. Thus, the police are trained in the psychological aspects of domestic abuse that the shelters and counseling centers concern themselves with, and those entities are trained in the criminal statutes and protocols that guide the police response.

The second strategic principle is that the coordinated response must be victim-safety centered. All policies and protocols established by the member agencies must be established with that central goal in mind. Monitoring and tracking systems should be developed to measure the efficacy and success of the various practices carried out by the agencies. Those practices should be backed by current and reliable research data that supports those practices in the context of victim safety. So, as an example, the success of the police department's arrest policy should not be measured by the sheer number of arrests, or the conviction rate of those arrested, but rather by the number of repeat offender cases the police respond to and the level of continued violence following the police department's intervention, both in cases where an arrest is made, as well as in those cases where the decision was made not to arrest.

The third strategic principle is that when a particular practice being carried out by a member agency is found not to be the most effective option to insure victim safety, then that agency must be prepared to change how it operates. The professional turf wars and agency inflexibility that have plagued the law enforcement mission in America for decades must be set aside for the good of the mission. When new practices are developed, they must be done so under the guidance and review of multi-agency committees that can ensure that proper criteria are being met. The law enforcement community, traditionally a conservative institution, has always had difficulty working with the social services community, traditionally liberal. In Duluth they realized that for the good of that community's domestic violence intervention mission, these walls had to be lowered or destroyed altogether.

The final strategic principle guiding the Duluth model is the critical importance of a clear and consistent response by the police and courts to cases of domestic abuse. First and foremost, the model calls for mandatory arrest of the *primary* aggressor. They attempt to avoid those situations where a police department, one following a strict mandatory arrest policy, arrests anyone accused of battering their partner, even a victim who may have struggled with their abuser and left physical evidence of her struggle in the form of scratches or marks. The model also calls for prosecutors to treat each case as unique, and to pursue prosecution based on the evidence in the case rather than using a standard plea bargain agreement to quickly dispose of the matter. Finally, the model recognizes that offender treatment services as an adjunct to prosecution is necessary for victim safety. Thus, such a program should include court-ordered treatment as an alternative to incarceration; however, with repeat offenders the penalty is increased in severity with each occurrence. To facilitate this objective an offender tracking system is utilized to ensure compliance with court mandates and to keep a dangerous offender from slipping through the cracks to continue their abusive behavior.

The North Carolina Model

Specifically relating to the police response, like any crisis, response, containment, and de-escalation are the first considerations, with remediation a necessary component once de-escalation has been achieved. In modern-day policing there are many different strategies; however, with domestic violence most departments now adhere to a similar model. The North Carolina Governor's Crime Commission (1998) outlined a response protocol for departments in their state to follow, one that exemplifies the most common response strategy currently being employed. For starters it mandates training for all police officers on the issue of domestic violence, and not just on issues relating to law, but also the psychological issues relevant to domestic violence. The protocol provides clear and decisive guidelines for containing the crisis. Officers are to respond quickly, approach cautiously, and then request entry to the house. If entry is denied, and there is evidence of ongoing violence, then the police have the right to make a forcible entry without a warrant in order to protect persons from further violence and potential injury. In either case, once inside the house, containment must take place immediately to prevent further violence. This is accomplished by officers separating all parties present, especially the abuser and their victim. If there is any doubt about which individual is the abuser, and tensions are still running high, then the police may initially handcuff both parties for their own safety.

Once the crisis is contained, de-escalation takes place by the officers calming the parties involved and beginning their investigation. Guidelines for officer interviews are as follows:

- Use supportive interview techniques.
- Ask the victim about previous incidents of abuse.
- Do not reveal to the victim what action is intended until all information has been gathered.
- Ask both the victim and suspect if they are in pain.
- Document victim and suspect's condition, demeanor, relative size, and evidence of injury.
- If the victim does not speak English, then a translator should be called in.

In addition to the victim and abuser, all witnesses to the incident, including children, should be interviewed. Additionally, the physical premises should be surveyed for any sign of struggle or other evidence that corroborates or refutes anyone's story. Pictures should be taken, when possible. Also, it is very important that officers inquire of all parties as they speak to them if there are any guns or other weapons in the house. If there are, those weapons should be seized by the police for safekeeping until such time that it is safe to give them back. Finally, once the situation is contained, the officers should determine if there is a valid **order of protection** in force against the suspect. An order of protection is a court order that prevents an individual from having any contact with the petitioner of the order, typically a spouse or significant other. In most states, a violation of such an order is a criminal offense.

Under this protocol a warrantless arrest, meaning an arrest at the scene by the responding officers, will be made if a felony offense has been committed. Additionally, if a misdemeanor offense is committed in the officers' presence, an arrest will be made. If a misdemeanor offense was allegedly committed prior to the officers' arrival, then this is where some flexibility is built into the protocol. In this case, any number of options can be pursued. The abuser may agree to an anger management or domestic abuse intervention in lieu of an arrest. The beauty of a multi-agency response protocol is that the agency providing such intervention can be immediately engaged while the police still maintain the leverage of potential charges.

Regardless of whether an arrest is made, the victim should be offered transport to a domestic violence shelter and assistance in securing an emergency order of protection against the abuser. If the emergency order is given, then the abuser will be precluded from having any further contact with the victim until the matter is resolved. To do so would expose the abuser to additional charges, up to and including prison time. Within a period of a few days, the court will hold a hearing on whether the order should be made permanent. Both sides have the opportunity to present evidence in such a hearing; however, if the judge sides with the victim, then the order will be made permanent, or in some cases for a period of up to two years.

Finally, the North Carolina protocol discourages a dual arrest where there is evidence of physical altercation by both parties. In these cases, it is recommended that the primary aggressor be arrested. The primary aggressor is the one who is responsible for perpetrating the violence, not necessarily the one who threw the first punch or initiated the argument. It is recognized that in many cases a victim throwing the first punch or attacking their abuser may be entirely justified, depending on their state of mind at the time and the extent to which they felt it necessary to defend themselves.

Chapter Summary

The crisis of domestic violence is one of the most frequent a police officer will confront. It can be a volatile and dangerous situation, both for the officer and the victim of the violence. Containment and de-escalation are critical, but remediation is of equal importance. Historically we have watched law enforcement move from the extreme of inaction, to the opposite extreme of mandatory arrest of all people accused of causing injury, perhaps even a victim who did so in self-defense. In our modern society the goal has shifted to a middle ground, one in which the safety of the victim serves as the primary goal. Such a goal necessitates an understanding on the part of those who respond of the reasons why a victim many times will not separate themselves from their abuser.

Thus, it becomes critical that the offender be offered the opportunity to seek treatment for their problem while the courts maintain some degree of leverage. For many crises, the odds of it being repeated are very low, or none at all. However, with domestic violence it is just the opposite. In fact, it is expected that an abusive episode will be repeated unless an aggressive intervention strategy is followed. That strategy necessitates that those agencies responding to domestic violence at various stages—police, prosecutors, the courts, abuse shelters, and counseling centers—do so in a coordinated way and with two goals in mind: to protect the victim of abuse from further violence, and to intervene in the life of the abuser in an effort to permanently change their problematic behavior.

Key Terms

Domestic abuse
Cycle of violence
Honeymoon phase
Tension-building phase

Acute violence phase
Battered spouse syndrome
Traumatic bonding theory
Psychological entrapment theory

Multifactor ecological theory
Order of protection

Discussion Questions

1. When deciding whether to arrest a domestic abuser, should the police consider the financial impact of the arrest on the abuser's family?
2. What are the positive and negative effects of a mandatory arrest policy for domestic violence?
3. Discuss some of the reasons why an adolescent exposed to domestic violence in the home is at a higher risk for juvenile delinquency.

8

The Victims of Crisis

LEARNING OUTCOMES

Upon completion of this chapter the student should be able to:

1. Define the costs of victimization to American society.

2. List the various victim typologies.

3. Summarize the types of victim services available in the community.

3. Explain some of the problems associated with victim eyewitness reports.

Chapter Outline

INTRODUCTION

The word **victim** has been used to describe essentially any person subjected to injurious circumstances beyond their control or provocation. For the person in that situation it is the worst type of crisis, one that has both immediate and possibly lifelong physical and emotional consequences. In this chapter we discuss the various victim typologies and their identifying characteristics, the emotional impact of victimization, intervention strategies employed by criminal justice professionals when dealing with victims, and an overview of the various remedial and preventative services available to victims of crisis. Essentially every crisis responded to by the criminal justice system has the potential for leaving physically and emotionally damaged people in its wake. The cost to society, both in terms of tax dollars and productivity, is a heavy one. It is, therefore, critically important that the criminal justice system develop the most effective strategies for responding not only to crisis, but also to its human aftermath.

VICTIM TYPOLOGIES

It is difficult to fit all victims of crisis into a neat and concise set of typologies. Some are targeted by those who victimize them, whereas others are passive observers to the event that traumatizes them. Some suffer physical trauma, others sexual trauma, and still others emotional trauma. Their symptoms may be short-lived, or they may last a lifetime. So it is not a homogenous group. For purposes of this text, we will categorize victims as either *violated, assaulted, uprooted, passive,* or *oppressed*. A discussion of each, along with any subtypes follows.

The Violated Victim

Some victims are physically assaulted on the outside, and others internally in such a way that it attacks the very essence of who they are, especially their sexuality. If the victim is a child or an adolescent, then their sense of identity is still developing, and it could potentially be impacted by a crime of this nature being perpetrated against them (Harmening, 2009). In this category of victims we include those who are sexually assaulted, both adults and children. Traditionally the word **rape** has been used to describe the act of sexual assault, but the statutes relating to sexual offenses are now much more complex, and most states now have multiple types of sexual offenses in their statutes, including such categories as **sexual assault**, **sexual abuse**, **predatory sexual assault,** and a host of others.

The prevalence of sex offenses in America is staggering. In 2009 there were 88,097 forcible rapes reported to police, down from 90, 479 the year before and a 20-year high of 109,062 in 1992 (www2.fbi.gov/ucr). These are only the reported rapes. The FBI statistics do not take into account the thousands of sexual assaults that go unreported for various reasons. Each of these thousands of microcrises carries with it the risk of permanent psychological damage to the victim. For those who respond to these cases, it is critical that the response be **victim-centered**. When the police respond to most crimes, their response is typically **offender-centered**, meaning their primary goal is to de-escalate the crisis, preferably by arresting the offender. With a case of sexual assault however, the primary concern of the responding officers must be the victim. Their response, if done correctly, can help to minimize the psychological trauma to the victim. If done incorrectly, however, it can exacerbate it. And a victim of sexual assault handled correctly will ultimately lead to the gathering of more credible evidence with which to convict the offender.

YEAR	NUMBER OF REPORTED FORCIBLE RAPES	RATE PER 100,000 POPULATION
1990	102,555	41.1
1991	106,596	42.3
1992	109,062	42.8
1993	106,014	41.1
1994	102,216	39.3
1995	97,470	37.1
1996	96,252	36.3
1997	96,153	35.9
1998	93,144	34.5
1999	89,411	32.8
2000	90,178	32.0
2001	90,863	31.8
2002	95,235	33.1
2003	93,883	32.3
2004	95,089	32.4
2005	94,347	31.8
2006	94,782	31.7
2007	91,874	30.5
2008	90,479	29.7
2009	88,097	28.7

FIGURE 8.1 UCR, Forcible Rapes Reported to Police.

TYPES OF SEXUAL ASSAULT   Before we move on, it is important to discuss the differences between the various types of sexual assaults. As previously mentioned, in the various state criminal codes around the country, there are many different categories of sex crimes. They are broken down by such things as the age of the victim, the number of years separating victim and offender, whether force or weapons were used, and the actual type of sexual activity that occurred. For our purposes we can fit them into just three categories: stranger rapes, acquaintance rapes, and statutory rapes. Each will have a slightly different type of response by the police and other crisis personnel.

When we talk about **stranger rapes**, we are really talking about what has traditionally been thought of as rape. These are cases where the victim is stalked and/or attacked without any prior contact with their attacker. They are the most brutal of rapes, and many end in murder. Others lack any display of violence, with the attacker gaining compliance by simply threatening the use of force, usually with a knife or gun. These cases are among the most difficult to prove, especially if the attacker is careful to leave behind no fingerprints or bodily fluids containing identifiable DNA.

In contrast to stranger rapes, **acquaintance rapes** occur when the attacker and victim know each other. It may involve co-workers, former intimates, or even a young couple on a first date. Sadly, it may also involve a father raping his own children. The common element in each case is an attacker who engages in some type of sexual domination over their victim without their consent, or the victim is simply too young to give consent.

The final category is what is commonly referred to as **statutory rape**, or one in which both parties are consenting; however, the victim is considered neither old enough to give such consent nor to understand the implications of their decision to engage in consensual sex with an adult. It is referred to as *statutory* rape because the age parameters are defined by statute. In reality, few if any state statutes actually refer to the crime in this manner, but opt instead for things like *sexual abuse, sex with a minor*, or *child exploitation*. This class of crime may even be a misdemeanor offense in some states if the victim is an older teenager, and the offender is close in age.

HISTORICAL ATTITUDES ABOUT RAPE   It was not so long ago when rape was looked at much differently by the criminal justice system in America. Victims were often accused by their attackers of actually inviting the assault with their style of dress or behavior, and many times the police agreed with them. Victims were oftentimes accused of being sexually promiscuous and ostracized by their communities. And whether or not the attacker was charged often depended on who they were or the color of their skin. Sadly, race played a role not only in determining who would be charged, but what sentence would be imposed. Prior to 1977, those convicted of rape could actually be sentenced to death in some states. Between 1930 and 1968, 455 convicted rapists were executed in America, nearly all of them African-American men accused of raping white women (Siegel, 1998). Very few white men ever received harsh sentences for raping Black women, and allegations leveled by Black women against Black men were seldom even investigated. In 1977 the U.S. Supreme Court permanently banned the use of the death penalty in rape cases, unless of course the victim was also murdered.

Perhaps the biggest impetus for a change in public perception came with the feminist movement of the 1970s. During this time, awareness was raised in many areas, including women's rights, equal pay, domestic violence, and certainly the criminal justice system's response to sex crimes against women. For the first time, acquaintance rape was pushed to the forefront. Prior to this time these cases were seldom brought to trial. They were perceived by the police and prosecutors alike as difficult, if not impossible, to prove. Consequently, many prosecutors were reluctant to move forward with criminal charges based solely on the statement of the victim (Estrich, 1993a). It was viewed in the same light as a husband raping his wife, another type of acquaintance rape. It was simply not thought of as a crime, except perhaps physical battery, if the victim had ever been intimate with her attacker, or was even a consenting date for dinner or a movie.

DATE RAPE   Also during this time, and for the first time, the term **date rape** was used, especially on America's college campuses, to describe a legitimate criminal offense that would no longer be tolerated. When the issue was finally studied, the rate at which young college females were being sexually assaulted was found to be extremely high. The Campus Sexual Assault Study (Krebs et al., 2007) found that 13.7 percent of undergraduate female students had been victims of a completed sexual assault. Of these, 4.7 percent were victims of a forcible rape, 7.8 percent were raped when they were incapacitated by alcohol or drugs, and 0.6 percent after being administered a **date rape drug** without their knowledge. In another widely cited study (Siegel, 2001), it was found that 673,000 of nearly 6 million females attending college at that time (11.5 percent) had been sexually assaulted. Equally disturbing is that only 12 percent of those reported the incidents to police.

RAPE SHIELD LAWS   In an effort to change not only the public's perception of rape victims, but also the way in which the male-dominated criminal justice system handled their cases, **rape**

shield laws were enacted around the country to prevent victims from in essence being put on trial themselves. Prior to these laws it was not uncommon for defense attorneys to make the victim's sexual history an issue in an attempt to argue that their sexual promiscuity somehow supported their client's belief that the victim wanted to have sex. In those cases where the victim was injured, it was not uncommon for the defense to even go so far as to argue that the victim wanted "rough sex."

Today, rape shield laws prevent a victim's sexual history from becoming an issue in court. Some states will allow it, but only after the judge has made the decision that to not allow such testimony would violate the constitutional rights of the accused (NCVC.org, accessed 07/02/2011). In most cases, an effort is made to prevent the victim's past reputation, especially her sexual history, from becoming an issue and causing a victim to be traumatized all over again during the trial. This more than anything is what prevented the vast majority of sexual assault cases from being reported to police in decades past.

THE POLICE RESPONSE   There is not a more victim-sensitive response the police make than to a case of reported rape. The initial response, if done correctly, not only ensures the collection of credible evidence, but also buffers the victim against additional trauma, and gets her, and in some cases *him*, immediately on the path to recovery. The response is so important that Scotland Yard now requires that every one of its officers who handles such a case be trained in the psychological effects of rape (McVeigh, 2010).

In most cases there will be no need for containment and de-escalation when an officer responds to a reported rape. Many times the victim will even wait for a length of time, perhaps even days, before reporting the incident. Remediation becomes the primary goal, which involves not only the collection of evidence, but also directing the victim to available resources within the community that can provide needed medical and psychological services.

In most cases the responding department will send two officers to a reported rape, both of whom should be properly trained in this area, and at least one of whom should be a female officer. In those smaller departments where the availability of a female officer is limited, then the department should have a written protocol allowing a female nurse or EMT to accompany the officer. The officer's response has three goals: to assist the victim in getting medical care, to collect the evidence needed to arrest and prosecute the attacker, and to advise the victim of available resources for counseling and other forms of victim assistance.

The officer's initial contact with the victim must be victim-centered. Although arresting the victim's attacker is certainly one of goals, the officer must give a clear signal to the victim that they are concerned first and foremost with their well-being. The officers should reassure the victim that everything will be okay, and that they will remain with them throughout the process. They should first ascertain if the victim is physically injured, and if so, then immediate medical care is pursued. If she is not seriously injured, then the victim should still be asked to agree to a medical exam by specially trained medical staff in the hospital emergency room. While discussing and preparing for this exam, the officers should be asking a few general questions about what happened, and if the crime was just committed, then information about the attacker's description must be gathered and broadcast to other officers working that jurisdiction. At this point, detailed questioning about the sexual assault, especially about the act itself, should be avoided. The officers should also be looking for evidence, but in a way that does not lead the victim to think they are more concerned about that than their well-being. Evidence can take many forms. Although crime scene technicians will more than likely process the scene for evidence, the responding officers will be responsible for protecting evidence that could be destroyed, such as the victim's clothes and undergarments. It is also critical that the victim not take a shower or bath until the medical exam has taken place.

After getting some basic information about what happened, and the victim's agreement to go to the hospital, then the officers will transport them there. It is important here that the female officer establish rapport and continually inform the victim of what is happening, and that she is safe. A male officer responding alone should be cautious to ask a female victim to allow him to transport her to the hospital. She is still emotionally decompressing from the trauma she just experienced at the hands of a male attacker. To get into a car with another male may be too much for her to handle at this point. Also, the victim should be asked to bring along a clean set of clothing to the hospital, and have it explained to her that the clothes she is wearing will be taken as evidence for analysis.

Once at the hospital, then specially trained medical personnel will take over. These are nurses and physicians who are trained in the collection of evidence while tending to the victim's medical needs. Their activities will include a head-to-toe physical examination during which any visible blood, urine, semen, or hair will be collected and preserved. To do this, they will utilize what is commonly referred to as a **rape kit**, or a prepackaged and sealed set of instruments used specifically for the collection of evidence. Once finished, then the kit will again be sealed and sent off for forensic and DNA analysis by the investigating detective or agency. Photos will be taken of any injuries to the victim, including the genital area, and the clothes she was wearing at the time of the assault will also be taken and forwarded for forensic analysis.

Only after the medical exam has been completed is a detailed interview of the victim attempted. During this interview the victim will be asked to recount every detail of the attack, including the sexual contact between her and her attacker. This may be extremely difficult for a victim, because in asking them to recount the events, the detective is asking them to experience their trauma all over again. Care must be taken by an investigator trained in this area to know when to discontinue the interview for a period of time. It is also recommended that a mental health professional, preferably from a local women's shelter, be standing by or even present during the interview. Many departments have written protocols and agreements in place for this type of assistance.

RAPE TRAUMA SYNDROME   It is important for anyone responding routinely to cases of rape or sexual assault to understand the symptoms associated with **rape trauma syndrome**. Victims of rape will often begin acting in erratic ways almost immediately after their assault. It may at first be confusing to an officer who responds to investigate the matter. Karmen (2010) points out that during the acute phase of this syndrome, which can last for two to three weeks following the attack, the victim may experience the following reactions:

- Revulsion, even toward herself
- Self-blame
- Extreme mood swings from anger to fear
- Sorrow and grief
- Disorientation

During this time the victim may also experience physical symptoms such as nausea, insomnia, and severe headaches.

The second phase of the syndrome is a longer-term period during which the victim attempts to cope with what has happened to her. Depending on the person, this phase could last from months to even years. During this time the person may experience recurring nightmares, strained relationships with men, a loss of sexual desire, and they may develop an intense fear of many different things they have somehow related to their attack. In the most extreme cases, the victim may experience a complete emotional breakdown, and may even demonstrate schizophrenic-like behaviors.

One important thing must be said about child victims of sexual assault. When an officer responds to such a case, they must keep in mind that they are dealing with a victim who will spend a lifetime battling the trauma of their abuse. How the officer responds can impact the child's perception of the event for many years to come. The officer must be careful not to further the child's trauma. If the child's own parent is the attacker, and the officers are there to arrest the parent, they must be cognizant of the fact that even though the parent has abused or assaulted the child, there is still an attachment to that parent, and to watch them be hauled away in handcuffs can be traumatic on its own, and may only deepen the child's negative perception of the larger issues. The child may even blame themselves not only for their own abuse, but also for their parent getting arrested. So the responding officer, while never wanting to place themselves or others at risk by not following accepted arrest procedures, should always be aware of the child-victim's presence, and attempt to anticipate the impact of their actions on the child's emotional development and well-being.

The Assaulted Victim

PASSIVE VS. ACTIVE VICTIMS   The second class of victims are those who are physically attacked, but without a sexual component. These victims are either **passive**, meaning they had no prior connection to their attacker, or **active**, meaning they were participants in the situation that led to their assault. Examples of the latter might include a fight, a riot, or an abused spouse. Unlike the violated victim, the response by police to an assault is more offender-centered. Certainly the first matter of importance is the welfare of the victim, so medical attention comes first. But once medical attention is rendered, then the responding officers attempt to gather as much information as they can, and as quickly as they can, in order to arrest the attacker. There are times when the officers arrive while the assault is still taking place. In such cases, containment and de-escalation are the first orders of business, after which the welfare of the victim is attended to.

Although the response to an assaulted victim tends to be offender-centered, if the victim is a passive one, then there is certainly the possibility of long-term psychological damage to the person. The responding officers must take care not to exacerbate their trauma by approaching the matter in an uncaring or cavalier manner. They absolutely must avoid lecturing the victim about how they shouldn't have been in a particular place, said a particular thing, or carried out a particular action that may have contributed the attack. Such statements only cast blame on the victim for their own attack, and self-blame for a victim will potentially lead to self-contempt over time, and self-destruction in the most extreme cases.

CHILD ABDUCTION AND THE AMBER ALERT   Finally, one additional type of crisis must be placed in this category, and that is the horrific crime of child abduction. It is a crisis that demands immediate action by multiple responders according to predetermined procedures and protocols. There are approximately 115 non-family abductions each year in America in which a child is detained overnight, transported at least 50 miles, held for ransom, or intended to be kept permanently or killed (NJCRS.gov, 2003). In almost all states now, when a child is abducted there is an **Amber alert**. This alert notifies the general public of the abduction, along with descriptive information about the child and the abductor. This allows the community at large to be on the lookout for the child, the suspect, and the suspect's vehicle.

The Amber alert, an acronym for America's Missing: Broadcasting Emergency Response, was established following the 1996 abduction and murder of 9-year-old Amber Hagerman of Arlington, Texas. Begun as a state measure in Texas, the alert has now become standard in all states. When it is triggered, the information is broadcast on radio and television stations, by satellite to the various receiving services, and even on LED billboards that have the ability to be programmed immediately with the information. The information can also be broadcast via SMS text messages. The criteria for the police initiating an Amber alert include the following (amberalert.gov):

- Law enforcement authorities must confirm that an abduction has taken place.
- The abducted child must be at risk of death or serious injury (as opposed to a parental abduction).
- There must be sufficient descriptive information available about the child, the abductor, or the abductor's vehicle to make the alert potentially useful.
- The child must be 17 years old or younger.

Although the Amber alert was not necessarily developed to address the problem of parental abductions, many states that have signed on to the protocol do use it for that purpose. To date, the system has contributed to the safe return of 540 abducted children (amberalert.com, 2011).

The Uprooted Victim

Some victims will require intervention on the part of criminal justice professionals who have not experienced a crime. These are the victims primarily of natural disasters who have lost their homes. We witnessed nearly a million residents of New Orleans being relocated following Hurricane Katrina. It has become known as the "American Diaspora." People were relocated as far away as Texas and Georgia (Tracking the Katrina Diaspora, 2006), and many of the children of that mass relocation experienced significant psychological problems in its wake (Pina et al., 2008).

Anyone who remembers as a child moving to a new city and attending a new school no doubt remembers how traumatic the experience was for them. To leave one's home and natural environment is not an easy thing, but when we moved as children to a new city we had significant social supports in place to ease the impact of the move. We had a new school, hopefully waiting with open arms, new friends, a new home, and the ability to return to our old home whenever possible to see old friends. In the case of Katrina however, these supports were not in place. Those who were relocated were among the poorest of New Orleans. Thus, few decisions about their relocation were made by them. They went to wherever FEMA forced them to go if they wanted food, housing, and health care. They had no nice houses waiting for them. They had temporary trailers or apartments, and more than likely moved to a city that simply did not want them there. On top of that, many left their friends behind, some of whom had died during the disaster, their pets, their jobs, and any hope for the future. Consequently, the relocation victimized many of them all over again.

Those who respond to such a large-scale crisis, especially those in decision-making positions, must be cognizant of the impact of uprooting people from their homes. When people get desperate they do desperate things. For the criminal justice professionals who respond, they must recognize that they are dealing with people who have been victimized by their circumstances, and that things like looting, stealing cars, and resorting to violence against one another are sometimes the result of that desperation.

One thing can be said about people, especially children, who lose their social identity by being uprooted from their natural environment: they run the risk of becoming a lifelong problem for society by replacing the social supports they left behind with juvenile delinquency, substance abuse, and adult criminality (ABA Center on Children and the Law, 2009). We haven't yet felt the full effects of Hurricane Katrina. When the children of the Diaspora have their own children, and they theirs, we will see the compounded effects of that macrocrisis.

The Passive Victim

Passive victims are those who are traumatized by simply observing another person being victimized. The most common form of this type of victimization confronted by criminal justice professionals are the children of an abusive home. More often than not, when a man physically or emotionally abuses his spouse or partner, there are children watching. It is estimated that over 3.3 million children each year witness domestic violence (American Psychological Association, 1996). It is one of the most traumatic things a child can experience, and it almost always has long-term implications, including juvenile delinquency, sexual promiscuity, and substance abuse (Witnessing Domestic Violence: The Effect on Children, 2002).

Those who respond to domestic violence must view the children present as additional victims of the abuse. They must take precautions not to increase the trauma already experienced by the children, but also should consider proactive measures. In addition to the abused spouse being advised of available services, such as shelters and counseling services, the children too should be offered services through the victim-parent. This can include counseling, mentoring (e.g., Big Brother, Big Sister), and academic intervention and other services offered through the school counseling office.

Another type of passive victimization involves those who are exposed daily to inner-city violence. They are adults and children who are forced constantly to look back over their shoulder the minute they leave their homes for work, school, or leisure. Maintaining such a hypervigilant demeanor will invariably begin to cause psychological strain. Parson (1994) lists some of the long-term effects, including a profound loss of trust in the community and the world, a hatred for self, a tattered system of internalized morals and ethics, and a breakdown of their inner and outer sense of security and caring. They are particularly vulnerable to traumatic stress illnesses resulting from a sense of **death immersion**.

The most effective response the criminal justice system can make to alleviate this type of victimization is to proactively address the problem of violence in the impacted neighborhoods. The response here is *preventative* in nature. A strong police presence in high-crime areas is necessary. Many cities have established police substations in these areas, and some have employed foot patrols by officers. It is critical that the people affected know that their neighborhoods are safe for them and their children. It is also important for those officers working these neighborhoods to become acquainted with those who live there, and to keep an open eye for children and adults who may be experiencing a traumatic stress response. They should have protocols in place for referrals to needed counseling and social services. They should also make an effort to organize the neighborhood. There is power in numbers, and when a neighborhood organizes to assist the police in cleansing their streets of gangs and drug dealers, those who live there can feel safer and more in control of their lives.

The Oppressed Victim

The final category we will discuss are those individuals who are subjected not to physical or sexual violence, but rather to economic and emotional oppression. These are people who live in

---

• **The Violated Victim**

Victims of sexual crimes such as sexual assault, sexual abuse, and sexual battery.

• **The Assaulted Victim**

Victims of physical violence. Includes both active and passive victims, as well as abducted children.

• **The Oppressed Victim**

Victims of economic, social, or emotional oppression or cruelty.

• **The Passive Victim**

Victims of observing and vicariously experiencing another's trauma.

• **The Uprooted Victim**

Victims of forced relocation and deculturation following natural disasters and large-scale crises.

FIGURE 8.2 Victim Typologies.

constant crisis due to their circumstances. It may be a woman living under the oppressive and emotionally abusive control of her husband. It could be those stuck in the web of a cult, and who are unable to see leaving as a viable option for fear of retaliation. And it could certainly be those living in abject poverty, and who feel helpless to do anything about it. Like any other type of victimization, oppression, after an extended period of time begins to have long-term psychological effects on the individual.

Oftentimes the lack of a criminal offense and privacy concerns preclude criminal justice professionals from intervening in the lives of these types of victims. However, the overriding concern for anyone who responds to crisis is the welfare of any potential victims. If it is determined that an individual is being victimized, even emotionally, then it is well within the realm of responsibility to at least offer assistance and services. This is especially true of children, and in fact there is a much higher bar of responsibility when it comes to child victims. Adults certainly can exercise their right to refuse help, but children cannot. If it is suspected that they are being victimized emotionally by a parent or cult leader, then action can and must be taken. In either case, state child and family services officers must be engaged to determine if it is appropriate to remove the child from their environment and circumstances. In the case of a parent, there are remedial steps short of removing the child that may be taken, such as mandatory counseling and ongoing observation by a case worker.

For those oppressed by their social circumstances, there are many opportunities for criminal justice professionals to cross their paths. This is where having a comprehensive understanding of the various victim and social services available in the community is critical. Those who respond to crisis, even the type of crisis that is not readily apparent, should always be prepared to intervene to the extent possible, even if it involves nothing more than advising the individual of available services and offering to take them there.

ISSUES & ETHICS IN CRISIS INTERVENTION
Contributory Blame in the Case of Rape

The principle of contributory blame has been used many times to deny victims of rape financial and other types of assistance made available through various government-sponsored victim compensation programs. In many cases, women using drugs at the time of their rape have been denied benefits and assistance. In these cases, the agencies overseeing the requests have ruled that their use of drugs was contributory conduct, and that the victims had essentially participated in their own assaults. As you can imagine, victims' rights advocates are outraged by this position.

Contributory blame is not a new concept in civil and criminal procedure. In civil cases, judgments are often made on the basis of contributory blame. The amount of the financial award is determined by the percentage of blame that is attributed to the plaintiff. In criminal proceedings, the amount of blame attributed to the victim is oftentimes the deciding factor in whether charges are even filed in the case. It also becomes an issue during sentencing proceedings. If blame can be attributed to the victim, then it is hoped, at least by the defendant, that the judge will consider that as a mitigating factor and impose a lighter sentence.

The question of whether a rape victim can ever be blamed for her attack however, has been hotly debated. One of the reasons our current "rape shield" laws were enacted was to prevent the defense from making a victim's sexual history an issue in the case in an effort to attribute blame to the victim. But a defendant still has a constitutional right to testify in their own defense and, in doing so, to testify to their state of mind at the time of the sexual contact and why they had developed that state of mind. Here is where blame can be cast onto the victim in the eyes of the jury. In such a case, "no" should mean "no." But a jury is never completely impartial or unbiased. A good defense attorney in a rape case will take every opportunity to use this reality to the defendant's advantage.

Discussion Questions
1. Should the way a female rape victim dresses and acts prior to the rape be considered as evidence?
2. If the victim had consensual sex with the defendant on a prior date, should this have a bearing on an alleged rape occurring during a subsequent date?
3. Do you believe it is possible for a female attacker to rape a male victim and, if so, how do you think the criminal justice system might look differently upon a male victim as opposed to a female victim?

VICTIM SERVICES

Almost every community in America has access to various resources to assist victims. They are numerous, and the type of services provided will depend on the type of victimization. It is important that those who respond to crisis have information on hand listing the services available to assist victims, and also to be prepared to facilitate to the extent possible the engagement of those services for the victims.

If it is a victim of crime, then some of the more common services found in the community include the following:

- *Victim compensation:* No matter the type of victimization, there is almost always a financial burden to the victim. It may be lost wages, medical bills, damaged property, or any number of other things. Many states and municipalities maintain a victim compensation fund designed to at least in part ease the economic strain on the victim. Most have

a maximum amount available to a victim. In Illinois for example, the fund, administered by the Office of the Attorney General, sets the maximum at $27,000 (Crime Victim
Compensation Program, 2011).

- *Victim advocacy:* Unfortunately when a person is victimized, their involvement doesn't
  stop once the offense is completed. The victim will no doubt have to testify during a trial.
  There may be a civil trial, and perhaps administrative hearings. A victim seeking justice
  may want to ensure their voice is heard by the sentencing judge. In many jurisdictions a
  victim advocate is assigned to assist the victim through all of these potential activities and
  more. Their goal is to ease the strain on the victim and to insure that the victim is not re-
  traumatized by the process.
- *Crisis counseling:* Sometimes a victim is so traumatized by the events that immediate
  psychological intervention is necessary. Many criminal justice agencies have established
  protocols for this service. Responding counselors are typically contracted for and paid by
  the agency rather than the victim. The goal is to deal with the immediate trauma in advance of referring them to longer-term counseling. Also, there are certainly times following a traumatic event, especially a sexual assault, when the victim may become suicidal.
  This short-term intervention may serve as a conduit for hospitalization or an involuntary
  psychiatric commitment in these extreme cases.
- *Emergency legal advocacy:* Oftentimes these services are provided by the state's attorney
  or DA in the particular jurisdiction where the offense takes place. In other areas govern-
  ment-funded legal assistance agencies take responsibility. In the case of a victim, especially
  a victim of domestic violence or stalking, there may be a need for an immediate order of
  protection or restraining order. Legal advocates have the ability to engage a judge and address the needed issue immediately. They may need to file a temporary guardianship petition on behalf of an abused elder, or an order placing a child in protective custody. Legal
  advocates are there to provide these and other services without delay.
- *Shelter/safe house:* Almost all medium- to larger-sized cities have a number of shelters available for the victims of abuse. Most have been established in response to domestic violence.
  Some are publicly advertised, whereas others maintain undisclosed locations and security
  measures. The latter are for those victims who are at high risk for further abuse. In most cases,
  at least certain members of the local police department are aware of those locations, and protocols are in place for officers to be quickly dispatched if the need arises. Some of these shelters
  are for women only, whereas others specialize in the care of abused women and their children.

In this same category are those entities that care primarily for the homeless. Sadly, there
is a high degree of victimization among the homeless population. Agencies that focus on these
individuals, such as the Salvation Army and other faith-based organizations, provide not only
crisis intervention services, including housing, but also remedial services such as job training
and substance abuse counseling. These agencies recognize that many people are victimized in
part because of their life circumstances, so they take a holistic approach in an effort to improve
a person's quality of life, and thus reduce the chances and opportunity for further victimization.

THE VICTIM-WITNESS

Many times when a police officer responds to crisis, the victim of that crisis, if it is a criminal
matter, is the one the officer must rely on for the necessary eye-witness evidence to arrest and
convict the offender. This sometimes creates a difficult situation, due to the effects of trauma on

memory and recall. Research has shown that our perception is less accurate in traumatic situations (Doctor and Shiromoto, 2009). A victim may be certain of the physical description of their attacker only to discover later that the person arrested looks much different. Stress increases a person's emotional response, and this increase acts to constrict a person's perceptual field. Their reported memories may be influenced by personal bias and prejudice or expectations related to the event. For example, a woman sexually assaulted in a particular ethnic neighborhood may erroneously report having been assaulted by a member of that ethnic group because she expects it to have been by virtue of the location. If the attack took place in the dark, and the victim was not able to get a good look at her attacker, then her perception may be influenced by her expectations as she begins to fill in the missing pieces.

One method that is sometimes used by the police to get accurate details from an eyewitness, even one with no conscious memory of the event, is **forensic hypnosis**. It is used when the stress and trauma of the event is preventing the witness from recovering memories that have either been repressed or not consciously processed at the time they were witnessed. In a state of heightened relaxation, or what hypnotists refer to as a **trance-state**, with the person's conscious mind no longer blocking the recovery of the pertinent memories, it is hoped that the person's recall of what they witnessed will take place with little effort.

Chapter Summary

Whenever there is a crisis of any type, chances are there are victims left in its wake. One of the primary missions of criminal justice professionals, especially the police, is to assist those victims and to protect them from further harm. Most of the time that is done reactively in response to calls for assistance, but there are also times when a police officer has the opportunity to assist proactively, and to help a person avoid further victimization by helping them secure needed services and resources. The cost of victimization to American society is heavy, both economically and in terms of lost productivity and social capital. Children who are victimized are at risk of all sorts of developmental problems, some of which may lead either to their further victimization during adolescence and beyond, or even worse, to them becoming the type of person who victimizes others.

It is imperative that the criminal justice system in America recognize the absolute necessity for victim services. Unfortunately, when budgets are cut, oftentimes things like victim services are the first to go. The fact is, those who control the budgetary apparatus likely have lived most or all of their lives having never had to endure the effects of physical, emotional, or sexual trauma. They tend not to perceive the need for what they have never needed. It is a problem that must be corrected through public policy and education if we are to break the deadly cycle of victimization that has so plagued modern American society.

Key Terms

Victim	Rape shield laws	Uprooted victim
Victim-centered	Rape kit	Passive victim
Offender-centered	Rape trauma syndrome	Oppressed victim
Stranger rape	Passive assault	Amber alert
Acquaintance rape	Active assault	Death immersion
Statutory rape	Violated victim	Forensic hypnosis
Date rape drug	Assaulted victim	Trance-state

Discussion Questions

1. Many minor drug offenders are serving time in America's prisons, especially in "3-strike" states. Given the oppressive nature of prison life, do you consider these individuals to be "victims of oppression," and therefore in need of victim services, or because they committed some type of crime, should we not consider them victims at all?

2. We have seen cases in America where an adult man is charged with statutory rape when the girl is nearly an adult and fully consenting. Do you consider this girl to really be a victim? What factors do you believe the criminal justice system should weigh when determining whether to criminally charge such a man, even though the letter of the law has been violated?

3. Should the government take any steps or feel any obligation to remove small children from gang-infested neighborhoods in order to proactively reduce the chances of them becoming victims of violence or long-term exposure to violence? Or would such a policy be beyond the scope of the criminal justice mission?

9

The Hostage Crisis

LEARNING OUTCOMES

Upon completion of this chapter the student should be able to:

1. Summarize the dangers associated with a hostage crisis.

2. List the various types of hostage-takers.

3. Explain the structure of the police hostage team.

4. Explain the response methodology of the police hostage team, and to list the various signs of a successful negotiation.

5. Summarize the psychological experience of the hostage during an active hostage crisis.

Chapter Outline

Introduction
    When Things Go Bad: The Case
       of Patrolman Robert Hester
    Other Hostage Disasters
Types of Hostage Situations
    Hostage Profiling Schemes
    A New Classification Scheme
       The Criminal Hostage-Taker
       The Ideological Hostage-Taker
       The Domestic Hostage-Taker
       The Frustration-Driven Hostage-Taker
       The Thought-Disordered Hostage-Taker

The Hostage Team
Response Protocol
    Initial Response
    The Task of the Negotiator
    Demands
    Danger Signs
    Signs of a Successful Negotiation
The Hostage Experience
    The Stockholm Syndrome
Chapter Summary

INTRODUCTION

One of the most stressful types of crisis a police officer may have to confront during their career is one involving a hostage. It is one in which a police officer's ability to effectively communicate may mean the difference between the life and death of an innocent person. It is a crisis that has the capacity to change on a moment's notice from calm to chaotic, and from inert to deadly. It is also one in which multiple contingencies must be in place and ready to rapidly implement in the event of changing circumstances. Police officers do a great deal of training to prepare for the hostage crisis. Negotiators, sharpshooters, and SWAT members all undergo specialized training to carry out their respective missions with one goal in mind: the safe release or rescue of the hostages.

When Things Go Bad: The Case of Patrolman Robert Hester

The case of Patrolman Robert Hester of the Memphis Police Department illustrates just how chaotic and deadly a hostage situation can become. The incident began on January 12, 1983, when Patrolman Hester and his partner responded to a residence in a predominantly African American working-class neighborhood in North Memphis to investigate an earlier purse-snatching (*Time*, 1983). Hester and his partner were allowed into the house where they found themselves outnumbered by 14 members of a strange religious cult who had been drinking and smoking marijuana all day. An official account of the incident (ODMP.org, 2010) describes the deadly events that followed. The two officers attempted to back their way out of the house but the intoxicated men became crazed and attacked them before they could reach the door. In the fight that ensued, Patrolman Hester's partner was disarmed of his weapon and shot in the face as he escaped through the door. He would survive. Patrolman Hester too was disarmed of his weapon, but was unable to escape. He became a hostage.

Other officers quickly arrived on the scene. One officer entered the house firing his service revolver. When he ran out of ammunition he exited, reloaded, and again entered the house firing. Still unable to free Patrolman Hester, he exited the house to retrieve a shotgun and made a third attempt, this time firing his shotgun as he entered the house. It is unknown how many of the occupants the officer wounded or killed that day. Unfortunately, as heroic as his actions were, he was unable to free Patrolman Hester, and a tense 30-hour stand-off began. It was a situation that began violently, and one that would only get worse as the crisis dragged on.

At the time of the incident, the Memphis Police Department's hostage negotiation team had only been in existence for a little over a year, and had little experience (*Daily News*, 2008). Ultimately they were unable to make any meaningful contact with Patrolman Hester's captors. While they continued their efforts to do so, a tactical team moved into position to storm the house if necessary. They were able to lower a microphone from the roof of the house to determine exactly what was happening inside. To their horror, they were met with the sound of Patrolman Hester screaming for help as he was severely beaten by his captors. Even faced with that reality, the tactical team was not allowed to immediately enter the house to attempt a rescue. The decision was made by the commander on the scene to allow the hostage negotiators to continue their efforts to affect a peaceful resolution to the crisis.

One can only imagine the chaos of the situation. An inexperienced negotiating team having little success; a tactical team wanting to rescue their fellow officer and being held back; and at least in the early hours, the sound of Patrolman Hester screaming for help. It was a crisis easily contained, but one where the presence of a hostage and a group of uncooperative hostage-takers made de-escalation difficult, if not impossible, without jeopardizing the safety of the hostage. After nearly 30 hours, long after Patrolman Hester's screams had subsided, the decision was made to allow the tactical team to make a rescue attempt by storming the house with tear gas and flash grenades. When they did they were met by gunfire, and all seven suspects still inside the house were shot and killed by the entry team. Sadly, Patrolman Hester was found beaten to death in a bedroom. It was later determined he had been killed nearly 12 hours before the assault.

Because of cases like the Memphis standoff, police departments in the United States have made great strides in the area of hostage negotiations. In every region of the country there are now highly trained and proficient hostage negotiators ready to move into action at a moment's notice. They are trained not only in the techniques of negotiation, but also in the key indicators that negotiation is no longer a viable option. They are trained in how to coordinate their efforts with other police units, such as tactical entry teams and police sniper units. There simply is no room for turf wars in an active hostage situation, and even less room for insecure or competitive professional egos. The overriding concern is the safe release of the hostages, and those officers engaged in this endeavor, regardless of the role they play, understand this important goal. With increased training and professionalism, the law enforcement community in America has for the most part overcome the types of obstacles that perhaps plagued the chaotic response in Memphis. There is now little hesitation on the part of the police in such situations, and more often than not the hostages are safely released or rescued.

Other Hostage Disasters

Unfortunately in other parts of the world the police have not been so lucky. We have witnessed many examples of untrained police and military units attempting a hostage rescue without first de-escalating the crisis. Many of these situations have had deadly outcomes. A few of the more highly publicized cases include the following:

• *Moscow Theater*:   On October 23, 2002, approximately 50 armed Chechen rebels took 850 people hostage in a Moscow theater. They were supporters of a separatist movement, and were demanding the withdrawal of Russian troops from Chechnya. At that time Russia was in armed conflict with Chechnya. The negotiations, which were chaotic and without design, failed after the imprudent involvement of numerous public officials and a promise to the hostage-takers that they would be granted safe passage to another country. After two days of failed attempts to get the rebels to end the standoff, and after the deaths of an increasing number of hostages, many of them executed, Russian forces introduced a chemical agent into the theater through its ventilation system and stormed the building shortly after. Their intent was to simply put everyone to sleep and then bring the hostage crisis to a peaceful conclusion. Unfortunately though, a number of the rebels had gas masks, and as the Russian forces entered the building a firefight broke out. When it was over, 39 of the rebels lay dead. Even those who were rendered unconscious by the gas were shot and killed where they lay. There were also at least 129 dead hostages, nearly all of them killed by the gas itself. The raid, and the entire manner in which the crisis was handled, was heavily criticized for its lack of organization and the methods employed by the government forces. In the middle of the crisis at least two people even managed to enter the theater to personally plead with the rebels. Both were executed (Dunlop, 2006).

• *Beslan School*:   The Beslan School hostage crisis, which has since become known as the Beslan massacre, also involved Chechen rebels seeking to end their armed conflict with Russian forces. On September 1, 2004, the rebels took more than 1,100 people hostage at Beslan School in the North Caucasus region of the Russian Federation. Among the hostages were 777 children. Like the earlier Moscow Theater crisis, attempts to negotiate the safe release of the hostages failed. On the third day of the stand-off the Russian forces stormed the school using heavy weapons, including tanks and rockets. During the next two hours a violent firefight took place that included police, military personnel, and even a number of local civilians who had arrived with their own weapons. Explosions were heard throughout the school as the rebels fought back. When it was finally over nearly 400 people, most of them hostages, lay dead. Among them were 156 children. Many others were missing and unaccounted for. Even to this day the Russian government is less than forthcoming with official information about the crisis-turned-disaster. Once again, it was a deadly example of a crisis that was perhaps contained, but not de-escalated to any degree before an assault was attempted. When heavy weapons were introduced the focus became less on the hostages and more on the hostage-takers, a deadly error in strategy (Dunlop, 2006).

 • ***Philippine Bus Incident***:   On August 23, 2010, Rolando Mendoza, a former police officer who had been fired for engaging in extortion, boarded a bus in Manila and took 25 people hostage, most of them tourists from Hong Kong. Mendoza was using the incident to protest his firing and to demand reinstatement. Initial attempts to negotiate with Mendoza appeared successful, as nine of the hostages were released without harm. During the next five hours, however, the negotiations began to break down, as Mendoza's demeanor became increasingly more aggressive. His brother, also a police officer, was allowed entry to the secure perimeter with a gun. After he was detained and disarmed, Mendoza's demeanor deteriorated even further, and he was now threatening to shoot hostages. Police finally moved to end the crisis when shots were heard from inside the bus. Rather than a well-planned tactical strike, however, the assault by police was chaotic and disorganized. For nearly an hour the assault team attempted to board the bus. They broke windows and fired their weapons into the bus while Mendoza used his hostages as human shields. Finally, a single shot from a police sniper ended the crisis, but not before eight members of a Hong Kong tourist group were killed. It was the deadliest attack on tourists in Philippine history, and the police were heavily criticized for how they handled the situation (Bloomberg, 2010).

The previous examples clearly demonstrate the need for a well-planned and proven protocol in the event of a hostage crisis. They also demonstrate the need for an established command structure to take control of a situation immediately and maintain that control. In a crisis situation of any type, control is not determined by rank, but rather by who is best qualified to supervise and command the situation. In the event of a hostage crisis, that person must be someone properly trained to understand the dynamics of a hostage situation, and the integrated use of lethal and non-lethal means to contain and de-escalate the matter in order to gain the eventual release of the hostages.

Before we look at the dynamics of an actual hostage crisis, we first must understand the different types of hostage situations. Each has its own type of hostage-taker, with differing motivations and expectations. It is critically important that those who respond to a hostage situation understand these differences. The response to a hostage-taker who does not want to die compared with one who expects to die, or even one who wishes to die, will be much different. This is just one of the factors that must be weighed by the person responsible for managing the crisis. To get it wrong may lead to the death of an innocent hostage.

TYPES OF HOSTAGE SITUATIONS

Hostage Profiling Schemes

A number of profiling schemes attempt to account for the most common types of hostage situations. The *Encyclopedia of Police Science* (Greene, 2006) identifies four types of hostage situations: *criminal*, *mentally ill*, *unorganized groups*, and *terrorists*. In the first category are those individuals who take hostages in an effort to facilitate their escape. These hostage-takers typically have no plans to take hostages, but it becomes necessary after being discovered in the commission of their crime. They use their hostages as human shields and bargaining chips. The most common example of this type of hostage-taker is the individual who robs a bank and is discovered by the police before they have a chance to escape the building.

The mentally ill hostage-taker is simply that, someone who suffers a mental illness, usually schizophrenia, and takes hostages for some irrational purpose. They may believe the world is being invaded by aliens, or that the CIA is following them, or some other belief that compels them to take hostages for reasons that may make sense only to them. They may also take hostages as a way of getting the necessary media attention to warn the world, or some segment of it, of an approaching danger. Mentally ill hostage-takers are not a homogenous group. They are similar only in their irrationality.

Unorganized groups typically take hostages during some spontaneous event like a prison riot. There is no cohesive plan or purpose for taking the hostages. It tends to be the natural inclination of a hostile and unpredictable group, especially inside the walls of a prison where the rioters know they will very quickly be met by overwhelming force. The hostages are used as human shields, bargaining chips, or worst of all, symbolic victims of the rioters' pent-up aggression and vengeance.

The final typology is the terrorist hostage-taker. They are among the most dangerous because they almost always are willing to die for their cause, and to take any hostages with them. The terrorist hostage-takers use their hostages to further some cause, although in recent years we have watched terrorist groups in places like Iraq and Afghanistan take hostages for the sole purpose of publicly murdering them in order to instill fear in the populace and to prevent them from working against the objectives of the group's terror activities.

A typology scheme utilized by the U.S. military (Jones, 2000) classifies hostage situations as *criminal*, *domestic*, or *terrorist*. The major difference from the previous scheme is the addition of the domestic hostage situation. This would include those situations in which a family member or an intimate partner takes someone hostage, oftentimes their own children. These situations play out every single day across the United States, and nearly all of them end peacefully. They typically are initiated by a divorce or relationship split, and suicide is oftentimes a real possibility. When children are involved, many times the hostage-taker will threaten to kill them purely out of vengeance toward the spouse or partner, or to make a final statement before they kill themselves along with the children. The domestic hostage-taker is perhaps the most common, and also among the most dangerous for the hostages.

A New Classification Scheme

The current text proposes a new scheme based on the psychological motivation of the hostage-taker. Perhaps nothing is more critical to the efforts of those responding to a hostage situation than an understanding of the hostage-taker's reasons and motivations for causing the crisis to happen. A classification scheme can facilitate this goal. Using this method we can classify hostage-takers as follows:

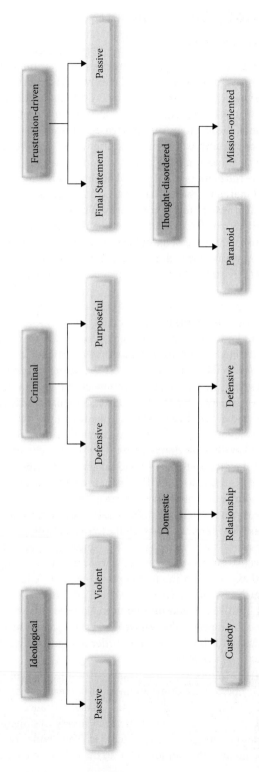

FIGURE 9.1 Classification Scheme for Hostage-takers.

THE CRIMINAL HOSTAGE-TAKER   The criminal hostage-taker is one who uses hostage-taking as a means to a criminal end, or they use hostage-taking as an unintended tactic to escape a particular set of circumstances. In the first case, the **purposeful-criminal hostage-taker**, hostage-taking is an intended tactic used for a specific purpose. An example is a hostage being held for ransom. Another is a hostage being held until a family member can withdraw money from their bank and return with it. And yet another example is the gang member being held by a rival gang until the hostage's own gang delivers quantities of drugs, guns, or money. In each case, the act of taking a hostage is one of the elements of the offense.

The **defensive-criminal hostage-taker** is one who initially does not intend to take hostages, but is forced to as events unfold. The most common is the bank robbery gone bad. When police show up outside the bank before the robber can make a getaway, they may take hostages in a moment of irrational judgment thinking they can use them as bargaining chips. Another example is the individual who enters a home or workplace to harm a specific person, and then takes hostages when it becomes apparent that the police have already responded to the scene. Unlike the purposeful-criminal hostage-taker, the defensive-criminal hostage-taker typically makes the decision to take hostages during the commission of another offense and while in a panic. They may be highly agitated and unpredictable as their situation worsens, and may even become suicidal.

THE IDEOLOGICAL HOSTAGE-TAKER   The ideological hostage-taker takes hostages to make a political, social, or religious statement of some type. The **violent-ideological hostage-taker** is willing to kill or be killed for what in their mind is a higher calling and purpose. Here we find what are commonly referred to as *terrorists*. We witnessed this type of hostage-taking at the Munich Olympics in 1972, the American Embassy in Tehran in 1979, and the numerous kidnappings that took place in Lebanon in the 1980s. In more recent years we have seen numerous hostages taken by radical Muslims in places like Iraq and Afghanistan, usually with deadly results. This type of hostage-taking is usually carried out for the purpose of drawing attention to some particular cause. For example, in the case of the Munich Olympics, its purpose was to draw attention to the Palestinian issue. These hostage-takers are extremely dangerous because in most cases the hostage-takers are prepared to die for their cause. They are also typically desensitized by training or experience to the pain and suffering of their hostages.

In contrast to the more violent type, the **passive-ideological hostage-taker** is less inclined to harm their hostages. For them, the message they are attempting to convey is the most important aspect of their mission, and many times their message is peaceful in nature. An example would be an animal rights activist who holds a corporate CEO hostage in order to get the message out about animal experimentation taking place inside the CEO's company. The underlying issues that prompt such hostage-taking can include environmental issues, abortion, access to pharmaceuticals and health care, and immigration, to name a few. Passive-ideological hostage situations almost always end peacefully. Those who participate in such hostage-taking see greater benefit in living beyond the hostage event in order to argue and protest their cause.

THE DOMESTIC HOSTAGE-TAKER   Perhaps the greatest number of hostage situations handled by the police in a given period are domestic in nature, meaning they involve hostages who are family members or significant others of the hostage-taker. Because there is an emotional connection between hostage and hostage-taker, sometimes a very dysfunctional one, these situations can be very volatile, and often have tragic outcomes. They typically involve deep-seeded emotional issues like attachment and abandonment, so the risk of an escalating crisis is high.

The first of the three domestic subtypes to be discussed is the **custody-related hostage-taker**. This type of case happens practically every day somewhere in America. It almost always involves a divorce and custody battle over the couple's children. Eventually either one parent refuses to give up custody, or they take off with the kids in defiance of a court order. In either case the police are called in, the parent barricades themselves with the children inside a house or hotel, and a hostage standoff begins. This is an extremely dangerous situation, especially if the parent is already suicidal. There is a heightened risk that the parent will kill the children before taking his own life. Never should the danger of a situation be underestimated because it involves the hostage-taker's own children.

The second subtype is the **relationship-related hostage-taker**. This type of case involves an individual, usually a man, holding his spouse or girlfriend at gunpoint following a breakup or divorce. It can happen wherever the hostage-taker is able to track down their target; at home, their place of employment, their church, or possibly even their school. Many times the hostage-taker has no intentions of taking a hostage when they approach the other individual. Most of the time they simply want to talk or make a last-ditch effort to convince the other person to take them back. They may be armed as a way of forcing the other person to listen to what they have to say, or as a way of manipulating the other person by threatening suicide if they refuse to take them back. When such an event is witnessed and the police are called, there is a high likelihood that a hostage standoff will ensue. At the heart of this type of hostage situation is the issue of abandonment. The hostage-taker perceives themselves as not being able to live without their target. It is one of the most dangerous and intense emotions the police will have to confront. In many cases the hostage-taker is simply unable to think rationally, or to consider any viable alternatives to the dangerous course of action they have chosen.

The third and final domestic subtype is the **domestic-defensive hostage-taker**. The police may show up at someone's house for a number of reasons. Perhaps they have an outstanding arrest warrant for someone inside, or maybe the sheriff is there to remove the occupants from a foreclosed house. They may be there to question someone inside about a recent crime, or to check on the welfare of the children after being notified by the school that one of them showed signs of physical abuse. Whatever the reason, there are frequent cases when the police approach a house only to have someone inside either take a shot at them, or display a gun through the door in a threatening manner. Obviously in either case there will be a strong police response, which may include even a tactical entry team. Oftentimes when the police show up in force, the person will barricade themselves inside the house with their family. Such a situation is certainly to be considered a hostage situation if the family members are not free to leave. In most such cases the hostage-taker has no desire or plans to harm their hostages, usually their own family members. They simply make an irrational decision in a moment of panic. Most such cases end peacefully.

THE FRUSTRATION-DRIVEN HOSTAGE-TAKER The next major category of hostage-taker is the frustration-driven person. These are people who use hostage-taking as a way of making a personal statement. They are not ideologically driven individuals who wish to make a political, social, or religious statement, but rather, people who are frustrated over some circumstance in their personal lives. They may be a **passive-frustration hostage-taker**, and have no intentions of hurting anyone, including their hostages. This type of situation was played out in the movie *John Q*, (New Line Cinema, 2002). It is the story of a father who takes hospital staff hostage until they agree to place his young son on a waiting list for a heart transplant after his insurance company refuses to cover the procedure. This type of hostage-taker seldom resorts to violence, and can almost always be talked down from their act of desperation.

In contrast, the **final statement hostage-taker** is one who has reached a breaking point, and the act of taking hostages is used to insure that their frustrations are heard by making the event as dramatic as possible. They tend to be people whose frustration has led them to take the most desperate of actions. Perhaps they hold hostage a judge after the judge sentences a family member to a lengthy prison term. Or perhaps they hold bank employees hostage after the bank forecloses on their home. The common characteristic of this type of hostage-taker is a frustration level that has caused them to feel as though they are simply out of options. Many, if not most of these individuals are suicidal, making it an extremely dangerous situation for the hostages. What sets it apart from the passive subtype is that these hostage-takers fully intend to end their situation violently, either with the death of the hostage, themselves, or both.

THE THOUGHT-DISORDERED HOSTAGE-TAKER   The final category of hostage-taker is the **thought-disordered** individual. This is an individual who by all measures is mentally ill and out of touch with reality. It is likely they would ultimately be judged incompetent to stand trial for their crimes due to their delusional thinking. Two subtypes are in this category. The first, the **paranoid hostage-taker**, is someone who suffers from the delusional belief that they are in some type of danger. They may take hostages as a way of bargaining their way out of their imagined situation. Or they may believe the hostages are somehow involved. In the latter case, the hostage-taker may target a particular company they believe to be involved in a plan to hurt or kill them. Or they may take a neighbor hostage under the delusional belief that the neighbor is a CIA agent tasked with spying on them. The paranoid is an extremely dangerous individual in this type of scenario. They feel they are in a corner with no way out, and any attempt to get them to think rationally will likely fail.

In the second subtype, the **mission-oriented hostage-taker**, the delusional hostage-taker believes they must take action against a particular person or group because of a perceived threat they pose, or because they are being directed by someone or something. For example, the mission-oriented hostage-taker may hold the members of a particular church hostage because God is telling them that a demon has infected the minds of its members. Or they may hold the employees of a bank hostage because they believe the bank is involved in a conspiracy to control the world. The mission-oriented hostage-taker believes they are doing the right and necessary thing. They differ from the paranoid hostage-taker in that they are not motivated by what they perceive as a personal attack or threat, but rather by what they believe to be a danger or threat to the larger social order or any of its subgroups.

The benefit of a classification scheme such as this is that those who respond, especially the hostage negotiators, can immediately adjust their response to what has been found to be the most successful de-escalation method for the particular type of hostage crisis they are responding to.

THE HOSTAGE TEAM

Regardless of the typology of the hostage-taker, the police response is the same. Someone who has been specially trained in hostage negotiations responds to attempt to bring the event to a peaceful resolution by negotiating with the hostage-taker. How they negotiate is in large part determined by the type of hostage-taker they are facing. Hostage negotiators are almost always police officers. In some cases there may be a behavioral specialist, such as a psychologist, present to assist. According to Dr. Laurence Miller (2007), crisis negotiations should be pursued in a team format. The team should be multidimensional and consist of the following core components:

- *Team leader:* The team leader is a person of rank who commands the crisis negotiation team. They are responsible for selecting its members, making sure all have been properly trained, and overseeing their actual deployment when a hostage crisis occurs. The team leader will interact with the on-scene commander and the tactical team leader at a crisis event to develop the most effective plans for either rescuing or negotiating the safe release of the hostages. If negotiations are attempted, then the team leader has full command of the process. It will be the team leader who will advise the on-scene commander when negotiations have failed, and a tactical entry may become necessary. In that event, then the tactical team leader will take charge of a rescue attempt.

- *Primary negotiator:* Once it has been decided that negotiations will be attempted, the team leader will select one of their personnel to be the primary negotiator. This selection will be based on the experience of the negotiator, the demographics of the hostage-taker, and the type of hostage event being negotiated. There may be cases when it is decided that a female negotiator may be more effective. Other situations may call for a male negotiator. Obviously the language of the hostage-taker must be considered. If the person's primary language is Spanish, then it may be best to select a Spanish-speaking negotiator. Sometimes the ethnicity of the hostage-taker must be considered. Responding to a crisis is not a time to simply use the next person in line as the primary negotiator. It is absolutely critical that the primary negotiator be able to build rapport with the hostage-taker. Thus it is also critical that the team leader select an individual they believe will have the ability to do so, and to take into consideration all factors when deploying them.

- *Secondary negotiator:* If the department has the luxury of having multiple staff trained to conduct hostage negotiations, then a secondary negotiator should be deployed to work beside the primary. The purpose for having a secondary is to take over if the primary is unable to establish rapport, or if the primary must take a break after hours of negotiating. The secondary negotiator works side by side with the primary in order to have full knowledge of the negotiations in the event that they must take over. The secondary is fully trained to serve as a primary negotiator, and may have done so in previous cases.

- *Intelligence officer:* This individual is responsible for finding out as much about the hostage-taker and the hostages as possible. It is helpful to know the background of the hostage-taker. Who are their family members? Do they have a history of violence? Were they recently terminated from a job? Any close friends? Do they have a religious background, and is there a religious leader with whom they have a relationship? All of these bits of information can be extremely helpful to the negotiator. Also, who are the hostages? Were they specifically targeted or randomly selected? The more the negotiator knows about the principal players, the more power they have. The intelligence officer must keep a steady flow of information coming to the negotiator. If the hostage-taker makes a cryptic comment, such as a vague reference to not wanting to return to prison, the intelligence officer immediately attempts to determine its relevance. Was the person ever in prison? For how long, and for what crimes? Do they have a parole officer? In the latter case, a person's parole officer typically has access to their entire psychosocial history. The intelligence officer would immediately track that person down and engage their assistance.

- *Communications officer:* In any hostage crisis, communication is a critical component. The communications officer is responsible for making sure all lines of communication remain open and unobstructed. This individual may be a dispatcher or a tech services officer from within the department. First and foremost, a method of communication must be established between the negotiator and the hostage-taker. Oftentimes this is done with a **throw phone**, a phone with a dedicated line the negotiation team attempts to get in the hands of the hostage-taker. If a phone already on the premises is to be used, the communications officer will attempt to ring the number and establish contact.

At any hostage situation there are a number of police units present that are being directed by separate commanders. It is important that all of these units are in constant communication. They may include tactical entry team members, snipers, uniformed patrol officers, and canine officers. The situation can become quite chaotic rather quickly unless there is a central dispatch center responsible for maintaining the lines of communication. The communication officer oversees this function. Additionally, they may be responsible for surveillance equipment. In many hostage situations, if the structure permits it, the tactical team will attempt to get a microphone and video camera inside the building to provide real-time feedback on what is happening inside. The communications officer must ensure that the information is in working order, and that the information is accessible by the negotiator. In the ideal situation, the negotiator works from a mobile command center, which also serves as the mobile communications center, equipped with all the necessary equipment to effectively carry out the task of negotiating the safe release of the hostages.

• **Public information officer**:   Given the nature of a hostage crisis, it almost always catches the eyes and ears of the news media while it is still in progress. The public information officer is responsible for the release of information to the media during and after the event. This task can potentially have serious implications, especially if the hostage-taker is monitoring the news. The PI officer must weigh the public's desire for information against the impact the release of that information will have on the safety of the hostages. To have erroneous or emotionally charged information make its way to the media could agitate the hostage-taker and create a more volatile situation. It is also important that no information be released about tactical plans, including videotape of the tactical entry team moving into position for an assault. The PI officer must do everything they can to protect the operation, and thus the hostages, from too much or inappropriate media coverage.

Following the event, it is the PI officer who then briefs the media on the outcome of the case, always making sure not to discuss evidence in the case, nor to violate the confidentiality of the victims. In a protracted hostage situation—some have lasted for days—the PI officer will hold regular briefings with the media to release as much information as possible without compromising the operation.

• **Team psychologist**:   Police officers may be trained to become very effective hostage negotiators, but they are not necessarily behavioral specialists. If the department has the luxury of a staff psychologist, or even one who is contracted by the department for such incidents, they can be an important addition to the team. A staff forensic psychologist can provide behavioral profiles of the hostages and the hostage-taker based on the available evidence and intelligence. This information can perhaps point to areas of weakness in the hostage-taker for the negotiator to attempt to exploit. They can provide on-scene risk assessments to assist the team in knowing when a hostage-taker is preparing to break off negotiations and harm a hostage. They can gauge the emotional impact of the incident on the hostages, and perhaps assist the negotiator in bargaining for the release of vulnerable hostages. A forensic psychologist can also study the comments and demands of the hostage-taker and attempt to determine their intentions from that information.

Another area where a staff forensic psychologist can play an important role in the process relates to the negotiators themselves. The task of negotiating the release of hostages can be extremely stressful for the negotiator, especially given that the skill of the negotiator may mean the difference between the hostages' safe release and possible harm. This responsibility can weigh heavily on the mind of a negotiator. The staff psychologist can monitor the behavior and reactions of the negotiator to look for signs that the stress is beginning to have a negative impact on their performance. When that becomes apparent, then it is the responsibility of the team leader to make the decision either to allow the negotiator to continue, or to have the secondary negotiator take over.

Finally, once the event is brought to its conclusion, the staff psychologist can take responsibility for any critical incident debriefing activities that take place. It is common for law enforcement officers to second-guess their performance. Hostage negotiators are no different. In those cases when the crisis turns out for the worst and hostages are harmed or killed, the team members are at risk of experiencing a significant stress reaction, and may even develop Post-traumatic Stress Disorder (PTSD) as a result of the experience. The benefit of having a staff psychologist as part of the team is that they will be in a position to monitor the team members for a period of time after the crisis to look for signs of a stress reaction, and to refer those in need of services to an appropriate provider.

RESPONSE PROTOCOL

Initial Response

Although it is important that the police response to a hostage crisis be adapted to the specific situation confronting them, there are some basic protocols that must be followed in almost every case. First, like any crisis, it must be contained by a secure perimeter so that all potential escape routes are cut off, and no one but the police are able to enter the area. It is absolutely imperative that once negotiations are under way they are not disrupted by bystanders, news media, or just curious citizens trying to get too close. Also, without the foreknowledge of what types of weapons the hostage-taker may have in their possession, it must be assumed that they have weapons capable of hitting targets at long range, such as a high-powered rifle. For this reason a containment perimeter must be established immediately.

After the area has been secured and the hostage team deployed, then the next critical task is to establish a communication link with the hostage-taker. Without this important step, no negotiations can begin. It is important to engage the hostage-taker immediately in order to distract them from considering a violent response to the police showing up. A communication link is made by any available means. There may be a telephone inside the premises that can be called by the police in hopes of having the hostage-taker answer. There may be a cell phone that can be called if the police have ascertained the number through their initial intelligence gathering. If there are no other options, the hostage team will attempt to use a throw phone. As the name suggests, this phone is designed to withstand the impact of being thrown inside a door or window, or even over a wall in an effort to get the phone into the hands of the hostage-taker so the negotiator can make contact. As a last resort, the negotiator will attempt to make contact over a bullhorn if no other means exist.

The Task of the Negotiator

Once communication is established, then the first task of the negotiator is to attempt to build rapport with the hostage-taker. According to Miller (2007), the following strategies can be employed by the negotiator for this purpose:

- The negotiator should open with a statement of introduction that conveys honesty and credibility, and a sense of confidence that the crisis will be resolved peacefully. An example might be as follows:

"This is Det. John Davis of the Chicago Police Dept. I'm here to listen to you, and to make sure everyone inside the building stays safe until we can resolve this matter peacefully."

- The negotiator should ask the hostage-taker what he likes to be called, and then address him accordingly. This shows respect for the hostage-taker, a great rapport builder. It is also true that people are more responsive when being addressed in a way family and friends do. The negotiator can take advantage of this conditioning process to facilitate a quick connection with the hostage-taker on an emotional level. If the hostage-taker fails to respond to this request, then the negotiator should use a name that conveys respect, such as Mr. or sir. Slang or nicknames should be avoided unless the hostage-taker indicates that they wish to be called by such a name.
- Voice modulation is important. The negotiator's voice should remain calm and steady. A high-pitched voice or a quickened rate of speech should be avoided in order to avoid the hostage-taker naturally mirroring those speech patterns and becoming further agitated. Also, the negotiator should adapt their speech to the level of hostage-taker's vocabulary. The hostage-taker will likely be agitated and confused already, so to talk above them will only confuse them more. Conversely, to try too hard to mimic their level of speech may be perceived as disingenuous and condescending. Finally, although profanity works in the movies, it doesn't in real life. Even if it is being used by the hostage-taker, the negotiator should avoid such speech. It could potentially agitate rather than calm the hostage-taker.
- In most cases the hostage-taker will want to express a lot of frustration, fear, anger, or other negative emotions right up front. The negotiator should allow the person to vent, but make an effort to control the situation so that the venting doesn't spiral out of control and agitate the person to the point of becoming violent. The negotiator can do this with their voice and limited responses. They should keep a calm and steady voice, and practice the active listening skills discussed in Chapter 3 of this text (i.e., minimal encouragements, paraphrasing, emotion-labeling, etc.). By allowing the hostage-taker to vent, it demonstrates the negotiator's interest in hearing what they have to say.
- The negotiator should keep the focus of the discussion on the hostage-taker and not the hostages. It is best to keep their focus as much as possible off the hostages. The negotiator should make an effort to determine the medical condition of the hostages, but they should make it appear as a secondary consideration to the hostage-taker's welfare. An example might be:

"Are you okay (name)? Are you in need of any medical attention? Does anyone else need medical attention? Is everyone safe?"

- The negotiator should downplay what the hostage-taker has done to this point, even if people have been injured or killed. The goal is to avoid further violence, so the negotiator should be encouraging and remind the hostage-taker that things have not gotten any worse, and that this is a positive step toward resolving the crisis. The negotiator must be careful not to sound as though nothing has happened and that everything will be okay, especially if people have been harmed. This will be perceived as disingenuous. The hostage-taker knows full well what they have done. To minimize it will sound like trickery. The goal is to focus away from what they have done, and instead onto something positive. The best way to do this is to focus on what they have not done, such as harm people, or in the event people have been harmed, that they have not further harmed any people.

- The negotiator should complement the hostage-taker for any positive actions taken. This plays to the desire we all share for positive strokes, especially from authority figures—a lasting remnant of the parent–child relationship. The goal is to create a pattern of constructive acts by the hostage-taker through positive reinforcement.

Demands

At the heart of any hostage negotiation is a series of demands. They can range from simple demands, such as a demand for food and water, to the more grandiose and complex, such as a demand for media access or a helicopter. A few cardinal rules are followed by hostage negotiators when dealing with demands. First and foremost, the hostage-taker never gets anything without giving something in return. To do so would reinforce and empower the hostage-taker. By making an even exchange the balance of power is not tipped by the dynamics of the demand, but instead remains the same, hopefully in favor of the negotiator. Consider the following exchange:

HOSTAGE-TAKER: *"I want some food in here now!"*

NEGOTIATOR: *"That shouldn't be a problem, but I need you to do something for me, okay? I need you to agree to keep this line open so we can talk. Can you do that?"*

The goal is to always get some concession without agitating the hostage-taker to the point of breaking off negotiations and possibly harming people. By gaining concessions, the negotiator maintains a bargaining position, and the hostage-taker is conditioned to expect this give and take with each demand. In reality, each time the hostage-taker does agree to give something up, the negotiator increases their power over the situation.

A few other rules are standard when negotiating with a hostage-taker. First, never solicit a demand, nor suggest something not specifically asked for. Additionally, never deliver more than what was agreed to. It would be wrong, for example, to deliver twice as much food than what was asked for in the belief that such a generous act will convince the hostage-taker to release people. In reality what it will do is empower the hostage-taker, and in their perception of things, increase their power and control. Also, the negotiator should avoid saying "no" to a demand. If the demand is realistic but not possible, then the negotiator should put off accepting or rejecting the demand, and instead shift the focus away from the issue. For example:

HOSTAGE-TAKER: *"I want a helicopter and a bag with $100,000 in it on board."*

NEGOTIATOR: *"Something like that will take some time. You need to work with me here. You mentioned earlier you were upset about losing your job. What kind of work did you do?"*

You can see in this exchange that the negotiator doesn't refuse the demand, but instead neutralizes it somewhat by shifting the focus to another issue without empowering the hostage-taker with a "yes," nor agitating them with a "no." There are times when the demand is simply not realistic. In this case the negotiator must be careful not to reinforce this type of thinking, but instead bring the negotiations back to a more realistic dialogue. For example:

HOSTAGE-TAKER: *"I want a helicopter on the roof, and I want the power shut off city-wide."*

NEGOTIATOR: *"I don't think I can pull that off. It would take days to power down the entire city. Let's talk about what we can do …"*

Sometimes the hostage-taker will set deadlines. The goal is to simply ignore the deadline, and deflect the conversation to another issue. The negotiator should never mention the deadline, and make every effort to keep the hostage-taker talking and focused on things other than the deadline. The longer the negotiator can keep the hostage-taker talking without getting agitated, the better the chances for a peaceful resolution to the crisis.

At some point in the negotiations the negotiator will begin to bargain for the release of hostages. This can and will be a counteroffer at the first opportunity the negotiator has after building some rapport with the hostage-taker. The general rule is to let the hostage-taker suggest how many will be released and negotiate from there. The negotiator should seek the release first of those who are the most trouble for the hostage-taker, such as children and anyone who might be injured. Care must be taken, however, not to cause the hostage-taker to change their mind. If they offer to release three hostages, and an attempt by the negotiator to get five released is met with immediate resistance, then it is best to back down and get the three out safely.

Danger Signs

At any point during the negotiations it is important for the negotiator to know when it is time to hand the operation over to the tactical team leader. Strentz (1993) has pointed out a number of indicators that point to a potentially violent outcome. They include the following:

- *A depressed hostage-taker who denies thoughts of suicide:* Any hostage-taker has considered the potential implications of their act, and many, if not most, have considered the possibility of taking their own life. When a hostage-taker who shows clear signs of depression or despair denies suicidal thoughts, then that is an indication that they are not being open and honest with the negotiator. Anytime a hostage-taker is not being candid with the negotiator it is a danger sign. It indicates that they have no desire for a legitimate dialogue with the police, and thus have no plans to make it out of their predicament alive.
- *No rapport:* No effective negotiations can begin until there is some amount of rapport established between the hostage-taker and the negotiator. There are times when rapport simply cannot be established because the hostage-taker refuses to have direct communication with anyone. They may have one of the hostages act as a go-between. Or perhaps they ask for a particular media person to act as the go-between, and then refuse any further communication until that person arrives. They may also suffer from a mental illness that precludes the negotiator from establishing rapport. Whatever the case, a lack of rapport must always be taken as a danger sign.
- *The subject insists on face-to-face negotiations:* It is never advisable for a negotiator to meet face-to-face with a hostage-taker, especially one who is armed, as most are. It indicates an ulterior motive on the part of the hostage-taker, perhaps a plan to take the negotiator hostage or to brandish a weapon and get the police to shoot and cause a "suicide by cop." A demand for a face-to-face meeting, especially a persistent demand, should always be looked upon as a sign of violent intentions.
- *Subject sets a deadline for their own death:* Anytime a hostage-taker discusses a deadline for their own death it should be taken seriously and considered a sign that they will likely either harm or kill the hostages just before killing themselves. When a person has made the decision to die, they become very egocentric. Any concern for their hostages will likely evaporate when they become singularly focused on their own death. For a negotiator, when such a deadline approaches and the hostage-taker discontinues their dialogue, that is when a decision must be made whether to let the deadline pass or to attempt a rescue with a tactical entry.

- *Verbal will:* When a hostage-taker begins discussing final arrangements, the final disposition of their personal property, or they ask that good-bye messages be relayed to loved ones, this is a sign that the crisis will potentially have a violent outcome unless some intervention is attempted. An experienced negotiator will attempt to deflect this type of talk and keep the focus on other issues, but if it persists, then a decision will have to be made about whether to continue the negotiations or attempt a rescue.

- *Refusal to negotiate:* A refusal to negotiate is always a danger sign. It typically means the hostage-taker has developed a plan, and that they have no desire to deviate from that plan. This happens often in cases where the hostage-taker actually selects his hostages, such as an individual who returns to their place of employment to kill those employees they feel are responsible for their termination. They have no need to negotiate because their plan to kill the hostages and then themselves is final. They hold them hostage to make them suffer and to demonstrate their power and control over them. They may also be holding the hostages to allow time for an audience to gather, especially the media. This gives them the chance to make a "final statement" of their frustrations before ending the episode with violence. If there is no attempt to negotiate then a negotiator is of no value. In this situation, the tactical team leader begins to prepare immediately for a tactical entry, or a sniper may be given the green light to attempt to bring the event to a close with a single deadly shot.

- *Hostage-taker insists on a particular person being brought to the scene:* This may be an attempt by the hostage-taker to gain an audience to their own death, either by suicide, or perhaps by provoking the police to shoot. Part of the important task of the intelligence officer is to learn as much as possible about the person the hostage-taker wishes to see, and why they wish to see them. If it is a person with whom the hostage-taker has an emotional connection, then it is critical that the negotiator understand the dynamics of their relationship. It is seldom advisable to have the person actually show up and make their presence known to the hostage-taker; however, if it is determined that the person is a symbol of safety, such as a parent or grandparent, then perhaps they will be allowed to speak over the telephone with the hostage-taker. If it is determined that the requested person has a strained relationship with the hostage-taker, then any contact must be avoided in order not to agitate the hostage-taker and cause them to become violent.

- *Isolation or dehumanization of hostages:* Whenever a hostage-taker isolates their hostages, or dehumanizes them by covering their heads, this is an extremely dangerous situation. It indicates that the hostage-taker views them only as objects that can be used to further their objective. Two things happen to the hostage-taker as a crisis wears on. First, as the adrenaline wears off and exhaustion sets in, their perception of events may shift, and what initially seemed like a workable plan may now begin to seem hopeless. The other thing that hopefully happens is that some type of rapport is established between the hostage-taker and at least some of their hostages. The more human the hostages become to the hostage-taker, the less likely it is they will be harmed. It is important for the negotiation team to determine the quality of the relationship that is being established between the hostage-taker and the hostages. Are the hostages being called by their names? Is there casual conversation taking place? Are the hostages being offered food and water? Such things are important to know, because if these types of things are not happening, then the hostage-taker has dehumanized their hostages, and the danger level rises dramatically.

- *Weapon is tied to the hostage-taker:* If a hostage-taker attaches a weapon to their hands, it is a good indication of two things. First, they don't intend to ever put the gun down. And second, they hope to shoot even in the event they are shot. This is especially true if they also have the barrel of the gun taped or tied to a hostage. A hostage-taker who does this is not necessarily suicidal. In fact, they may very much want to escape, especially if the gun is attached to a hostage. This is a situation where eventually the hostage-taker will expose themselves to the police as they walk to an escape vehicle. However, it is not a situation for the cops surrounding the hostage-taker to begin shooting. The hostage-taker has every intention of killing the hostage if they are shot, and chances are they will be successful. Rather, this is a situation that requires the skill of the negotiator to convince the hostage-taker to expose themselves at just the right location, and an expert sniper to immobilize the individual with a single shot. It must be assumed that if the hostage-taker were to escape, the hostage will in fact be killed at some point.

- *Excessive ammunition and multiple weapons:* This indicator speaks for itself. Anyone who has armed themselves with excessive amounts of weaponry and ammunition is preparing to make a defense, and likely has no intentions of being arrested. They fully realize they will not survive the assault, and their goal is to take as many people with them as possible. In a hostage situation, this becomes an extremely volatile situation, especially if the hostage-taker is also isolating and dehumanizing the hostages.
- *No clear demands, outrageous demands, changing demands:* The final indicator is the hostage-taker who simply does not negotiate clearly and consistently. They are not necessarily looking for a way out of their predicament. In most cases they are simply stalling for time. They may be trying to build up the courage to make a final statement, or perhaps they simply don't have the courage to do so, at least not by committing suicide. They may be enjoying the attention they are getting, or the power and control they perceive themselves as having. They may be mentally ill, or they may even be a juvenile. A juvenile hostage-taker is always an indicator of potential violence because of their inability at times to truly understand the finality of death or the implications of their actions. They may also commit violent acts for symbolic and grandiose reasons, which adults tend not to do. This makes it ever more likely that they may take a dramatic step at some point during the standoff. It also makes it more difficult to negotiate with them in the same way as an adult.

As is true with all indicators of potential violence, it is the job of the negotiating team to weigh all the available evidence that either supports or argues against the probability that a violent act by the hostage-taker is imminent. Obviously it is not a scientific process. Much depends on the experience of the team members and their ability to properly read the hostage-taker. When it becomes apparent that the danger level is rising to the point of placing the hostages in imminent danger of being harmed, there is no option at that point but a tactical entry. If done correctly, and time permitting, the tactical team is prepared and in place before the negotiations reach this point. They hopefully have been able to insert a microphone and perhaps even a micro video camera inside the hostage location to get the layout and to determine exactly where the hostages are located. They also hopefully can identify what type of weaponry the hostage-taker has, including the presence of any bombs. With this type of intelligence, the tactical entry team is prepared to move in through a predetermined entry point on their team leader's command.

Signs of a Successful Negotiation

Just as there are indicators that signal danger during a hostage crisis, there are also those that point to success. Strentz (2006) points out 11 indicators that a peaceful resolution to the crisis can be achieved. They are as follows:

- *A trusting relationship with negotiator:* It is imperative that a hostage-taker trust the person with whom they are negotiating. The more they do, the greater the likelihood of a peaceful outcome. This trusting relationship will be evidenced by the hostage-taker talking less about demands, and more about what is really on their mind.

- *Talk of personal needs and issues:* When the hostage-taker begins to personalize and talk about personal needs and concerns, again, it is a very good indicator that a peaceful resolution will be reached. The hostage-taker may begin to portray themselves as a victim, and to discuss their troubles with the negotiator.

- *Longer periods of talk:* One of the primary goals of hostage negotiations is to keep the hostage-taker talking. When they are talking they typically are not thinking ahead and planning, nor are they ruminating about the future and getting themselves depressed and suicidal. Silence is never a good sign, nor is it when the negotiator has to work at keeping the hostage-taker talking. When they talk freely however, and remained engaged for longer periods of time, especially when the talk is less about demands, then that is an excellent sign that the negotiator has established a trusting relationship with the hostage-taker. Once again, there is no better sign that a peaceful resolution will be reached.

- *Non-violent subject:* If no one has yet been harmed, then it is a good indicator that the hostage-taker has no intentions of doing so. Certainly there are exceptions to this rule, such as in the case of terrorist hostage-takers, but aside from that type of situation, non-violence, especially if the hostage-taker has no history of violence, is an excellent indicator of success.

- *Expectations have been reduced:* An experienced negotiator will be able to focus the hostage-taker away from unrealistic demands. When the hostage-taker no longer demands such things as helicopters, large amounts of cash, or the release of friends and colleagues from prison, then they likely have accepted that their original plan has failed. A good sign is when their demands shift to things relating to personal safety, and to their treatment by the police and the court system. They may now demand a lawyer, or to be incarcerated in a particular jail to await trial. In any case, when demands shift to post-event plans and expectations, there is an excellent chance that the crisis will end peacefully.

- *A decrease in threatening behavior:* When a hostage-taker decreases their violent talk or actions, this is a good sign that exhaustion may be taking hold. As we learned in Chapter 2, when the body remains at an elevated stress level for a period of time, eventually the internal mechanisms that protect the individual from the effects of stress begin to fail. This is when exhaustion sets in and the individual can no longer think as clearly. This is a desired state to get the hostage-taker to, and is precisely why the negotiator will stall for as much time as possible.

- *Humanizing hostages:* It is always a good sign when the hostage-taker refers to the hostages by their names. They are no longer just objects to further the hostage-taker's plan. It is a sign that the hostage-taker has made an emotional connection with the hostages. This makes it increasingly more difficult for the hostage-taker to bring harm to them. The humanizing of hostages is a sign the negotiator should always be on the lookout for.

- *Passing of deadline without incident:* When a hostage-taker issues a deadline, and then the deadline passes without incident, there is a good chance that a peaceful outcome will be achieved. If the ultimatum given by the hostage-taker involves killing a hostage though, this is when the negotiator must make an informed decision about the hostage-taker's intention to follow through. If there are indicators that they will in fact harm or kill a hostage, it may then become necessary to attempt a tactical entry to rescue the hostages.

- *Release of hostages:* This is almost always a good sign, especially if the hostages being released fail to improve the hostage-taker's position with their release. For example, if the hostage-taker begins releasing children and other vulnerable hostages, this is a good sign. A hostage-taker wanting to force a demand without the threat of a tactical assault is best served by keeping children as hostages. No negotiator or tactical commander wants to risk the death of children during a tactical entry unless it is absolutely necessary. The negotiator will actually construct a list of hostages, and develop a priority list in the event the negotiation leads to an agreement to release some of them. If those the negotiator seeks to get released first are the ones the hostage-taker seems unwilling to release, then this certainly is less of a positive sign. In fact, it may be a sign that the hostage-taker is releasing those who are most dangerous to them, such as adult men. There is likely a zero-net gain in the negotiator's position by this type of hostage release.
- *Routine exchange of material goods for hostages:* This indicates a trusting relationship between hostage-taker and negotiator. It indicates that the hostage-taker is becoming more focused on needs rather than on demands. With each exchange the hostage-taker is further conditioned to release additional hostages in return for something else. It also continues to facilitate a sense of trust between the hostage-taker and the negotiator when the negotiator complies with the agreed-upon exchange and demonstrates their willingness to negotiate in good faith.
- *Defensive threats:* At some point the hostage-taker may shift from offensive to defensive threats. An offensive threat is one in which the hostage-taker threatens to take an action if the police do NOT follow through on something. For example, the hostage-taker may threaten to kill one hostage every hour until a helicopter is brought to the roof of the location. In contrast, a defensive threat is one in which the hostage-taker threatens an action if the police DO follow through on something. For example, a hostage-taker may threaten to kill a hostage if the police attempt to enter the location. This type of defensive threat is guaranteed not to be acted upon without the police initiating it. Thus, they are in a position to effectively manage the threat. This type of threat also indicates that perhaps the hostage-taker is becoming more concerned about their own safety, always a good sign to a negotiator.

Eventually, with enough positive signs that the negotiation process is working, the negotiator must make an effort to end the crisis. Ending a hostage crisis is similar to a salesman *closing* the deal. An experienced negotiator knows that the timing of the attempt is important. To attempt to bring the crisis to an end too early may cause the hostage-taker to regroup their thoughts and accuse the negotiator of manipulating them. To wait too long may give the hostage-taker time to think about what has transpired and their reasons for doing what they did. They may get angry all over again, or if they spend too much time thinking about their legal predicament, especially the real possibility of losing their freedom, then a sense of hopelessness and despair may set in, and they could become suicidal.

When the negotiator feels the time is appropriate they will seek the hostage-taker's commitment to bring the crisis to an end. It is then a matter of the negotiator and hostage-taker agreeing to a **surrender ritual**, or the manner in which the hostage-taker desires to end the crisis. To some extent, when a hostage-taker agrees to bring it to an end and release the hostages, their concern becomes how the world will perceive them. Some want the police to pull up close to the location and spirit them away in a squad car without the public getting much of a glimpse. Others want to walk out proudly, and in full view of the cameras. Some even want the tactical team to tackle them when they walk out in order to give the appearance of toughness, and of not

ISSUES & ETHICS IS CRISIS INTERVENTION

The Case of Patricia Hearst: Willing Participant or Victim?

Patricia Hearst was born into one of the wealthiest families in America, the granddaughter of publishing giant William Randolph Hearst. Her name became a household word in early 1974 when she was reportedly kidnapped by the *Symbionese Liberation Army*, a radical left-wing political group active in America during the early 1970s. The nation watched as demands were made by her captors. Then, on April 15, 1974, to everyone's shock, Hearst was caught on surveillance tape wielding a military-style gun during the robbery of the Sunset District branch of Hibernia Bank. Shortly thereafter, a communiqué was released by Hearst under the pseudonym "Tania" in which she stated she was now committed to the goals of her captors. A warrant was immediately issued for her arrest and, in September 1975, after being added to the FBI's most wanted list, she was arrested in a San Francisco apartment along with other SLA members.

During her trial, defense attorney F. Lee Bailey argued that Hearst had been a victim of brainwashing after days of physical and sexual abuse. A number of psychiatrists, some appointed by the court, agreed, and argued that Hearst had in fact developed the *Stockholm Syndrome*, which only then was finding its way into the professional literature and lexicon. They argued that Hearst had been subjected to a form of thought control similar to the victims of the Maoist regime in communist China. According to the experts, Hearst was at risk due to her youth and limited involvement in politics.

The prosecution in the case argued that Hearst had acted of her own free will, regardless of any brainwashing activities that may have occurred. They pointed to the fact that after she was arrested and booked into jail, she listed her occupation as "urban guerilla," and later refused to testify against any of the other SLA members. The prosecution also had experts to support their position. They argued that Hearst had simply embraced the radical ideology of the SLA and had willingly joined in their cause.

In the end, the jury returned a verdict of guilty, and Hearst was sentenced to 35 years in prison. But that would not be the end of the case. After serving just 2 years of her sentence, President Jimmy Carter commuted her sentence and she was released from prison. She would later be granted a full Presidential pardon by President Bill Clinton on his last day in office. Nearly two decades after a surveillance camera in Hibernia Bank of San Francisco caught one of the most famous images of the 1970s, the case was now finally put to rest with the stroke of a presidential pen.

Discussion Questions

1. Do you believe it is possible that Patricia Hearst had been brainwashed by her captors to the point that she no longer acted of their own free will, as her attorney argued during her trial?
2. In what ways does the Hearst case differ from that of a gang member being indoctrinated by a gang and committing violent crime at the behest of the gang's leadership?
3. How much do you believe politics or some other circumstance unrelated to Patricia Hearst's psychological state at the time of her crime played a role in her commutation and eventual pardon?

going willingly. However, if the hostage-taker wishes to surrender, it is not a good time for a negotiator to demand that they determine the method of surrender. Every effort should be made to comply with the hostage-taker's wishes without risking someone's personal safety in the process. For example, a hostage-taker cannot be allowed to walk out with their weapons in hand to personally surrender them to the police. In this case the negotiator must deny the request without giving the appearance that they are demanding the method of surrender. Instead they will shift the hostage-taker's focus away from their demand and allow them the autonomy to choose an alternative.

THE HOSTAGE EXPERIENCE

Much has been written about the experience of a hostage during a protracted crisis. Movies have been made and books written about the psychological changes that occur. And there are no doubt changes that do occur, especially if there is contact between the hostages and their captor. Sometimes a hostage-taker may lock their hostages up in a room or vault and have little contact. This form of dehumanization inhibits the development of any amount of rapport being established between the two that could cause some beneficial psychological changes to occur. This same dehumanization occurs when the hostages have bags placed over their heads.

The Stockholm Syndrome

In those instances when there is contact, excluding hostage situations where the hostages are family members or individuals known to the hostage-taker, then the opportunity exists for what has come to be known as the **Stockholm Syndrome**, a psychological change that takes place in a hostage that can lead them to form an emotional bond with their captor. This change has been described by F. J. Ochberg (1978) as:

> *The positive feelings of the captives toward their captor(s) that are accompanied by negative feelings toward the police. These feelings are frequently reciprocated by the captor(s). To achieve a successful resolution of a hostage situation, law enforcement must encourage and tolerate the first two phases so as to induce the third and thus preserve the lives of all participants.*

When hostages are impacted by this dynamic, they begin to experience positive and supportive feelings toward their captors. They may even identify with them in such a way that they actually turn against the police officers who are attempting to free them. This type of change is encouraged by the activities of the negotiator, though not apparent to the hostage-taker or the hostages, because allowing such a connection to develop may very well keep the hostages alive. For this reason the negotiator may attempt to humanize the hostages at every opportunity. They will refer to the hostages by their names, or they may tell the hostage-taker things about the personal lives of the hostages, such as how many children they have or any medical conditions that may be present. The more information the hostage-taker has about their hostages, the greater the likelihood that they too will humanize them, and with that, the greater the possibility that the Stockholm syndrome will develop.

The syndrome gets its name from an incident that occurred in 1973 at the Sveriges Kreditbank in Stockholm, Sweden. On August 23rd of that year, two armed men entered the bank firing their weapons at the ceiling. One of the men, a prison escapee named Jan-Erik Olsson, announced to the approximately 60 terrified employees "The party has just begun" (Lang, 1974). The two robbers allowed all but four of the employees, three women and one man, to leave. For the next 131 hours the four hostages were held inside a bank vault with dynamite strapped to them. There they remained until being rescued by the police five days later.

Following their rescue, the hostages exhibited some attitudes that were not expected. They participated in numerous media events in the days following their captivity, and it was clear they were actually being supportive of their captors. They talked about how they feared the police and their efforts to rescue them, and how their captors protected them. One of the female hostages later became engaged to one of the hostage-takers, and another assisted with their defense fund. Those who studied the behavior of the hostages came to understand that what had happened was that the hostages had formed an emotional bond with their captors during their time in captivity, a bond that continued even after their rescue.

The Stockholm Syndrome is the result of positive contact between the hostage-taker and their hostages. It is bidirectional in its effect, meaning the hostage-taker can be equally as impacted as the hostages. The more the hostage-taker humanizes the hostages, doing things such as using their names and carrying on casual conversations with them, the more likely it is that the Stockholm Syndrome will take hold. When it does, it could even lead to a situation where hostages actually refuse to leave when given the opportunity. In the case of the hostages, Dr. Joseph Carver (2011) describes four conditions that must be present in order for the syndrome to develop. They are as follows:

- The presence of a perceived threat to one's physical or psychological survival, and the belief that the hostage-taker would carry out the threat.
- The presence of a perceived small kindness from the abuser to the victim.
- Isolation from perspectives other than those of the hostage-taker.
- The perceived inability to escape the situation.

Exactly what it is that causes this change in a hostage's behavior has been the subject of many varied psychological theories, most of them well beyond the scope of this text. There are, however, a few basic factors that undoubtedly contribute to this phenomenon. First is the role of **identification**. We tend to connect on an emotional level with those who are like us in some way. People who have served in a particular war, such as Korea or Vietnam, identify and connect with others who served in that same war. People who work in a particular profession, such as police and firefighters, tend to connect with others employed in those same professions. And, unfortunately, those who engage in criminal conduct tend to connect with other criminals. We are social beings, and for whatever reason the evolutionary process has left us with an innate emotional attraction to other like-minded people.

So how does this relate to the Stockholm Syndrome? In most hostage situations where this syndrome could potentially develop, the taking of hostages was not a planned event. So most hostage-takers are not emotionally prepared for the drama and danger that follows. When they look out and see 25 police officers pointing guns in their direction it can be a very stressful event. The hostages too are stressed, and for obvious reasons. A hostage-taker will almost always threaten harm in the opening minutes of a hostage crisis. They do this as a means of gaining immediate control over their hostages. The unavoidable fear that follows is highly stressful for the hostages. So suddenly both hostage and hostage-taker are sharing in the stress of the moment and, with a little positive contact between them, the identification process may begin. In a sense, the hostage-taker is held captive by the police, and the hostages by the hostage-taker. The more the hostage-taker perceives themselves as a victim, the greater the likelihood they will identify with the real victims, the hostages.

The other dynamic that contributes to the development of the Stockholm Syndrome goes back to the parent–child relationship. We all remember times as a child when we tried our hardest to please our parents, even when they were being a bit critical. It is the natural tendency of a child to want to please those who hold authority over us, especially the parents. When children are disciplined, they typically don't become vengeful and rebellious. After a few minutes of anger, they typically endeavor to please the very parent who disciplined them in an effort to regain their affection. Even children who are sexually and physically abused will commonly seek to please their abuser and win their affections. Some have suggested that the experience of a hostage is a similar process. They unconsciously attempt to please their captor as a critical parent figure. In the case of both the child and the hostage it is ultimately an unconscious effort to avoid further negative outcomes in the relationship that causes an emotional bond to their parent/captor to develop.

Chapter Summary

The hostage crisis is one of the most complex sets of behavioral and psychological dynamics a police officer will ever encounter. It is a situation where everything done by the police has a singular purpose: to save the lives of the hostages. Law enforcement has fine-tuned the techniques of hostage negotiation to the point where most hostage situations now end peacefully. It is also an area where the communication skills learned on the street far outweigh any knowledge gained in the classroom. Thus it is only specially trained police officers who engage a hostage-taker, or, if the crisis occurs in a correctional setting, an equally well-trained correctional officer will take the lead. Neither profession relies on a psychologist or psychiatrist to do the task for them. There simply are no better individuals for the job than the men and women who engage such people on a daily basis, and thus gain the needed experience to know from what a hostage-taker says and how they say it that violence is imminent, or that deep down all they really want is to be heard and then surrender their cause.

As effective as the hostage negotiation process has become, there are still cases, unfortunately, where nothing will prevent the hostage-taker from resorting to violence. In those cases it is up to the experience of the negotiator to know when it is time to hand the situation over to the tactical commander to attempt a rescue by force. If they do, there is a good chance that a hostage might in fact be killed. But there is also a good chance that hostages who would otherwise be killed might be saved. The hostage situation brings out the best in law enforcement and corrections. Done correctly, it is a crisis where many different techniques and methods come together to engage a deadly situation with precision and timing. In most cases the hostage-taker has no idea they are being manipulated into a demeanor that will facilitate a peaceful resolution, or in the event that a peaceful resolution is not part of their design, then into a position where the police can either affect an arrest or immobilize the individual before they have the chance to react and harm their hostages.

Key Terms

Purposeful-criminal hostage-taker
Defensive-criminal hostage-taker
Violent-ideological hostage-taker
Passive-ideological hostage-taker
Custody-related hostage-taker
Relationship-related hostage-taker
Domestic-defensive hostage-taker
Passive-frustration hostage-taker

Final statement hostage-taker
Paranoid hostage-taker
Mission-oriented hostage-taker
Hostage team leader
Primary negotiator
Secondary negotiator
Intelligence officer
Communications officer

Throw phone
Public information officer
Team psychologist
Verbal will
Dehumanization
Surrender ritual
Stockholm Syndrome
Identification

Discussion Questions

1. Watch one of the many Hollywood films in which a hostage crisis is depicted and discuss the typology of the hostage-taker using the scheme presented in your text.
2. Discuss the police response as depicted in the film. Was it effective? What problems were encountered?
3. Discuss the experiences of the hostage(s), as depicted in the film. Was there any depiction of the Stockholm Syndrome developing?

Recommended Hostage Films

The Taking of Pelham 123 (1974)
Dog Day Afternoon (1975)
Die Hard (1988)

The Negotiator (1998)
John Q. (2002)

10

Responding to Mass Panic

LEARNING OUTCOMES

Upon completion of this chapter the student should be able to:

1. Explain the concept of mass panic.

2. List and define the various types of mass panic.

3. Summarize the psychology of mass panic, and define relevant factors such as the Schelling incident, deindividuation, and contagion.

4. Describe the police response to mass panic, and to explain why preparedness, command and communication, and contingency planning are important.

Chapter Outline

INTRODUCTION

THE SUMMER OF SAM

The onset of mass panic is as spontaneous and chaotic in humans as it is in a herd of animals being approached by a single predator in search of a meal. In 1976 and 1977 a single human predator, David Berkowitz, crippled an entire city with fear (A&E Biography, 2008). Berkowitz, the infamous *Son of Sam* killer, brought New York City to a standstill with his string of murders. He targeted mostly young women, but didn't hesitate to attack any young man who happened to be present when he selected his target. Once the police determined that the attacks were connected, and that the gun used was the same .44 caliber revolver, a task force of over 200 detectives was formed to hunt the killer down. By the time they finally did, six young people had been murdered, and seven others wounded.

As Berkowitz carried out his murderous crimes, New York City was paralyzed by fear ("Summer of Sam," 1999). People remained in their homes at night. Young girls went outside only if absolutely necessary, and then only during daylight hours and with an escort. Many brunettes dyed their hair, thinking the killer was only interested in a particular look. People armed themselves. And businesses closed their doors early for lack of business, and for their own safety. Entire sections of the city simply shut down during the hours of darkness. Mass panic had set in.

THE BELTWAY SNIPERS

A more recent example of a fear-induced panic in America is the case of John Muhammad and Lee Malvo, the "Beltway snipers," whose deadly acts during a three-week period in October 2002 resulted in 10 homicides, all shot from long range, with five others wounded. Like Berkowitz before them, Muhammad and Malvo created such a panic in the multistate Washington, D.C., area, a panic made worse by the fact that they were killing their victims from long range with no advance warning, that people drove for miles to locations outside the beltway just to gas up their automobiles. Others avoided department stores, and many parents kept their children home from school. If a person had to be outside for any length of time, the goal was to keep moving and to maintain cover if possible behind walls, vehicles, trees, or anything else that could possibly prevent a clear shot. During Berkowitz's murder spree, people at least held the belief that by being hyper-sensitive to their surroundings they could possibly thwart an attack by not allowing strangers to approach to within shooting range. In the case of Muhammad and Malvo, however, no one felt safe (Moose and Fleming, 2006).

Although these examples clearly show how a community can be overtaken by fear and panic in response to criminal acts, even those carried out by a single perpetrator, there also are times when panic sets in following natural or man-made disasters, during times of unrest and rioting, or in response to desperate social conditions. In all cases, panic is the result of a loss of control, and almost always requires some type of intervention, sometimes on a massive scale, to contain and de-escalate the tension and potential destructiveness. There are times, such as during the 1992 L.A. riots, when the police simply contain the crisis with no immediate effort to de-escalate the violence. In the case of the L.A. riots, as discussed later in the chapter, the results were devastating. And then there are times, such as a moving riot, when the police are forced to attempt to de-escalate without first containing the crisis. Before we discuss methods and practices for responding to the crisis of mass panic, we will look first at the various types of mass panic that have been experienced by American society.

TYPES OF MASS PANIC

The method of containing and de-escalating a mass panic is in large part determined by the underlying factors that led to the crisis. Some may require police or military force, whereas others just logistical support and needed supplies. The goal is neither to overreact nor under-react to the crisis, and thus make containment and de-escalation more difficult. A widespread sense of panic can be agitated or empowered by an improper police response, so those who respond must do so with the appropriate level of intervention. We can look at mass panic as being driven by four different types of motivating factors:

Fear-driven Panic

As we discussed in the chapter on the psychology of crisis, when fear sets in, our natural biologically driven instinct is either to run or stand and fight. In cases of extreme fear we may simply freeze and become incapacitated. When fear sets in on a large scale, and entire groups of people in tandem are overcome by this response, then the opportunity for mass panic presents itself. We witnessed this following the events of September 11, 2001, as people and institutions all across the country panicked to different degrees, ranging from hypervigilance to near hysteria. Certainly at Ground Zero in New York City, the spot where the World Trade Centers stood as the events of that day began to unfold, there was mass panic, and understandably so, as people attempted to escape the danger out of fear for their lives. Most thought additional attacks were imminent. Millions of people attempted to leave lower Manhattan all at once, most of them walking. And as the unknown of that day continued, the level of panic only increased.

No type of panic will spread quicker if not contained than a **fear-driven panic**. People become very egocentric as they shift into a sort of survival mode to escape or avoid the source of fear. This frame of mind has the potential to spread quickly to others, even absent sufficient evidence to support the level of fear being experienced. When people see others run in fear they tend to follow. It's like yelling "fire" in a crowded theater. Once the panic sets in it takes on a life of its own. Fear-driven panics are oftentimes associated with evacuations. When a hurricane approaches landfall for example, it is imperative that an effective evacuation plan be in place. Such a plan is the first line of defense against mass panic. When people can clearly see that someone is in control of the situation, and that order can be maintained, then they feel safer regardless of the danger. This is the very reason why high visibility by the police and others who respond to situations where mass panic could potentially break out is so important.

Desperation-driven Panic

This type of panic is spurred on usually by a lack of resources or basic sustenance. Whereas those in the grip of a fear-driven panic tend to run away from something, those experiencing a **desperation-driven panic** are running toward something, usually the source for some needed item, such as food or water. This type of panic can be extremely dangerous, especially if resources are insufficient to take care of everyone's needs. This type of panic is often seen following a natural disaster. Following Hurricane Katrina's landfall in New Orleans in 2005, this was precisely the type of panic that set in, as the situation quickly deteriorated to the point of hopelessness for many. People were without food, fresh water, housing, and proper medical care for a number of days. The desperation was apparent in the messages that were visible on the rooftops of many of the flooded houses, many of which had the word "HELP" spelled out with paint, clothing, bed sheets, or whatever household items they could gather together before the flood waters forced them to their rooftops. People resorted to violence and uncontrolled looting in an effort to survive the disaster.

Unlike a fear-driven panic, which can spread rapidly and disrupt the public order, a desperation-driven panic can very quickly lead to mass violence, and must be contained and de-escalated quickly. Those panicked by fear tend to activate the *flight* component of their autonomic response system. Those motivated by desperation tend to do just the opposite and activate the *fight* component of that system, which enhances their ability to acquire what is needed in order to decrease their level of desperation. As we have witnessed many times in America and around the world, otherwise peaceful and law-abiding people have the capacity to riot, loot, and even kill if their level of desperation reaches a critical level. People tend to reach this level quicker if there is a perceived lack or loss of control by the police and others responsible for bringing relief to those affected.

Anger-driven Panic

On April 29, 1992, a Ventura County, California, jury that included no African Americans announced its acquittal of three of the officers involved in the beating of Rodney King, and a fourth officer on all but a single charge. What followed was the deadliest riot in U.S. history. Out of anger and frustration, people took to the streets and began burning, looting, and worst of all, killing innocent people. When it was over, 53 people lay dead, with nearly 3000 more injured, and more than 3100 businesses damaged or destroyed. The financial impact of the riot exceeded $1 billion (Cannon, 1999).

The L.A. riots of 1992 is a deadly example of an **anger-driven panic**. It was sparked by the verdicts in the trial of the four police officers, but the fuel that really fed the fire was years of tension between the LAPD and the city's minority populations. Allegations of police brutality and discriminatory enforcement were a daily occurrence. Adding to it was Chief Darryl Gates, a battle-hardened cop who had come up through the LAPD ranks, and who was accused by Black and Hispanic residents of being insensitive to their complaints, and of doing little to control the harsh enforcement policies of his officers (*New York Times*, April 16, 2010). This pent up anger toward the police department finally reached its boiling point and exploded following the verdicts in Ventura County. Their anger was not so much over the beating of an African American man by four white police officers, but more so over the anger and frustration of what in their collective mind amounted to decades of state-sponsored oppression by the LAPD.

An anger-driven panic is typically very violent and dangerous. Moral and ethical controls very quickly break down, as people suddenly justify their actions by the actions of others. Those who attempt to de-escalate the panic from within risk their own safety, as group hysteria quickly takes over. Looting, burning, and killing escalate out of control until the police can eventually contain and de-escalate the crisis. It is a time when those in close proximity to the crisis either choose to participate, thereby acting out their own anger and frustration, or they choose not to participate, and either make an effort to escape the violence or remain in harm's way to protect their property. An anger-driven panic is extremely dangerous for essentially every person involved, regardless of which side of the crisis—those who respond, those who agitate, or those who simply try to get out of the way—they happen to be on.

Another type of anger-driven panic, and one often seen in America in the 1960s and 70s, is the political demonstration. Not all such demonstrations are violent in nature, but there have always been those groups that attempt to make their point by causing as much mass panic and damage as possible. In those earlier decades, truly a period of American radicalism, such demonstrations were a common occurrence in the urban areas. Whether it was sparked by the Civil Rights Movement, the Vietnam War, American Foreign Policy, or the disparity between rich and poor, the potential for violence and mass panic was always present. In our modern day we continue to see this type of violent demonstration, most recently the 1999 World Trade Organization (WTO) riots in Seattle, where nearly 40,000 demonstrators attempted to disrupt the WTO Ministerial Convention being held in the city that year (SPD After Action Report, 2000).

Excitement-driven Panic

The final type of mass panic is often seen, paradoxically, following an event that generally makes people happy. The **excitement-driven panic** often begins with a celebration of some sort, such as the type that follows an important sporting event like the Super Bowl or World Series. People demonstrate their excitement usually in acceptable ways at the start, but as the level of excitement grows, the outward demonstration of that excitement grows with it. An excitement-driven panic is less dangerous perhaps than the other types of panic, with most injuries occurring accidentally, but many times, especially as the police move in to contain and de-escalate the matter, violence does break out.

One factor that often contributes to the escalation of an excitement-driven panic is the presence of alcohol. Alcohol skews the thinking and reasoning of most people, and makes it more likely that they will follow the actions of the group rather than a more sensible option. This has been seen time and again on college campuses across America. What begins as a self-contained party erupts into a excited panic once the destructive behavior begins. And when the police show up, it is often then when the matter escalates into a moving riot. An excitement-driven panic can also be non-centralized, and may break out in various locations simultaneously across a city or region. This has become commonplace following important sporting events, and the police now mobilize in anticipation of this type of panic. Their immediate goal is to keep the excited behavior contained, and then to quickly move in to de-escalate the matter before it has the opportunity to turn violent.

THE PSYCHOLOGY OF PANIC

The psychology of mass panic can be discussed in terms of two qualitatively different sets of variables. We will begin by discussing those factors that contribute to the onset and agitation of an excitement or anger-driven panic, and then follow that with a discussion of the factors contributing to the fear and desperation-driven panics.

Excitement and Anger

Unlike the fear and desperation-driven panics, the panic in these cases is quite intentional, at least in its beginnings. Panic is the desired effect. It tends to be confrontational toward the police. Thomas Schelling (1960) first described the behavioral dynamic of an anger or excitement-driven crowd. He wrote:

> It is usually the essence of mob formation that the potential members have to know not only where and when to meet but just when to act so that they act in concert. Overt leadership solves the problem; but leadership can often be identified and eliminated by the authority trying to prevent the mob action. In this case the mob's problem is to act in unison without

overt leadership, to find some common signal that makes everyone confident that, if he acts on it, he will not be acting alone. The role of "incidents" can thus be seen as a coordinating role; it is a substitute for overt leadership and communication. Without something like an incident, it may be difficult to get action at all, since immunity requires that all know when to act together.

The incident Schelling spoke of has become known as a **Schelling incident**. It is any occurrence that has the capacity to set off panic-driven behavior once a crowd has gathered. Some incidents have this capacity simply because they have done so in the past, and because the crowd has become conditioned to react in like manner when it happens again. For example, in America, winning a national sports championship has in some cities served as a Schelling incident, one that has often incited excitement-driven panic. The crowd is already present, and once they're out on the street following the victory, it takes very little to initiate the excitement. The Schelling incident signals to people in the crowd what others are likely to do and, because of the media attention such occurrences have in the past received, people come to expect that others in the crowd will overturn cars, start fires, and break windows. This expectation emboldens people and prepares them psychologically to participate in such behavior.

In terms of the anger-driven panic, the Schelling incident is almost always the act or occurrence that elicits the anger. For example, the L.A. riots were set off by the acquittal of the four white police officers who were charged in the beating of Rodney King in 1991 following a high-speed chase. The African American community was outraged, and the acquittal served as the Schelling incident for this nation's worst riot. When the verdict was announced, people expected others in the neighborhoods affected to take to the street to demonstrate their anger. Police misconduct has always been a very clear signal for people to assemble and demonstrate their anger. Most of the time it is peaceful, especially when the demonstration has been organized by non-violent leaders or activists. Other times however, especially when it is a spontaneous gathering with no leadership, the chance of the demonstration becoming a dangerous anger-driven panic is greatly increased.

Even in those cases where a demonstration is organized, there is still the possibility of a Schelling incident unleashing a panic. For example, there have been many demonstrations in America that began as peaceful actions, but at some point a window is broken, a police officer strikes a demonstrator, or perhaps it's something as simple as someone running through the crowd and yelling loudly. Any of these events can serve as a Schelling incident, causing an otherwise peaceful demonstration to suddenly turn dangerous. The speed with which it does will depend on the level of conditioning in that particular crowd, or the degree to which the crowd expects such behavior. In a more economically depressed area, the type where the police have traditionally been more active and aggressive in their enforcement of the law, the expectation is higher. In contrast, in those areas where the police are less active, such as the more affluent neighborhoods in any particular community, the expectation is significantly lower due to the lack of opportunity for conditioning.

Once such an incident occurs, what is it that compels otherwise law-abiding people to join in and participate in the panic-driven event, perhaps even violating the law in the process? Two perceptions must take place in the individual before they join the chaos and do things they otherwise would not have considered acting alone. First, they must perceive that the cost of their actions is low, meaning the likelihood of the police singling them out and arresting them is low. When they reach this perception, or when they consciously act in spite of the cost, then they go through a process of **deindividuation** (Festinger, 1952). This occurs when individual participants immerse themselves in the group to the point of losing their sense of self-identity and becoming anonymous participants with less personal responsibility. They begin to feel, think, and act in ways more consistent with the group than with their own character and beliefs. According to Gustave Le Bon (1895), the group eventually reaches a **collective mind** and, once it does, individuals who have willingly set aside their individuality begin to conform their behavior to the perceived norms of the group. And because people are highly suggestive in this state, having set aside their self-control, the various emotions and attitudes of the group spread rapidly. Le Bon referred to this as **contagion**.

Le Bon argued that when the crowd develops this collective mind it replaces private self-awareness with primitive instinctual urges. So his views are evolutionary in this sense. He believed that because the participants act without the self-control present in their individual behavior, they necessarily act from the unconscious storehouse of evolutionary urges and instincts. He viewed the group as savage and uncivilized, thus having the potential for destructiveness and violence. In Le Bon's view, throughout Man's evolutionary history it was the protection of the group in times of danger and conflict that allowed for the survival of the individual members of the group. The required actions of the group in those times likely involved violence and warfare. So in the evolutionary view, the internal pressure to follow such a course of behavior when thrust into a group situation that could potentially elicit such behavior has become instinct in humans. Unless cognitively mediated, that instinct will be acted out and the individual will deindividuate, adopt the emerging norms and expectations of the group, and participate in behaviors they otherwise would never have considered while acting alone.

Fear and Desperation

This type of mass panic tends to be unintentional and non-confrontational toward the police, at least until such time that the police become perceived as obstacles to alleviating the fear or desperation. To contrast these dual perceptions of the police we can look at the previously mentioned Beltway sniper case and the events of September 11, 2001. In both cases a fear-driven panic had set in, paralyzing significant geographic areas of the country. The police were supported by the populace in both instances. The police were viewed as agents of safety and security, and their directives were accepted without question. In contrast, we can look at the events in New Orleans following Hurricane Katrina. What followed the levies breaking was both a fear and desperation-driven mass panic. People were not having basic needs met. They needed food, water, and medical care. Widespread looting began and, while many of the looters were simply opportunists, the police very quickly became perceived as obstacles to those who were truly desperate. People became confrontational toward the police, and the police reciprocated. Events very quickly spiraled out of control, and New Orleans became a very dangerous city in the midst of its panic.

Whether it's the fear of a serial killer or the desperation of hungry and scared people, the panic that sets in can quickly spread and worsen. Like excitement and anger-driven panic, there is typically an incident that sparks the panic. But it is more abstract and internal than things like breaking glass or an unpopular jury decision. People do not deindividuate in a fear or desperation-driven panic. Instead they experience what might be described as **hyper-individuation**. Rather than taking on a group mentality, they instead take on an *everyone-for-themselves* demeanor. They become egocentric to the extreme, looking out for themselves and family, possibly even to the detriment of others. The incident that sparks the panic in the individual is the perceived loss of control over the situation. It is a situation that quickly feeds on itself. As more people panic, the loss of control becomes more apparent, causing the panic to spread.

We can look at the examples already discussed to see this process in action. In the case of the Beltway snipers, people reached a point where they no longer felt safe outside. They had lost control over their own safety, not knowing if a high-powered bullet would be awaiting them at the gas station or grocery store. People were beginning to panic and, as others around them panicked, with the police reinforcing the panic by instructing people to restrict their activities, the individual panic very quickly became a multistate, fear-driven mass panic. As people in the military will attest, there is nothing more frightening than the unknown. A sniper can cripple an entire battalion of soldiers with a few well-placed bullets from a silenced rifle. The same reaction was witnessed during the wars in Iraq and Afghanistan when a new type of weapon, the *roadside bomb*, began to take a devastating toll on American soldiers. Although soldiers are trained not to panic, the emotional cost of not knowing when and where the next explosion would occur will for many be apparent the rest of their lives.

In the case of Hurricane Katrina, the loss of control was realized when it became apparent that no rescuers were immediately coming. As people grew hungry and in need of clean water and shelter, panic set in. The more panicked people became, the more hyper-individuated they became. They looted and pillaged, and many took up arms against their own neighbors to protect themselves and secure needed rations. Certainly, as previously stated, there were opportunists among the panicked masses—those who were deindividuating in the midst of an excitement or anger-driven panic—but the majority of those caught in the disaster were just trying to survive the crisis. Fear and desperation had set in, and the longer the crisis continued without containment and de-escalation by police and emergency personnel, the greater the level of fear and desperation.

Figure 10.1 provides a comparison between the two classes of mass panic discussed.

	Anger & Excitement-driven	Fear & Desperation-driven
Initial Demeanor toward Police	Confrontational	Non-confrontational
Loss of Control	Intentional	Unintentional
Onset of Panic/ Motivating Factor	External-Schelling Incident	Internal–loss of Control
Individual Psychological Response	Deindividuation	Hyper-individuation

FIGURE 10.1 Comparison of Mass Panic Types.

THE POLICE RESPONSE TO MASS PANIC

The police are in a very tough and unpredictable position during a mass panic. They may be perceived as rescuer by some and repressor by others. Their actions are so critical because they will many times determine the course of the panic. Their *under-response* in the case of an excitement or anger-driven panic will cause the individuals involved to perceive a lower cost of participation, and thus speed up their deindividuation. In contrast, their *over-response* in the case of a desperation or fear-driven panic may cause the individuals involved to perceive them as an obstacle to their immediate needs, and thus intensify their hyper-individuation. And finally, the very presence and demeanor of the police may in some cases serve as a Schelling incident that can potentially cause an otherwise peaceful demonstration to become an anger-driven panic with the capacity to rapidly spread.

The L.A. Riots of 1992

We need only to look at the L.A. riots of 1992 to see an example of the first scenario. From the very beginning of that crisis there was a lack of response, even with clear indications of what was about to happen. By 9:00 P.M. of the first night, April 29th, the riots had spread to approximately 50 square miles, with only 400 to 500 police officers in the area (Rosegrant and Falkenrath, 2000). The sheriff of L.A. County, Sherman Block, had offered LAPD Chief Daryl Gates a contingent of 500 deputies; however, Gates refused, believing his department was fully capable of containing and de-escalating the crisis. Governor Pete Wilson, seeing the situation rapidly deteriorate, ordered the California National Guard to mobilize. Unfortunately they were hours from the scene, and most of the guard troops were untrained for this type of crisis.

By the following morning an estimated 50,000 people had taken to the streets of South Central L.A., many of them carrying weapons they had looted from gun stores. And while the riots certainly began as an anger-driven demonstration by enraged members of the African American community following the acquittal of the officers charged in the Rodney King beating, by the next morning people of all races, ages, and income levels had joined in the melee. What had started as an anger-driven panic had become predominantly an excitement-driven panic, fueled in part by the lack of response on the part of the LAPD. Even when the National Guard did arrive, they were mostly constrained from using force. The local news was even reporting that the soldiers were unarmed. This lowered even further the perceived cost of joining the conflict, and the riots worsened. In the end, 53 people lost their lives, and thousands more were injured, in what would be America's deadliest riot.

Hurricane Katrina

In contrast, the panic following Hurricane Katrina provides a clear example of an over-response by the police. Certainly it was an under-response by FEMA and other relief agencies, but the reaction of the police only exacerbated the desperation felt by many as the flood waters surrounded them. Aside from the horrendous relief effort that followed the disaster, the chaotic conditions throughout the city, along with the chaos and frustration that was occurring within the ranks of the police department itself, caused the police who remained to focus primarily on restoring order through force. They immediately announced that looting would not be tolerated, even by those desperately seeking basic commodities (NewsMax.com, September 3, 2005). Governor Blanco, referring to the National Guard troops who were mobilizing, stated publicly, "these troops are fresh back from Iraq, well trained, experienced, and battle tested, and under my orders to restore order in the streets. They have M-16s and they are locked and loaded. These troops know how to shoot and kill and they are more than willing to do so if necessary, and I expect they will" (CNN, September 2, 2005).

In addition to their focus on restoring order through force, the police from various jurisdictions actually prevented people from fleeing New Orleans to the safety of suburban areas such as Gretna City and Crescent City, instead turning them back at the bridges leading into their cities (*New York Times*, September 10, 2005). In doing so the police only intensified the desperation-driven panic. Additionally, those who maintained firearms for their own protection were ordered to surrender them to the police or National Guard. Seizures and house-to-house searches were carried out without warrants, and in some cases guns were confiscated by force. Those who refused to surrender their firearms risked being arrested.

The events in New Orleans following Katrina clearly show what happens when the police place themselves in opposition to the panicked masses during times of desperation. People will resort to whatever measures they feel necessary in order to protect their families. By taking on the role of enforcers, the police unavoidably were perceived not as rescuers, but as obstacles to safety and sustenance. The more force they applied, the greater the panic became until order could finally be restored a number of days later.

The Seattle WTO Riots

Finally, one additional example of how the police can impact the course of a mass panic is the response by the Seattle Police Department to the demonstrations held during the World Trade Organization's meeting in Seattle in November 1999. Tens of thousands of protestors prepared to demonstrate during the meeting, with some even planning to peacefully shut down the conference by blocking the delegates' access to the meeting venues (Oldham, 2009). The demonstrators represented a number of groups opposed to the WTO's policies, among them labor unions and environmentalists. What began as a planned and properly permitted peaceful demonstration quickly deteriorated into an anger-driven panic when the Seattle Police Department overresponded with the use of tear gas, rubber bullets, and concussion grenades. Even infuriated residents of the city joined the demonstrators after witnessing the police department's use of force against peaceful demonstrators.

The situation in Seattle was exacerbated by the establishment the first day of a 7:00 P.M. curfew on much of the downtown area, and the next day a 25-block "no protest zone." Both directives, entirely unnecessary, only empowered the police to intensify their aggressive response. The widespread use of tear gas continued, and hundreds were arrested for violating the orders. The police were out to control the streets, and they were willing to do it by force if necessary.

By the next day, with widespread criticism of the police department's tactics being voiced, the police did in fact change their tactics and abandoned their use of non-lethal weapons. From that point on, very few demonstrators were arrested. In the end, charges were dropped against essentially all the demonstrators who were arrested for violating the curfew and no-protest zone. Within days of the demonstration, Chief of Police Norm Stamper and the assistant chief responsible for WTO planning, Ed Joiner, both announced their retirements. Pursuant to their directives, it had been a misguided effort to contain and de-escalate by force a crisis that really had not reached the level of a true crisis by the time the intervention was initiated. Intervention was perceived instead by the crowd as suppression of free speech and lawful activities. A crisis that existed only in the minds of a few police commanders and planners quickly erupted and became a real crisis. Paradoxically, the police finally contained and de-escalated the matter by simply constraining their own efforts to do so.

Elements of the Police Response

In each of the cases discussed above, the police response negatively impacted the course of the panic. In some respects the police became their own worst enemy in their efforts to contain and de-escalate the crisis to which they were responding. So we are left then with the question, how should the police respond? How can they avoid inadvertently exacerbating the situation by their presence and response? And more importantly, how can they respond in a way that maximizes their efforts to quickly contain and de-escalate the matter? There are some important considerations that are common to the police response to any type of mass panic; *preparedness, command and communication,* and *contingencies.*

ISSUES & ETHICS IS CRISIS INTERVENTION

When the Police Spy

The ability to assemble and protest has long been viewed as a sacred constitutional right in America. Even when it is anticipated that such protests will become violent, the police have traditionally taken a reactive stance toward the groups involved and their individual members. The need to protect the freedom to assemble and voice an opinion has always outweighed the desire by the police to get the upper hand by infiltrating such groups and actively collecting intelligence on their activities in advance of a planned protest or demonstration.

During the 1970s, when demonstrations relating to the Vietnam War and Civil Rights often turned violent and chaotic, the FBI established a secret program called COINTELPRO (Counter Intelligence Program) that was given the task of infiltrating and disrupting radical groups such as the Weather Underground and the American Indian Movement (AIM). The methods their agents employed, which came to the public's attention only after an FBI office was broken into by activists who removed COINTELPRO files found on the premises and released them to the press, oftentimes involved violating the constitutional rights of their targets. Following a congressional investigation into the activities of the FBI and other law enforcement agencies in their efforts to carry out the goals of COINTELPRO, which included even subversive activities against Martin Luther King, Jr., new safeguards were put in place to hopefully prevent such abuses of power in the future.

Following the events of September 11, 2001, the American law enforcement community once again found itself weighing the Constitutional rights of those who disagreed with their government against the need to gather intelligence and disrupt future calamity. Once again law enforcement agencies, especially the FBI, began to infiltrate and gather intelligence on groups exercising their constitutional right to free speech.

In 2008, an FBI informant and an undercover Minnesota sheriff's deputy spied on political activists in Iowa City before the Republican National Convention held later that year in St. Paul, Minnesota. It was discovered that the informant had been planted by the FBI among a group described as an "anarchist collective." The group was meeting regularly in Iowa City, and one of their stated goals was to organize street blockades to disrupt the Republican convention later that year. The sheriff's deputy, acting independent of the FBI, had infiltrated a group known as the "RNC Welcoming Committee," a group that was also planning to protest at the Republican National Convention.

While members of the FBI were ultimately indicted in the 1970s for their COINTELPRO activities (all were later pardoned), the activities uncovered in Iowa were well within the parameters of the law, especially the post-9/11 Patriot Act. But because of the negative public reaction to those and other similar cases, such activities and methods are now used more judiciously, essentially only in cases where terrorist activities are suspected.

Discussion Questions

1. Should the police be concerned about the constitutional rights of those who intend to riot if necessary to protest their disagreement with the government over some political issue?
2. How far should the police be allowed to go to gather intelligence on radical political groups that have the potential for violence (i.e., wiretaps, infiltrations, dirty tricks)?
3. Conduct some basic internet research on "COINTELPRO." Discuss the five major groups the FBI targeted with their secret operation. Was the FBI justified in their investigation of any of the five?

PREPAREDNESS   Preparedness is perhaps the most important consideration in the police response to contain and de-escalate a mass crisis. Many in Seattle and New Orleans felt the police over-responded due to their lack of preparedness and planning. In a sense, they too became panicked, and one of the first rules of policing is to maintain control through an appropriate level of force if necessary. When the police perceive a loss of control in a group situation their natural inclination is to resort to force. The lower the level of control they perceive themselves as having, the higher the level of perceived risk to their personal safety, and thus the level of force rises to confront that perceived risk. Loss of control by the police, as well as their ability to maintain control, is directly related to their level of preparation. Preparedness for a large-scale crisis involves training and planning for any possible scenario, having in place protocols and predetermined action plans for mobilizing personnel, and above all, having sufficient personnel and equipment to effectively contain the crisis while reducing to the extent possible the level of risk to the individual officers.

COMMAND AND COMMUNICATION   The second major consideration in any type of mass crisis is command and communication. Many of the problems we have discussed to this point were the result of poor command and communication. When a large-scale crisis erupts, there must be no question as to who is in charge at each operational level, and the orders of those who are in charge must be clearly communicated to those on the front lines of the crisis. Just as importantly, important information must be communicated back up the line so the command staff has a clear and real-time picture of what is happening. Law enforcement has always been weighted down by interagency competition. Unfortunately there is no real pecking order in American law enforcement. During the L.A. riots, not only did the LAPD have jurisdiction to respond, but so too did the L.A. County Sheriff's Department and the California Highway Patrol. In theory, it is the sheriff who serves as the chief law enforcement officer in any particular county, because sheriffs are elected officials and thus answerable to the public. But there are no laws requiring that a chief of police take on a subservient role to the sheriff of their county, nor to the director of the state police. They all have autonomous and equal jurisdiction, and typically, it is only professional courtesy that determines who will answer to whom. In the case of the L.A. riots, this interagency competition boiled over, and the end result was that officers from departments other than the LAPD who were mobilized and ready to assist were not cleared to be on the street in time to help contain the crisis during its earliest stages.

CONTINGENCIES   Finally, there must be contingencies in place. It is not enough to plan for something like the WTO meeting in Seattle, expecting it only to be a large peaceful demonstration. There must be some amount of intelligence gathering, within the guides of constitutional constraints, to determine what's happening beneath the surface of such a planned event. For example, are there agitators preparing to disrupt any peaceful demonstrations? Is there a specific event or circumstance planned that could potentially serve as a Schelling incident and turn a peaceful demonstration into an anger or excitement-driven panic? There must be contingency plans in place in the event of a changing situation. In New Orleans there were no doubt plans to patrol and prevent looting during and after Hurricane Katrina, but when the levies broke the situation changed dramatically, and the police were not prepared for the crisis that followed. What began as a disaster-related response that should have resulted in a low level of panic among the populace, rapidly deteriorated into a desperation and fear-driven panic requiring a much different type and level of response by the police.

Rules of Engagement

The one consideration that is not universal, but instead must be adapted to the type of crisis being responded to, is the **rules of engagement**. These rules, or guidelines, determine the collective demeanor the police will take toward the citizenry, and the level of force they are willing to use or threaten to use in response to the actions of the group. General guidelines include the following:

ANGER OR EXCITEMENT-DRIVEN PANIC   The goal of the police response in these situations is to make it readily apparent that there will be a high cost of participation for people choosing to involve themselves. This means a strong police presence is necessary. People leaving a sporting event in a highly excited state must come face to face with the police as they leave the venue. Additionally, the police can use barriers, or even position themselves, in a way that **cuts the crowd**. There is power in numbers, and the danger of a Schelling incident greatly increases the larger the crowd becomes. By strategically cutting the crowd, it channels people into smaller groups separated by the police. This increases the perceived power of the police, which in turn increases the perceived cost of participation.

In the event of a potential large-scale, non-centralized panic, such as the anger-driven panic that sparked the L.A. riots, another form of cutting the crowd is positioning the police in a way that prevents the crowd's consolidation. It involves anticipating potential "hot spots," and then saturating those spots with a heavy police presence. In the case of the L.A. riots, by establishing a containment perimeter, and then essentially allowing hotspots within that perimeter to be populated and consolidated, the LAPD only exacerbated things by greatly decreasing the perceived cost of participation for those who joined the rioting.

So the goals of the police when an anger or excitement-driven panic is threatened or expected is to proactively confront the threat with a strong presence, and to take steps to prevent a large crowd from consolidating and shifting the perceived balance of power in favor of the crowd. Additionally, when a panic is not yet apparent, as was the case at the Seattle WTO meeting, the police must be judicious in their use of force so as not to become the Schelling incident that incites the panic. Their use of force must be commensurate with the amount of disruptive behavior being demonstrated. In the case of the WTO meeting, it was a non-violent attempt by demonstrators to block access to the meeting that caused the police to resort to the use of tear gas and other non-lethal weapons. Had they constrained their use of force, and instead either negotiated with the demonstrators or simply moved the meeting venue, perhaps the widespread panic would not have happened as it did.

FEAR OR FRUSTRATION-DRIVEN PANIC   The police response in these situations should be directed at preventing the level of fear or frustration from rising to the level of a widespread panic. This should be done in a non-confrontational way, with the police acting as problem-solvers rather than enforcers. In the case of a Katrina-type crisis, the police must respond *in* force without responding *with* force. They must be well prepared for any eventuality, and anticipate when a lack of response by relief agencies will incite a panic. The police must also have a strong public relations effort to assist their efforts. To prevent fear or frustration from deteriorating into a widespread panic, it is critical to communicate with the public, and to reassure them that the police will be responsive to their needs. If it's a natural disaster, then the police should be highly visible with mobile or temporary community assistance centers that are strategically located in areas of high risk for looting and violence. If it's a situation like the D.C. sniper case, then the police should maintain close contact with the public with periodic and regular updates. Additionally, the police again should make themselves highly visible to instill a sense of safety in the minds of the public.

Chapter Summary

Unfortunately so many times in America we have seen situations that deteriorated into mass panic because the police were simply unprepared or understaffed. When it does, then the police have no choice but to contain and de-escalate the crisis through the use of force. Since the events of September 11, 2001, the law enforcement community, with the help of the U.S. Homeland Security Department, has become much more adept at preparing for mass panic. Protocols are now in place for the quick mobilization of manpower and resources in the event of a large-scale crisis. Mutual aid agreements are in place to provide police departments the authority to aid other departments outside their jurisdiction. And training has been greatly expanded for those who plan and coordinate crisis response for police departments.

The law enforcement establishment is very good at learning from its own mistakes, and events like the L.A. riots, Hurricane Katrina, and the Seattle WTO demonstrations have provided much to analyze and learn from. They have learned that to simply contain a crisis, as the LAPD did, is insufficient as a tactic by itself. People lost their lives because of the police department's lack of response. They have also learned that to respond with force when people are hungry and desperate, as the New Orleans Police Department did following Hurricane Katrina, is counterproductive to containing the crisis in its earliest stages. And they have learned, as the Seattle Police Department did, that the response and demeanor of the police can sometimes turn a peaceful demonstration into the very anger-driven panic they are trying to avoid.

Mass panic is one of the most difficult types of crisis to contain and de-escalate. To avoid its rapid spread, or to prevent it from even happening at all, requires preparation, command and communication, and contingency planning on the part of the police. The right type and level of response can calm the sleeping giant that lies dormant in every group waiting to be awakened by the sounds of breaking glass, tear gas canisters, or the cries of desperate people. The best response to any mass panic is the one that prevents it from happening in the first place, or in the event that it has already begun, from worsening to any significant degree.

Key Terms

Fear-driven panic
Desperation-driven panic
Anger-driven panic
Excitement-driven panic

Schelling incident
Deindividuation
Collective mind
Contagion

Hyper-individuation
Rules of engagement
Cuts the crowd

Discussion Questions

1. Do you believe the government's response to the disaster in New Orleans following Hurricane Katrina was in part influenced by the demographics of the population in New Orleans at the time?

2. Describe a recent anger or excitement-driven panic that was reported in the press, and specifically the "Schelling incident" that set off the panic.

3. Discuss "deindividuation," and describe a time when you experienced this phenomenon.

11

The Cult Mind-set and the Doomsday Crisis

LEARNING OUTCOMES

Upon completion of this chapter the student should be able to:

1. Explain the nature and structure of a cult.

2. List and describe the various cult typologies.

3. Summarize the profiles of the various types of cult members.

4. Describe the dangers posed by cults, and the best practices for police intervention.

Chapter Outline

INTRODUCTION

THE 1960S AND A NEW AMERICAN LIFESTYLE

During the 1960s a new lifestyle emerged among America's youth, that of communal living. It was a new social paradigm that offered a type of utopian existence, an egalitarian system into which young people could escape the melee of war, political assassinations, and racial segregation that had overtaken America. Many young people who took up the communal lifestyle were searching for something new and positive in their lives. Some were escaping military conscription, others the law, and still others any involvement in traditional society. Most experimented with hallucinogenic drugs, dabbled in the eastern religions, and engaged in uninhibited sexual practices. The age of the modern cult had begun.

By the end of the 1960s, communes had sprung up all over America, particularly on the West Coast, and what began as a social experiment in utopian living had in many cases become the antithesis of such a lifestyle. The great proliferation of illicit drug use, along with a growing apathy toward the Vietnam War and the winding down of the American Civil Rights Movement, the two predominant energizing forces of the day, was leading to a social malaise that was causing America's youth culture to turn in on itself. The other reality of the latter part of the 1960s was the emergence of many new and bizarre ideologies that were heavily influencing segments of America's youth. Some were new apocalyptic interpretations of traditional religious teachings. Others, both peaceful and militant, promoted the idea of a new world order based on the viewpoints of some particular group. And still others, ranging from the strange to the absurd, sprung out from such odd sources as science fiction, pyramidology, Druidism, and even UFOs. It was inevitable that these emerging viewpoints and the communal lifestyle would eventually come together. When they did, they gave rise to a whole new social phenomenon, the *cult*.

The distinguishing characteristics of these early cults included an isolationist lifestyle, a cutting off of all ties to the dominant culture and its institutions, and in almost every case the presence of a charismatic leader who maintained absolute control and authority over the group. The leader typically was the author of the ideologies and beliefs that formed the group's corporate identity and purpose. In many cases these cult leaders were significantly older than their typical members, which only added to their ability to maintain an authoritarian demeanor. The leaders served the group in the capacity of mentor and protector, and in some cases even God. They instructed their members on how to live their lives, how to raise their kids, how to meet their needs without engaging the institutions of the dominant culture, and most importantly, what to believe. Most established rules the group members were expected to follow, and in some cases even a system of negative consequences for violating the rules.

It wasn't long before those with ulterior motives began to establish such groups for the sole purpose of exploiting those they enticed to join. This exploitation would take many forms, but typically involved either financial or sexual exploitation. In some cases the members of a particular group were even coerced into carrying out criminal acts at the leader's behest. Drug usage and "free love" were typically condoned, and even promoted in such groups as manipulative devices. For the most part these groups went relatively unnoticed against the backdrop of the more highly publicized radical groups of the day. While these groups carried out routine bombings, hijackings, and riots, the cults were seen as relatively small and harmless groups of misguided young people who would eventually grow up and return to mainstream society out of necessity. This view quickly changed on the morning of August 9, 1969, when five people, including actress Sharon Tate, were found gruesomely murdered in Tate's Los Angeles home. It became one of the most highly publicized crimes in American history, and the trial that followed of a frustrated musician named Charles Manson would provide the public its first real glimpse into the darkness of an American cult, and even more chilling, into the distorted and manipulative mind of its leader.

One of the consequences of the Manson case was that the American criminal justice system became more acutely aware of cult activity around the country, and the potential dangers they posed for innocent people as well as for their own members. In recent times we have witnessed some of the tragic consequences of these groups: the mass suicides at the *People's Temple* in Jonestown, Guyana (1978); the deaths of the *Branch Davidians* at their compound in Waco, Texas (1993); and the attempted mass killings by *Aum Shinrikyo* in the Tokyo subway system (1995). All were considered cults, and all ended in tragedy. But law enforcement has to this point been relatively unsuccessful in proactively investigating and interrupting the destructive intentions of these groups. Not only is their right to assemble constitutionally protected in America, but they tend to be such closed groups that law enforcement in most cases is completely helpless to infiltrate them to any significant degree.

In this chapter we will look at the problem of cults, especially those espousing violence against innocent people, and the challenges faced by the criminal justice system in America in its efforts to effectively confront this problem. We will look at the beliefs that guide different cult typologies, the psychology of the cult mind-set, and the circumstances that lead to a cult spiraling out of control and resorting to violence. We begin by exploring the characteristics of those groups we commonly identify as cults.

WHAT IS A CULT?

In its simplest form, a **cult** is a group of people who abandon their involvement in the dominant culture, and instead affiliate as a subcultural group holding a common belief system and a separatist worldview. In abandoning the dominant culture, they typically live communally in a location far removed from the watchful eyes of neighbors and passers-by. If they do remain in a populated area, they typically take great steps to maintain the secrecy of their group and its beliefs. Cult members neither vote nor involve themselves in civic affairs. They educate their children within the group, and oftentimes seek no medical treatment outside the group, or at the most, limited treatment for medical emergencies. For financial support and subsistence, any assets owned by the group's members will typically become communal assets upon joining. Some cults generate revenue through the sale of a product or service. And still others engage in some type of criminal enterprise.

In almost all cases, the members of a cult will demonstrate a persecution mentality. They hold to the belief that secrecy and isolation are necessary in order to prevent the dominant culture from taking their children, seizing their assets, and arresting their leaders. The leaders of these groups promote this type of thinking in order to validate the group's separatist beliefs and to strengthen their position as protectorate of the group. It is a manipulative device that has been used by essentially every cult leader of the last 40 years to instill in their members an unquestioned loyalty to them and their beliefs. The group views the dominant culture as the enemy that will destroy them if given the opportunity, and it's only by the protective hand of the leader that it can be prevented. Even mainstream political leaders have employed this strategy; chief among them, Adolph Hitler in 1930s Germany.

TYPES OF CULTS

Cults can be defined by their beliefs and intentions. We will look at four typologies: *violent-apocalyptic*, *passive-apocalyptic*, *social-isolationist*, and *new world order*. Each of these typologies, in addition to the common elements just described, has a unique set of characteristics that distinguishes it from all the others. It is important for law enforcement and child protective agencies to understand the characteristics of each in order to effectively evaluate their risk level for criminality, violence, child abuse, or even mass suicide, and to what extent that risk is present before, during, and after some type of confrontation with law enforcement or other government entities. This understanding can assist authorities in minimizing the potential for death and destruction by allowing them to anticipate the cult's likely reaction when confrontation becomes necessary. It can also facilitate effective investigation and intelligence-gathering activities that will better assist authorities in anticipating when violence or child abuse may be occurring within the group, thus requiring immediate intervention. Before we look at the personality and behavioral characteristics of individual cult members, we will first explore each of the cult typologies. We will look at their typical doctrinal beliefs, the outcomes they hope to achieve, the methods they employ for recruitment and retention of group members, and their typical response to real or perceived confrontation.

Violent-apocalyptic Cults

The distinguishing characteristic of these types of groups is their belief that the end of the world as we know it is imminent and that they have the ability to help usher in the final outcome through some type of violent action. Most find their origins in extreme religious beliefs. They typically believe that a violent and prophetic event will occur that will result in a new and cleansed world in which only the spiritually pure shall exist. Of course most such groups consider themselves to be the only humans deserving of salvation, which only acts to reinforce their cultic views. They may stockpile weapons to prepare for the final battle, and are willing to perpetrate violence against innocent people in an effort to usher in the apocalypse. When they are confronted by authorities, they may view the confrontation as an effort by Satan or some other dark force to prevent the final outcome they so vigilantly await. The combination of these beliefs and available weaponry creates an extremely dangerous situation for those who attempt to intervene in the group's activities. They will protect their perceived role as benefactors of the newly cleansed world, and will look upon anyone attempting to intervene as an agent of an enemy that endeavors to deny them this role.

Violent-apocalyptic cults come in one of three forms, depending on the source of their doctrinal beliefs. They include the following:

• **Biblical:** These groups base their beliefs on a literal interpretation of the Christian Bible, especially the Book of Revelations and other prophetic passages. The interpretation they rely on is typically one provided by the group's leader, who spends a great deal of time instructing the group on the various aspects of that interpretation, and instilling in them a belief in the infallible nature of those teachings. The leaders of these groups typically portray themselves as prophets who have been specially selected by God to lead the group safely through the coming apocalypse to achieve their eternal salvation.

• **Quasi-Biblical:** These groups also find a basis for their beliefs in the Bible, once again the Book of Revelations and the other prophetic passages, but they tend to add things to create an entirely new storyline. For example, they may adopt the corporate belief that they are the reincarnated members of a lost tribe of Israel, or that their leader is Jesus Christ in the flesh, having returned to earth to lead and protect the group as the apocalypse nears. They may adopt new writings, typically those created by the leader, as divinely commissioned addendums to the Biblical writings. Whereas the Biblical groups are led by an extreme literal interpretation of Scripture, the quasi-Biblical groups subordinate scriptural teachings to those of the group's leadership.

• *Secular:* These apocalyptic groups base their existence on a non-Biblical set of beliefs that still point to an imminent apocalyptic event. They may pattern their beliefs and practices after those of the ancient Druids, the Mayas, the mythic gods of Greek antiquity, or even modern New Ageism. Most are a mix of pagan religion and fantasy, and almost always the leader of the group places themselves at the center of their doctrinal spectrum. In most cases it is the leader who creates every aspect of the cult's religion. Like the others, the group members of a secular apocalyptic cult look to their leader as their spiritual guide and protector in the face of the coming darkness and turmoil.

Regardless of the type of apocalyptic cult, according to a report filed by the Canadian Security Intelligence Service (1999), these groups share common elements:

1. Apocalyptic beliefs: As previously stated, these groups all anticipate a violent end to the world as we know it. They view themselves as being among those who will survive the apocalypse, and in many cases the only ones who will survive. They view this inevitable end as a necessary and prophesied step to cleansing the world of its evil and sin. Although they all view a higher power, perhaps even their own leader, to be the force that will usher in the final conflict, violent-apocalyptic groups believe they can help it along through their own violent and provocative actions. Most of these groups maintain a belief in their own invincibility, a belief that is only energized and reinforced by their apocalyptic doctrines.

2. Dualism: This is the belief that the world is a battle ground of sorts between good and evil. This belief only reinforces their perceived need for isolation, and in the more violent groups, the need to stockpile weapons and ammunition. Of course every such group views themselves as being on the side of good, which again only increases their willingness to perpetrate violence against those they perceive as being on the side of evil. In most cases, these groups view themselves as standing alone on the side of good. There simply is no middle ground. Those not affiliated with the group are necessarily evil, and thus viewed as the enemy.

3. The persecuted chosen: Most apocalyptic cults view themselves as persecuted by evil forces in the world due to their chosen status before God or another divine entity. This can lead some such groups to make plans for defending themselves against anyone they perceive as a threat, to include the police and child welfare workers. To believe they have nothing to lose and everything to gain, namely some eternal metaphysical existence for their martyrdom, creates a very dangerous situation for those who must intervene, especially if the cult has weapons at their disposal.

4. Imminence: Most apocalyptic groups believe the end is fast approaching. Prophecies and visions by the group's leader are oftentimes used to support this notion, and to instill in the members a sense of urgency about taking the necessary steps to ensure their salvation. Sometimes these steps may be violent in nature. This sense of imminence instills a "nothing to lose" mentality in the members, making them extremely dangerous if violent action is part of the group's mandate.

5. Determinism: Because these groups believe they are on the side of good, and because they believe it is predetermined that they will exit the final conflict as victors, they tend not to fear the consequences of provoking or obstructing authorities. They view themselves as having little to lose by taking whatever action is necessary to protect their cultic lifestyle. Again, their sense of invincibility, which is only reinforced by their deterministic views, makes them extremely dangerous to those attempting to intervene in some manner.

6. Salvation through conflict/enemy eradication: Violent-apocalyptic groups view their own perseverance in the face of conflict and persecution preparatory for salvation. They tend to constantly be on alert for confrontation, and they perceive any threat to the group, including inquiries by law enforcement, as evil in nature. This then justifies violent action to eradicate such evil. Believing they are always on the side of some divine right, and that such confrontation will move them closer to salvation once they necessarily prevail, greatly diminishes any hesitancy on their part to become confrontational or violent.

EXAMPLE: AUM SHINRIKYO ("SUPREME TRUTH")   On March 20, 1995, at the height of the morning rush hour on Tokyo's subway system, one of the busiest in the world, packages resembling lunch containers were left on five subway cars after being punctured with umbrellas at a predetermined time. A thick substance, later determined to be a liquid form of *sarin*, was seeping from the containers as hundreds of commuters moved in and out of the cars. In the minutes that followed, people began gasping for breath as blood gushed from their nostrils and mouths. In the panic that followed, thousands were sickened or injured, many seriously, with at least 12 people dying from inhaling the poisonous gas.

It was quickly determined by Japanese authorities that a group called Aum Shinrikyo was responsible for the attacks. They were not unknown to Japanese officials. In fact, that very day the police were planning to raid a number of the group's properties. It was believed that an insider had tipped off the group about the coming raids, and that the attacks were carried out in an effort to divert attention and resources away from the group. The raids were in fact carried out, and police discovered stockpiles of weapons, explosives, chemicals, and even biological warfare agents such as anthrax and Ebola. It was estimated that the amount of sarin that could have been produced from the chemicals on hand would have been sufficient to kill upwards of 4 million people (http://www.factsanddetails.com).

A number of people were ultimately tried, convicted, and sentenced to death for the Tokyo subway attack, among them the group's founder, Shoko Asahara. Asahara preached an apocalyptic message—a mix of Buddhism, Christianity, and the predictions of Nostradamus—that predicted the end of the world occurring in 1996. He preached that only the members of Aum Shinrikyo would survive a great nuclear war that would bring about mankind's demise, a war that would be initiated by an American attack on Japan. His religious practices included a mix of yoga, the use of LSD, and some rather strange cleansing rituals, which included being hung upside down for periods of time and being subjected to electric shock therapy. Asahara held himself out as the first "enlightened one" since Buddha. He claimed the ability to cure physical illness and to increase a person's intelligence and emotional well-being.

Under Asahara's leadership the group accumulated a great amount of wealth from the operation of various communal businesses. Additionally, Asahara required new members to sign their assets over to the group. Aum recruited many wealthy young people from elite families who brought with them significant assets. Most were college-educated people who were simply tired of their everyday existence, and who sought something new and exciting to believe in. Aum answered that need with the group's apocalyptic doctrine and ascetic lifestyle. It eventually became the fastest-growing religion in Japan, boasting an estimated 40,000 members worldwide, with a number of international offices, including in America.

In recent years, Aum Shinrikyo, at least one segment of it, under a new name and leadership, has made efforts to return to a more spiritual existence. Another segment remains loyal to Asahara and his teachings, and this faction remains under constant surveillance by Japanese authorities. Aum Shinrikyo also remains a designated foreign terrorist group by the United States and other countries. On May 28, 1993, a large seismic disturbance was recorded in the desert near West Victoria, Australia. Passers-by reported seeing a bright flash of light. There was speculation that the blast was a nuclear device. Ground zero of the blast was found to be property owned by Aum Shinrikyo (Bryson, 2001). Consequently, they remain under the watchful eyes of the world's intelligence services.

Passive-apocalyptic Cults

The **passive-apocalyptic cult** is marked by many of the same characteristics as the violent-apocalyptic typology; however, what distinguishes the two is the extent to which they are willing to engage in violence in an effort to bring about the apocalypse. Passive-apocalyptic groups tend not to engage in violence unless provoked. Many such groups will actively stockpile weapons; however, they take a more defensive posture toward their use. They tend not to view themselves as having the ability to bring about the final apocalypse through their own actions. Rather, they endeavor instead to be ready when the time comes, and to protect from mainstream society their lifestyle and cultic practices.

Like their violent counterpart, these groups can be Biblical, quasi-Biblical, or Secular in nature. Many times the doctrinal beliefs to which they adhere are the creation of the group's leader, and invariably the leader will place themselves at the center of those beliefs. They may present themselves as God, or at least God-like in nature, or they may teach that they are the reincarnation of a famous person in history. Others will add fantasy and science fiction to the doctrinal mix, and may even teach their members that they are in fact of an alien nature. The beliefs that are ultimately adopted by a cult are limited only by the imagination of its leader and the extent to which they can teach those ideas in a believable manner and inspire their members to follow them without question.

EXAMPLE: HEAVEN'S GATE   The Heaven's Gate cult is one of the more bizarre examples of an American cult. Established in the 1970s by Marshall Applewhite and Bonnie Nettles, the group held the belief that the earth was about to be "recycled" in some manner, destroyed and rejuvenated, and that the only way to survive it would be to leave it as soon as possible. Applewhite's belief system involved a strange mix of Biblical apocalypse, computer technology, and a belief in UFOs. He believed and taught his followers that travel to other worlds and dimensions was a possibility. He and Nettles held themselves out as "the Two," the two witnesses spoken of in the New Testament Book of Revelations (11:3). Traveling across the country under various names, they managed to gain a small following, eventually taking up residence with nearly 40 of their followers in a rented communal mansion near San Diego. To pay their expenses and provide sustenance, the group established a Web development company, and enjoyed some success. The mansion in which they lived was later found to be wired throughout with monitors, computers, and other forms of technology.

On March 26, 1997, Applewhite and 38 of his followers were found dead in the mansion. Each appeared to have committed suicide. All were found lying in their bunks with a purple cloth covering their faces and upper torsos, and each wore an armband that read "Heaven's Gate Away Team." During the subsequent investigation videotapes were found in which Applewhite described the circumstances leading to the mass suicide. He described how the Hale-Bopp comet was approaching the earth, and that behind it would be a spaceship waiting to transport the group members to safety. The suicide was necessary in order for their souls to be released from their bodies, thus allowing them to travel to and board the waiting spaceship. In a strange twist, the subsequent autopsies revealed that Applewhite and six male followers had previously been surgically castrated. The cause of death in each case was found to be poisoning by a mix of phenobarbital and pudding laced with cyanide and arsenic (CNN, March 27, 1997).

Social-isolationist Cults

In contrast to the apocalyptic groups, **social-isolationist cults** are not motivated by a final armed conflict that will usher in the end of days. Rather, they are motivated primarily by their desire to simply live an isolated existence free of outside influence. These groups can, and do, oftentimes have a religious basis for their isolationist lifestyle, but they may also espouse a purely secular set of beliefs. Unlike the apocalyptic groups, many of which may resort to violence to help usher in a final conflict they believe to be imminent, isolationist groups tend to avoid contact with mainstream society, except for recruiting activities. Unlike the apocalyptic groups, isolationist groups do not view themselves as being purified or prepared in some way for an imminent event. Rather, these groups, whether founded on spiritual or secular ideas, perceive a need for isolation in order to protect a particular lifestyle. It is often a lifestyle that would be viewed in a negative light by mainstream society. Some examples include the following:

- Polygamist groups
- New age groups
- Wiccan/witchcraft/Satanic groups
- Groups espousing adult-child sexual interaction
- Alternative religious groups

The more deviant of the isolationist groups almost always have an authoritarian leader who takes measures to shield the group from any contact with the outside world. The leader may even establish a security force within the group that is charged with keeping the outside from getting in, and the inside from getting out. The more authoritarian the group, the more its members are pressured to cut off all contact with family and friends outside the group. Members are "instructed" constantly on the beliefs and practices of the group, almost all of which are dictated by the leader, and there may even be a harsh disciplinary system in place to deal with members who demonstrate too much independence or violate the group's rules. The leaders of these groups are viewed as having either divine knowledge or some special wisdom that transcends that of a normal human. Their directives are almost always viewed as absolute and beyond question.

EXAMPLE: THE PEOPLE'S TEMPLE   The tragic events that took place in the jungles of Guyana on November 18, 1978, became one of the most publicized events in U.S. history. It was here that 918 members of the People's Temple, including the group's leader, Reverend Jim Jones, died after drinking cyanide-laced Flavor Aid. Those who refused were shot, and it was later determined that Jones died from a self-inflicted gunshot. It was one of the saddest episodes in the history of American cults. Among the dead were entire families, and at least 270 children (trutv.com).

The People's Temple began as a relatively mainstream Christian church in Indianapolis in 1956. But Jones was also a devout communist, and he believed the church should espouse such egalitarian values. In the church's early days, as Jones moved his organization from Indianapolis to California, there was a focus on racial integration and poverty. Jones was held in high esteem by local politicians and civic leaders. He required his congregants to wear common clothes so the poor members of the church would not feel out of place. He organized shelters and food pantries, and provided rent assistance and job training. While in Indiana, Jones was even appointed to the Human Rights Commission. His church recruited heavily from the African American community, one of the few white churches to actively do so at that time.

Eventually Jones's communist beliefs began to more heavily influence his ministry, and when it did the People's Temple began its transformation from Christian church to isolationist cult; a transformation that would eventually lead it to the jungles of Guyana. Jones referred to his new paradigm as *Apostolic Socialism*. He began to preach a message that included Marxist philosophy, and the idea that Jesus was a communist. Members were now asked to donate all their material possessions to the church in return for the church meeting all their needs. He also began to devalue the Bible, and described it as nothing more than a tool for the subjugation of women and minorities. He even began to attack the traditional Christian conception of God, referring to it as a "sky God," who in reality was no God at all. This doctrinal shift had the effect of alienating Jones from the traditional churches in the community, which only added to his growing paranoia.

The further away from traditional doctrine Jones took his Temple, the more bizarre his teachings became. He began to fake healings with confederate church members as a way of attracting new members. Members were taught to avoid their families, and to consider the other church members as their primary family. Jones began to act erratically, and it wasn't long before he was teaching that he personally was a special manifestation of Christ, and thus of a divine nature. People who left the church were harassed and threatened. A small army of armed members surrounded Jones everywhere he went.

Eventually the media in and around San Francisco began to report on the odd beliefs and behavior of the People's Temple and its members. Former members were telling stories of abusive practices, drug abuse, and financial fraud occurring within the church. With media scrutiny increasing, Jones ordered his followers to follow him to a piece of land the church leased in Guyana. It was there they would establish a socialist paradise free from the oppressive influence of American capitalism. By late 1978, over 900 members of the Temple had relocated to the People's Temple Agricultural Project or, as it was informally known, "Jonestown."

Once established in Guyana, Jones rapidly began to decline emotionally. He completely abandoned Christianity, now believing he was the one true God. He used illicit drugs on a regular basis, and he became increasingly more paranoid as time passed. Eventually word leaked to family members in America that members who wished to leave Jonestown were not being allowed to. Additionally, there were allegations of physical, emotional, and even sexual abuse occurring in the village. It was later reported that Jones was having ritualistic sex with both men and women in the village, and possibly even children (Reiterman and Jacobs, 1982).

In an effort to address the concerns he was hearing in his office, California congressman Leo Ryan agreed to travel to Jonestown to see the conditions there. He flew in to a small airstrip near the village with journalists and aids. His goal was to speak to members of the Temple to determine if they were in fact being abused and prevented from leaving. On November 17, 1978, Congressman Ryan arrived in Jonestown, and was given a tour of the facilities by Jones's wife, Marceline. The next day, satisfied that only a few people truly wanted to leave, and agreeing to take them with him, the congressman returned to the airstrip to depart for California. What happened when they arrived at the clearing in the jungle was captured on the video camera of a

Violent Apocalyptic
Focus is on the end of the world and the group's continued existence in another dimension of experience, with a perceived ability to facilitate its coming, and a willingness to do so through violent actions.

Biblical

Quasi-Biblical

Secular

Passive Apocalyptic
Focus is on the end of the world and the group's continued existence in another dimension of experience, but typically without the perceived ability to facilitate its coming.

Social-isolationist
Focus is on living an alternative lifestyle free of interference by the members and institutions of mainstream society.

New World Order
Focus is on facilitating a re-ordering of mainstream society, through violence if necessary. In order to be more consistent with the beliefs of the group.

Cultural

Environmental

Geopolitical

Fantasy

FIGURE 11.1 Cult Typologies.

dying journalist for the world to see. A truck full of Temple members approached and opened fire, killing Congressman Ryan and four others, and wounding 11 more.

Immediately following the killings at the airstrip, Jones summoned his followers to the main pavilion, and there he advised his followers that the congressman had been killed, and that to avoid the torture that would now be perpetrated on them, he directed them to drink the poison-laced drink. Parents were ordered to first poison their children, and then to lie beside their bodies while they drank the poison themselves. In the end, it was the greatest loss of American civilian life in a non-natural event until being surpassed by the tragic events of September 11, 2001. To this day, Leo Ryan remains the only U.S. congressman in history to have been murdered in the course of his official duties.

New World Order Cults

New World Order cults are not concerned about an apocalyptic event that will mark the end of the world. They endeavor instead to re-order society in a particular way that is more consistent with their beliefs. They tend not to be religious in nature, and they may very well engage in violence. Unlike the apocalyptic cults, these groups are not waiting for some final event. Instead, they view themselves as agents for the desired change. Thus they may resort to violence as a way of initiating that change. Some of the more common types of new world order cults are as follows:

• **Cultural:** These groups desire to change the structure of society in some way. They may seek to make the culture of a particular minority group the dominant one, or they may seek to eliminate minority groups altogether. They may wish to eliminate the authority of the police, and to perhaps create a new world order in which young people control the institutions of society.

• **Environmental:** These groups are radical environmentalists who view the protection of the environment as paramount. They typically live communally in places far removed from America's urban jungles. Unlike the social-isolationist groups that wish only to protect a particular lifestyle, which may have an environmental theme, these groups endeavor to transform society, by force if necessary, to adopt their lifestyle as the predominant cultural paradigm. They may engage in ecoterrorism if they believe it will further their objectives.

• **Geopolitical:** These groups have a political basis for their affiliation. They may be secessionists wanting to start their own country, or perhaps they wish to establish a new political party with the goal of taking over the government through the election process. They may be tax protestors, or extreme constitutionalists. They may be right-wing militia types, or left-wing revolutionaries. Many everyday people will admit to having similar sentiments, but what sets a cult apart is their secrecy and their cohesion as a group.

• **Fantasy:** These cults can take on a wide range of group identities. They tend to find their inspiration in science fiction or fantasy, where the line between reality and fiction is blurred. They may desire a world that resembles the setting of a particular board game or video game. Perhaps they may be computer-oriented, and endeavor to bring about a world where computers control human beings. They may pattern their daily lives after the legends of King Arthur, or the characters of J. R. R. Tolkien. If the fantasy after which they pattern their lifestyle includes a violent element, then there is a risk that the group could perpetrate this same level of violence in their efforts to act out their fantasy roles.

EXAMPLE: THE MANSON FAMILY   The Manson family murders are among the most notorious crimes in American history. Not only did the gruesome events of August 1969 mark a symbolic end to the idealistic 1960s, but they brought into full public view the reality of cult life in America. In a two-night violent crime spree, seven people in two separate houses were brutally murdered by members of the Manson family. Once it came to light that the murders were connected, and that members of a cult had committed them, Americans became captivated by the story, and by the trial that followed.

In 1967, Charles Manson was a 32-year-old unemployed ex-convict living in a small apartment in Berkeley, California. Still on parole for a series of crimes, Manson had spent half of his life behind bars, where he learned to play the guitar and write songs. In the Haight-Ashbury district of San Francisco, Manson became known as a sort of mystic-musician who moved between singing his songs on the street and espousing a counter-culture philosophy to anyone who would listen. Within a short time he and a following of mostly young females were living communally on an abandoned ranch outside Los Angeles that once served as a movie set. It was here, where unrestrained drug use and sexual activity were part of the group's daily lifestyle, that Manson gained full control of the minds of his young followers.

In late 1968 Manson was introduced to the Beatles' *White Album*, a seemingly innocuous circumstance that would set in motion a series of events that would culminate in the deadly murder spree in August 1969 (Bugliosi, 1974). Manson believed the album contained coded messages meant specifically for him and his group of followers. His obsession with the album led to a vision of a new world order in which Blacks would annihilate whites and declare Manson their leader. He referred to this coming race war as "Helter Skelter," after the title to one of the songs included on the *White Album*.

By August 1969, Manson had become agitated that the expected race war had not yet happened. He therefore decided the time was right to initiate the war himself by committing a serious of random and heinous crimes, believing the authorities would accuse Blacks. Manson hoped this would set off a violent reprisal by whites, and the race war would begin. They began their attacks on the night of August 8th, when Manson instructed four of his followers to go to a house in Los Angeles he had previously visited at a time when another person lived there, and to kill everyone inside. The house was now inhabited by actress Sharon Tate and her husband, Hollywood director Roman Polanski. Polanksi was away on business; however, his wife, now eight months pregnant, was inside sleeping, along with three of her friends. Before entering the house, the group of Manson followers killed a teenage boy in his car as he was leaving the location.

The bloodbath that followed was one of the most gruesome killings in American history. No one was spared. Even the pregnant Tate was brutally stabbed nearly 20 times as she pleaded for the life of her baby. Abigail Folger, heiress to the Folger's coffee fortune, was stabbed a total of 28 times. When the city awakened to the news of the senseless killings, people were shocked at the brutality of it. But Manson and his followers were not finished. The very next night Manson and six of his followers selected another house, this one again a place Manson had once visited when different people lived there, and again ordered his people to kill its inhabitants. Inside, Leno and Rosemary LaBianca were awakened at gunpoint by Manson and his followers, who proceeded to brutally stab them to death.

In all, seven people died in the two-night crime spree. The LAPD initially denied any connection between the murders. On August 16th, Manson's ranch was raided by the L.A. County Sheriff's Department, and 25 members of the family were detained in connection with an auto theft ring. One of those family members, Susan Atkins, informed two cellmates of the family's involvement in the Tate and LaBianca murders. Those cellmates eventually informed the police of Atkins's statements, and in short order Manson and four of his most loyal followers were charged with first-degree murder. All were eventually convicted and sentenced to death; however, the death sentences were eventually overturned when California abolished the death penalty. All but Susan Atkins, who died in prison of brain cancer in 2009, remain incarcerated to this day, over 40 years since their convictions.

CULT PERSONALITIES

Those who fill the ranks of a cult tend to fall in one of three categories based on their position and duties within the cult, and their general personality characteristics. These personalities are *leader, enforcer*, and *follower*. Together they create a unique dynamic that allows a cult to flourish, and to protect it against threats from both inside and outside the group.

The Leader

Obviously the most important person in any cult is its leader. In most cases it is the leader who establishes the group, recruits the initial members, and most importantly, develops the ideology that will guide the group. Tobias, Lalich, and Langone (1994) have compiled a list of the most common characteristics of a cult leader. They point out that cult leaders are extremely charming and persuasive. They are also masters at manipulation. Their goal is to acquire and maintain absolute control over their members. Most have a history of juvenile delinquency, and have learned through experience how to con someone for financial or sexual gain. They are almost always sexually promiscuous, and make sex a part of the cult experience. Most could be described as antisocial, with no empathic connection to others and no sympathy for those experiencing some sort of despair. Their behavior can be very erratic, and they tend to be pathological liars.

When you look in the past lives of cult leaders, you tend to find some common themes. First, they tend to come from dysfunctional homes, and thus they never fully acquire such attributes as love, compassion, and morality. They are almost always conflicted about their self-identity during adolescence. This conflict can relate to their sexuality, their occupational or career goals, or their religious beliefs. Most have difficulty with relationships and social competence. And almost always, as a way of compensating for their personal deficits, they develop a grandiose view of themselves and their purpose in life. They also tend to experience failure in their adult lives prior to their cult experience. Many try legitimate careers and lifestyles before eventually failing. Marshall Applewhite, the leader of the Heaven's Gate cult, was fired from his job as a college music professor due to his emotional problems. Reverend Jim Jones was a respected minister until he began resorting to fake healings in an effort to attract new converts and financial resources, something the local news media eventually exposed. Shoko Asahara, who was born near totally blind, was a trained acupuncturist before being kicked out of the business for running an unlicensed pharmacy.

Cult leaders are masters at exploitation. Most have a history of exploiting people and situations since adolescence. In terms of their cult activity, they prey upon people who are impressionable, and who likely have a history of being exploited in some way. They offer themselves as a savior-figure who will protect them from further exploitation. The more vulnerable these converts are, the more likely it is that they will follow the leader without question. What the cult leader gives them is hope, and hope can be a powerful motivating force. This hope may come in the form of a promised afterlife, or perhaps a better set of circumstances during this one. Above all else an effective cult leader understands the power of hope, and how to use it to their advantage.

The Enforcer

The one thing a cult leader fears most is being exposed as a fraud and losing control of their grip on the group members. In almost every cult there are those who make up the leader's inner circle of friends and followers. These are people who are trusted by the leader to carry out their orders without question. Many times these enforcers are people who have been with the leader since the very beginning. Some may very well believe the leader's doctrine, whereas others may simply see it as an opportunity to do something that meets their particular needs in some way. The leader may even pay the enforcer with money or special privileges for their loyalty. They tend to have antisocial personalities with histories of crime and violence. Some may even choose to remain with the cult in order to hide out from the law.

One thing that is true of enforcers, the cult leader seldom demands their loyalty to their beliefs and doctrines, only to him personally. They are relied upon to serve as disciplinarians within the group, always keeping a watchful eye for a member who may have doubts and become a threat to the group's continued existence. In the more volatile groups, the enforcers may even be relied upon to perpetrate violence against other cult members, or even public authorities and

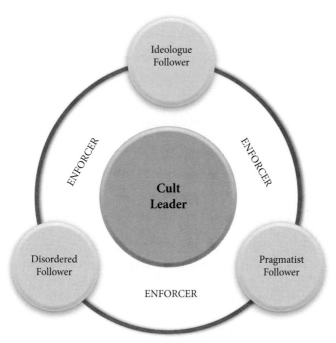

FIGURE 11.2 Structure and type of cult membership.

officials. For Charles Manson, it was Tex Watson who carried out his violent orders to brutally kill seven innocent people. When the few survivors of Jonestown finally told their stories, they described how when Jim Jones called them to the pavilion that dreadful day, they noticed armed men quietly surrounding the group. And of course we learned that these enforcers were the ones who shot and killed anyone refusing to drink the poison.

The **enforcer** plays a critical role within the group. They increase the power of the leader with the implied threat of action in response to disobedience or disloyalty. Even if this action is non-violent in nature, their presence still buffers the leader against internal threats. The enforcer also prevents the establishment of alliances within the group. They develop their own intelligence-gathering networks, leaving the group members unsure who can be trusted and who cannot. The resulting paranoia benefits the cult leader. On the one hand they instill an uneasy obedience, and possibly even fear in the members, and on the other an emotional dependence on the leader as their benevolent savior. The end goal for the leader, of course, is to gain complete control of the person's mind through their manipulative methods. The enforcers are a critical necessity for achieving this desired goal.

The Follower

For any cult to remain viable there must be a supply of loyal followers. They are the ones who provide the group the needed funds to exist communally, either by signing over their own assets, engaging in criminality, or working for it; who spread the group's message both inside and outside the group, assuming the latter is a desired goal; and who participate in the recruitment of new members. The follower is not part of a homogenous group. They may have different motivations for joining the group and staying with it. Followers can be grouped into three broad categories: the *ideologue*, the *pragmatist*, and the *disordered*.

- **Ideologue:** This individual is part of the cult because they truly believe in the message being proffered by the group's leader. Many members of Aum Shinrikyo were well-educated professionals who had the ability to provide themselves a comfortable life. Many joined the group and signed over their assets, however, because they truly believed Asahara's message. The ideologue is attracted to the group more by the message than by the lifestyle. They may also be the first to leave the group when the leader begins to deviate from the original message.

- **Pragmatist:** These people are attracted to the group less by the message and more by the lifestyle. They are typically people who have been disenfranchised by the dominant society or have experienced some major problem that left them unable to live on their own and provide for their own sustenance (i.e., unemployment, divorce, bankruptcy, etc.). The majority of the people who ultimately died at Jonestown were African Americans from the poorer areas around San Francisco. Jones's Christian socialism allowed them to avoid the types of hardship being experienced by many minorities during that particular time. Also, by affiliating with a cult made up mostly of African Americans, these followers were suddenly no longer part of a minority community. The pragmatist is attracted by the stability and security the cult offers. The effective cult leader understands this, and uses it to their advantage by playing the role of protector to gain their loyalty.

- **Disordered:** These cult members tend to be emotionally unstable, and may even suffer from any number of psychological disorders. They may have little interest in the group's ideology, or it may actually reinforce and strengthen their delusional thought processes. They may have a history of rejection, social isolation, and a general lack of attachment to caregivers. These people are tailor-made for the cult experience, and will respond immediately to a charismatic leader. They respond less to the message and lifestyle of the cult, and more to the relationships and sense of connectedness cult affiliation offers. For those who suffer delusional thinking, the cult offers a feeling of normalcy without the fear of institutionalization. Disordered members are easily exploited, and thus they may be called upon by the group leader to carry out certain tasks that will purportedly benefit the group in some way. These tasks may include criminal offenses.

THE CULT THREAT

Without a doubt, a cult can be dangerous. As we have pointed out in this chapter, many innocent people around the world have lost their lives as a result of cult activity. The threats they pose are many, depending on the type of cult it happens to be, and the type of intervention attempted by authorities. They may carry out a terrorist-style attack on an unsuspecting public, as in the case of Aum Shinrikyo. There may be the threat of mass suicide, as in the case of the People's Temple and Heaven's Gate. Or they may adopt a criminal lifestyle and perpetrate violence and other criminal acts against innocent people, as in the case of the Manson family. And finally, they may retaliate with violence and firepower if authorities intervene in a manner that threatens their lifestyle or continued existence. We witnessed this in the case of the People's Temple and, more recently, in February 1993, at the Branch Davidian compound outside Waco, Texas.

One of the primary goals of the criminal justice system in relation to cults is to identify a growing threat before it is acted upon by the group's members. The previously cited Canadian Security Intelligence Service Report (1999) lists a series of early-warning signs that may point to a cult's eventual use of violence.

- *Intensification of illegal activities:* One of the telltale signs that a cult may have violent intentions is their procurement of weaponry, chemicals, or other materials that could potentially be used for destructive purposes. This could indicate that the group is taking defensive measures against a perceived threat, but it also could point to some type of planned proactive action by the group. In the case of David Koresh and the Branch Davidians, the ATF was well aware of the fact that they were stockpiling weaponry. It was reported that over 8000 pounds of ammunition, parts for automatic weapons, and even hand grenades, had been shipped to the compound (Time, 1993). It was this fact that compelled them to seek a search warrant to raid the Davidian compound in February 1993, a mission that went terribly wrong and cost the lives of four federal agents and six Davidian in the initial assault. It was later learned that Koresh was preparing his group for a final apocalyptic battle with non-believers, a battle he believed was imminent.

- *Humiliating circumstances:* For Reverend Jim Jones, nothing was more humiliating than to have a U.S. congressman visit his compound, question his practices, and then attempt to depart with members of the group who wanted to leave. The greatest threat to a cult leader is being exposed as a fraud or having their power and control over the group called into question. Congressman Ryan did just that, and at a time when Jones was becoming increasingly more paranoid as a result of excessive drug use and mental illness. The result of course was the congressman's murder, followed by the mass suicide of Jones and his followers.

Any situation in which people or agencies in positions of authority call into question the practices of the cult creates a dangerous situation. Not only do such actions give the appearance of subjugating an omnipotent leader to the authority of those bringing the questions, but it suddenly makes the leader look a little more human and a little less divine. It may be child welfare authorities looking into allegations of child sexual abuse, or even something as minor as county authorities questioning zoning infraction. For the group's leader, the humiliation comes in not being able to stop such an inquiry, and further, in being subjected to various types of sanctions if they try.

The other major source of humiliation for a cult leader is when prophecies do not come to pass. Prophesying major events is a manipulative device used by cult leaders to control and exploit their members. It keeps them focused on a future event, and gives the group some justification for existing. When a prophesy fails it can create a dangerous situation. Leon Festinger (1956) was one of the first to describe a phenomenon in which a cult is actually strengthened following a failed prophecy. The failed prophecy leads to what Festinger called a **disconfirmed expectancy**. The result is a dissonance between two cognitions, which creates an uncomfortable psychological state. On the one hand the cult members have placed their complete trust in the group leader and his prophecies. But on the other hand, the prophecy did not come true.

You would think that in such a case, the members would realize that the leader is a fraud and move on. But as Festinger found in his study of cults, just the opposite oftentimes happens. People do not enjoy the psychic tension that accompanies **cognitive dissonance**. For someone who has invested much in the cult experience, to simply admit their mistake and move on is simply unbearable. So instead they attempt to rationalize the failed prophecy in a way that will eliminate the dissonance. Most of the time this rationalization simply involves accepting without question the group leader's explanation as to why the prophecy failed. This not only eliminates their dissonance, but in most cases actually strengthens their trust in, and loyalty to, the group leader.

The danger arises when the group leader's explanation involves a form of displacement, meaning they cast the blame for the failed prophecy on an outside source. The stronger the blame, and the more forceful the response, the easier it is for the members to believe the explanation, or

ISSUES & ETHICS IN CRISIS INTERVENTION

The Line between Religion and Cult: The Case of Warren Jeffs and the Fundamentalist Church of Jesus Christ of Latter Day Saints

In August 2011, Warren Jeffs, the president and self-proclaimed prophet of the Fundamentalist Church of Jesus Christ of Latter Day Saints (FLDS), was sentenced to life in prison by a Texas jury for sexually assaulting two young girls, ages 12 and 15. The older of the two gave birth to Jeffs's child. During the trial evidence was offered showing that Jeffs had sexually assaulted a number of young girls over the years, including his own niece when she was just 7 years old.

The case began when Texas law enforcement authorities and child protective personnel raided the FLDS compound in April 2008 after receiving a hotline tip that children in the compound were being sexually abused on a wide scale. Although the hotline tip turned out to be a hoax, police did see a number of young girls who appeared to be pregnant. Additionally, Jeffs's own journals were discovered in which he detailed his abusive practices, including the forced marriages of young girls to adult men. As a result of this evidence, over 400 FLDS children were removed from the FLDS community and taken into protective custody.

By all accepted measures, the FLDS was a cult. Its members lived in isolation from mainstream society and maintained their own system of beliefs and cultural practices, most of which originated in the mind of Warren Jeffs. In reality the FLDS was nothing more than a criminal enterprise that provided a steady supply of vulnerable victims to a group of sexual predators under the guise of God-sanctioned marriage. Eventually, Jeffs and 11 other adult men would be charged with crimes relating to the sexual exploitation of children.

Just one month following the initial raid however, the Texas Supreme Court ruled that there was not enough evidence to support the removal of the children from their homes, and ordered that they be returned to their families within 10 days. Many came to the FLDS's defense over the issue, and even the ACLU stated publicly, "Exposure to a religion's beliefs, however unorthodox, is not itself abuse and may not constitutionally be labeled abuse" (2008). Unfortunately those beliefs, in the case of the FLDS, included arranged marriages of young girls to adult males, and their subsequent sexual abuse, the extent of which would be sadly confirmed in the coming trials.

America has always been conflicted over its definition of "religion," and thus the institutions of American society have typically erred on the side of caution when intervening in the affairs of a religious organization. The question must be asked whether the FLDS children were failed by people and agencies that turned a blind eye because they were unable to see the cult for the religion that shrouded it.

Discussion Questions

1. Should the authorities intervene anytime children are found to be living in an isolated community, religious or otherwise, to ensure they are being treated and educated appropriately?
2. Discuss your definition of "religion." At what point do you believe a religious organization becomes a cult?
3. For the FLDS, underage marriage was a tenant of their religious practice. For some Native American groups, the use of peyote, an illegal hallucinogen, is protected under the Constitution as a tenant of their religious practice. Both are illegal in mainstream society. Why should the use of peyote be allowed, but not underage marriage?

at least to allow themselves to repress any lingering doubt. In order for the leader to save face, he may deem it necessary to retaliate against the parties responsible for the failed prophecy, which may be the police, a local judge or politician, or even the non-believing citizens with whom they co-exist. This is exactly what happened with the Manson family. When the race war Manson predicted did come to pass, he blamed it on the laziness of African Americans, and then decided to jump-start the war by killing innocent white people and making it appear as though the murders had been committed by Blacks. It was a classic example of a cult leader reducing the dissonance following a failed prophecy by rationalizing a cause and displacing the group's aggression onto innocent people. In the end, Manson only strengthened his position among his followers.

- *Relocation to a rural area:* Anytime a group relocates to an isolated location it is a sign that the group, or the group leader, feels threatened in some way. Such a physical isolation is almost always accompanied by a psychological isolation, as the group adopts a "bunker" mentality. Their posture turns defensive, which only increases the group members' loyalty to their leader and his doctrine. Relocation is typically precipitated by an event, one which threatens the continued existence of the group and its lifestyle. It could be just about anything that excites the paranoia of the group or its leader. For Jim Jones and the People's Temple it was a series of exposés in the local newspaper that led them to abruptly flee to the jungles of Guyana.

A mass relocation by any suspected cult should be considered a danger signal. An isolated location allows for greater ease in the stockpiling of weapons, and also for military-style training by group members outside the watchful eyes of the authorities. Such a relocation may signal that the group is preparing for a violent defense against an imagined attack, but it may also point to a violent offensive action, as in the case of Aum Shinrykio. And, as previously discussed, a sudden relocation may be used by the leader as a manipulative device to redirect the focus of his followers following a failed prophecy. The failure may be blamed on an action by outside entities, thus allowing the leader to avoid accusations, or even quiet suspicions among the group members, of false prophesy, and necessitating their immediate relocation to either defend themselves or to take an offensive action that will purportedly speed up the fulfillment of the prophecy.

- *Increasingly violent rhetoric:* When a cult leader begins to feel threatened or increasingly paranoid, either because they truly believe they are under attack or because they are attempting to manipulate their members to shift their focus away from a failed prophesy or some other embarrassing event, such as the leader getting arrested for some petty offense, then the rhetoric will invariably grow more violent. It is also a way for the leader to psychologically prepare his followers if his intent is to direct them to perpetrate violence against innocent people. An analogy is a football coach who prepares his team for a game by hitting the lockers and using extreme competitive language. By the time they hit the field they are in a frenzy and eager to externalize their pent-up aggression on the opposing team.

- *Struggle for leadership:* An internal struggle for the group's leadership is always a sign that violence may occur, especially internal violence involving the various factions vying for control. Many cult members have been attacked or killed for taking sides in favor or against a particular leader. Once again, this type of scenario may be used to justify violence outside the group if a leader convinces his followers that such an internal struggle is a sign that the coming apocalypse is imminent. It may be enough to push an already paranoid and mentally ill leader over the edge and cause him to order his followers to carry out violent acts against innocent people.

THE POLICE RESPONSE TO CULT ACTIVITY

Constitutional Limitations

It is no easy task for law enforcement to act proactively when it comes to cult activity. Cults have a constitutional right to exist in America and, further, they have a right to believe and behave as they wish, so long as no laws are broken. Traditionally, the criminal justice system in America has been terribly unsuccessful in dealing with cult activity. Their typical first contact with a cult is either to look for a missing person the family believes is living with the group, or to check on the welfare of children after rumors surface of child abuse or neglect. In the first instance, if the individual is an adult and living with the cult voluntarily, then there really is nothing for the police to do but to report back to the family that their family member is there and that they wish to remain. In the second instance, if the children appear healthy, and there is no sign of abuse or neglect, then once again there really is nothing that can be done. As much as the cult may seem to most, including the police, to be abnormal or even oppressive, precautions must be taken not to violate their constitutional rights.

So how do police agencies respond to an active cult? First of all, the police must recognize that their mission is not only to protect the public from the violent actions of a cult, but also to protect innocent members of the cult itself, especially children, from violence. So the first step for law enforcement is to attempt to understand the nature of the cult, and the makeup of its membership. Thus, intelligence gathering becomes the first crucial step. If information is developed about the existence of a cult, then the police should attempt to ascertain the following:

- Type of cult (apocalyptic, social-isolationist, new world order)
- Guiding doctrines
- Trigger event (a major event anticipated by the cult that may trigger violence)
- The identity of the group's leadership (criminal history, past violence, social history)
- Source of the group's funding
- The group's membership (identities, ages, missing persons, etc.)
- Weapons acquisition
- Immediate concerns (allegations of child abuse or neglect, forced detention)

Obviously if there are allegations of victimization, or if there is evidence of illegal weapons being stockpiled, then the police must act as they normally would. Whether the response will be non-confrontational, or a full tactical assault, will depend on the circumstances. As we witnessed in the case of the Branch Davidians in Waco, Texas, if a tactical response is attempted without proper intelligence and secrecy, the result can be disastrous.

In most cases there will be no direct evidence of ongoing illegality. Without it, the police have no ability to do wiretaps, search warrants, or subpoena financial records. Thus intelligence gathering becomes a matter of watching, listening, and building relationships with people who may have contact with the group, or the actual group members. One thing that is absolutely critical, especially when dealing with an apocalyptic type cult, is that the police avoid unnecessary confrontation with the group. Such confrontation may unleash a **spiral of amplification**, or a confirmation of the group's apocalyptic beliefs, and lead to unnecessary violence on the part of the cult members. In fact, friendly engagement with the group may actually serve a much better purpose. It allows the police to gather intelligence by being in close proximity to the group, and it acts to diffuse any tension between the groups that can contribute to a spiral of amplification. Some groups, however, especially violent-apocalyptic groups, make friendly engagement unlikely, if not impossible. With these groups, active intelligence gathering becomes critical, and may include surveillance and even infiltration by undercover officers.

As intelligence is gathered on a particular cult, there should be an ongoing analysis of the data to determine if the group is preparing for violent actions, including its own mass suicide, and if immediate action by the police is warranted. It is critical that an investigator be assigned to the matter that is trained in the area of cult investigations. Any type of proactive action by the police, including search warrants and wiretaps, must be based on **probable cause evidence**, or in other words, a level of evidence that extends beyond merely a hunch or rumor. This probable cause evidence is indicated in an affidavit that is submitted in support of a judge's authorization to conduct the operation. Sometimes certain patterns of behavior and otherwise unremarkable actions by cult members may be acceptable as probable cause, indicating perhaps that a mass suicide is imminent for example; however, it requires that the investigator drafting the affidavit have sufficient expertise to make those determinations and analyses. This expertise must be clearly indicated in the actual affidavit, and it makes it much more likely that a judge will authorize the action.

If an event does take place, such as an attack on innocent people or clear evidence of child abuse, then the police response must be swift and calculated. If intelligence is being gathered on a particular group, then a response plan should be in place for a rapid response. The action taken will depend on the event that has taken place. One thing the police must avoid at all costs is a standoff similar to the one with the Branch Davidians. To the extent possible, efforts should be made to separate the group's leader from the other group members and disrupt any channels of communication. This may be difficult, especially when the leader is growing increasingly more paranoid and refusing to leave the group's compound. If a standoff does result, then an experienced negotiator must be brought in who understands the cult mind-set, and who understands that confrontation may unleash a spiral of amplification and endanger those inside, including any children present. Like all forms of crisis intervention, the initial goal when responding to a cult situation is to contain and de-escalate the crisis.

A New Federal Protocol

Deputy Attorney General Phillip Heymann (1993) proposed a number of changes in federal law enforcement protocol following the disaster at Waco. His recommendations included the following four elements:

1. **A well-equipped and highly skilled tactical team** that has completed extensive training in complex hostage/barricade incidents. This team should be sizeable enough to establish a perimeter around the incident location to keep people out, especially the media. In many cases the presence of cameras only emboldens the group leader, and may even prompt them to commit violent acts in order to make a public statement. The team should also be trained in the use of the most current non-lethal weapons technology.

2. **Trained and experienced negotiators** who are supported by research relating to techniques for peaceful resolution. Negotiators must understand the cult mentality, especially that of its leader, and recognize when tensions inside the location are approaching dangerous levels.

3. **Behavioral science experts** who can advise negotiators at the scene of changes in the situational dynamics, and make tactical recommendations based on those changes. These experts must be people who have researched and studied cult behavior, and fully understand the relationship between the actions of the tactical team and the spiral of amplification within the cult.

4. **A command structure** that can develop an overall strategy for de-escalating the situation. One of the problems at Waco was the lack of a cohesive command structure. There was interagency squabbling over who was in charge, the ATF or the FBI, and many important decisions were being made by people who were not even at the scene of the incident. There must be no doubt about who is in charge of an incident such as Waco. The person(s) in charge must be at the scene of the incident, and must have clearly delineated plans for any possible contingency.

Chapter Summary

The problems posed by modern-day cults will not go away anytime soon. As our modern techno-society becomes more complex and diverse, it is likely that cult activity will only increase. People will continue to search for new meaning in their lives, with the vulnerable and disenfranchised being especially susceptible to the manipulative methods of cult leaders. Many cults have been, and will continue to be non-violent. So long as no laws are broken, these groups have a constitutionally protected right to assemble and exercise free speech. In terms of crisis intervention, non-violent groups pose less of a threat to the safety and welfare of innocent people. Violent cults on the other hand, and those likely to resort to violence when threatened, must remain under the watchful eyes of law enforcement. The police must identify these groups in their earliest stages, and develop new methods of surveillance and intelligence gathering in order to keep an eye on their activities. The police must also avoid confrontation when it is unnecessary, and make every effort to better understand the mind-set and doctrines of these groups, along with patterns of behavior that may signal that violence or mass suicide is imminent.

Key Terms

Cult
Violent-apocalyptic cult
Apocalyptic belief
Dualism
The persecuted chosen
Imminence
Determinism

Salvation through conflict
Passive-apocalyptic cult
Social-isolationist cult
New World Order cult
Enforcer
The ideologue
The pragmatist

The disordered
Disconfirmed expectancy
Cognitive dissonance
Spiral of amplification
Probable cause evidence

Discussion Questions

1. Reflect on someone you know whom you think might be attracted to affiliate with a cult under the right circumstances. What are the characteristics of that person's personality that led you to believe this?
2. Do some basic internet research on the siege at Waco, Texas, of the Branch Davidian compound in 1993. Discuss the initial police response, and whether you feel it was appropriate given the information and intelligence that was available to them at the time.
3. Discuss the "spiral of amplification," and some ways in which the police response could potentially trigger and intensify this dangerous circumstance.

12

The Crisis of Mental Illness

LEARNING OUTCOMES

Upon completion of this chapter the student should be able to:

1. Describe the problem of mental illness in the context of the criminal justice mission.

2. Summarize the traditional police and corrections response to mental illness.

3. List and define some of the more common types of mental illness faced by crisis responders.

4. Summarize the accepted best practices for responding to mentally ill offenders, victims, suspects, and inmates.

Chapter Outline

INTRODUCTION

Crises involving the mentally ill have long been considered among the most dangerous to which a police officer can respond. They are volatile, unpredictable, and many times involve individuals who have lost their ability to think rationally. They are dangerous not only for the police, but also for those who stand at the center of these crises. Unfortunately, a mentally ill individual wielding a knife looks no different to most police officers than any other violent offender. For the police, the same rules of engagement and force apply, and many times an individual in need of mental health intervention instead ends up on the receiving end of a police officer's use of deadly force, force that almost always is ruled justifiable and appropriate under the circumstances. Avoidability is seldom one of the criteria by which police shootings are measured. Consider the following examples:

- In May, 2010, 36-year-old Keith Briscoe was standing in front of a Winslow Township, Pennsylvania, convenience store smoking and drinking a soda. He was neither armed nor trying to harm himself. In fact, Briscoe was repeating a daily routine before attending his therapy session at Steininger Behavioral Care Services a few blocks away. People inside the store knew him and no complaint had been filed. When a police officer showed up and demanded that he quit loitering and leave the premises, a fight broke out. It took four additional officers to finally subdue and handcuff Briscoe. When they got off his body they discovered he had quit breathing. Briscoe later died at a nearby hospital (Nark, 2010).
- On May 10, 2009, officers in San Jose, California, were called to the home of Daniel Pham, a 27-year-old Vietnamese man who reportedly was threatening people with a knife. Dispatchers advised the responding officers that the department had previously responded to Pham's residence, and that he was known to be mentally ill. Upon arrival the officers confronted Pham, who was standing in his backyard smoking and still holding the knife. As the officers pointed their guns at Pham and ordered him to drop the knife, Pham moved toward them with the weapon raised in the air. The officers immediately opened fire, killing him instantly (CBS News, Cbsnews.com, 2009).
- On November 6, 2008, Washington, D.C., police were called to the condo of David Kerstetter by a neighbor and maintenance man who found his front screen torn and the front door open. David was last heard from the night before by his mother, who said he had called her from a payphone extremely paranoid. David was diagnosed with bipolar disorder, and had previously attempted suicide. During the call to his mother he told her *they* had locked him out of his own house, and that *they* had killed his dog. It would be the last time she would ever talk to her son. When two police officers entered the condo, they found Kerstetter in a bedroom wearing only his boxers and holding a knife. Within moments of confronting Kerstetter the officers shot and killed him (Cherkis, 2008).

Handling cases involving mentally ill people can be a dangerous endeavor, both for the person with whom the police come in contact, and for the police. According to official FBI Uniform Crime Reports, during the period from 1997 to 2006, there were 1058 officers assaulted in America, and 13 feloniously killed while responding to calls involving mentally ill people (FBI, Fbi.gov, 2007). Many, if not most people suffering a mental illness will react negatively to the presence of the police, and this reaction tends to cause a like reaction by the officers involved as they resort to their training and take a defensive posture for self-protection. As soon as each reaction is apparent, which is oftentimes immediate, then a tension builds that can cause the situation to escalate and become very volatile. The police are neither accustomed to, nor trained to, de-escalate themselves in the midst of a tense situation. Sometimes very quickly in these situations they reach a point of no return, and their defensive posture shifts into offensive mode as they take the necessary steps to de-escalate the matter through the use of force.

THE PROBLEM OF MENTAL ILLNESS

In each of the cases described previously the officers' actions were found to be justified. The question, however, is whether things could have been done differently to avoid taking a mentally ill person's life. Could they have reacted in some alternative manner prior to reaching the point of no return when offensive action was perceived as necessary to de-escalate the situation? Traditional police training makes no distinction between sanity and mental illness when it comes to the use of deadly force. A person with a knife who is in close proximity to the officer and approaching in a threatening manner creates a deadly force situation regardless of their ability to think rationally. Police officers have a great deal of discretion in how they deal with a situation, especially the less serious ones. Their first inclination is typically to confront the situation directly. In the case of a man with a knife, rather than wait for a mental health officer to arrive, a luxury many departments lack, they will almost always confront the individual from a safe distance in an effort to get them to drop the weapon. In many cases, especially with someone like David Kerstetter, who suffered extreme paranoia among other symptoms, confrontation will only exacerbate an already dangerous situation.

Although almost all correctional institutions have staff counselors and psychologists to assess inmates with some type of mental illness, and to assist in any crisis situation involving a mentally ill inmate, the police don't have access to that level of assistance, at least not out on the street. They are forced to rely on each other, which is why it is so critical that officers be trained to deal with situations involving mentally ill offenders, suspects, witnesses, or people they just happen to come across during a routine shift. They must have at least a rudimentary knowledge of the more common types of mental illness, the symptoms that are generally seen, and the actions to be avoided to prevent a situation from escalating out of control unnecessarily.

Traditional police academy training includes very little on the subject of mental illness. In Illinois for example, police officer cadets are required to complete 480 hours of instruction prior to being certified. Of that amount, only eight hours of behavioral science instruction is mandated (ILETSB website, 2010). And of that amount, a good portion of time is spent on things like communication strategies and police officer stress. At the end of the day the total time spent on mental illness may amount to only a couple hours. The training mandated is certainly not commensurate with the amount of time officers spend dealing with mentally ill people. Consider the following:

- In the first nine months of 2006, the LAPD had 46,129 contacts with people suspected of being mentally ill. Of those, 709 had attempted suicide and 4686 were taken into custody for an involuntary commitment and psychiatric evaluation (Reuland, Schwarzfeld, and Draper, 2009).
- The Lincoln, Nebraska Police Department reported that in 2002 it handled over 1500 cases involving mentally ill persons, and that it has spent more time on these cases than on burglaries, felony assaults, or traffic accidents involving injuries (Cordner, 2006).
- In 2000, officers in Florida transported more than 40,000 people for an involuntary 72-hour psychiatric evaluation. This number exceeded burglaries (26,087) and aggravated assaults (39,120) handled during the same year (McGaha and Stiles, 2000).

So the first major problem in the police response to mental illness is a lack of training on how to effectively respond to, contain, and de-escalate such a crisis without the need for heightened or deadly force. The second problem, and one closely related to the first, is the perception among police officers that mentally ill people are always more violent than non-mentally ill people, a perception that is not necessarily supported by the available research (Harris and Lurigio, 2007). This, of course, causes an officer to immediately enter a situation in a more heightened state of readiness and with an expectation that some level of force will be necessary. The combination of these two reactions only increases the potential for a violent outcome if a confrontation occurs.

TYPES OF MENTAL ILLNESS

Before we proceed further, it is important to discuss some of the major classes of mental illness police and correctional officers may be forced to confront in the course of their duties. These various disorders have recognizable symptoms, and all have the potential to contribute to, or actually be the cause of, a crisis requiring the intervention of police or correctional officers. In this section we will review three classes of psychological disorders: *thought disorders, mood disorders,* and *anxiety disorders*. It is important that those who respond to crisis understand these classes of disorders and the dangers associated with each.

Thought Disorders

Thought disorders are characterized by a person's disordered thinking and, in the more serious cases, a general disconnect from reality. The most common disorder in this class is schizophrenia. According to the Diagnostic and Statistical Manual of the American Psychiatric Association (2000), in order to be diagnosed with schizophrenia, a person must typically demonstrate at least two of the following:

• *Delusions*:   When people hold extremely irrational or unrealistic beliefs, they are said to be delusional. They are beliefs that are fixed and unchangeable in the person's mind even when confronted with evidence to the contrary, and for the most part include content that is improbable or impossible. For example, a person who believes they will turn into a tree if water hits them would certainly be considered a delusion. Different types of delusions include the following:

— Delusions of control: When the person believes their thoughts and actions are being controlled by some entity.

— Nihilistic delusion: A belief that the world is ending. At the time of the writing of this text there is a widespread belief that the world will end in 2012, the end of the Mayan calendar. This would not be considered a delusion, because it is a popular belief held by many, and for which there is some evidence in support, regardless of how questionable and discredited that evidence may be.

— Delusional jealousy: An obsessive belief that a spouse or lover is having an affair.

— Delusion of guilt or sin: A false sense of guilt that incapacitates the individual. An example would be the man who feels so much shame and guilt over his habit of masturbating that he severs his own penis with a knife.

— Delusion of mind being read: This is a paranoid type delusion in which the person truly believes their mind is being read, or perhaps that some type of transmitter has been implanted in their brain to allow their thoughts to be read.

— Delusion of reference: This is a false belief that something outside the person's own experience actually relates to them. An example would be the person who thinks a news commentator is actually sending them secret messages through the television.

— Erotomania: The false belief that another person, typically a famous person, is in love with them. This type of delusion, once it becomes an obsession, can be very dangerous for the object of the delusional person's affection.

— Grandiose delusion: A person's belief that they have special powers or abilities, or that they are somehow famous or connected to a famous person.

— Persecutory delusion: Another paranoid-type delusion which leads the person to believe someone is after them, usually the police or spies from another country.

— Religious delusion: Many people hold to religious beliefs that are based in their own faith, but when a person crosses the line into delusional religious belief they tend to see themselves as taking on supernatural qualities. They may think they are God, or perhaps an angel.

— Somatic delusion: These are delusions relating to one's body or bodily functions. The person may think they have a tumor, or perhaps parasites eating their internal organs.

- **Hallucinations:** The second DSM-IV diagnostic criterion is the presence of hallucinations. Whereas delusions are false beliefs held by the person in the face of evidence to the contrary, hallucinations are false perceptions experienced without the corresponding sensory input, or a failure to perceive things that are in the person's sensory field. A *positive* hallucination is experiencing something that is not there, such as hearing voices or seeing miniature people running around on the ground. In contrast, a *negative* hallucination occurs when the person is unable to experience something that is there, such as not being able to see a particular picture on the wall, or not seeing their own arm and arguing that it is not there.

- **Disorganized speech:** The third DSM-IV criterion is disorganized speech. This is typically the first symptom a responding police officer will encounter. People in the midst of a schizophrenic episode will oftentimes talk rapidly and nonsensically. Their speech patterns may be excited or panicked, and they may simply make repetitive sounds or repeat single words or phrases rather than actually speak.

- **Grossly disorganized or catatonic behavior:** Like their speech, a person having a schizophrenic episode may also display the same level of disorganization in their actions. They may be pacing erratically, or even in a fetal position. It is their actions and speech which almost instantly will signal to a responding police officer that mental illness may be a factor.

SCHIZOPHRENIA There are a number of different types of schizophrenia, each with its own characteristics and symptoms. Some present greater challenges and dangers to responding police officers due to their unpredictability and the underlying thought processes that contribute to the onset of the schizophrenic episode.

- **Paranoid schizophrenic:** Individuals suffering from this disorder can be extremely dangerous. They are typically fixated on the false belief that someone is out to get them, or that they are being persecuted in some manner. They are hypervigilant to an extreme degree, always looking over their shoulder or out the window. What makes them dangerous in a crisis situation is that the police may inadvertently reinforce their delusional thinking, causing them to resort to violence to avoid confrontation or capture by their perceived persecutor. They may be armed as a way of protecting themselves against their perceived threat. If alcohol or drug use is involved, the danger increases.

- **Disorganized schizophrenic:** The disorganized schizophrenic is typically incoherent. Disorganized speech and behavior are almost always present, and delusional thinking and hallucinations are common. There may be no consistent theme to their thinking. They can be erratic and unpredictable and, again, if alcohol or drug use is involved, their behavior may become even more so.

- **Catatonic schizophrenic:** The individual suffering from this type of schizophrenia typically causes or contributes to no type of crisis beyond their own medical crisis. The catatonic individual is usually withdrawn and unresponsive, and they may show very little movement. At times they may also assume unusual postures, such as curling up in a fetal position. Obviously they are a danger to no one in this condition. The goal of the first responder is to simply comfort them until they can be transported to a hospital for medical and psychiatric care.

• ***Residual schizophrenic:*** When an individual is no longer experiencing a schizophrenic episode, and the delusions and hallucinations have either lessened to a significant degree or stopped altogether, the residual effect is often quite devastating for the afflicted person. Symptoms include a depressed mood, and a loss of interest in life. They lack motivation, and their ability to communicate with others is greatly diminished. During this time an individual may become suicidal, and as discussed in the chapter on suicide, first responders must always take precautions when dealing with a suicidal individual.

Mood Disorders

In contrast to thought disorders, people with **mood disorders** may have no delusional thinking or hallucinations. Their symptoms are primarily extremes in how they feel, either extreme excitement or agitation, or more commonly, varying degrees of depression. There are times when their mood is so extreme that it does affect their ability to think rationally. Some people with severe depression have even reported experiencing hallucinations during their most severe episodes.

DEPRESSION There are two predominant types of mood disorders: **depression** and bipolar disorder. Everyone experiences periods of depression, most of the time related to some personal issue, but people who are diagnosed with major depression may have no idea why they feel as they do. To be diagnosed with a major depressive episode, the DSM-IV-TR requires at least five of the following during the same two-week period:

- Depressed mood most of the day, nearly every day, as indicated by either subjective report (e.g., feels sad or empty) or observation made by others (e.g., appears tearful). **Note:** In children and adolescents, can be irritable mood.
- Markedly diminished interest or pleasure in all, or almost all, activities most of the day, nearly every day (as indicated by either subjective account or observation made by others).
- Significant weight loss when not dieting or weight gain (e.g., a change of more than 5 percent of body weight in a month), or decrease or increase in appetite nearly every day. **Note:** In children, consider failure to make expected weight gains.
- Insomnia or hypersomnia nearly every day.
- Psychomotor agitation or retardation nearly every day (observable by others, not merely subjective feelings of restlessness or being slowed down).
- Fatigue or loss of energy nearly every day.
- Feelings of worthlessness or excessive or inappropriate guilt (which may be delusional) nearly every day (not merely self-reproach or guilt about being sick).
- Diminished ability to think or concentrate, or indecisiveness, nearly every day (either by subjective account or as observed by others).
- Recurrent thoughts of death (not just fear of dying), recurrent suicidal ideation without a specific plan, or a suicide attempt or a specific plan for committing suicide.

For the truly depressed person, these symptoms are experienced without an apparent cause. Many people suffer episodic depression related to certain life circumstances. Others experience depression related to drug and alcohol use. But major depression, as defined by the DSM-IV-TR, is a debilitating disease with no apparent cause, and no successful intervention short of medication.

In decades past, severely depressed people were even administered electric shock (electroconvulsive therapy) as a treatment alternative, and a few even underwent "transorbital lobotomy," a procedure in which part of the brain was actually traumatized with an instrument similar to an ice pick. Neither of these treatment methods was successful in bringing about a lasting change.

BIPOLAR DISORDER   A second type of mood disorder, and one that can be extremely dangerous for those who confront people suffering from the disorder, is **bipolar disorder**, also called *manic-depressive disorder*. People diagnosed with this disorder will experience periods of elevated mood, energy, and cognition (mania), as well as periods of depression. Typically the two extremes are separated by periods of relatively normal functioning, and psychotic-like features, such as delusions and hallucinations, are sometimes experienced at the extremes.

Those diagnosed with bipolar disorder must be approached with caution if they are in the midst of a personal crisis. If in the manic stage, their judgment can be significantly impaired, and their actions erratic. They may experience paranoia and delusional thinking, and thus they may perceive those who respond to help as dangerous in some way. If in the depressive stage, these individuals may become suicidal, and all the dangers discussed in detail in the chapter on suicide may be present. At times, the symptoms of bipolar disorder will be magnified if the individual cycles between the two extremes rapidly. Either on the way up to a manic state, or on the way down to a depressive state, the frustration and desperation experienced by the individual over their perceived inability to control the fluctuations in their mood can lead to a sense of hopelessness and the dual risks of erratic judgment and suicidal ideation.

Anxiety Disorders

Anxiety disorders are a class of disorders that are marked by abnormal amounts of fear, worry, or uneasiness. At their extreme, these disorders can have physical symptoms such as chest pains and shortness of breath. A person suffering from a severe anxiety disorder may be entirely unable to function normally without some type of therapeutic intervention, to include medication. One of the common outcomes with people suffering from these types of disorders is a reliance on drugs and alcohol to deaden the pain and calm the anxiety. Unfortunately most of the time drugs and alcohol only worsens the problem. They oftentimes have significant problems with personal relationships, and with trusting other people. They have a difficult time holding down a job, and they may act out the desperation they feel with displays of anger. This anger may be turned against those who respond to offer help and intervention, and the affected person may project onto these same people their negative self-evaluation and feelings. If they are in the midst of an anxiety episode, which many of them are during a personal crisis, then they have the capacity to behave in unpredictable and erratic ways.

- *Generalized anxiety disorder:*   These individuals experience constant worry and anxiety over everyday situations in their lives. The level of anxiety they experience is typically inconsistent with the level of stress expected of the situation causing the anxiety. They are highly irritable and may experience some level of paranoia. These people tend to always appear on the verge of crying.
- *Panic disorder:*   These people typically suffer brief attacks of intense fear, and may have physical symptoms that mimic a heart attack. The focus or cause of their fear may not always be apparent. Usually people in the midst of a panic attack are less of a risk for two reasons. First, they are usually incapacitated by their panic, and are simply unable to act in offensive and aggressive ways. And secondly, people suffering a panic attack are usually open to the idea of intervention in order to relieve their intense fear or worry.

• *Obsessive-compulsive disorder:*   These individuals experience distressing, persistent, and intrusive thoughts, and the need to repeatedly perform a specific act or ritual. They may experience delusional thinking, and may develop superstitious ideas about the acts or rituals they feel compelled to repeat. For example, they may suffer the persistent belief that if they were to discontinue their pattern of walking in circles, then the Earth would break apart and swallow them. The danger for those who respond to offer help, especially the police, is that their actions may run the risk of causing the person to become desperate if they believe the responding officers intend to stop their persistent behavior, thus exposing them to whatever circumstances they believe will result. The more deadly or dangerous the perceived outcome, the more desperate they will become in the presence of the police if they believe they are there to either remove or transport them to jail.

• *Post-traumatic stress disorder (PTSD):*   Much has been written about this disorder, especially since the end of the Vietnam War. With more recent wars in Afghanistan and Iraq, it again has found its way to the forefront of media reporting, as thousands of young soldiers have returned home to experience the ongoing effects of battle-induced stress. They report having flashbacks and being constantly on their guard and hypersensitive to their surroundings. They isolate themselves even from loved ones, and experience extreme levels of anxiety and depression at times. Unfortunately there is a high level of alcoholism and drug use among PTSD victims. The danger to crisis responders is the extreme agitation these people experience, and their inability to decompress once they become agitated. They may become violent or suicidal, and in some cases may even flash back during a crisis event to the circumstances that led to their diagnosis, causing them to lash out even at those attempting to help.

• *Separation anxiety:* Some people become so emotionally dependent on others that they have an inability to separate from them for any length of time, and almost no ability to do so permanently. This syndrome is oftentimes seen in cases of divorce and domestic violence, and can be extremely dangerous for all involved, including those who respond to domestic crises involving such persons. The idea of separating, even in a marriage or partnership that is toxic and dysfunctional, is so frightening and unthinkable to the individual that they oftentimes resort to violence in an irrational attempt to prevent the other from separating. There is a high risk of violence, not just for the victim-partner, but also for any children who may be present. Murder-suicide is a common outcome in these cases, as is a hostage crisis. Those who respond to cases involving these types of individuals, especially the police, must do so with great caution. They will be seen as facilitating the separation that has the person desperate and panicked.

THE EFFECTS OF DRUGS AND ALCOHOL

It is not uncommon for heavy drug and alcohol use to cause psychotic-like symptoms, either during a person's period of intoxication, or during their subsequent withdrawal (Curran, 2004; Zoric et al., 2007). According to the DSM-IV-TR, a diagnosis of substance-induced psychotic disorder must meet the following criteria:

• Presence of prominent hallucinations or delusions
• Hallucinations and/or delusions develop during, or within one month of, intoxication or withdrawal from a substance or medication known to cause psychotic symptoms.

- Psychotic symptoms are not actually part of another psychotic disorder that is not substance induced.
- Psychotic symptoms do not only occur during delirium.

As the diagnosis suggests, this type of psychosis is the direct result of the drugs or alcohol being ingested by the individual. The onset and severity of the symptoms will depend on the type and amount of the drug ingested, and the duration of use. For the police officer who responds to a crisis involving such a person, the symptoms will appear the same as those presented by a mentally ill person, and the dangers are also the same. The same precautions should be taken, however, if it can be determined that the individual is suffering from substance-induced psychosis; it is important that a medically supervised detoxification be pursued. This may impact an officer's decision to do an involuntary commitment to a hospital or mental health center where such a detoxification can be accomplished. An involuntary commitment should be considered if the individual in crisis is still actively using the drug or consuming the alcohol. They are experiencing psychotic symptoms because the substance is having a toxic effect on their brain. To continue doing so is certainly an indication that the person has become a danger to themselves, and in most states that is the primary criterion for doing an involuntary commitment.

INTERVENTION STRATEGIES

Crisis Intervention Teams: The Memphis Model

In 1988 the Memphis Police Department instituted a program designed to reduce violent encounters with the mentally ill, and to provide a more effective response to situations involving mentally ill people. The program involved the formation of a specialized **crisis intervention team**, or **CIT**. Each member of the team received advanced training from community mental health professionals, family advocates, and mental health consumer groups. According to the department's official website (Memphispolice.org), the unit was established for the purpose of developing a more "intelligent, understandable, and safe approach to mental crisis events." Since that time the **Memphis Model** has become the standard among law enforcement agencies nationwide.

Today, essentially every geographic area has law enforcement officers trained as CIT members. They are officers who can respond immediately when a situation arises involving someone with an apparent or suspected mental illness. The officers are not only trained to deal with the immediate situation in a way that reduces the chance of violence or use of force, but they also serve as conduits for the medical or psychiatric care the individual may need. CIT members work in partnership with community mental health centers and drug and alcohol treatment centers to facilitate this goal.

In Memphis and other jurisdictions where CITs are deployed, there is an immediate response whenever a suspected mentally ill individual is in crisis. The CIT officers are trained in de-escalation techniques and, where possible, the goal is to avoid incarceration, instead diverting the individual to the appropriate intervention. CIT members are trained to recognize the signs and symptoms of various types of mental illness, and to avoid the types of confrontational police behaviors that will escalate the situation. There is a recognition that traditional police methods that attempt to invoke a person's rational judgment and common sense simply don't work in many cases with the mentally ill. In the past, when a properly trained officer was not at the scene, many times the police response would only aggravate and escalate the situation to the point where the use of force, sometimes deadly force, would become necessary. The Memphis Police Department has outlined the following benefits that have been realized since training and deploying CIT officers:

- Crisis response is immediate
- Arrests and use of force have decreased
- Underserved consumers are identified by officers and provided care
- Patient violence and use of restraints in the ER have decreased
- Officers are better trained and educated in verbal de-escalation techniques
- Officer injuries during crisis events have decreased
- Officer recognition and appreciation by the community has increased
- Less "victimless" crime arrests
- Decrease in liability for health-care issues in the jail
- Cost savings

The CIT concept has been widely studied to determine its effectiveness. Compton et al. (2009) looked at differences in the use of force preferences and perceptions among CIT and non-CIT officers. Their hypothesis was that CIT-trained officers would select lower levels of force to respond to an escalating psychiatric crisis, and perceive non-physical methods as being more effective. The researchers had both groups of officers complete a survey involving three scenarios, each depicting an escalating psychiatric situation. Their task was to select a preferred action in each scenario. As a group, their preferred actions escalated across the three scenarios; however, the CIT-trained officers chose less escalation. Additionally, the CIT-trained officers reported less of a decline in their perception of the effectiveness of taking non-physical actions. The results suggest that the CIT program may be an effective approach to dealing with the mentally ill.

To evaluate the effectiveness of the Greater St. Louis CIT, Tyuse (2006) looked at the disposition of cases involving individuals experiencing psychiatric crises in the first year of the program. All were cases in which a CIT member responded. The Greater St. Louis CIT program consisted of over 600 members representing 38 police departments and various mental health entities. A total of 1259 CIT reporting forms were reviewed, covering incidents occurring between July 1, 2005, and June 30, 2006.

During the period covered by the study, CIT members completed a reporting form with each and every contact involving a person experiencing a psychiatric crisis. Team members had four possible options for resolving a situation:

1. Resolve the situation on the scene, allowing the individual with the mental illness to remain in the community.
2. Arrest the individual and place them in protective custody.
3. Access behavioral health response services (e.g., crisis outreach, crisis telephone counseling, etc.).
4. Transport the individual to a partner hospital with psychiatric services.

Following the resolution of each case, the CIT members who responded were required to complete a CIT reporting form to detail what took place, including which of the above outcomes was achieved. Figure 12.1 provides a detailed picture of the types of individuals with whom the CIT members interacted and attempted to help, and a summary of the outcomes achieved.

Most of the St. Louis subjects (89 percent) were either transported or referred to a mental health facility, and of that number, 56 percent were admitted involuntarily to the hospital by police or family members. These individuals were successfully diverted from jail, and into the types of services they most needed. It is also important to note that in only 4 percent of the cases (52) was force used,

Subject/Incident Characteristics	%	(N)
Behaviors Evident at the Time of Incident		
Uncooperative (Angry or Hostile)	14.0	(175)
Disorientation/Confusion	11.0	(140)
Depressed	11.0	(137)
Drug or Alcohol Use (at time of incident)	29.5	(372)
Transported to Hospital or Treatment Facility	89.0	(850)
96-Hour Affidavit Completed?		
Yes	55.5	(633)
No	5.0	(56)
Unknown	39.6	(451)
Arrested?		
Felony	6.0	(70)
Misdemeanor	.1	(1)
No arrest	93.0	(1142)
Use of Less-than-Lethal-Force	4.0	(52)
Injuries to Individual	3.0	(37)
Injuries to Law Enforcement Officers	.7	(9)

FIGURE 12.1   Greater St. Louis CIT Results.

and deadly force in only one of those incidents. The author concluded that the program was a success. Those most in need of services were in fact diverted into those services in the majority of cases. In the past, prior to programs and training like CIT, many of the officers would have found themselves in an escalating situation with no apparent way out but by the use of force. Instead, in the vast majority of these cases, there were officers present who had gone through CIT training and who knew how to de-escalate the situation without resorting to force, and in the process avoided potential injury to themselves, their fellow officers, and the mentally ill individuals with whom they came in contact.

CIT in the Correctional Setting

The CIT model has also been adapted to the correctional setting. Nowhere are the dangers associated with mental illness more real than in a correctional institution, whether it is a county jail or a state or federal prison. Not only is mental illness easily exacerbated in such a setting, but those charged with maintaining order are for the most part unarmed. Traditionally, jails and prisons have taken a very hardline approach to maintaining control. The threat of force is ever-present, and staff will not hesitate to use it when necessary. There tends to be little room for negotiation because to do so would shift the perception of power in favor of the inmates. The downside to this unilateral approach is that the mentally ill tend to go unnoticed and untreated until a crisis demands some type of intervention. Even then intervention may come in the form of punishment and isolation rather than treatment.

Cattabriga et al. (2007) studied the effectiveness of CIT in Maine, and specifically its efficacy within the correctional setting. Maine launched the program statewide in 2005 after recognizing that they were inadequately prepared to deal with the problem of mental illness. Staying true to the Memphis Model, their training focused on the following issues:

1. How to recognize and understand the various psychiatric disorders
2. The use of de-escalation skills to calm and reassure mentally ill people
3. Linking officers with mental health service providers in the local community

To determine the program's effectiveness, data was collected through a number of different methods, including surveys of correctional officers and a review of jail incident reports. The results indicated that the training was effective in preparing officers to deal with the mentally ill. CIT incidents were more frequently resolved through de-escalation techniques rather than by force. During the period of the study, inmate and staff injuries were also reported to be lower. Thus, the program was found to be an effective strategy.

Essentially all state and federal prisons now have a CIT or similar type of program. Two problems are faced in a prison setting. First is the basic problem of dealing with the mentally ill and keeping people safe, but a second problem, and one that is just as critical to address, is the possibility that the actions of a mentally ill inmate may serve as the spark that ignites larger-scale violence or disruptive behavior among other members of the inmate population. In a prison setting violence begets more violence. It is therefore critical that properly trained staff be available to move in immediately when a mentally ill inmate's behavior begins to escalate.

Unfortunately many county and municipal jails do not enjoy the benefit of having CIT personnel to respond to such a crisis. The vast majority of these jail facilities in America are in rural areas, with many holding a maximum of 50 inmates or less. These counties and municipalities may lack the funding to support such training, or they may simply not see the need for it. In these cases, it is the regular jail staff who must respond to each and every type of crisis, and perhaps even jail staff who have had no specialized training in the area of crisis intervention. As these smaller facilities, and the people who run them, find themselves more and more inside a courtroom being held liable for an inadequate or improper response to a mentally ill inmate, the perceived need for training in this area will continue to grow, and hopefully the availability of needed funding will grow with it.

DE-ESCALATION TECHNIQUES

Like any other type of crisis, the primary goals of the first responder are containment and de-escalation. Most such crises are single-person events, and thus containment is usually not an issue unless the individual is eluding contact with the police. If they are considered dangerous or potentially dangerous, then containment becomes a critically important task. Once contained, then de-escalation becomes the primary focus. As discussed in Chapter 6, de-escalation is a five-step process during which the officer must *engage, establish rapport, listen, offer an out,* and *gain commitment.* It is first and foremost a process of empathic listening, or listening with a sincerity, that is apparent to the person in crisis. And then help is offered, and in a way that reassures the person in crisis that the effort is more than simply a ruse to get them to jail. People in crisis can become hypersensitive to the words and actions of the police. When an officer is not sincere, chances are it will be perceived as insincerity by the person in crisis.

In terms of the actual techniques of de-escalation, we can review those discussed in Chapter 6 of the text.

• **Engagement:** De-escalation begins the moment the CIT officer approaches the person in crisis. The officer should do so in a non-threatening manner. This means that to the extent possible without jeopardizing their own safety, they should approach with their hands free of any weapons. They should also be aware of changes in the person's demeanor as they approach. The person will signal through their words and actions when the officer begins to cross the boundaries they have established. The officer should be cognizant of these boundaries, and make every effort not to cross them without the person's permission. This show of respect will be an important step in building rapport.

It is important that only one CIT officer approach and attempt to communicate with the person. People in crisis are confused and highly emotional to begin with. More than one officer attempting to communicate with them can be very confusing, as their ability to process data from multiple sources is diminished. When this happens, an already confused individual will simply focus back on the event or circumstance that pushed them into their personal crisis. For rapport to be established, the person must connect with a single officer on a personal level. To facilitate this, the officer should identify themselves in a calm and professional voice. They should avoid sounding authoritative or overly friendly. The former will be perceived as a threat, and the latter as a ruse. The officer's introduction should be followed by a simple purpose statement, such as "I'm only here to help you."

• ***Establish rapport:*** In order to create an atmosphere of trust, it is essential that the officer build rapport with the person in crisis. **Rapport** is a relationship of trust and, when it is established, the officer is in a much better position to get the person in crisis to respond to their requests. There is no better way to begin this process than to ask the individual's name. This personalizes the exchange, and also demonstrates sincerity on the part of the officer. If the individual appears nervous or paranoid, the officer should immediately address those fears by assuring the person that no one is going to do anything to harm them. The officer's goal at this point is to get the person to focus entirely on them.

If the individual is highly emotional, the officer should attempt to de-escalate the person in a calm and non-judgmental way. One of the best methods for de-escalating high emotionality is to get the person talking. Questions unrelated to the person's immediate problem can work for this purpose, such as "Are you from around here (name)?" The officer should be looking for things that are apparent about the person that can serve as a point of connection. For example, many young police officers now have tattoos. It is a practice that has gained a great deal more popularity and respect in recent years. If there are tattoos apparent on the person in crisis, then perhaps the officer could use that as a point of connection by stating something like, "I can see your ink (name), tell me about it."

Anything that can be ascertained from the person's appearance or circumstances that is non-threatening to the individual to talk about is worth exploring in an effort to build rapport and focus attention away from the crisis at hand. However it must be done carefully and in a way that shows sincerity. For example, men will connect almost immediately with other men who have similar military experiences. This is a powerful subject for building rapport; however, if the officer is not a military veteran, then it may be best not to bring up that particular subject, because it could cause the person in crisis to view the officer in a less favorable light. It may also be viewed by the person as insincere and coercive. Honesty is critical in this situation. Also, the officer must be very careful to shift the focus away from a particular subject if it becomes obvious that it is suddenly causing the individual to become more emotional and agitated.

Whatever actions the officer takes, they should be careful to inform the person before doing so. Any sudden or unannounced movements may be wrongly perceived by the person in crisis as an aggressive act. People in crisis typically experience heightened paranoia, especially if they have a history of being institutionalized. The officer should avoid movements that will intensify this paranoia. Instead, they should announce what they are planning to do in advance, and ask the individual if they are okay with it. This allows the person to feel some sense of control over the situation.

• *Active listening:* Concurrent with, and following the, establishment of some degree of rapport, the officer should simply listen. Much of the time this is all the person really wants, someone who will listen to their problems and show a sincere concern for their situation. The officer should avoid trying to get the person to discuss their problems. It is best to allow them to do it on their own terms. Chances are once rapport is established the individual will begin to talk about their problems with little prompting by the officer. It will usually require little more than a comment or question, such as "What can I do to help, (name)?"

When a person in crisis is talking, it is critical that the officer listen and not interrupt. They should acknowledge their understanding of the person's words both verbally and non-verbally. Eye contact and head nods are important. It signals to the person in crisis that the officer is attentive to their words. The officer should avoid "why" questions, and should reassure the person with comments like, "I understand, (name)," or perhaps, "I understand why you're upset, (name)." The goal is to keep the person talking with promptings like, "can you tell me about …," or "(name), I'm interested in hearing about …." If the person believes the officer sincerely cares about their situation, then again the chances of averting further escalation are greatly increased. Some of the main verbal techniques used for de-escalation—*minimal encouragements, paraphrasing, emotion-labeling, open-ended questions, "I" messages,* and *effective pauses* were all discussed in detail in Chapter 3 of the text.

Many times the person in crisis will again emotionally escalate while talking to the police. The responding officer must be ready to act quickly to de-escalate this flair-up when it happens. The more emotional a person is the less rational they become. A mentally ill person can very quickly become a suicidal person. It is imperative that the officer attempt to guide the person's attention away from the source of their emotion. The officer should remain calm and speak in a reassuring voice. They should also watch carefully for signs that the person is about to become violent toward themselves or others. The behavioral cues that the officer must be aware of include the following:

- The person begins to nervously scan the area around them
- They no longer attend to the officer's words
- An obvious quickening in their rate of breathing
- Cadence-like behaviors, such as rocking their head or counting under their breath
- Sudden laughing or extreme emotionality

When it becomes apparent that the person is about to behave in potentially harmful ways, even in spite of the officer's calm and reassuring words, then the officer must be ready to act. At this point the person will likely be focused on nothing else but their own immediate circumstances. As a last resort the officer should become authoritarian and loud. They should demand that the person look at them now and stop what they're doing! The officer should try not to sound panicked, but rather like an authoritarian parent. They should continue their demands until they regain the person's attention. If they are not successful, then for the person's own safety, non-lethal forms of force must be considered in order to safely subdue the person and transport them to a place where they can get the help they need.

Once the situation has been de-escalated and the person has committed to ending the crisis, then the CIT officer is trained to serve as a conduit to community mental health resources. Whereas in the past the person in crisis would have been taken either to the hospital or to jail, now a trained CIT officer is aware of all the available resources in the community, and through various written protocols and mutual aid agreements is able to assist the person in getting the appropriate type and level of intervention they need.

COMMUNITY RESOURCES

It is critical that all first responders, whether CIT trained or not, have an understanding of the various resources available in their communities to meet the needs of people in crisis, especially the mentally ill. The police are trained to respond to, contain, and de-escalate a crisis, but not necessarily to remediate and prevent further crisis. They must rely on other resources to carry out these functions. It is therefore in everyone's best interest to be aware of community resources, and to develop interagency agreements and protocols.

If we look at any particular community we will find a number of different government, private, and faith-based entities who endeavor to ease the suffering of those experiencing some type of crisis. A review of resources available in the metropolitan Atlanta area revealed over 100 different organizations involved to varying degrees in the counseling and intervention fields. We can break them down into six major categories:

• *Primary care facilities:* These are inpatient, residential facilities such as hospitals, drug and alcohol treatment centers, and mental health centers. Their goal is to treat the person's immediate problem aggressively, sometimes even without their consent, and to do so under some level of observation and case supervision by a medical doctor or psychologist. In most states, the police have the ability to "petition" a person into a psychiatric facility involuntarily if they are deemed a danger to themselves or others. A mentally ill individual who is incapacitated by their condition and unable to provide basic self-care is in most cases considered a threat to themselves, and thus they can be transported to an appropriate facility for a mandated observation period after which the attending psychiatrist will make a determination regarding continued commitment.

In the case of drugs and alcohol, it is a little less clear because the mental illness may be related to chronic alcoholism or drug addiction. Mental health centers will typically not accept someone under the influence of drugs or alcohol, and hospitals may not accept them involuntarily if there is no indication of mental illness apart from their addiction. Drug and alcohol treatment centers are even less flexible in terms of involuntary commitments and, in some states, they are simply precluded from doing it. Many times an involuntary commitment is not necessary, and the person in an alcohol, or drug-related crisis will voluntarily choose to go to a detox unit. Some treatment centers have a medically supervised detox unit, whereas others do not. Those that don't will require the individual to first be detoxed in a local hospital, and then transferred to the treatment center for inpatient counseling.

• *Counseling centers:* Many times a crisis can be de-escalated simply by talking to the person(s) involved, or perhaps by having one party to the crisis leave for the night. In the past, the police viewed their involvement as stopping there. But today a CIT member, or any other officer, will refer the people involved to the appropriate intervention, and may even facilitate that referral by making the initial contact. When immediate inpatient intervention is not warranted, there are counseling centers of many types that provide services on a periodic outpatient basis. Some of the predominant outpatient counseling centers include the following:

• Drug and alcohol treatment centers
• Veteran's centers (PTSD)
• Adolescent behavioral therapy centers
• Marriage and family counseling centers
• Outpatient mental health centers

Outpatient interventions tend to be less intensive than their inpatient counterparts. They are longer term and usually require a weekly appointment. Some programs, especially those for adolescents, may require multiple nights each week, with each night having a different purpose. For example, there may be a group therapy night, a recreation night, and an education night, depending on the type of program. Many outpatient counseling programs make use of group therapy sessions. They are powerful forums for expressing feelings in a safe setting, getting immediate and honest feedback, and with a trained professional present to guide the exchange in a way that provides the most benefit to the participants.

• *Support groups:* Support groups are an excellent type of intervention. As the name implies, these are groups of people with similar circumstances who simply meet on a regular basis to provide each other support. They tend to do so with limited structure, and without a professional counselor being present. By far the most successful and widespread support group is *Alcoholics Anonymous.* Every CIT officer will likely have a listing of local AA meetings being held in their community. Some of these groups are open, meaning anyone can attend, whereas others are closed, requiring the group's approval in order for a person to attend. Rather than professional counselors, these groups have group leaders who take responsibility for organizing and maintaining the group. These leaders are typically people who have had a history of success with the particular problem the group was organized to confront. For example, an AA group will likely be led by an individual with many years of sobriety.

Over the last 40 years the number of support groups in America has grown dramatically in most communities, mostly the result of the anonymity these groups offer, and the successes reported by the advocates of AA. We now have support groups for essentially every major problem afflicting society. Those following the AA model include *Narcotics Anonymous, Gamblers Anonymous, Sex Addicts Anonymous, Overeaters Anonymous, Debtors Anonymous,* and *Suicide Anonymous,* to name a few. Also, many others do not follow the 12-step model of AA. There are support groups for people suffering from depression, bipolar disorder, schizophrenia, and even extreme anger. All can be effective interventions, and it is important for those responding to crisis to have a clear understanding of the various groups present in their communities.

• *Advocacy groups:* Sometimes a person in crisis is in need of more than one type of assistance. Perhaps in addition to a mental illness they are also dealing with homelessness, HIV, the need for job training, or maybe medical and dental care for their children. Advocacy groups are sometimes the best place to start in getting the holistic help needed. These groups are a conduit to intervention services, and they also are heavily involved in seeking legislation or city codes favorable to the specific issues they attempt to address. Most advocacy groups are organized around a single predominant issue, such as homelessness, HIV-AIDS, veterans' needs, teen pregnancy, and juvenile delinquency, to name a few.

• *Faith-based providers:* These are sometimes excellent resources for the police to be aware of. They are intervention services provided by churches. The benefit to these types of services is their lack of bureaucracy. They are able to provide immediate services most of the time, and are typically staffed by very dedicated and purpose-driven volunteers. Some will attempt to convince the person being helped to seek membership in their particular church, but for the most part this type of activity is minimal, and many faith-based organizations make no such effort at all. Because faith-based organizations provide their services under a perceived spiritual mandate, they have the potential not only to remediate the immediate crisis, but to have a life-changing impact on the people they help.

ISSUES & ETHICS IN CRISIS INTERVENTION

A Question of Responsibility: The Case of Andrea Yates

In June 2001, Texas resident Andrea Yates made national headlines when she methodically drowned her five children in a bathtub. She had previously been diagnosed with severe postpartum depression and postpartum psychosis, and had been taking twice the recommended dose of the antidepressant Effexor. She had a history of suicide attempts and hospitalizations, and her psychiatrist had recommended that she and her husband have no further children, and that she not be left alone with her kids. Compounding her problems were certain fundamentalist religious beliefs that led her to believe she and her children were evil and doomed to perish in the fires of Hell.

Yates confessed to police that she drowned her children, after her husband left for work. When she had completed her horrific act, leaving her last victim floating in the bathtub, she called the police to report what she had done. She then called her husband and said simply "it's time" over and over. When the police arrived, they found the other four young victims lying on a bed in the master bedroom.

During her trial, both sides agreed that Yates suffered from severe mental illness at the time of her crimes, but the prosecution argued that she still had the mental capacity to understand right from wrong. Under Texas law, in order to successfully argue an insanity defense, it must be shown that the defendant was so incapacitated by mental illness or defect at the time of their crime that they had lost that ability. In spite of her mental illness, the following year Yates was convicted of capital murder and sentenced to life in prison with the possibility of parole after 40 years.

In 2005, the Texas Court of Appeals reversed Yates's conviction, but not because of the severity of her mental illness. During her original trial a world-renowned forensic psychiatrist, Dr. Park Dietz, testified on behalf of the prosecution that Yates likely had gotten the idea of drowning her children from an episode of *Law & Order*. Dietz's testimony supported the argument by the prosecution that Yates had acted in a premeditated and calculated manner, and had actually planned her crimes. It was later discovered however that the episode Dietz had referred to never aired in that marketplace, and that Yates could not possibly have watched it. Based on the weight of Dr. Dietz's testimony, the conviction was overturned, and a new trial was ordered.

On July 26, 2006, the jury in the new trial agreed that Yates was sufficiently impaired at the time of her crimes to prevent her from understanding the implications of her acts. The jury found her not guilty by reason of insanity, as defined under Texas law. She was committed by the Texas courts to a state psychiatric hospital, where she will remain until such time that her doctors determine she has sufficiently recovered from her mental illness to be released.

Discussion Questions

1. Do some basic Internet research and discuss the differences between a verdict of "not guilty by reason of insanity" and one of "guilty but mentally ill."
2. Do you believe Andrea Yates should be required to spend her life incarcerated in spite of her mental illness? Why or why not?
3. What is the difference between a person being incapacitated by mental illness or by extreme drug abuse? Either could argue they had no awareness of the implications of their actions. Should they be treated the same under the law?

• ***Shelters:*** Many times the only way a crisis can be de-escalated is to get the person to a place of safety where their basic needs can be met. Essentially every urban area in America, and many rural areas, is serviced by a number of different shelters where people can be taken by the police and dropped off for the help they need. The two most common types of shelters are domestic violence and homeless shelters.

When the police respond to a domestic violence call, many times an abused spouse will not wish to file a complaint, and if there is no sign of injury or violence, then the police are limited in their ability to arrest the purported abuser. Most police departments follow a protocol that requires their officers to provide the victim of domestic violence information about their various options, including safe transport to a domestic violence shelter. In many communities, domestic violence shelters are set up to take in the victim's children also. The locations of these shelters are many times confidential and non-publicized. Others are in the open; however, they may have substantial security in place to prevent an abuser from coming to the shelter and perpetrating violence against a spouse or other family members.

Homeless shelters provide for the basic needs of the homeless. Most are operated by organizations that also provide other services, such as job training, drug and alcohol treatment, and GED preparation. They may also provide a daily food pantry and temporary quarters for homeless families. Homeless shelters come in many different types and, again, it is important that the police be aware of what types of services are available in their communities for this population. They are highly susceptible to victimization, and a significant percentage of crisis calls in any particular community will likely involve the homeless.

Chapter Summary

The crisis of mental illness has long been a problem for law enforcement. Police officers are trained to respond to overt behavior, rather than to the underlying causes of that behavior. Correctional officers are trained to respond in a similar fashion in order to maintain control of the jail or prison population. In the past, both professions have been terribly unresponsive to the problems and needs of all but the most seriously mentally ill. In recent years, however, that has started to change. With the creation of crisis intervention teams composed of officers specifically trained to respond to cases involving the mentally ill, the focus is shifting from enforcement to advocacy. And by engaging resource agencies within the community through written protocols and mutual assistance agreements, the law enforcement community is creating a response apparatus that reduces the potential harm to the person in crisis and the responding officers, and increases the odds that remedial and preventative efforts will be successful.

Key Terms

Thought disorder
Delusion
Hallucination
Mood disorder

Depression
Bipolar disorder
Anxiety disorder
Crisis intervention team (CIT)

Memphis Model
Engagement
Rapport

Discussion Questions

1. Discuss the concept of personal responsibility, and whether you believe the mentally ill should still be held accountable for their crimes.

2. Do some basic Internet research, and then discuss the differences between the verdicts of "guilty but mentally ill" and "not guilty by reason of insanity."

3. Do you believe the criminal justice system should recognize a difference between a mentally ill person who is psychologically impaired and an intoxicated person who is chemically impaired? Assuming both commit the same crime, and both are unable to understand the implications of their actions, should they be treated differently?

13

The Institutional Crisis

LEARNING OUTCOMES

Upon completion of this chapter the student should be able to:

1. Summarize the nature of the prison riot.

2. List and define the various riot typologies, and the dangers posed by each.

3. Explain the psychological principles at play during a prison riot.

4. Summarize the accepted best practices for responding to a prison riot, and the various solutions available to those attempting to de-escalate a prison riot.

Chapter Outline

INTRODUCTION

THE PRISON RIOT: A DEADLY RECORD

The prison system in America has always been a breeding ground for crisis, especially riots. Over the years we have witnessed many deadly riots, most of them culminating in the deaths of inmates, correctional officers, or both. It is a crisis that typically involves hostages and lengthy negotiations. Containment is typically accomplished quickly by the physical structure of the prison itself; however, de-escalation can be a lengthy process, one made more difficult by the false sense of freedom the inmates enjoy during the course of the crisis. It is this same sense of freedom that makes a prison riot, even when contained and with negotiations under way, a tinder box. Most of the time the inmates are as much a danger to each other as they are to any hostages they may have taken. Some of the more notable prison riots that have occurred in modern times in America include the following:

- **Attica Correctional Facility, New York:** On September 9, 1971, nearly 1000 inmates revolted following the shooting death of inmate and political activist George Jackson at California's San Quentin Prison. Inmates took control of the prison, along with 33 hostages. Negotiations lasted for four days, but when they finally reached an impasse on a key point, then–Governor Nelson Rockefeller ordered that the prison be re-taken. When it was over, 39 people lay dead, including 10 prison guards and civilian employees. It was later determined that the hostages were all killed by friendly fire. Attica remains the deadliest prison riot in U.S. history (*Time*, 1972).

- **McAlester Prison, Oklahoma:** On July 27, 1973, the riot at McAlester Prison broke out after inmates became frustrated with overcrowding and the inability of staff to control prison violence. From the beginning of 1970 until the time of the riot, official records of the prison recorded 19 violent deaths, 40 stabbings, and 44 serious beatings of inmates. During the riot there were numerous beatings, stabbings, and the murder of three inmates. Twenty-one hostages were taken in the chaos, but all were eventually let go alive. During the riot many of the prison's buildings were set ablaze by the inmates. In all, 24 buildings were destroyed, making it the costliest prison riot in U.S. history, with damages in excess of $20 million (oktrooper.com, 2010).

- **New Mexico State Penitentiary:** On February 2, 1980, inmates overpowered guards in a spontaneous riot that became one of the most gruesome in U.S. history. The riot lasted 36 hours and left 33 dead, all inmates. A number of guards were taken hostage, although all were released alive after being severely beaten, and in some cases even raped. The scene inside the prison during the riot was mass chaos. Gangs were battling other gangs, and some of the most dangerous inmates were giving orders. Many of the inmates who died were informants who were being kept in protective custody. A group of rioters managed to blowtorch their way into the protective custody cellblock, drag the inmates from their cells, and brutally torture and kill them. Many of the dead were dismembered, some of them while still alive (*Time*, 1989).

- **Atlanta Federal Penitentiary**: In November, 1987, inmates at the Federal Penitentiary in Atlanta, Georgia, seized control of the facility after the State Department announced plans to send 2500 Cuban nationals in U.S. custody back to Cuba. Many of the detained nationals arrived on U.S. soil during the Mariel boatlift in 1980 and were subsequently convicted of crimes. When the detained Cubans heard the announcement that they were being returned to Cuba they rioted. Their principal demand was that they not be repatriated. Over a period of 11 days the rioters took more than 100 hostages and burned down much of the facility. They eventually surrendered and released all of the hostages. The only death to occur during the incident was an inmate shot by a prison guard reportedly to protect a co-worker (*New York Times*, 1987).

- **Chino Prison:**   On August 8, 2009, a riot broke out at the California Institute for Men in Chino California, 35 miles east of Los Angeles. The riot was blamed on overcrowding and racial tensions. During the single night of violence 249 inmates and 8 prison employees were injured, though none fatally. The riot also caused an estimated $5.2 million in damage to the facility. Following the riot a panel of federal judges ordered the California Corrections Department to reduce its adult prison population by 40,000 by the summer of 2011 (*LA Times*, 2009).
- **Folsom Prison:**   California's Folsom Prison has had a long history of violence. In October, 2010, 8 inmates were injured after a fight broke out in a dining hall involving over 100 inmates. In August 2010, correctional officers fired into a crowd of rioting inmates after other methods failed to stop the violence. Five inmates were wounded by the gunfire, and two others were injured by other inmates during the 30-minute riot. Five inmates were injured during a riot involving hundreds of inmates in September 2008. In April 2002, 24 inmates and 1 guard were injured during a riot in the prison yard when rival Mexican gangs battled. In September 1996, 1 inmate was killed and 13 wounded during a riot. Six guards were also injured in the violence (KCRA.com, 2010).

It is clear to see that a crisis inside the walls of a penitentiary can be a deadly situation. Group behavior tends to overpower any rational attempt by individuals to quell the violence. It is also deadly because those who commit the most heinous acts do so with the belief that they can very easily fade into the crowd once prison officials regain control. An inmate who cooperates with a post-riot investigation does so at great peril. This reality is well established among the prison population. Many times even those inmates who are attacked and injured refuse to cooperate and identify their attackers. Retaliation is considered the only viable form of justice among the inmate population.

Before we look at the psychology of the prison riot, it is important to identify the various riot typologies. The type of riot will determine the potential level of violence, especially toward hostages, and the appropriate response by prison or police officials.

TYPES OF PRISON RIOTS

Martin and Zimmerman's Classification Scheme

There have been a number of attempts to look at prison riots in terms of typologies. Some have attempted to do so in terms of the motivation of the rioters. Others have looked at riots in terms of precursory conditions inside the prison. Martin and Zimmerman (1990) Classified prison riots into a typology scheme involving six different types:

- *Environmental conditions:*   One of the main factors associated with prison riots over the years has been the deplorable condition and overcrowding of many of America's prisons. There has traditionally been a reluctance among politicians, especially at the state and local level, to dump tax dollars into improving the conditions inside their prisons, or to construct new prisons to relieve the overcrowding. It is simply not viewed as a priority. America takes a rather conservative approach to criminal justice. There is little compassion for those incarcerated, especially those imprisoned for long periods of times for heinous crimes. Unfortunately this view does not take into consideration the safety of prison staff who must work each day in conditions where violence could erupt at any moment as a result of tensions related to poor conditions and overcrowding.
- *Spontaneity:*   These riots tend not to have a collective cause or reason. They often begin with a fight, an aggressive action by correctional officers, or even the unruly behavior of an inmate. The precursory event is only the spark that ignites the fire. Once a sufficient number of

people join to allow inmates the perceived ability to fade anonymously into the unruly or violent episode, then a group mentality sets in and the riot begins. There are no leaders in a spontaneous riot, no demands or objectives. Instead it tends to be a mass release of aggression and frustration directed at prison officials, other inmates, or the physical structure itself. These types of riots are extremely dangerous because they are unplanned and uncontrolled.

- *Conflict*:   There is much conflict inside a prison. In fact, its entire social structure is based on conflict. Survival of the fittest is the dominating principle, and conflict is the means by which the fittest is determined. There is constant tension among the prison population on many different levels. There is tension between individual inmates, between rival gangs and ethnic groups, and between inmates and prison staff. Many times this tension manifests itself in the form of violence. Large-scale conflict between rival gangs or between inmates and prison staff can very easily turn into a riot.

- *Collective behavior/social control*:   It is difficult to control a population of inmates who have no desire to be controlled, and who know full well their rights under the law and the U.S. Constitution. But control is exactly what a prison attempts to do. Prison officials control every aspect of an inmate's life during their incarceration. They control the inmate's movement, their daily activities, their meals, and even their shower and personal hygiene. At times this extreme amount of control can cause tensions to increase, especially if it involves the removal of privileges for a particular reason. Eventually this increased tension can lead to a planned and organized riot by the inmates in an effort to effect some change, usually an easing up of the amount of control the prison staff maintains over them.

- *Power vacuum*:   Every prison has a hierarchy of power among its inmates. In today's environment, the power within a prison is usually related to gang affiliation. The most powerful gang is in control, and the leadership of the gang is usually determined by its leadership outside the prison. Many times there are multiple gangs, with no single gang having all the power. They have protected turf outside on the yard and in the common areas inside the facility. One gang may control the basketball courts for example. Another may control the weightlifting area. They may even control the prison economy, which is typically a bartering system involving such items as cigarettes. Inevitably there are times when the leadership of these gangs is left with a void following someone's release or transfer. When this happens rival gangs may attempt to exploit the situation to their own benefit and increase their power. This, of course, can lead to a protracted struggle that may involve violence and rioting until power is again consolidated.

- *Rising expectations*:   In the latter half of the 1960s a prison reform movement began in America that endeavored to improve the conditions inside America's prisons. This movement was backed by many people not in prison, including civil rights lawyers and liberal politicians. The end result was a new era in American penology. Inmates were now given access to educational resources, religious practice, mental health treatment, and job training. There was a greater focus on rehabilitation rather than using prisons strictly for punitive retribution. With these new rights, however, inmates became more empowered and expected more than the system was willing to give. Examples have included more access to television, violent rap music, or even email and the Internet. Any time expectations inside a prison are not met, tensions increase, and eventually may cause a riot to erupt with violence directed at the prison administration.

Useem and Kimball's Model

In another popular theory, Useem and Kimball (1989) looked at prison riots from the perspective of prisoner perceptions and the strength of the administration's control over the inmates. At the heart of their theory is the belief that all riots are a function of eroding administrative structures. The specific causes proffered by Martin and Zimmerman explain only half of the

Inclination to Riot

		YES	NO
Ability to Riot	YES	NORMAL RIOT CONDITIONS	RIOT-PRONE
	NO	RIOT-PRONE	SAFE PRISON

FIGURE 13.1 Levels of Proneness.

equation, or, as Useem and Kimball argue, the strength of the inmates' *inclination* to riot. For them a second factor is needed to fully explain the causes of a prison riot, and that is the *ability* of the inmates to riot in the first place. This last factor they attribute to a breakdown in the prison administration. When factors such as those described by Martin and Zimmerman increase the inmates' inclination to riot, and an ineffective administration fails to properly control that population, thus increasing the inmates' ability to riot, then violence becomes more likely.

Useem and Kimball categorized a prison's proneness for a riot based on these two factors. Their scheme is essentially a vulnerability scale with four possible levels of proneness, as illustrated in Figure 13.1. At one extreme is a prison with poor conditions and an administration unwilling or unable to deal with it. In this case, a riot should be expected as a normal outcome of these two factors. At the other extreme is a prison with acceptable conditions, few grievances among the inmates, and an administration that is receptive to the needs of the inmates while maintaining a level of strength and professional competence to effectively control the inmate population.

Each of these classification schemes has its limitations. Martin and Zimmerman's scheme is perhaps too general to have much utility in terms of understanding the etiology of the prison riot. It is not enough to suggest that "conflict" may be one of the causes of a riot. It seems common sense that some form of conflict is necessarily involved. It also seems inadequate to suggest that "rising expectations" may lead to a riot. Expectations are likely always on the rise in a prison environment, yet in the vast majority of cases this does not lead to rioting.

With regard to Useem and Kimball's scheme, they leave two very important questions unanswered; that is, what causes a prison to move from "proneness" to "actual"? And how is it that a prison considered "safe" under their scheme can experience a riot? Unless there is a correlation between proneness, as they measure it, and a history of actual rioting, then it seems that their theory loses its utility rather quickly.

For purposes of our study, we will offer a new classification scheme for the prison riot, one based on the demographics of today's inmate population and, more importantly, the near total control of gangs inside the prison walls. Also, any classification scheme should have some utility in terms of prevention. The descriptors we apply should point to the areas where preventative measures need to be targeted.

A New Classification Scheme

THE GRIEVANCE RIOT   The first type of prison riot we will look at is the **grievance riot**. This category includes two subtypes: *conditions* and *lifestyle*. The first subtype includes those riots that results from the conditions in which the inmates are forced to live. Many of the riots of the 1960s and 1970s, the most active era in modern American history for prison riots, were the result of the deplorable conditions in which the inmates lived. Overcrowding, bad food, lack of clean bedding, and broken plumbing are just a few examples. The prison reform movement began in part because of the condition of America's aging prisons. Since that time, many new prisons have been constructed across the country. Additionally, the various courts in America have made numerous rulings relating to inmate rights. The result is a vast improvement in prison living conditions, except perhaps for the overcrowding issue. The likelihood of such a riot has been greatly reduced as a result.

The second type of grievance riot is related to inmate lifestyle. Even in the best living conditions there are still grievances. Examples might include a demand for more access to religious practices, job training, and computers. Perhaps a demand for more time outside, or more athletic equipment. This type of grievance can be related to anything that is, or could be part of the inmates' daily routine. One example that has been hotly debated is the idea of making prisons smoke-free. Many states still do not have smoke-free prisons out of fear that such a move will lead to increased assaults on staff and riots. A 2001 survey of 51 U.S. prisons with smoking bans found that only two reported any type of violence relating to the ban; however, 20 percent reported increased staff-inmate tensions (Hammond and Emmons, 2005).

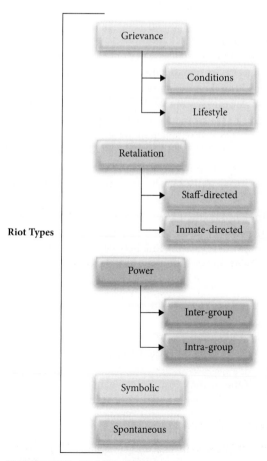

FIGURE 13.2   Riot Typologies.

THE RETALIATION RIOT   The second major category of prison riot is the **retaliation riot**. This deadly type of riot is one in which violence is either *staff-directed* or *inmate-directed*. Although the days of inmate brutality have largely passed, there are still prisons that have gained a reputation on the part of their correctional officers for being overly authoritarian and physical. This type of behavior can certainly lead to increased tensions and, if bad enough, the inmates may feel compelled to riot as a way of getting media attention, or simply to exact retribution against the correctional officers. In this latter situation there may be hostages held by the inmates in order to improve their bargaining position; however, there will no doubt be those who are tortured or killed at the outset of the riot for purposes of revenge.

The second subtype, *inmate-directed*, is the more common type of prison riot, and certainly the most common cause of violence inside the prison. As previously stated, the vast majority of inmates in America's prisons are affiliated with one gang or another. In any given prison multiple gangs operate. Membership in these gangs is based largely on ethnicity. The gangs live by a particular code, and one of the standard provisions of that code, regardless of the gang, is that violence and disrespect by a rival gang, or any of its members, will be met with retribution, usually in the form of more violence. Another provision of that code is that gang members always back up their brothers. Consequently, it is not uncommon for an attack by one gang member on another to end up in a full-blown riot in the prison yard or cafeteria.

THE POWER RIOT   The third category in our riot typology scheme is the **power riot**. This type of riot can be both *inter-group* and *intra-group*. There was a time when every prison had a definite hierarchy of power among its inmates. A prison population was typically controlled by one person who had a cadre of loyal lieutenants under him to assure compliance among the inmates. Those days, however, are long over, as gangs now wield the power in any particular prison. Seldom is there only a single gang in control. Rather it is a sharing of power among a few of the more powerful gangs. Most of the time this sharing of power is carried out peacefully. But there are times when rival gangs resort to violence in an effort to gain more power and control. This violence can erupt into a full-blown riot, either planned or spontaneously in response to an attack by a rival. This type of inter-group power riot can be deadly, especially if it is a planned event, in which case a large number of weapons may be present in anticipation of the violent action.

According to the U.S. Department of Justice (2010), prison gangs are self-perpetuating criminal entities that can continue their operations outside the confines of the penal system due to the extensive networks they have developed over the years. They play an important role in drug trafficking, and in many cases are the link between the drug traffickers and the street gangs. The Justice Department identifies the following as being among the most powerful prison gangs currently operating:

- **Aryan Brotherhood**:   Also known as AB, there are two factions, one located in the California Department of Corrections and the other within the Federal Bureau of Prisons. The AB's members tend to be Caucasian, and they are highly organized even outside the prisons. They are an extremely violent gang, and their primary activities involve drug trafficking and murder-for-hire.
- **Barrio Azteca**:   One of the most violent gangs currently operating inside America's prisons. Its members are typically Mexican nationals or Mexican Americans. They are most active in prisons throughout Texas and the Southwest. Their main activity outside prisons is smuggling narcotics across the U.S.–Mexican border. They are also involved in a number of other criminal enterprises, including extortion, kidnapping, and smuggling illegal aliens across the border.

- **Black Guerrilla Family**:   Founded in 1966 at San Quentin State Prison in California, the BFG is a highly organized paramilitary gang with a supreme leader and a central committee. A majority of its members are African American, and they are active primarily in prisons in California and Maryland. Like the other gangs, outside the prison they are involved in drug trafficking and an assortment of other criminal enterprises.

- **Dead Man Incorporated (DMI)**:   A violent prison gang that originated in the 1980s and operates primarily out of the Maryland Department of Corrections. Its members are predominantly white. They have recently begun recruiting new members in the Virginia prison system. One of its members assaulted a law enforcement officer for the sole purpose of getting incarcerated in a Virginia prison to begin recruiting new members. Outside the prison the gang's members have committed murders for hire, acts of intimidation, and have engaged in drug trafficking.

- **The Texas Syndicate**:   One of the largest and most powerful gangs operating on both sides of the U.S.–Mexico border. The syndicate is a highly structured gang composed primarily of Mexican nationals or Mexican Americans. They are highly involved in drug trafficking, and control the drug trade in entire regions of the Southwest. They have a direct relationship with certain Mexican drug cartels, in addition to an alliance with Los Zetas, a paramilitary organization employed by the cartels.

- **Tango Blast**:   A predominantly Hispanic gang operating throughout the Texas prison system that originated in the 1990s among gang members entering prison from Austin, Dallas, Fort Worth, and Houston. The original purpose of the gang was to provide protection to those who had no interest in joining an established prison gang. As interest in the gang grew among Hispanics entering the Texas system, eventually eight different affiliated groups were formed. Texas officials now worry that the gang is of a sufficient strength to challenge the Texas Syndicate for control of illegal activities within the prison system. Unlike the other gangs, the Tangos do not appear to be highly active outside the prisons. Members tend to migrate back to their street gangs upon release.

- **Mexican Mafia**:   Formed in the late 1950s in the California Department of Corrections, it is a loosely structured criminal organization with strict rules imposed on its members, who are predominantly Mexican-American males from Southern California street gangs. Like the Texas Syndicate, the Mexican Mafia maintains relationships with drug traffickers, and they are highly involved in the drug trade in the southwestern and Pacific regions of the United States. Other reported sources of income for the gang include gambling and prostitution inside the prison system, and extorting drug distributors on the outside.

- **Nazi Low Riders**:   A violent California-based gang that maintains a white supremacist philosophy. The gang's members are predominantly Caucasian males with a history of street gang activity. The gang operates primarily in prisons in the southwestern and Pacific regions of the United States. They are heavily involved in the drug trade and the extortion of independent drug dealers and members of other white power gangs. Outside the prisons they are involved in many different types of criminal enterprise, including identity theft, money laundering, and robbery.

- **Public Enemy Number One**:   Reportedly the fastest-growing Caucasian prison gang in the United States. The gang operates mainly in the California prison system, and to a lesser extent in locations throughout the northeastern, Pacific, southwestern, southeastern, and the West-Central regions of the United States. The gang espouses a white supremacist philosophy and maintains alliances with both the Aryan Brotherhood and Nazi Low Riders. Like the other gangs, outside the prisons its members are engaged in a wide array of criminal enterprises.

All of these gangs, and an assortment of others, are extremely violent. They maintain such a demeanor as a way of surviving the harsh realities of prison life. They also use violence as a way of securing a position of power among the prison population. Power is everything in a prison. Those who hold the power can control the illegal activities inside the prison, everything from drugs and gambling, to prostitution. Those in power can control the prison economy, the work assignments, who gets what territory on the yard, and who will be subjected to some form of prison justice for their actions. When a gang's hold on this power, or any part of it, is threatened by a rival gang, then violent measures may be employed in an effort to remove the threat. Such violent measures can very easily lead to a riot involving rival gangs.

A less common type of riot is the intra-group power riot. There are times when a gang experiences internal conflict among its own members. When this happens there may be a power struggle for control of the gang. The gang may splinter into factions. The possibility of violence by one faction against the other is very real when this happens.

In reality, the gangs operating inside America's prisons are now highly organized, and for the most part are controlled by a leadership structure outside the prison. For this reason intra-group conflict and violence is much rarer than conflict between rival gangs. Also, modern gangs are in the business of making money, almost always in illegal ways. Those in positions of gang leadership understand what it takes to operate a lucrative business, and one of the most important things is the cooperative efforts of everyone involved. Conflict in the gang will only diminish its ability to generate income. For this reason, internal conflict is typically avoided at all costs, and when it occurs, it is dealt with quickly by the gang's leadership.

THE SYMBOLIC RIOT   The fourth category of prison riot is the **symbolic riot**. Prison inmates are not oblivious to the news. In fact, they are quite up to date on the world's daily happenings. With so much time on their hands, they have little else to do at times but read, watch television, and in some cases surf parts of the Internet that are not restricted. Many times in the past prison populations have taken up a particular cause to support. These causes have included civil rights, the anti-war movement, and bringing fairness and equity to our justice system. At times their support for a cause may compel them to demonstrate that support, and one of the most dramatic forms of demonstration a prison population has at its disposal is a destructive prison riot. It gets a great amount of media coverage, and allows the inmates the possibility of voicing their support to a national audience. As mentioned at the beginning of this chapter, the 1971 riot at the Attica Correctional Facility in New York, the deadliest in U.S. history, was in part a symbolic riot in response to the death of inmate and prison activist George Jackson at San Quentin earlier in the year.

THE SPONTANEOUS RIOT   The final category of prison riot is the **spontaneous riot**. These riots occur like a spark setting off a wildfire. Typically it begins with a fight or some other disturbance, and very quickly escalates out of control when inmates see an opportunity. This opportunity may be signaled by an overpowered correctional officer, or perhaps by the quick departure of correctional officers from the cellblock, followed by its lockdown. The spontaneous riot may be sparked by the destruction of a piece of equipment, or by lunch trays being thrown across a cafeteria. It takes very little to cause the controlled behavior of individuals to quickly fade into the chaos of group excitement, agitation, and panic. Once it does, no one is safe, and it is likely that a large amount of prison property and infrastructure will be damaged or destroyed.

RIOT PSYCHOLOGY

Deindividuation

What happens in the minds of those who turn violent during a prison riot and commit atrocities they never would have considered otherwise? Although there certainly have been planned and premeditated prison riots in America, even those have tended to spiral out of control very quickly to take on the appearance of a spontaneous event. Even with some form of leadership in place trying to control the inmates, it still becomes very chaotic and deadly, as inmates seize upon the opportunity to damage and destroy property, or to attack prison staff or other inmates.

To understand the psychology of this type of behavior we turn again (see Chapter 10) to Leon Festinger's research on the phenomenon of deindividuation. Festinger (1952) was the first to look at an individual's increased capacity for violence and aggression as a member of a group, in contrast to their actions when acting alone. Festinger believed that a person can become so immersed in a group that they no longer perceive themselves as acting individually within that group. He referred to this as deindividuation (first described in Chapter 10), when a decrease in self-awareness and self-evaluation leads a person to commit acts they would never have considered while acting on their own. Festinger researched this phenomenon with memories of WWII, and more specifically the Holocaust, still fresh in the collective mind of the academic community. Many wondered how it was that these seemingly Christian men could kiss their wives and children goodbye in the morning, travel to work, and then spend their day slaughtering Jews in the gas chambers. Not only did they deindividuate themselves ("I was only following orders"), but they deindividuated their victims, seeing them only as a single dehumanized group with no individual identities.

A more recent example is the American massacre of innocent civilians in the Vietnamese village of My Lai in 1968. Over 300 women, children, and elderly men were brutally murdered, some sexually assaulted, by American soldiers searching for enemy combatants. These were American soldiers, accustomed to the rules of engagement; however, on that day something happened. After being given orders to enter the village and aggressively seek out the enemy, these young American soldiers became abusive and violent. Within minutes their abusive behavior turned to murder. The soldiers began rounding up and killing entire families of unarmed civilians. Babies were shot in their mother's arms. It was one of the most brutal and shameful episodes in American military history. Ultimately the brutality of that day, once news of it leaked to the press, would hasten America's departure from Vietnam.

And an even more recent example is the behavior of American Soldiers at Abu Ghraib Prison in Baghdad in 2004 during the Iraq War, where torture and humiliation of Iraqi prisoners took place in direct violation of international accords and the military's own policies. There is a certain degree of deindividuation that is a normal part of military life, but in Abu Ghraib that deindividuation increased as the soldiers there felt a singular purpose to retaliate against the Iraqis for killing American soldiers. Their ability to evaluate their own behavior in a proper context was greatly diminished by this deindividuation process and their dehumanization of the Iraqi prisoners. In short, as is also true in the case of My Lai, the soldiers were no longer acting as individuals, being directed by their own moral convictions and ethics, but instead were completely immersed in the group and acting out the perceived goals and motivations of the group.

According to Festinger's theory then, deindividuation impacts the group dynamic in three ways, all of which can be related to the prison riot:

- *Less inhibition*: When a person is no longer acting as an individual, but rather as a member of a group, then there is no need for inhibited behavior. It's as if they pack away their sense of self temporarily and forget about it. Their behavior is no longer constrained by personal values, but instead only by the perceived values of the group. If those group values are grounded in violence and confrontation, then the deindividuated person will have little problem being violent and confrontational without the immediate self-perception that they are violating their own personal values. And because they are able to rationalize their group actions without threatening their sense of self, this makes the deindividuated person indeed dangerous. Many times after people have participated in atrocities and are interviewed later, they seem like different people. Many speak about their actions in bewilderment, unsure how they could have engaged in such behavior. In such cases the individual's sense of self has been reintegrated. They are back to being directed by their own moral and ethical standards, and they may even find their own past behavior objectionable.

- *Heightened responsiveness*: With increased deindividuation there is a heightened sensitivity to external inputs and a greater level of responsiveness to those inputs. As a riot unfolds, and deindividuation begins, people become highly responsive to what they see and hear around them. If people around them are destroying things, they are much more inclined to join the destructive behavior. And because their level of inhibition is also decreasing, they do so with little internal dialogue or regulation.

- *Adherence to group norms*: When deindividuation occurs, individual norms and standards are replaced by the perceived norms and standards of the group. With heightened sensitivity to the external inputs that define these norms and standards, and a decreased level of inhibition, the individual willingly behaves in ways that are consistent with the new standards of the group. This is especially dangerous in a prison setting, because inmates to a large extent have already adopted a new set of standards in order to survive prison life. Thus they are already primed to adhere to group norms. During a riot, when the predominant group norms are to control, destroy, or even kill, those norms are willingly accepted and adhered to by the deindividuated inmate.

Adherence to group norms requires an obedience to a level of authority or direction over and above an individual's own internal set of moral and ethical standards. This blind obedience could be to another person, or it could be to an ideal. The Nazis for example, were blindly obedient to the idea of exterminating a race of people, and also to the individual commanders handing out the orders to do so. This obedience is the result of deindividuation. It is what compels people to commit atrocities, and to make them appear at the time as the acceptable thing to do. And with little internal conflict compelling them to turn away from such behavior, and with their inhibitions lowered, they become responsive to the behaviors of those around them and allow their own moral and ethical standards to fade into those of the group's.

MILGRAM'S OBEDIENCE STUDY Dr. Stanley Milgram studied this phenomenon of obedience, and in 1962 carried out one of the most famous experiments in the history of psychology. His "Obedience" study (Milgram, 1974) involved having volunteers administer varying levels of electric shock to an individual who was attempting to learn a series of word combinations. If they answered correctly and remembered the learned combination, then they moved on to the next word pairing. If they did not answer correctly, then the volunteer administering the test was instructed to deliver the shock. With each incorrect answer the level of shock was increased up to a maximum of 450 volts. The volunteers were told that the study was to determine the effects of punishment on the learning process.

In reality, of course, there was no shock at all. The person answering the questions, who appeared to be randomly selected, was in fact an actor. Milgram was not studying the effects of punishment on the learning process, but rather to what extent someone would follow orders and administer punishment to another human, even if it violated their own moral standards. The actor was seated in another room out of the volunteer's view, and after a certain level of shock they began to make audible noises ranging from low sighs of discomfort to outright screams. The actor also demanded at various points during the testing process to be released from the restraints that were purportedly holding him to his chair, and which the volunteer was allowed to inspect prior to beginning the test.

To everyone's amazement, 65 percent of the volunteers in the study continued to administer the electric shock all the way to the maximum 450 volts, even with the actor screaming in apparent pain and demanding to be released. Only one refused to go beyond the 300-volt level. Most of the volunteers, during a debriefing in which they were told the truth about the study, explained that they had administered the level of shock they did because they were following the rules of the experiment. They were being obedient to the researcher who explained to them the rules and requirements of the procedure prior to beginning. In short, their obedience to the researcher and the requirements of the study caused them deindividuate and administer what they thought was an electric shock to another person, even when that person was feigning distress.

THE STANFORD PRISON EXPERIMENT   Another study worth noting, and one that was no less controversial than Milgram's was the Stanford Prison Experiment (Zimbardo, 2007) carried out by Dr. Philip Zimbardo at Stanford University in 1971. In the study, Zimbardo set up a mock prison in the Psychology Department at Stanford, and then randomly assigned 24 males to serve either as inmates in the mock prison or as prison guards. His goal was to study the phenomenon of deindividuation inside a prison setting. What he found was that deindividuation occurred in both the prisoners and the prison guards. In fact, what was intended to be a two-week simulation was discontinued after only six days due to the sadistic-like behavior of the guards, a circumstance that was worsening as time went on. The guards had resorted to such tactics as humiliation and deprivation to gain the inmates' compliance, and they did so with no prior directives to use such methods.

Zimbardo concluded that the changes in character taking place in the prison guards and inmates alike was the result of deindividuation. The guards were becoming evil and the inmates pathologically passive. Both were now taking on a new group character, complete with new expectations and norms. Although none of the guards would normally have been abusive to other people in their daily lives, in the mock prison setting it was becoming easier and easier.

So the psychology of the prison riot is such that people will become less inhibited because they no longer see themselves individually, but as a member of a group. They become increasingly more responsive to the actions of those around them. And because they no longer self-evaluate as they do in an individuated state, they become accepting of, and obedient to the norms and standards of the group. It can be argued that this happens even quicker in a prison setting because deindividuation is actually one of the goals of the prison system. Inmates are known by their inmate numbers. They wear uniforms. And their daily lives are almost entirely void of any sense of individualism. Making matters even worse is the prevalence of gang affiliation among inmates, a factor that decreases even further their sense of individualism.

Unlike a riot outside the prison walls, where it could potentially take some effort to get people to abandon their self-evaluation and join in, a prison riot happens with the slightest provocation. Inmates are primed to react with violence because for the most part they have already become obedient to the group norm among inmates that violence and disrespect are to be met with the same, and in like measure. It is a deadly situation in which the participants lose all inhibitions, and become hyper-responsive to the actions of those around them.

THE CRISIS RESPONSE

The prison crisis is one that is essentially contained by the infrastructure itself. Though some have, few prison riots have the ability to spread beyond the immediate or general area of the prison in which it erupts. And there is essentially no chance of it spreading to areas outside the prison. So the primary goal in responding to a prison crisis is rapid de-escalation in an effort to avoid further death and destruction.

When a crisis does break out inside the prison walls, specifically a riot in which the inmates have gained some control of persons or territory, then the administration essentially has three options available to them. They can de-escalate the crisis by force (the *tactical* solution); they can attempt to negotiate an end to the crisis (the *negotiation* solution); or they can attempt to wait out the rioters and allow the crisis to die out on its own (the *waiting* solution). In a study funded by the U.S. Department of Justice (Useem et al., 1995), researchers looked at each of these options against the backdrop of actual prison riots that had been successfully resolved to determine when each option should be attempted.

The Tactical Solution

The tactical solution can involve either a planned **tactical strike** or a **riot squad maneuver**. The most important consideration in determining which to use and when to use it is the presence of hostages or the likelihood of violence being perpetrated against vulnerable inmates. When the likelihood is high that the inmates will torture or kill hostages or other inmates, then a planned tactical strike becomes necessary. Such a strike is unannounced, and makes use of the element of surprise if possible. The timing of the strike is also important. If possible, the strike force reacts in the same manner as the police do in an active shooter situation. There are benefits to moving in immediately once the riot begins. This disallows the rioters the opportunity to organize and come up with their own plans for when a tactical strike occurs. It also prevents them from separating any hostages and securing them in locations that are more difficult to penetrate rapidly.

The two key elements in deploying a rapid tactical response are intelligence and preparation. Preparation comes through training, and having action plans for essentially any scenario that may unfold. It includes plans for rapid deployment of the tactical team, and a predetermined command structure to direct the operation. The team should have a thorough knowledge of the layout of the prison in order to maximize the speed with which they are able to reach any hostages, and the necessary weaponry—stun grenades, non-lethal weapons, and firearms—to diminish the inmates' ability to react to the assault.

The other main element, intelligence, is crucial to the success of any tactical operation. In any prison, intelligence gathering is an ongoing and necessary task. It allows the administration to be aware of any dynamic among the inmate population that could potentially lead to a crisis. It can also give the administration a head start in understanding the inmate leadership during a riot, which of those among the inmates could potentially be influential during negotiations, and any potential conflicts that may arise among the inmates under the stress of a protracted crisis, such as among rival gangs. Additionally, this type of intelligence may provide critical information that the operational commander needs in order to determine if an immediate tactical strike is necessary, or if negotiations should be attempted first. Certainly if it is believed that hostages or other inmates will be tortured or killed regardless of negotiations, then an immediate strike will be necessary.

Tactical intelligence is also critical once the crisis has begun. This type of intelligence is obtained primarily from staff and inmates who have escaped the crisis, and from security systems within the riot area. This type of intelligence may include information about the location of hostages, inmate intentions and plans, the presence of weapons, and the most effective entry points for a tactical strike. Once again, this intelligence is critical in determining if an immediate strike is necessary. Those escaping the crisis may have knowledge that certain hostages or inmates will be tortured or killed regardless of any negotiations. In this case the operational commander will likely order an immediate tactical strike.

The second option in the tactical solution is the riot squad maneuver. Unlike the planned tactical strike, this option does not seek to take advantage of the element of surprise. In fact, just the opposite is true. The riot maneuver is a show of force. Its goals are to divide, isolate, and intimidate the inmates. The maneuver is a controlled entry into the riot area of a large and well-equipped force of officers. They move as a group, protected by riot shields and armed mostly with non-lethal weapons such as riot clubs, rubber bullets, and pepper spray. It is hoped that such a show of force will compel the inmates to discontinue the riot, but if it does not, then the goal of this action is to divide and isolate groups of inmates who can then be restrained by force if necessary.

Obviously such an action is likely not going to be attempted if hostages have been taken, unless the action coincides with a tactical strike. To do so would give the inmates time to harm or kill the hostages. It is best used when intelligence suggests that significant property damage will take place unless the riot is stopped. Also, before such a maneuver is attempted, it is critically important that intelligence be gathered relating to the type and amount of weapons that are present among the inmates. Like any use-of-force situation, force will be met with the same or greater force when and where necessary. Obviously if the inmates have somehow secured firearms inside the prison, then a riot maneuver will not be attempted.

The Negotiating Solution

The second option available to the prison administration in the event of a riot is the negotiating solution. These negotiations can be either **direct negotiations** or **third-party negotiations**. In the first instance, prison staff conducts the negotiations. Essentially every prison system in the country has access to a negotiating team. They are primarily either prison staff or state police, or in the case of the federal system, the FBI. These teams are specially trained to negotiate with prison inmates, and to deal with the special problems posed by negotiating with an incarcerated population.

One of the most important considerations when attempting this option is to ensure that someone is in a leadership position among the inmates, either an individual or a committee. Negotiations should not begin until some semblance of leadership is apparent inside the prison. Also, it is important that those negotiating on behalf of the prison not be in positions of authority in the prison. It is not beneficial to the situation for inmates to negotiate with someone they know to have the authority to make immediate decisions, such as wardens or assistant wardens. Many times the negotiators are able to buy time by carrying inmate demands to a higher authority. This option is lost if the negotiator is the higher authority.

The cycle of the negotiation, as described by Useem et al. (1995), will begin with **exaggerated demands**. The extent to which they are exaggerated will depend on the leverage the inmates have in terms of hostages or the potential to destroy property or infrastructure. The more leverage they have, the more exaggerated the demands will likely be. The goal during this phase is to get the inmates to abandon these demands and begin the process of realistic negotiations. During this initial phase the prison negotiators will be careful not to give in to any inmates' demands, nor to make counteroffers. To do so will only empower the inmates with the belief that they have more negotiating power than they actually do. During this phase, rather than use the word "no," negotiators will recast inmate demands so they can be met, but without empowering the inmates. For example, consider the following exchange:

Inmate: "We want ten cases of good whiskey now! If we don't get them, then we start burning this place down!"

Negotiator: "Whiskey is a problem. I know you guys are thirsty though. Can we send in some soda or Gatorade?"

In the earlier chapter on crisis communications we discussed the idea of hooking a person's "adult" ego state. That is exactly what the negotiators attempt to do during this initial phase. Once they are successful, then the inmates hopefully will discontinue their exaggerated demands and get down to the business of resolving the crisis. Negotiations at this point can progress in one of three different directions, although most negotiations will have elements of all three:

• *Bargaining*:   In this scenario, there is a legitimate give-and-take that takes place between negotiators and inmates. Inmates make demands, and negotiators make counter- demands and offers. The goal is to reach a mutual agreement for the release of any hostages and to bring an end to the crisis. This type of negotiation is appropriate when a riot is a planned and organized event, and when there is a definite leadership structure in place among the inmates.

• *Problem solving*:   There are times, especially during a spontaneous riot when hostages are taken simply because they are in the wrong place at the right time for the inmates to gain control over them. These types of hostage situations do not begin with an end-goal in mind. It is more like, "we have hostages, now what do we do?" In these cases the focus of negotiations is more to solve the immediate problems the inmates face, and to de-escalate the situation in a way that is acceptable to them. It is less about bargaining, and more about coming to an agreement on how the inmates can get out of their current predicament with their physical safety assured.

• *Situation management*:   In the previous two negotiation types, it is presumed that some amount of de-escalation has taken place inside the prison to allow for such negotiations to begin. In those situations that remain very fluid, however, perhaps with rival elements vying for leadership or with aggressive acts continuing unabated, then the focus of negotiations becomes the management of the crisis in an effort to de-escalate it to the point that effective negotiations can begin.

At any time during each of these three negotiating scenarios a tactical strike may become necessary in order to rescue and protect hostages. In some cases the negotiators are not made aware of the tactical plans in order to avoid their own behavior tipping off the inmates. Even subtle changes in voice inflection or attentiveness may become apparent to an observant inmate. In other cases their negotiations may be used to gather intelligence for a tactical strike. Ultimately it is the situation commander who will make the decision to discontinue negotiations and carry out an assault. If the killing or torturing of hostages is taking place, or if intelligence suggests such acts are imminent, then such a strike will likely be ordered and carried out immediately. If the strike force is not yet fully deployed, and such violence is occurring or about to occur, then it is up to the negotiators to do their best to manage the situation, and to buy enough time for the tactical team to deploy and begin their assault.

Assuming negotiations are underway, one of the tasks of the negotiator is to know when enough is enough, or when an **impasse** has been reached. This is the point when effective negotiations are no longer possible, typically because the inmates refuse to change their demands or to take the negotiations seriously. When this point is reached, then the negotiator will likely issue an ultimatum. This ultimatum can be delivered in two different forms. The **use-of-force ultimatum** is just that, the decision by the negotiating team, and verbalized to the inmates, that the rioters must surrender control immediately or else be subjected to an overwhelming amount of force as the riot squad moves in. In most cases this ultimatum will be enough to bring the crisis to an end. If, however, the inmates are holding civilian or prison staff hostages, then this ultimatum must be used with caution. To announce such an ultimatum is to also essentially announce how much time the inmates have to carry out whatever deadly or destructive acts they choose to do.

The second type of ultimatum is the **issue ultimatum**. When negotiations reach an impasse because of a particular issue that simply cannot be met, the negotiating team can announce that the issue is dead and beyond discussion. It is hoped that this ultimatum will cause the inmates to see the situation in a realistic light and return to a more productive dialogue. This type of ultimatum may be used when there are hostages and the situation is such that a tactical strike may endanger their safety.

One final issue that must be addressed in a discussion of negotiation is the use of third-party negotiators. Over the years there have been many instances when third-party negotiators successfully resolved a prison crisis. It is typically the inmates who request an objective third party to hear their grievances. Those selected may be lawyers who specialize in prison reform, media professionals with a reputation for fair and accurate reporting, or religious leaders who are respected in their communities or perhaps socially active. These third-party negotiators can play several roles:

- *Initiators of conversation:* There are times when the inmates simply refuse to even talk to prison administrators. In this type of situation a third-party negotiator can be very effective in initiating dialogue between the two parties.
- *Guarantors to a promise:* There will likely always be some level of distrust between prison administrators and inmates. It is simply the nature of the relationship. When promises are made, or agreements reached between the parties, a third-party negotiator serves as a witness and bolsters the inmates' trust that the agreements will be honored.
- *Mediators:* Perhaps the most important role played by a third-party negotiator is that of mediator. They act as an objective negotiator with no vested interest in anything but the peaceful resolution of the crisis. Through their involvement the issue of distrust is lessened because neither side is talking directly to the other. Both parties can also feel assured that coercion and dishonesty in the negotiations is lessened by the third party evaluating both positions in advance of delivering it to the other side.
- *Government bargaining chips:* The use of a third party, especially if demanded by the inmates, can be used as a bargaining chip for the release of hostages, or even some of the hostages. If the inmates want their story to be publicly aired, then they may be willing to give something up for the chance to have a third party enter the negotiations who they can trust to report events accurately and fairly, including the inmates' grievances. A third party does not act as an agent for the prison administration, but rather for the peaceful resolution of the crisis.

Although third-party negotiators can have major benefits in a prison crisis, the prison administration must still be careful who they allow to act in this capacity. Caution must be taken to avoid individuals with their own political agenda, or with preconceived ideas about the prison or its staff. Steps must be taken to insure that the third party does not take it upon themselves to

ISSUES & ETHICS IN CRISIS INTERVENTION

Prison Privatization: A Prison-Industrial Complex?

As state and federal budgets continue to decline in America, the idea of prison privatization has again become a hotly debated issue. Proponents say private prisons can be operated more efficiently than government-owned facilities, which translates into reduced financial costs to the taxpayer. Opponents, however, have voiced numerous concerns, including concerns related to a private facility's ability to respond to crisis within its walls. The use of force, including deadly force, has been used often in America's prisons to break up fights and riots, and to save the lives of correctional officers and other prisoners. The question arises whether private contractors will have personnel with sufficient training to use force in legal and proper ways, as police and correctional officers are trained to do.

Some have questioned the constitutionality and ethics of private corporations detaining American citizens. Most agree that with the proper statutory authority private prisons are constitutional; however, not all agree on the ethics. By their very nature, corporations in America endeavor to turn a profit for their owners. Is it ethical to make money on someone else's misery? Government prisons of course make no money, aside from the various prison industries that are operated with inmate labor. The revenues from those endeavors however are entirely insufficient to operate any single prison. And what if the revenue generated by a private prison is insufficient to remain viable? Can a prison just close its doors? Does it file bankruptcy? If it does, are the prison's creditors then the new owners?

There are also many issues concerning oversight. In today's environment there is little chance that abuses occurring within a prison will go unreported to the outside world. But this may not be the case in a private prison, where the corporation owns and controls every aspect of the prison infrastructure. How will we be certain those abuses are not occurring? To what extent will government oversight be effective? We have witnessed in the banking and financial services industries how ineffective government oversight can be at times in its effort to prevent corruption and abuses of power.

And, finally, some would suggest there is an immediate conflict created when a prison is privatized. With a government-owned prison, the goals of the prison and the governmental entity funding it are the same; to rehabilitate the prisoner as quickly as possible to allow for their return to society. But a private prison will benefit most from keeping the prisoner incarcerated for as long as possible. Is there a danger that the politically powerful owners of private prisons may actually lobby legislators for longer sentences? It certainly seems like a possibility, given the track record of many other American corporations in recent years.

The debate over prison privatization will only increase in the years ahead. Those who see it as a moneymaker will continue to advocate for the concept. Those concerned more about human rights and social justice will likely fight against it. And caught in the middle are the politicians who ultimately will be responsible for the industry's rapid growth or steady decline through their legislative efforts. They will be influenced both by money and by social concern. Which will win the day is yet to be determined.

Discussion Questions

1. Discuss whether you feel it is ethical and appropriate for government to contract with private prisons.
2. If you believe private prisons are an acceptable option, do you also believe that privatization of police departments is a viable option for reducing the cost of public safety?
3. Do you believe a correctional officer's loyalty to a corporation, rather than to a governmental entity, is a potential benefit of privatization, or a potential danger?

act on the inmates' behalf, or to raise new issues. The prison administrators must have a means of monitoring the negotiations to avoid situations where a third party may start communicating with subtle suggestions supporting or even directing the inmates' actions.

The Waiting Solution

The final strategy for handling a prison crisis is the **waiting solution**. One unavoidable reality faced by rioting inmates is that in the end they have no place to go. Few prison rioters have ever escaped during a riot, and arguably in our modern day the probability of being able to do so is almost zero. In situations where there are no hostages, nor the likelihood of inmates being attacked and possibly murdered, then the waiting option may be the best. It is hoped that by stalling for time, inmates will simply grow tired of the crisis and discontinue their action.

The waiting solution can be both passive and active. With the **passive waiting** option the prison administration makes no effort to increase the discomfort of the inmates. They provide ample food and water, and are responsive to the inmates' daily needs and necessities. The negotiators may refuse to discuss issues, or they may stall for time, but they otherwise avoid increasing tensions between the two parties. It is hoped that eventually the crisis will lose its steam and the inmates will simply quit.

With the **active waiting** option the prison administration does make an effort to increase the discomfort of the inmates. They may refuse food and water, cut off the electricity, or pipe in loud, continuous music in an effort to make sleep more difficult. They may do this with limited negotiations, or while refusing to negotiate at all. It is hoped that the discomfort alone will be sufficient to cause the inmates to bring their action to an end.

Chapter Summary

The prison crisis is one of the most volatile and deadly situations that can occur within the criminal justice system, especially if hostages are taken. The prison environment creates a behavioral dynamic among inmates that can be violent and unpredictable. When a crisis does erupt, prison administrators have three options available to them: attack, negotiate, or wait them out. Only after an analysis of the situation by highly trained personnel using all available intelligence is an option selected. If hostages are in imminent danger, then it is likely that a tactical strike using the element of surprise will be carried out. If there are no hostages, or if there are, but prison officials have confirmed that they are neither harmed nor in imminent danger, then it is likely that negotiations will begin, possibly even using a third-party negotiator.

Researchers and practitioners in the field of corrections are constantly looking for improved systems, methods, and practices that will accomplish the dual goals of incarceration and rehabilitation while reducing the dangers present whenever hundreds of individuals with violent and troubled histories are housed together for lengthy periods of time. Making matters worse in our present day is the prevalence of well-organized gangs inside essentially every prison in America. The days are long over when prison guards with little education and making minimum wage salaries were expected to work in over-crowded prisons their entire career without succumbing to laziness, complacency, or even corruption. Sadly, many of them did. Today's correctional officer is likely a college graduate, career-minded, and, because of union representation, now making an acceptable wage with attractive benefits. Their jobs are among the toughest, and when a crisis erupts, their initial actions can mean the difference between a cafeteria disturbance that is quickly contained and de-escalated and a full-blown prison riot with the potential for death and destruction.

Key Terms

Grievance riot
Retaliation riot
Power riot
Symbolic riot
Spontaneous riot
Tactical strike

Riot squad maneuver
Tactical intelligence
Direct negotiations
Third-party negotiations
Exaggerated demands
Impasse

Use-of-force ultimatum
Issue ultimatum
Mediator
Waiting solution
Passive waiting
Active waiting

Discussion Questions

1. Many prison riots take place because of the freedom inmates are given to roam and congregate in places like the prison yard and cafeteria. Should inmates be allowed such freedoms, or do you believe they should be isolated from each other for the duration of their incarceration?

2. Should gang affiliation be allowed inside a prison? Or should members of the same gang be housed in separate areas of the prison and not be allowed to intermingle?

3. Discuss ways in which you believe a prison could be made riot-proof.

14

Crisis in the Courtroom

LEARNING OUTCOMES

Upon completion of this chapter the student should be able to:

1. List and define the various types of crisis that can occur in a courtroom.

2. Describe the obstacles to maintaining a secure courtroom.

3. Explain the risk continuum and the use of risk assessment profiles.

4. Summarize both reactive and proactive courtroom security measures.

Chapter Outline

INTRODUCTION

DEATH IN THE COURTROOM

The odds of a crisis occurring within the four walls of any particular courtroom in America are quite high. After all, it is here where victims and their families must face their attackers, where prison and death sentences are handed down, where marriages are dissolved, and where children are taken from their parents. Seldom in a courtroom is a matter resolved to the satisfaction of all parties involved. It is a place of high tension and visibility, where a deadly crisis can break out at any given moment. This reality played out on August 7, 1970, at the Marin County Courthouse in San Francisco when one young man armed with numerous weapons entered a courtroom and set off a deadly chain of events.

In the latter half of the 1960s, and into the 1970s, there was a robust prison reform movement in America. This movement was directed from inside of the prison walls, and was essentially an African-American movement. They were the victims of a criminal justice system that not only enforced the law inequitably, but one that sentenced a disproportionate number of African Americans to prison when compared to white offenders. Consequently, American prisons were filled with African Americans, some convicted of relatively minor offenses. The conditions inside the prisons tended to be horrid. Inmates were given little opportunity to rehabilitate themselves through educational services. Adequate medical treatment was lacking. Some religious practices were disallowed. African-American inmates especially were not given full access to the courts. And in many cases inmates were not given consistent opportunities to exercise or to leave the dankness of their cells for any length of time.

One of the leaders of the prison reform movement was Black Panther leader George Jackson (*Day of the Gun*, 2002), who in August 1970 was serving a one-year to life term in California's San Quentin Penitentiary for a $70 robbery, and was now charged, along with two others, in the brutal murder of a guard at Soledad Prison. On the day of the courtroom violence, Jackson's 17-year-old brother, Jonathon, armed with multiple weapons, stormed into the courtroom and armed a defendant in another Guard killing case, along with his brother's two co-defendants who were present as witnesses. Next they took Judge Harold Haley, the district attorney prosecuting the case, and three of the jurors hostage, and attempted to escape in a waiting van. Jonathon Jackson's intent was to trade the hostages for the release of his brother from prison.

With essentially no procedures or contingency plans in place to contain such a crisis, the sheriff ordered his officers to hold their fire as the van departed with the hostages. However, before even leaving the courthouse grounds, a group of correctional officers who were nearby in a training exercise, opened fire as the van approached their location. In the ensuing gunfire, Jonathon Jackson and two of the inmates were killed. As they were being assaulted, one of them executed Judge Haley with a single shotgun blast to the neck. The third inmate, the prosecutor, and one of the three jurors were all seriously wounded. It became the bloodiest courtroom violence in American history.

In more recent times America witnessed another courtroom tragedy unfold in Atlanta, Georgia. On March 11, 2005, Brian Nichols, who was being retried after a mistrial on charges of forcibly detaining and sexually assaulting his former girlfriend, was alone with a much smaller female sheriff's deputy in a holding cell area when he overpowered the deputy with a near fatal punch to the face. The deputy had removed his handcuffs to allow him to change from his jail uniform into civilian clothing for the day's court session. With the deputy bleeding and unconscious, Nichols retrieved her .40 caliber semi-automatic duty weapon from a lockbox, and began moving through the court complex. But Nichols had something more important on his mind than escape at that moment. He was seeking out the judge and prosecutors assigned to his case, in addition to his victim.

Nichols entered Judge Rowland Barnes's courtroom from behind the judge's bench and immediately shot him in the back of the head, killing him. He then scanned the room for the two prosecutors, but they were not present yet. As he stepped from the bench he shot the court reporter, Julie Brandau, killing her. He then moved to the witness room where he expected to find his former girlfriend and victim, but she had not yet arrived. In the chaos that followed, Nichols entered a stairwell in an effort to escape the building. Sgt. Hoyt Teasley, a sheriff's deputy who had just arrived for his shift, caught site of Nichols descending the steps and proceeded to chase him. As Teasley exited to the outside in pursuit, Nichols turned and opened fire before Teasley could even draw his weapon, striking him in the abdomen. Within minutes he bled to death while Nichols made his escape. He would be apprehended 26 hours later, but not before murdering an off-duty federal agent who was working on his house when Nichols robbed him (Wikipedia.com, accessed May 10, 2011).

These are two examples of the worst kind of courtroom crisis, but there are smaller and no less dangerous crises occurring every day in America's courtrooms. Defendants attempt to escape or attack those testifying against them, judges are threatened or attacked, family members of victims attack their attackers as they sit at the defense table, people attempt to bring weapons into the courtroom, defendants and victims alike attack attorneys, and there are even times when opposing attorneys attack each other. These types of crises are not always preventable, but with the proper protocols in place, and a heightened level of vigilance on the part of the court's security personnel, many can be prevented, and when a crisis does occur, it can be contained and de-escalated quickly.

THE SCOPE OF THE PROBLEM

Few studies have ever been conducted to determine the true extent of the problem of courtroom violence. Those that have attempted to quantify this type of crisis have reported some alarming results. Calhoun (2000) looked specifically at violence directed at federal judges. He found that between 1980 and 1993 there were 3096 threatening communications and assaults made against federal judges. Of the threatening communications, 242 involved later more serious actions, and 118 of the reported incidents involved an actual attack. Since 1979, three federal judges have been assassinated.

According to Weiner et al. (2000), the reported incidents of inappropriate or threatening communications to federal judges have risen dramatically since then. They report that from 1997 to 1998 alone there were over 700 inappropriate or threatening communications to federal judges that raised concerns about the potential for an attack. They point out the disruptive effect this unavoidably has had on the functioning of the federal judiciary. The U.S. Marshal's Service, the agency responsible for the protection of federal judges and for the safety of their courtrooms, has been forced to significantly increase the resources committed to this endeavor, to develop new protocols and threat assessment techniques, and to make judicial and courtroom security the primary concern in the design of new federal courthouses.

The authors also detail a survey carried out by the Pennsylvania Court Administrator regarding violence against state court judges in Pennsylvania. The survey found that of 1112 judges, 12 had been attacked in their own courtrooms, and 533 had been the target of a threatening action. One in three judges (35 percent) reported that they had changed their judicial conduct "somewhat" or "a great deal" as a result of acts committed against them or an associate. This change in conduct oftentimes impedes the goal of maintaining a free and open court system.

In a further look at the dangers faced by state court officials, Stephen Kelson (2001) reported the findings of a survey conducted by the David County, Utah, Bar Association. The survey was sent to 161 members in the county, with 81 percent responding. The survey found that 13 percent of those responding had been physically assaulted at some point, with 59 percent reporting that they had been threatened at least once by a client, an opposing party, or another interested person in a litigation. The survey found that one of the most likely places for violence to occur is in the courtroom. Kelson reported that in one 22-day period, security officers in the 2nd District Courthouse in Davis County confiscated 829 weapons from people entering the courthouse. These weapons included clubs, throwing stars, razor blades, pen knives, belt-buckle knives, filed-down wrenches and screwdrivers, and a number of different types of homemade weapons.

To get an idea of the extent of this problem, and to witness it firsthand, one need only go to a popular website, *www.youtube.com*, and input a few keywords to search for actual video footage of courtroom violence. As of this writing, a search of the keywords "courtroom fight" revealed 515 videos, many of them showing violent attacks against defendants, witnesses, and courtroom personnel. A search of the keywords "judge attacked" revealed 1060 videos, and a search of "courtroom brawl" revealed 575 videos. This type of search may be lacking in scientific methodology, but it certainly provides much anecdotal evidence pointing to the problem of violence in the courtroom.

There is no doubting the danger present in a courtroom. The National Institute for Occupational Safety and Health (1996) identified sheriffs and court bailiffs as having the second-highest workplace homicide rate, 15 times the national average, trailing only taxicab drivers. It is a breeding ground for crisis, as emotions run high, and with the target of revenge only feet away. It is a constant juggling act to protect the safety of those in the courtroom without defeating the constitutional principles of a free and open trial, due process for civil litigants, and the ability of a defendant to face his or her accusers as an innocent person till proven guilty. The court must also avoid circumstances that may be seen as **prejudicial**, or those things that could potentially taint a jury's perception of any aspect of the trial. For example, to shackle a defendant during trial certainly makes that person appear guilty, and may impact a juror's perception, even unconsciously so, in a way that casts the defendant in a negative light in spite of the evidence. It is a problematic juggling act that to this day has not been fully resolved to everyone's benefit.

OBSTACLES TO A SAFE COURTROOM

Four problems contribute to the level of violence seen in America's courtrooms: a lack of funding, a lack of preparedness, complacency on the part of court personnel, and an unsafe infrastructure. Any of the four can create a dangerous situation.

The Problem of Funding

The funding problem has always been, and likely always will be a problem. Essentially all courts are funded by taxpayer dollars, and therefore they compete with schools, roads, and public utilities for whatever funding is available. A number of circumstances and perceptions many times cause court security to be placed very low on the funding priority list. They include the following:

- Most taxpaying citizens will never have contact with the court system, and therefore their level of concern for funding expensive security measures, rather than the things that do touch their lives, such as schools and roads, tends to be low. Politicians are of course beholden to these voters, so their voting records tend to mirror the values of the voting majority.

- There is a misperception, even among those holding the funding purse strings, that a courtroom must surely be a safe place because of the presence of police officers. As we have already seen, nothing could be further from the truth. In many courthouses, if not most, even police officers are not allowed to enter a courtroom armed. Instead they are required to secure their weapons in gun lockers in an area of the facility protected by security personnel.
- Although the news media is very good at reporting the most deadly courtroom attacks, they greatly under-report all others. Because of this lack of exposure, the problem seems less than what it really is, and leads to a "it'll never happen here" mentality.
- Politicians and taxpayers tend to view criminal justice professionals as having the ability to defend themselves without expensive security measures. Further, for reasons that can be debated, there is a lower level of concern for the safety of lawyers in our society than perhaps for other citizens. And finally, those attacks on defendants that are highly publicized are usually applauded by the public. What they don't realize is that many times innocent people are injured in those attacks, including courtroom security personnel.

The Problem of Preparedness

A second major obstacle to maintaining a safe courtroom is a lack of preparedness. This is especially true in rural courthouses where training in new protocols, techniques, and technology is often lagging behind the more urban areas. It is also true that in many smaller jurisdictions, courtroom security is carried out by sworn deputy sheriffs who may be rotated in and out of a courtroom security detail. One week or month they may be on the street enforcing the law as a police officer, and then suddenly find themselves in a courtroom doing security. Juggling these multiple missions and mind-sets can distract from their ability to effectively carry out the mission at hand. Also, in these types of situations supervisors may expect standard police training to be sufficient for preparing a deputy for a security detail in the courthouse. In fact, the two are sufficiently different that specialized training must be provided for this type of detail.

One additional issue that oftentimes gets in the way of preparedness is the fact that many court jurisdictions rely on retired police officers for courtroom security. This is essentially an institutionalized practice all across the country. Although retired police officers are certainly dependable and qualified on many levels, the fact is they are retired. Physically they tend not to be in any shape or condition to forcibly restrain people when a crisis erupts. They are not as hyper-vigilant as they once were as police officers, always ready to react to even the slightest of threats, nor are they as excited, or even interested in further training on new techniques and technology. The fact is, a modern courtroom needs to be staffed with career-minded security professionals who have received special training to properly carry out their mission.

The Problem of Complacency

The third major obstacle to maintaining a safe courtroom is complacency. This problem was demonstrated with a deadly result in the case of Brian Nichols in Atlanta. The female deputy who accompanied Nichols alone to a holding cell to allow him to change into civilian clothes prior to court had befriended him. When another deputy suggested she have someone go with her, she shrugged it off and refused the help. It was exactly what Nichols had been waiting for. The deputy had let down her guard. She had set aside all of her training and security protocols because she thought Nichols was her friend. As soon as she removed one handcuff, Nichols violently attacked her, nearly killing her in the process.

Another instance of an officer's complacency leading to deadly results is the case of Jeffrey Erickson, the "Bearded Bandit," a former police officer and ex-Marine who robbed eight banks in the Chicago suburbs in the early 1990s before being apprehended. According to reports (*L.A. Times*, 1992), at the conclusion of a hearing on July 20, 1992, at the federal courthouse in downtown Chicago, two deputy U.S. Marshals, a male and a female, were transporting Erickson and seven other federal defendants back to the Metropolitan Correctional Center a few blocks away. Somehow Erickson had obtained a handcuff key, and had surreptitiously unlocked his cuffs inside the elevator leading to the parking garage. When the door opened, the male deputy walked ahead to retrieve the transport van, leaving the female deputy alone with eight federal defendants. It is important to note that Erickson was also charged with shooting and wounding a police officer in the course of his string of bank robberies. His violent nature was not unknown to the U.S. Marshal's Service.

As they waited for the van Erickson made his move. With one swift movement, he struck the female deputy, knocking her unconscious and seriously wounding her. He next removed her service weapon, and then made his break through the parking garage. By the time the other deputy realized what had happened, it was too late. Erickson shot and killed him where he stood. As he ran up the ramp to exit the garage, it was a courtroom security officer, a retired Chicago cop, who fired upon Erickson, hitting him in the back. Erickson returned fire, striking and killing the officer. Realizing he was mortally wounded, Erickson placed the gun to his chin and ended his own life.

The case of Jeffrey Erickson is one where the U.S. Marshals had been lulled into a sense of complacency by the daily routine of prisoner transport. To have attempted a transport of eight dangerous defendants by only two U.S. Marshals was a recipe for disaster. They were not anticipating the potential hazards when a small-frame female deputy was left alone with the eight defendants; any one of whom could have easily overpowered her. A proper threat assessment of Erickson, who had already attempted to kill one police officer, would have dictated special precautions and procedures, especially when moving him between locations.

The problem of complacency can be deadly for any criminal justice professional. But the demands of both a police and correctional officer's jobs preclude them from becoming too complacent. Things are always happening during any given shift, and neither officer gets easily lulled into the belief that nothing dangerous will happen. For a courtroom security officer, however, who follows routine procedures and protocols on a daily basis, and who may go for long periods of time without facing a crisis, the risk of becoming complacent to some degree is quite high.

THE RISK CONTINUUM

How do we measure the potential danger associated with any particular courtroom proceeding? Many different types of hearings and activities occur in a courtroom. Many are related to civil proceedings where there is no possibility of anyone going to jail. Others are criminal in nature, and may range from misdemeanor offenses resulting in probation, to cases of homicide that could potentially result in the defendant being sentenced to death. It is important that a classification scheme be used, not only to properly staff a potentially dangerous situation, but also to avoid the overuse of resources where they are not necessarily needed.

Risk Assessment Profiles

THE MINNESOTA MODEL There are a number of **risk assessment profiles** in use throughout the criminal justice system in America. One of the more comprehensive schemes was

Risk	Civil Trial	Criminal Trial
LOW	Anti-trust Bankruptcy Contracts Environmental FOIA Labor suits Condemnations Personal injury Product liability Tort claims	Auto theft Burglary Embezzlement Forgery Counterfeiting Fraud Larceny Theft Perjury Public Corruption
MODERATE	Civil rights Deportations Foreclosures Seizures/forfeitures Tax violations High-profile media	Assaults Extortion Terrorist threats Stalking Firearms violations Obstruction of justice RICO Armed robberies Sex offenses High-profile media Anti-government/treason
HIGH	Violent criminal history	Mass/serial offenses Escape Homicide Kidnappings Bomb attacks Narcotics trafficking

FIGURE 14.1   Inherent Risk Level/Trial Type.

developed by the State of Minnesota, Conference of Chief Judges (1997). They developed a risk profile based on the inherent risk level of both the trial and the participants. Figure 14.1 reflects their formulation of the inherent risks associated with the various types of courtroom proceedings held in their particular State. They break it down between civil and criminal proceedings, with three different risk levels in each category. As you can see, the more violent the crime, the higher the inherent risk of the subsequent criminal trial. For civil proceedings they tend to correlate inherent risk with the degree to which the participant is at risk of losing something, such as their right to live in America (deportation), their home (foreclosure), or their money (tax violations).

The Minnesota model also looks at the participants in the court proceedings. Figure 14.2 reflects their formulation of the inherent risk levels of the participants in the proceeding. Although most civil proceedings are considered low risk, that changes if one or more of the participants has an emotionally charged interest in the proceeding or a history of violence apart from the current proceeding.

By looking at both of these inherent risk levels, the Minnesota model can then categorize the court proceeding along a threat continuum, from level 1 (low risk) through level 4 (high

Risk	Civil Trial	Criminal Trial
LOW	Class actions	Defendant not present
MODERATE	Jury trials Prisoner petitions Pro se actions High-profile/ media intensified Threat assessment—moderate rating Strong identification and ideological views with known threat groups	Defendant not in custody—on bond Threat assessment—moderate rating High-profile/media intensified Probation or parole violators Highly emotional/inner relationships Multiple defendants Repeat offender(s) Anti-society behavioral characteristics
HIGH	Highly emotional/ inner relationships Associated violent history or actions Threat assessment—high rating	Strong identification and ideological views with known threat groups Threat assessment—high rating Escapee from custody or commitment Violent actions/ outbursts while in custody Defense or plea based on insanity Mass or serial sexual predator Murderer/ contract killer Protected witness Multiple defendants Defendants with violent criminal history

FIGURE 14.2   Inherent Risk Levels/ Participants.

risk). This then allows for the sheriff and others charged with securing the courtroom to establish a particular risk environment based on the risk level. This will provide a guide for appropriating resources absent additional information that may necessitate increasing the risk level of a particular hearing. Illustration 14.3 shows the Minnesota model's risk matrix.

Other jurisdictions attempt to create a risk profile only from the participant's background. According to a report filed by the Task Force on Court Security of the New York State Unified Court System (2005), the courts in New York City use a color-coded card system to identify high-risk defendants in criminal trials. In their courts, whenever the Department of Corrections brings an incarcerated defendant into a courtroom for any reason, that individual is identified by a card as either not an elevated risk (blue card) or an elevated risk (red card). This card then allows the judge and the court security personnel to immediately identify high-risk individuals based on a history of violence, prior escape attempts, gang affiliation, or a history of suicide attempts.

The downside to this type of system is that it only concerns itself with criminal proceedings, and then classifies participants based only on their personal history. There are many high-risk civil proceedings, and many times in both civil and criminal court when a participant with no personal history of violence snaps during an emotionally charged point in the proceeding. It is therefore important for any risk profiling scheme to anticipate those moments based on the type of proceeding taking place. This provides a baseline risk profile for the deployment of a minimum level of resources based on the proceeding type, with the possibility of enhancing those resources based on the history of the participants.

Docket	Stage	Trial Risk	Participant Risk	Risk Level
CIVIL	Pretrial	----------------------	-------------------------	Level 1
	Trial	Low	-------------------------	Level 1
			Moderate	Level 2
		Moderate	-------------------------	Level 2
	Post trial	Low	-------------------------	Level 1
			Moderate	Level 2
CRIMINAL	Pretrial		Low	Level 1
			Moderate	Level 2
			High	Level 3
	Trial	Low	-------------------------	Level 2
			Moderate	Level 3
			High	Level 4
		Moderate	-------------------------	Level 3
		High	-------------------------	Level 4
	Post trial	----------------------	-------------------------	Level 3
			High	Level 4

FIGURE 14.3   Minnesota Model's Risk Matrix.

PROFILING THE EMOTIONAL RESPONSE   Another way of profiling risk in the courtroom is to look not at the type of proceeding taking place, but rather at the substance of the proceeding, and then gauging its potential for creating an atmosphere of heightened emotionality. While every courtroom sees the full gamut of emotions play out on any given day, there are essentially four predominant emotions that may cause the participant to act-out those emotions in a negative way. At the low end of the risk continuum is *inconvenience*. No one enjoys being in a courtroom. It takes time out of your day, and if you happen to be one of the participants, there is every chance the affair may cost you some money. If you are a witness, perhaps you are there against your will through the power of a subpoena. Many people in a courtroom are inconvenienced by their mandatory presence. Some may get quite passive-aggressive during their participation, or they may get angry to the point of raising their voice at the judge or attorneys. Seldom does being inconvenienced in a courtroom cause someone to resort to violence. Although this is where the risk profile may take into account the background of the participant. If the individual is known for a hot temper and violent outbursts, then the risk environment may be elevated by those responsible for securing the courtroom.

The second predominant emotion is *frustration*. This usually results when a feeling of helplessness sets in. It is the *cornered animal* syndrome, and many times it causes the very same reaction in people. An example might be a municipality bringing suit against a homeowner to remove a particular type of fence that is in violation of some city ordinance, a circumstance that will no doubt cost the homeowner a great deal of money. Whenever someone faces a governmental entity in a courtroom it can be extremely frustrating. The same is true with a corporate entity. An example might be a hospital or a credit card company suing someone for past due bills. A person in such a situation, especially one who has tried to pay their bills on time, can very quickly be overcome with feelings of helplessness, as if it is them against the entire world, including the judge. Depending on the person's personality, this frustration can lead to a violent

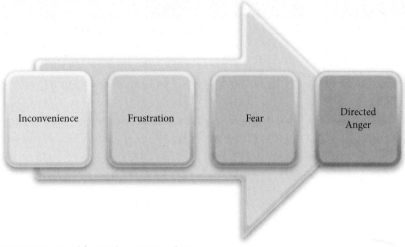

FIGURE 14.4   Risk Continuum/Emotions.

outburst. In some cases the person's background or ideology may cause this frustration to boil over quicker and more intensely than normal. For example, a tax protestor who finds himself in court facing the IRS or some other taxing authority should certainly cause a heightened security response over and above what is normal for such a proceeding.

The next predominant emotion that may be demonstrated in a courtroom is *fear*, typically the fear of losing something; a spouse, custody of children, financial assets, freedom, or even one's life. Fear in its activated form is panic. It is a powerful motivator, and anytime it is anticipated that a panic could potentially erupt in the courtroom, a high level of security must be present. A good example is a person about to be sentenced to life in prison or death. In civil court it might be a hearing where the judge is about to take from a parent custody of their own children. Panic can erupt as easily in a civil proceeding as it can in a criminal proceeding, sometimes even quicker.

The final emotion that may find its way into the courtroom, and the most dangerous, is *directed anger*. This emotion goes well beyond frustration, and is more calculated than the typically spontaneous panic response. This emotion is directed at a single individual or group of individuals present in the courtroom. Examples might include the family members of a murder victim coming face to face with the accused in the courtroom and attacking him in a violent outburst. It might include one of the parties to a divorce proceeding attacking the opposing lawyer. Or it might involve a defendant in a criminal trial attacking the prosecutor or judge. Directed anger is the most dangerous circumstance that can be present in a courtroom. It must be anticipated based on the circumstances of the hearing and the interpersonal dynamics present in the courtroom. This is where intelligence gathering is critical. Security personnel must be aware of who is in the courtroom, and their relationship to the defendant, plaintiff, witness, or victim.

A Comprehensive Profiling Scheme

Although the Minnesota model provides for risk assessment by looking at the type of proceeding and the background of the participants, a more effective scheme might add a third component, that being the potential for increased emotionality based on the circumstances of a particular

	Civil Family	Civil Economic	Civil Protective	Criminal Non-violent	Criminal Violent
Non-elevated	Non-contested divorce Family services—compliant parties	Bankruptcy Small claims Product liability	Protective order—Petitioner only	Initial appearance Misdemeanor trial	Video arraignment Status hearings
Elevated	Contested divorce Family services—non-compliant parties Parental rights	Foreclosure IRS Proceedings Tax Protestor Partner lawsuits Seizures/ forfeitures Land disputes	Protective order—defendant present Involuntary commitments	High-profile/media Defendant in custody attention Victims present Verdict Sentencing Contempt of court	Trial Defendant in custody Victim family present Bond hearing Initial appearance Gang involvement Verdict
Dangerous	Contested divorce—child custody or prior threats Family services—child removal	Tax protestor w/ prior threats Lawsuits w/prior threats	Protective order—defendant present w/ prior threats	Significant fraud victims present Victims present—prior threats	Verdict—Victim family present Sentencing Defendant testimony Opposing gang present

FIGURE 14.5 Risk Matrix.

hearing rather than relying only on the hearing type. For example, it may seem a low-risk hearing to bring a restrained defendant into a courtroom for an arraignment. With no jury present, and the arraignment in many cases being a formality that takes no more than a few minutes, the judge may allow the defendant to remain handcuffed. Consequently, on its face it may seem low risk, and few resources may be allocated to securing the courtroom. But if the victim's family members happen to be present in the courtroom, or perhaps both the victim's and the defendant's family, then the potential for violence is increased dramatically. Therefore any profiling scheme should consider a simple arraignment high risk in every instance when the crime is a violent one and someone has been victimized, especially when the victim has been murdered or sexually assaulted.

A new profiling scheme might therefore classify court proceedings appearing on the daily docket as *non-elevated risk, elevated risk,* or *dangerous,* based on the underlying circumstances of the hearing and the potential for heightened emotions. This scheme provides a matrix that categorizes all court proceedings in one of five general categories; civil family, civil economic, civil protection, criminal non-violent, and criminal violent. It then assigns a risk level based on the circumstances of the hearing. Figure 14.5 illustrates a sampling of the types of hearings and their associated risk levels.

With this type of matrix, there are a maximum of 15 different risk environments that must be planned for, with a predetermined minimum resource allocation for each environment. As specific circumstances warrant them, additional resources can quickly be allocated. For example, the initial arraignment of a murder defendant is classified as *dangerous.* Thus the appropriate level of resources is committed in order to secure the courtroom. If however it is found that a large number of the victim's family are present and waiting to enter the courtroom, then additional resources over and above the predetermined allotment can be mobilized to meet the increased potential for a crisis inside the courtroom, or even outside the courtroom if the defendant's family or gang members are present.

PROCEDURES AND PROTOCOLS

It's not enough to simply have a profiling scheme. A courthouse security operation must also have the plans in place to prevent a crisis from ever happening, and to quickly contain and de-escalate a crisis when one erupts. We will look first at the *proactive* measures that must be in place in order to properly secure the courtroom. We will look at the courtroom, the transport and movement of prisoners, and pre- and post-hearing activities such as allowing a detained defendant to change into civilian clothing prior to appearing in court. Following that we will look at the various *reactive* measures to be taken in the event of a crisis.

Proactive Measures

A number of deadly courtroom crises over the years could have been prevented had appropriate proactive measures been taken. We have already discussed the primary reasons why those measures were not taken. When they are however, they tend to work very effectively. Following is a discussion of a few of the more important proactive measures.

PRISONER TRANSPORT   We begin our discussion with one of the most dangerous points in a criminal court proceeding, at least one in which the defendant is detained: the transport of the defendant to the courthouse. Many larger modern courthouses are connected to the jail in some manner, either by tunnels or caged walkways between the two buildings. In the vast majority of counties and municipal jurisdictions around the country, however, getting from one building to the other requires a short drive. This creates an extremely dangerous situation, depending on the severity of the crime and the defendant's history of violence.

According to a study conducted by the National Institute of Justice (1997) in response to the sharp increase in courtroom violence, the safety of personnel responsible for transporting and monitoring prisoners in the courtroom was the biggest concern at that time among court personnel. The study found that a majority of court security and prisoner transport personnel were males between the ages of 40 and 50 years old who had completed some type of security training in preparation for their jobs. Many of these personnel, however, reported that they felt unprepared to maintain a secure courtroom. Fewer than half of the reporting agencies provided their personnel training in the proper operation of transport vehicles and the special considerations relating to prisoner transport. Also, less than half of those same agencies reported providing their security personnel training in the use of restraint devices. Restraints are never more important than while moving a prisoner from one location to another. Leg irons, handcuffs, and belt restraints are all used in various combinations; however, if not used properly, they can be compromised by a determined prisoner. The NIJ study recommended that security personnel responsible for transporting of prisoners be required to attend at least 80 hours of classroom instruction in these various areas.

Many departments have detailed protocols in place for the transporting of prisoners. The Virginia Department of Criminal Justice Services (1999) has published sample procedures for this type of detail. Among other things, these procedures require the following when transporting a prisoner:

- Prisoners should only be transported in a caged vehicle that provides a barrier between them and the security personnel transporting them. All window and door handles in the rear of the vehicle should be removed.

- In the event that a caged vehicle is not available, then the prisoner should be transported in the front seat of the vehicle. In either case, the prisoner should always be transported with their hands handcuffed behind their back, palms outward. Only in the case of pregnant, injured, or handicapped prisoners should the transporting personnel deviate from this restraint requirement.

- No single security personnel should ever transport more than one prisoner in a non-caged vehicle. It is always preferable to have two personnel assigned to a transport vehicle. In the event that the vehicle is a non-caged vehicle, then the prisoner should still be transported in the front seat, with the second security officer taking a position behind the prisoner in the rear seat.

- It is critical that the prisoner be searched before putting them in the vehicle. It is also important to search the vehicle to ensure that no contraband is present. In the previously discussed case of Jeffrey Erickson, the transporting officers did not conduct a thorough search prior to moving them from the courthouse. Erickson had somehow obtained control of a handcuff key and was hiding it in his hair. This of course allowed him to free himself and kill a deputy U.S. Marshall and an armed court security officer before being mortally wounded himself. It is not a stretch, especially in the smaller jurisdictions, to consider the possibility that someone friendly to the prisoner might possibly gain entry to the transport vehicle and stash a handcuff key or weapon, knowing the time and date when the prisoner will be transported.

- The prisoner must be kept under observation at all times, and at no time should the prisoner be allowed to carry on a conversation with anyone. In the event of a longer transport, and the prisoner needs to use bathroom facilities, assuming they are of the same sex, then the security officer should keep the prisoner under observation. If they are of the opposite sex, then the security officer should still maintain as much control as possible. At no time should the prisoner be allowed in a bathroom with another person, and the bathroom should be searched prior to allowing its use by the prisoner.

- Finally, upon arrival at their destination, the prisoner should not have their restraints removed until they are inside the facility, in a secure location, and the receiving authority is present to take custody of the prisoner. If the facility has an enclosed garage, then the prisoner should not be removed from the vehicle until the door to the outside is closed. If there is no enclosed receiving area, then the transporting officers should visually inspect the area before exiting the vehicle. If the prisoner is a high risk for escape or violence, then it is important that additional security personnel be notified of the arrival to provide additional security while the individual is walked into the facility. This is especially true if the prisoner is a member of a violent gang or an ideologically motivated group.

Essentially all departments that have written procedures and protocols for transporting prisoners follow these same guidelines. The critical components of a prisoner transport are preparation, control, and observation. If the proper searches are conducted at the outset, the proper restraining devices used, and sufficient personnel involved in the transport to maintain visual observation of the prisoner, then the likelihood of escape or injury to the security personnel is greatly diminished.

PRE- AND POST-HEARING ACTIVITIES   A number of activities require court security personnel before and after a hearing takes place. The nature of these activities will depend on the nature and risk level of the hearing itself, and whether a detained defendant is present. For a detained defendant, no exception should be made to the requirement that the prisoner be kept in a secure location at all times. If a change of clothes is required, that too should be done in a holding cell or other secure location. It is also important that a defensive barrier be maintained between the defendant and the security personnel. Brian Nichols in Atlanta was able to escape because he was allowed to change clothes in the same physical location as the lone officer guarding him. A few simple rules of thumb should guide the prisoner's activities outside the courtroom:

- Upon arrival at the courtroom area, the prisoner should be secured in a holding cell and not removed unless being escorted to the courtroom by security personnel.
- Clothing changes should take place inside the holding cell.
- At no time should an unrestrained prisoner be alone with a security officer, especially one carrying a weapon or keys to either a gun locker or secure doors.
- When a prisoner is moved to the courtroom, they should be moved in restraints, by a secure route if possible, and by two security personnel. Those restraints should not be removed until just outside the door of the courtroom, assuming it is a hearing that necessitates the prisoner being unrestrained, such as a jury trial. At no time should the prisoner be allowed to converse with non-security personnel except their lawyer.

Unfortunately a majority of small courthouses in America have no secure routes to escort prisoners from a holding cell into the courtroom. In this type of scenario it is important to make a secure route through the public area. If the individual is a high-risk prisoner, then the area through which he or she will be escorted should be cleared to the extent possible. In this case it is critical for additional security personnel to be present in order to control and observe the crowd for anyone intending to assist in the prisoner's escape.

Finally, procedures should be in place for the prisoner to converse with their lawyer before and after the hearing. The prisoner has a constitutional right to do this, and privacy is guaranteed. These conferences should not be allowed to take place in the courtroom, except immediately before the hearing, and in preparation for the hearing. Once the hearing is concluded, then the prisoner should be removed immediately from the courtroom in a controlled manner, and once again restraints should be used outside the courtroom. If an attorney-client conference is to take place, then a secure windowless room should be utilized. The prisoner should remain in restraints, and immediately upon completing the conference the prisoner should be searched thoroughly for contraband. It is also appropriate to pat down the lawyer and observe the inside of any briefcase, but only for weapons. To the extent possible, the conference should remain under visual observation, but to listen in on the meeting is prohibited by law as a violation of the defendant's constitutional right to consul. At no time should the prisoner be allowed to speak on a cell phone during the meeting, and the lawyer must be advised of this.

In the event of a hearing without a prisoner being present, such as a civil matter or a criminal hearing with a defendant who is out on bond, pre- and post-trial activities will depend on the risk level of the hearing. If adversaries are coming face to face, such as a contentious divorce, then the security personnel should anticipate areas where they may come in contact, including outside the courtroom and in the parking lot. Sufficient personnel should be made available to prevent a violent outburst. If things get extremely contentious during the hearing, then security personnel should control the departure of all participants at the hearing's conclusion. The adversaries should be escorted from the building by different routes to the extent possible, and the most at-risk participants should be escorted all the way to the doors of their vehicles.

If the hearing will bring together the family members of a victim and the defendant, then sufficient security personnel must be detailed to prevent a confrontation between the two groups. These volatile situations often erupt into small riots once outside the courtroom. It is important to brief both groups prior to the hearing about what to expect, and the ramifications of any aggressive acts while on the premises. The two sides must be kept separate, both outside and inside the courtroom. If in the opinion of the security team there will be violence between the two groups if they mix, then once again their egress from the courtroom should be controlled by the security personnel. One side should be quickly escorted from the building before the other is allowed to leave.

Like the transportation of prisoners, the keys to safely carrying out pre- and post-hearing activities are preparation, control, and observation. Security personnel must anticipate potential security problems based on the risk level and specifics of the hearing, and be prepared for any eventuality. They must control not only a detained defendant, but also essentially everyone else involved in the hearing, including observers. They must control movement, contact, and actions, and always be vigilant in their observations, not only of their physical surroundings, but of the people in close proximity to the hearing. They must be able to detect subtle cues on the faces, and in the actions of all parties to know when tensions are present and building.

COURTROOM SECURITY   The judge controls the courtroom, however, if security personnel believe a crisis is about to erupt, they have the ability to announce their alarm, halt or postpone the hearing, and take immediate steps to prevent the crisis from happening. Security personnel must be vigilant to detect subtle cues on the faces and in the actions of the participants to know when tensions are rising to the boiling point. Thus a sufficient level of security inside the courtroom is critically important. Security personnel must be prepared to subdue a hostile individual; to protect the judge, jury, lawyers, witnesses, and even the defendant from an attack; and to prevent the escape of a prisoner taking part in the proceeding either as a defendant or a witness.

The level of security present in the courtroom is determined by the risk level of the proceeding itself. If we return to the State of Minnesota's Conference of Chief Judges Security Manual (1997), we find four different levels of security being recommended, each being a combination of court security personnel and deputy sheriffs with full arrest powers. In many jurisdictions, these are one and the same. The four levels include the following:

- **Level one:** In a level-one hearing no security is recommended. This would include a very low-risk civil or criminal proceeding in which no defendant is present. This might include such proceedings as motion or status hearings. Many of these hearings amount to very short procedural-type proceedings where no one but the lawyers and the judge are present in the courtroom.

- **Level two:** This level is a moderate-risk civil proceeding in which the participants are present in the courtroom. It may be a hearing that has been contentious, with one person suing another, or perhaps a divorce case. It is recommended that either a court security officer or a deputy sheriff be present in the courtroom during a level-two hearing.

- **Level three:** This level is a moderate-risk criminal trial or a criminal post-trial with an in-custody defendant. The latter may include a sentencing hearing or a motion hearing seeking the release of a convicted defendant pending an appeal. In this case it is recommended that a minimum of a court security officer and a deputy sheriff be present. This does not include those security officers detailed specifically to guard the prisoner. Also, it is important to note that these are minimum standards. In the event a risk assessment has determined that the potential for violence has increased significantly, then additional personnel will be assigned.

- *Level four:* This level of security is for a high-risk proceeding, such as the trial of a violent offender when the family members of the victim are present. In this case the manual recommends a minimum of two deputy sheriffs and one court security officer. Obviously, those in charge of security must do a risk assessment of every high-risk proceeding to determine if additional personnel are needed.

In addition to these minimum levels of security, the manual also recommends a **one-on-one-plus-one detail** to secure any prisoners in the courtroom. This means that each detained prisoner will have a minimum of one security officer detailed specifically to secure them, with an additional officer in the courtroom. So if two prisoners are present, then a minimum of three security officers will be detailed to secure them over and above the officers detailed to secure the courtroom. If three prisoners are present, then a minimum of four security officers will be detailed over and above those detailed to secure the courtroom.

One of the important considerations for the security detail is where to place themselves in proximity to the participants. The goal is to provide maximum security without being conspicuous to the point of distracting the jury or other participants. It is also important that the security detail not be too obvious in securing a detained defendant in front of a jury. The courts could potentially find this as being "prejudicial," or having the potential to influence the jury's opinion toward the defendant in a negative way.

Inside the courtroom, it is important for security personnel to act as buffers between potential aggressors and victims, and to cut off any routes of escape. In a high-risk trial, the following must be considered:

- Security personnel must be positioned to intercept a sudden aggressive advance on the judge, jury, or a witness.
- Security personnel must be positioned between a detained defendant and any route of escape.
- In a high-risk trial where the defendant could potentially be attacked by the victim's family or perhaps rival gang members, a security buffer must be positioned between them. Here again, security typically will not stand directly behind a defendant because of the prejudicial aspects; however, they do typically sit in a location to the rear of the defendant, between them and any potential attackers. It is also common in this situation for undercover security personnel to take seated positions behind the defendant as if they are there to observe the trial. This allows the uniformed personnel to reposition to other parts of the courtroom without compromising the safety of the defendant.

Reactive Measures

THE CRISIS ALERT   When a crisis breaks out in or around the courtroom, it is imperative that the response be quick to contain and then de-escalate the event. Just like schoolchildren practicing a fire drill over and over until it becomes automatic, court security personnel must do the same. They must be prepared to immediately activate their response plan in such a way that security personnel throughout the courthouse know the nature and location of the crisis, and how and where to respond. The way this plan is activated of course is through the communication grid in use by the security personnel. It is important that all personnel be on the same communication system, and there be a centralized dispatch center to direct personnel when the response plan is activated.

Regardless of the type of crisis, there must be an immediate effort made by security personnel in close proximity to announce the crisis in a few short words. This announcement should identify the nature of the crisis and the location. Many different notification schemes are in use around the country; however, a simple one makes use of colors to identify the nature of the crisis. For example:

- **Code red (escaped prisoner):** When this crisis is announced, the courthouse is immediately locked down, and a predetermined individual takes charge of the situation from a temporary communications center. Security personnel advance to all points of egress within the building, while others aid in the protection of people present in the building. Once all points of egress are covered, then a search team begins a systematic search of the building, either from bottom to top, or vice versa. Search dogs are also utilized to the extent possible. On the outside of the building, additional personnel, perhaps even patrol officers, take responsibility for establishing a perimeter around the building. The temporary communications center should be established at whatever location within the building where security cameras are monitored. Done correctly then, the building is immediately locked down, a perimeter is established outside, citizens are protected by armed officers, and a search team, perhaps even S.W.A.T. trained, conducts the systematic search for the escapee. By announcing the location, such as "CODE RED, 3A!" signifying an escaped prisoner from courtroom 3A, then responding personnel can respond in the direction of the crisis to maximize their containment efforts.

- **Code blue (hostility in the courtroom):** When this crisis is announced, then the primary response is to get additional personnel inside the courtroom as quickly as possible to contain the violence. It may be family members attacking a defendant, or rival gang members fighting it out. All public exits should be locked down to prevent people guilty of committing a crime from walking out. The exits should remain closed until an "all-clear" signal is given. Obviously the important thing in this case is to get manpower inside the courtroom as quickly as possible, not only to separate the hostile parties, but to prevent injury to innocent spectators or participants.

- **Code white (weapons used):** There is not a more dangerous situation than this. Perhaps a weapon is smuggled into the courtroom, or perhaps a prisoner disarms an armed officer, or maybe one of the lawyers has carried the weapon to court in their briefcase. It is true that in many jurisdictions, lawyers who routinely come to the courthouse, and who are known to security personnel, are allowed to pass by security devices in the same manner as police officers. In any event, when a weapon is used, armed personnel must move toward the crisis quickly and safely. As they do, they must also direct innocent bystanders to immediately evacuate the premises in a direction away from the crisis, with the responding officers acting as a safety buffer as they evacuate.

Anytime a weapon is used, especially a gun, then the designated S.W.A.T. team must be activated immediately while officers on patrol establish a perimeter outside the building. Once again, points of egress must be locked down and covered; however, unarmed security personnel must remain out of harm's way. When a weapon has been used, and the individual who used it has escaped, only a trained S.W.A.T. team should conduct a search of the building. Although it is best to lock down the building and the people inside in the event of an escaped prisoner, if there is a weapon involved, then it is imperative to evacuate the building prior to the tactical team conducting their search. Also, this too is a case where it is imperative that a temporary communications center be immediately established with a designated commander taking charge of the scene.

• **Code orange (hostage situation):** In the event of a hostage crisis, which almost always involves the use of a weapon, and may even start out as either a code red or white, using our sample scheme, then the procedures are the same as a code white, only in this case a designated hostage negotiator is dispatched immediately to the scene. Once it is determined there are hostages, then the initial goal is containment only, with security and S.W.A.T. personnel setting up a perimeter around the crisis area and completely evacuating the building and immediate area. If the situation appears stable, meaning the hostage taker is not hurting anyone, then no attempt should be made to de-escalate the situation by force. It is imperative that personnel move to contain the situation until the hostage negotiator arrives on scene. As discussed in Chapter 9, once the negotiator is on-scene, that person is in charge. They attempt to make contact and de-escalate the crisis, while tactical personnel prepare to de-escalate by force on the negotiator's command. When that command is given, then the negotiator immediately hands over command of the scene to the tactical commander, typically the S.W.A.T. team leader.

• **Code green (potential violence):** One additional situation should be mentioned that requires additional security personnel being deployed. There are times when a trained security officer can tell when tensions in the courtroom are rising, even before any violent outbursts occur. In this event the officer may announce that the potential for a crisis exists, and have additional personnel deployed to either the courtroom or just outside the door. Once again, the amount and movement of security must not unduly disrupt the decorum of the court proceeding.

These are just a few examples. In reality, many code systems are a great deal more comprehensive. There may be codes for medical emergencies, for escorting disrespectful spectators from the building, or for personnel to respond to take into custody a defendant who has just been convicted or had their bond revoked. There may be codes for clearing the courtroom for a juvenile matter, for requesting technical assistance with courtroom equipment, or perhaps for requesting a replacement officer. There can be as many codes as a reasonable person can remember.

The important considerations when preparing for a crisis in the courtroom is threefold: communications, command structure, and response protocols. Any protocols, in order to be effectively carried out, must be practiced. Training is crucial, but unfortunately too many court security forces across the country spend little time in training. As we have pointed out, the court system in most jurisdictions is greatly underfunded and overburdened by a caseload that is ever-increasing. Training is oftentimes looked at as a luxury that can be easily sacrificed, especially the type of training that would require shutting down a courtroom for a few days in order to practice realistic response scenarios.

TRENDS IN COURTROOM SAFETY

Courthouses around the country continue to explore new and safer ways of carrying out the activities of their criminal and civil courts without compromising the individual rights of the participants. A number of new methods have been introduced, to include the following:

Video Arraignment

One of the best ways to prevent a crisis from taking place in the courtroom, at least one perpetrated by a detained defendant in a criminal proceeding, is to simply not have them present. Because the Constitution guarantees a defendant the right to be presumed innocent and to face their accusers, the court system is limited in the extent to which it can keep a defendant from being present in the courtroom. One of the times when it can is during an **arraignment**, a short hearing during which the presiding judge advises the defendant of what they are charged with, and asks how they wish to plead to the charges. No witnesses or victims are usually present, and the government has no ability to reject or argue the defendant's plea. In almost all cases the defendant will plead not guilty, after which the judge will set a trial date, or perhaps a hearing date in advance of the trial to rule on whether sufficient evidence exists to go forward with the charges, or on issues relating to the defendant's bond, or to hear pre-trial motions from either the prosecution or defense.

Many jurisdictions, especially the larger ones, are now taking advantage of video-conferencing technology to do video arraignments. Some also use it for bond hearings. It allows the judge and defendant to come face to face without the defendant ever leaving the jail, assuming they are detained. It completely removes the dangers associated with transporting prisoners to the courthouse at a time shortly after their arrest when their emotions are typically elevated, making them unpredictable as they face for the first time an uncertain future. With no defendant in the courtroom, there are typically no friends, family, or fellow gang members present either. It creates a safer environment for the judge, the lawyers, the security personnel, and the general public.

One of the early assessments of the effectiveness of video arraignments was conducted by the Alaska Judicial Council (1999). They looked specifically at the courts in Fairbanks, Alaska, where video technology has been used in some form since the 1980s. In questioning participants in the Fairbanks court system, the researchers found two major objections to the use of this technology. The first was the limitation it places on attorney-client communications. Obviously, it does not allow for private conversations between a defendant at the jail and a defense attorney participating from inside the courtroom. Some jurisdictions have attempted to overcome this objection by having the defense attorneys participate from the jail, a circumstance that many defense attorneys object to, or by placing a telephone on the defense table and one at the jail to allow for private communications during the hearing.

The second objection noted was that video conferencing diminishes the formality and seriousness of the proceeding. Some of those questioned indicated their concern that defendants would not take such a proceeding as seriously, and that it would take away the deterrent effect of being in a courtroom face to face with a judge. There was a concern also that a defendant might feel as if they don't really matter, and that their case is just another among many being herded through the justice system. Some judges have attempted to diminish this effect by instructing the defendants beforehand that they are considered to be in an actual courtroom and that any unruly or disrespectful behavior will not be tolerated. The judge may also use this opportunity to advise the defendants, however many there are, that their cases will be dealt with individually and with the full amount of attention paid to cases in which the defendant is present in the courtroom. The Fairbanks study found that most participants in the court system, including the defendants themselves, were satisfied with the use of video in the courtroom. They found it to be efficient and safe, and provided recommendations for its expanded use.

A more recent assessment was conducted by the Pennsylvania Commission on Crime and Delinquency (2004). The authors of the study found a wide array of benefits to video conferencing in the courtroom. From an operations perspective it saves time because there is less exchange between the judge and the defendant. There is a reduced need for the transportation of prisoners, less personnel needed to conduct the arraignment, and less costs associated with the arraignment process. From a safety perspective, there is reduced risk to everyone involved in the arraignment; the judge, lawyers, security officers, the public, and the defendant themselves. The Commission's recommendations included expanding the use of video for all arraignments, to use it for arraignments to be held after the court's normal hours of operations, and to begin using it for hearings other than just arraignments.

ISSUES & ETHICS IN CRISIS INTERVENTION

The Use of Stun Belts in the Courtroom

In some jurisdictions around the country, an effort has been made to reduce courtroom violence by requiring felony defendants in custody to wear a "stun belt" while in the courtroom. The belt, which is under the clothing and out of view of the jury, has two prongs that deliver a 50,000-volt shock when remotely activated. The shock incapacitates the person for up to 30 minutes. As effective as it may seem, the courts have not been so quick to look favorably on such a device. Their objections are threefold. First, the use of any restraining device can prejudice a jury, meaning it can give the appearance of guilt to an individual who is presumed innocent till proven guilty. Secondly, its use may impede a defendant's ability to assist in their own defense. And thirdly, some courts have called such a device offensive to the dignity of the judicial process.

The courts, including the U.S. Supreme Court, have ruled time and again that any type of restraining device used in the courtroom must be used only as a last resort, and only after a clear and present danger of violence has been assessed. Thus, the use of a stun belt as a matter of practice has been found to be inappropriate in some jurisdictions, and convictions have been overturned on appeal because of its use. The courts have also ruled in certain jurisdictions that it is not the sheriff's decision when to use a stun belt, but rather the judge's. This has caused controversy because it is the elected sheriffs who are primarily responsible for the security of our nation's courthouses. In making this decision, the courts have placed courtroom security in the hands of judges who likely have never been trained in security matters.

The use of stun belts, and other seemingly non-intrusive devices, will continue to be a topic of debate that pits the law enforcement apparatus responsible for courtroom security against the legal community and its desire to protect the constitutional rights of defendants. It is an issue not easily resolved.

Discussion Questions

1. Discuss whether you believe devices such as a stun belt should be used as a matter of routine with violent defendants held in custody while in the courtroom.
2. In what ways would the use of a stun belt prejudice a jury?
3. In what ways might the use of a stun belt, or other such device, impede a defendant's constitutional right to assist in their own defense?

New Courthouse Designs

It wasn't until recent years when courthouses were designed specifically with safety in mind. All across this country, court is routinely conducted in facilities that are as old as a hundred years or more. Many have been reconfigured or expanded, and never in a way that has improved safety a great deal. When a building was never designed with safety in mind in the first place, it becomes extremely difficult to ever fully secure it no matter how many improvements are made.

For new courthouses there are now design standards that make safety the primary consideration. A well-designed courthouse can maximize the containment of a crisis while security personnel move quickly to de-escalate the matter, hopefully with little or no damage to property or injury to the people. The infrastructure is the first line of defense against a crisis. It should minimize the opportunities for escape, maximize the safety of judges, and prevent contact between prisoners and the public.

One of the most important design elements in any new courthouse is the flow pattern. The optimal design is one in which there are multiple circulation patterns within the courthouse, none of which cross or comingle with the others. According to standards developed by the Judicial Council of California (2006), a courthouse should be segregated both horizontally and vertically, meaning the points of entry and the routes of movement throughout the building should be separate for the general public, judges, and any detained prisoners. This system of **zoning** provides for three circulation systems throughout the building, with the point of convergence being the courtroom. These circulation systems include the following:

- ***The Public Circulation System***: This system allows for access through a public entrance to all public service areas of the building, which would include the circuit clerk, the tax assessor, county treasurer, and the like. The general public, after passing through a security screening, can move through this zone without escort. Because they are high-traffic areas, those areas making up the public zone should be located on the bottom floors. The public circulation zone extends to the secure doors of the courtroom, but not beyond.

- ***The Restricted Circulation System***: This zone includes those areas that are off-limits to the general public unless allowed admittance, to include the courtrooms, the judges' chambers, the security officers' area, and the jury room. This zone may also include areas used by attorneys to interview witnesses or prepare for trial. The restricted zone has a separate entrance to the building that is kept secure. This entrance is used by judges and security personnel, and may also be used to usher jurors in and out of the building. This zone may even include a secure parking area. If done correctly, the general public will never come face to face with a judge except when he or she is on the bench hearing cases.

The courtroom is considered part of the restricted zone. Although the public does have access, it is only at specified times, and under the watchful eyes of courtroom security officers. A courtroom should never be left unlocked and unattended. When it is, then it becomes part of the public zone, and it opens up the possibility of weapons being hidden inside. When not in use the courtroom may be accessed from the more secure zones, but never from the public zone. It should remain locked.

- ***The Secure Circulation System***: The final zone is the one through which prisoners are escorted. This is the zone where the highest level of security is expected. Ideally, entry to this zone is through either secure, video-monitored doors from inside the building, or a secure **sally port** from the outside. A sally port is essentially a secure garage. When a prisoner is transported to the courthouse, the transporting officers announce their arrival through an intercom outside the sally port door. Once security personnel visually inspect the driver via a monitor and confirm their identity, then they remotely open the door for the vehicle to enter. Once the vehicle is inside then, security personnel close the door behind them before the prisoner is removed from the vehicle.

Each step of the way in the secure circulation zone is protected by a locked door in front of and behind all personnel. Movement through the zone is possible only by security personnel unlocking doors from a remote location after visually inspecting via a monitor those seeking access to any particular corridor or room. Prisoners being brought to the courthouse leave the sally port, and by a secure elevator used only in the secure zone, are brought to a holding area that is separated from the courtroom by yet another locked door. Detained prisoners never cross paths with, nor are they even seen by, anyone but security personnel until they enter the courtroom. Even security personnel inside the secure zone should not have keys to the locked doors. The secure zone should essentially be a jail within the courthouse, and prisoners should have no route of escape if they were to get away from their security escort.

The Utah State Courts (1987) have established their own design specifications for new court facilities. They also require independent circulation zones in order to maximize security, and include the following additional requirements:

- Each courtroom should have a clear separation between the spectator area and the *well,* or the area where the attorneys and other participants sit. Never should spectators be allowed to cross this barrier to gain physical access to any participant in the hearing. Some courtrooms, including those at the Cook County Courthouse, the nation's largest courts facility, separate the spectator area from the well with a bullet-proof glass. Spectators are able to hear the proceeding via a speaker system. Access to the well from the public zone is through a single door that is guarded by security personnel.

- The judge's bench should be of a height and size that will impede a hostile advance by someone in the courtroom, and also provide protection in the event of gunfire. Additionally, the door to the judge's chambers should be behind the bench to allow for a quick escape in the event of a crisis inside the courtroom.

- Furniture inside the courtroom should be designed without hidden recesses where weapons or explosives could potentially be hidden during periods when court is not in session.

- The judge's desk should be equipped with a silent duress alarm, and also a cautionary alarm to allow the judge to beckon security personnel to the courtroom if tensions are expected to rise, such as during emotional testimony or a particularly harsh sentencing.

A well-designed building is one of the best methods for containing and de-escalating a crisis in the courtroom. Many of the most tragic courtroom crises that have taken place in recent years could have been prevented had they been in a building with secure and non-overlapping circulation zones. In theory, a detained prisoner should never be able to escape once inside the building, yet Brian Nichols not only escaped from a courts facility in Atlanta, but then killed a man for no reason once on the outside. No amount of proper building design can eliminate complacency on the part of security personnel, but with the right design the end result of an officer's complacency can be greatly lessened.

Chapter Summary

Anyone who has spent time in a busy courts facility can easily see it is a breeding ground for crisis. It is a place where lives are changed forever at the drop of a judge's gavel. And it is a place where victims and their families come face to face with those who victimized them, perhaps for the very first time since the event that led to the proceeding. In courtrooms we see people losing their homes, their spouses, their children, and their freedom. The courtroom is where crisis is remediated and prevented long after it is contained and de-escalated by first-responders on the street. But these activities often lead to a new level of crisis, especially for those on the negative side of the court's remediation. It is thus imperative that those in positions of planning and authority always plan and train for the worst, and have contingencies in place for every possible scenario.

Key Terms

Prejudicial

Risk assessment profile

One-on-one-plus-one detail

arraignment

Zoning

Public circulation system

Restricted circulation system

Secure circulation system

Sally port

Discussion Questions

1. Perhaps one way to make courtrooms safer in America is to disallow any and all observers during a hearing except by closed-circuit television. Discuss your views on this. Would such a move violate some principle of American justice in your view?

2. Other than the cases discussed in this chapter, research a reported case of courtroom violence on the Internet and discuss what went wrong in terms of security protocols.

3. Discuss the idea of letting detained defendants change into civilian clothing prior to a trial, and how that relates to the concept of "prejudice."

15

The Cost of Crisis: When the Helpers Need Help

LEARNING OUTCOMES

Upon completion of this chapter the student should be able to:

1. Identify the various types of stress impacting criminal justice professionals.

2. Explain the impact of the police culture on an officer's response to stress.

3. Describe both PTSD and PTS and their diagnostic criteria and stages.

4. Describe accepted intervention strategies, including the critical incident stress debriefing and psychological first aid.

Chapter Outline

Introduction
    The Emotional Cost of Responding
       to Crisis
    Defining Police Stress
The Role of the Police Culture
Post-Traumatic Stress Disorder

Police Trauma Syndrome
Proactive Interventions
    The Critical Incident Stress Debriefing
    Psychological First Aid
Chapter Summary

"Whoever fights monsters should see to it that in the process he does not become a monster. And, when you look in the abyss, the abyss also looks into you."

—FRIEDERICH NIETZSCHE

INTRODUCTION

THE EMOTIONAL COST OF RESPONDING TO CRISIS

In this final chapter we turn our attention to a type of crisis that until recent years was oftentimes ignored to the point that de-escalation eventually became impossible. It is the crisis of *self* experienced by those who devote their daily lives to containing and de-escalating the crises of other people. Nietzsche summed it up perfectly long before we had psychological labels and diagnostic criteria to describe the problem. The implications of "looking into the abyss" are oftentimes more than a person can handle. From 1990 through 1998, 22 Chicago police officers committed suicide. During that same period 20 LAPD officers did the same. And in a slightly longer period, from 1985 to 1998, 87 NYPD officers took their own lives (Aamodt and Werlick, 1999). These statistics are staggering, and although media attention is always focused heavily on police officers killed in the line of duty, there is seldom mention made of this other sad reality.

Anyone who routinely deals with human misery is prone to pay an emotional price at some point. Our biological inclination is to run from trauma and despair. But those who respond to crisis make a career of running toward such conditions in an effort to contain and de-escalate whatever type of crisis it happens to be, sometimes multiple and different types of crisis during the same 8-hour shift. The stress of doing so can take its toll. But there is an added element that only a certain few are forced to deal with—police officers and correctional officers—and that is the strain of constantly being on their guard for someone intending to perpetrate violence against them. It is this constant hypervigilance that tends to magnify and compound the emotional strain of responding to crisis on a daily basis.

In this chapter we will look at the effects of stress specifically on police and correctional officers. We will look at the precipitating factors that lead to the onset of stress-related disorders, the signs and symptoms of these disorders, treatment alternatives, and perhaps most importantly, preventative measures that can be taken to alleviate the effects of stress before it manifests itself in the form of a full-blown psychological disorder such as post-traumatic stress disorder (PTSD).

DEFINING POLICE STRESS

An officer who had reluctantly followed through on a referral for counseling was asked to describe his greatest source of stress on the job. He responded that it was the "fucking bosses and their fucking procedures!" The counselor looked into the officer's empty eyes and asked him how often he awakened in the middle of the night in a cold sweat after having a night-mare about his bosses? With his simple question the counselor had exposed the monster in the shadows that had quietly been stalking the officer for years. The officer knew it was there, but to confront it was to admit defeat. The monster was the toxic residue of every dead body, every abused child, every screaming burn victim, every dead cop, and every hopeless junkie that had been packed safely away in the dark reaches of his mind over the years. The monster was the emotional hole left behind each time the officer lost a piece of himself to the devastat-ing effects of untreated stress, a hole that widened with each traumatic day on the job until it simply swallowed him up and he could no longer climb his way back out.

(HARMENING, 2009)

- **VICARIOUS STRESS**
Stress that results indirectly from interacting with or observing others in crisis

- **OCCUPATIONAL STRESS**
Stress resulting from the demands, risks, and dangers experienced while on the job

- **PROFESSIONAL STRESS**
Stress resulting from the organizational-logistical demands of the job

FIGURE 15.1 Types of Police Stress.

Most people are lucky enough to live an entire lifetime without enduring the sights, sounds, and smells of traumatic events. Police officers are not so lucky. Depending on the location where they work, they may have to confront trauma every single shift. Even in the smaller rural settings, trauma is a frequent occurrence. It may be the result of some form of violence being perpetrated by one person against another, or an accidental trauma, such as a traffic accident or deadly fire. Practically everywhere a police officer turns they are forced to interact with people in crisis. Thus one form of stress a police officer experiences is the stress related to vicariously experiencing the crises of others. We are biologically programmed to experience sympathetic arousal in response to someone else's emotional display (Harmening, 2009). When we attend a funeral we feel the grief of the family members. At a graduation we can't help but feel the same sense of promise and anticipation that the graduates feel. For a police officer, these vicarious emotions are fear, despair, hopelessness, hatred, and essentially every other stress-producing emotion, many times in varying combinations and at the same time.

One of the realities of the police culture is that officers simply do not talk about their emotions, especially those experienced vicariously. Cops are expected to be professional, tough, and emotionally strong. Imagine an officer sitting around a squad room talking about how he wanted to cry while handling a call involving a husband and wife dispute. It simply doesn't happen, and with no way to mediate the stress by externalizing it, it tends to eventually build up to a point of critical mass.

In addition to **vicarious stress**, as discussed above, police officers also experience **occupational stress**, or the stress associated with maintaining a hypervigilant demeanor, and constantly being on their guard for some type of violence being perpetrated against them or other officers. Obviously policing is among the most dangerous of professions. At every turn a police officer can be harmed or killed. A great deal of police training is intended to better prepare the officer to anticipate and proactively thwart an attack, sometimes by taking the life of the would-be attacker. This requires that the officer constantly be on the lookout for any and all signs of danger. Such a demeanor tends to keep the officer's autonomic nervous system in an aroused state for extended periods of time. As we discussed in Chapter 2, this hypervigilant demeanor will naturally lead to stress as the body's efforts to maintain equilibrium begin to weaken. Actually suffering an attack of some type will only amplify this stress as the officer repeatedly relives the event and becomes even more hypervigilant upon returning to duty. This is the primary type of stress suffered by correctional officers, most of whom witness very little actual trauma, thus limiting their exposure to vicarious stress.

The third and final type of stress experienced by police and correctional officers alike can be thought of as **professional stress**, or the stress related to the organizational-logistical demands of the profession itself. For a police officer, this type of stress may be related to the following:

- Shift work and its impact on an officer's family.
- Unproductive management styles and the paramilitary nature of the police organization.
- Unnecessary paperwork.
- Minimal sentences for criminal offenders.
- Lack of training and equipment.
- Lack of respect by the public.
- Antagonistic cliques and subcultures within the department.
- Self-doubts about performance.

This is also a type of stress experienced to a large degree by correctional officers as well as the police. All one needs to do is sit with a group of cops or correctional officers in any type of setting and you'll see how preoccupied some are with these types of stressors. Both professions are run as paramilitary organizations, but, unlike soldiers, cops and correctional officers enjoy the freedom to openly criticize their departments, their bosses, and even their professions without fear of reprisal. The downside to this type of freedom is that it tends to breed even more criticism, especially among the younger, more impressionable officers. Once an officer adopts an antagonistic demeanor toward their department, their supervisors, or their profession, then their potential for job satisfaction is greatly diminished, which in turn will invariably have a negative impact on their performance, their emotional resilience, and even their personal lives. This latter outcome is oftentimes the most stressful circumstance of all for many police and correctional officers. It is a cycle that, once begun, is difficult to break. The stress of the job affects their personal lives, which diminishes further their job performance, which in turn creates even more stress and tension at home. It feeds on itself until a breaking point is reached and intervention becomes necessary.

THE ROLE OF THE POLICE CULTURE

As we previously stated, one of the reasons stress can be particularly devastating for a police officer is because of their inability to effectively deal with it in ways that will diminish its lingering impact. This circumstance is directly related to the police culture, or the behavioral expectations imposed on police officers by their peers. Kurtz and Williams (2008) found that masculine social structures in the law enforcement profession create a situation where officers have few viable options for managing their stress, and the options that are accepted, such as excessive drinking and aggression, are oftentimes unhealthy and unethical. Unfortunately these and other options that are informally accepted by the police culture ultimately create even more stress, which only compounds the accumulated stress that led to the unhealthy coping behaviors in the first place.

The police culture is empowered in large part by an *us vs. them* attitude among the officers. As many men and women in blue have proudly pointed out, there are only two types of people in this world, police officers and everyone else! In order to survive and be effective in their jobs, it is viewed by most police officers as an absolute necessity that they present themselves to the public as fearless, authoritative, and uncompromising. To facilitate this, they adopt a particular identity, the police identity. It is a narrowly defined identity that allows little room for deviation. It tends to consume any personal identity developed during childhood and adolescence. For most people, their identity is the sum total of many things; what they believe, their interests, and their sexuality, among other things. But for a police officer, once they inevitably adopt the police identity, it becomes the sum total of their uniform, their mission, and the brotherhood to which they belong. This reality is illustrated perfectly by another favorite saying among police officers; "being a cop is not what I do, it's what I am!" Unfortunately one of the expectations of this identity is to never cry, never admit defeat, and never ask for help when the demons inside begin to stir.

Correctional officers have a slightly different identity and set of expectations that limits their available options for dealing with stress. Most importantly is the absolute need to avoid any display of weakness in front of the inmate population. Although police officers have intermittent periods of occupational stress, for correctional officers it is almost constant. The fear of attack is ever-present in a prison setting. The more stress correctional officers experience, the more they endeavor to hide any outward manifestation of that stress. The end result, like police officers, is a significant amount of accumulated stress that is left unmanaged, and a professional identity that encourages unhealthy coping strategies to deal with the stress.

A report by the New Jersey Police Suicide Task Force (2009) found that from 2003 to 2007 the rate of suicide among males ages 25 to 64 was 14.0 per 100,000 in the general population and 15.1 among police officers. Sadly, the suicide rate among correctional officers was 34.8, illustrating the magnitude of the problem among this population. The report concluded that among criminal justice professionals—police and correctional officers—the major obstacles to effectively dealing with stress include the following:

- A law enforcement culture that emphasizes strength and control
- Negative perceptions and distrust of mental health providers
- The stigma associated with seeking help
- General concerns about the loss of privacy
- Embarrassment and shame

The police culture is a double-edged sword for those officers who choose to immerse themselves in it. It can bolster an officer's ability to physically protect themselves, but it can just as effectively cause their emotional decline.

POST-TRAUMATIC STRESS DISORDER (PTSD)

Post-Traumatic Stress Disorder, or simply PTSD, is most commonly the diagnosis given to criminal justice professionals suffering the debilitating effects of accumulated stress and trauma. First introduced as a psychological disorder in the third edition of the *Diagnostic and Statistical Manual of Mental Disorders* of the American Psychiatric Association (1980), a PTSD diagnosis was historically reserved for combat veterans. Until the Vietnam War, it was referred to in various ways, including *shell shock, battle fatigue*, and even the *thousand-yard stare*. Then in the first edition of the *Diagnostic and Statistical Manual of Mental Disorders* (1952) it was identified as *stress response syndrome*.

A key catalyst for the eventual inclusion of PTSD in the DSM was the Vietnam War and the emotional problems experienced by a large number of veterans in its aftermath. Most of the research done on the disorder has involved Vietnam vets. In 1983 Congress authorized a significant study of the effects and prevalence of PTSD among this population of military veterans. The study was conducted by the National Vietnam Veterans Readjustment Study (NVVRS), and the results reported in *Trauma and the Vietnam War Generation: Report of Findings from the National Vietnam Veterans Readjustment Study* (1990). The study found that 30 percent of all male veterans of the Vietnam War, and 26 percent of all female veterans, had suffered the effects of PTSD during their post-war lives.

Eventually PTSD came to be understood in terms of anyone suffering the effects of trauma and stress; crime victims, victims of natural and man-made disasters, adult survivors of child abuse, and those professionals—police and correctional officers among them—who respond to such events, and who face their own stressful circumstances for an extended duration of time. The effects of PTSD can be disabling, and oftentimes can prevent the individual from leading a normal life. Many police and correctional officers attempt to "white-knuckle" their way through each day on the job, but as their ongoing stress continues to accumulate, their likelihood of an eventual disabling breakdown only increases.

In terms of symptoms, those associated with PTSD can be grouped into three different categories. **Re-experiencing symptoms** includes a recurrence of thoughts and dreams related to the traumatic event(s) that led to the disorder's onset. It becomes impossible for the individual to block the recurrent images, and the images act to increase the stress fueling the disorder. Many police officers who have been in shootings have reported recurrent dreams in which the shooting is relived, only with more negative outcomes. Common examples that have been reported include the officer being unable to pull the trigger of their duty weapon, or actually shooting, only to watch the bullet dribble out the end of the barrel and fall to the ground. In the most extreme cases, these recurrent images may even begin to impact the individual's perception of the actual event.

Avoidance symptoms and **hyperarousal symptoms** are typically the two categories that are most easily noticed by supervisors and co-workers. The avoidant officer will start to isolate him or herself, and will appear to lose interest in their job. They may start cutting corners and leaving things undone. Their physical appearance may become disheveled. Even those previously known for taking pride in their appearance may start showing up for work in unclean and wrinkled uniforms. There was a time when this type of behavior was collectively referred to as **officer burnout**. Then the consensus was that all the officer really needed was a little time away from the job, or perhaps some time off the street. Unfortunately though, when PTSD sets in, time off will have no bearing on its intensity, and may even aggravate the problem by causing the officer to isolate themselves even further.

In contrast to the avoidant officer, the hyperaroused officer may display symptoms that appear just the opposite. This is the officer who snaps while on the job. They may become abusive, and disregard procedures or their professional ethics. They may also appear paranoid, especially toward their supervisors or other investigative agencies they perceive as being out to get them. The hyperaroused officer is always on edge, and will appear to have gotten little sleep between shifts. Their judgment typically becomes significantly impaired, and citizen complaints against them are likely. Unlike the avoidant officer, the hyperaroused officer may continue to socialize with other officers, and may do so while sacrificing much-needed sleep. They may also drink frequently and to excess, and may even become abusive to their fellow officers, or worse, to their own family.

POLICE TRAUMA SYNDROME

One of the problems with applying a PTSD diagnosis to police and correctional officers is that while they do suffer its effects and demonstrate the same classic symptoms as military veterans and those who have experienced some type of trauma, they don't always meet the DSM-IV-TR criteria for the diagnosis. For example, criterion A requires that the traumatic event to which the person is exposed elicits a response that involves "intense fear, helplessness, or horror." Police officers tend not to have these types of reactions. They are trained to separate their emotions from the traumatic event and respond behaviorally. In fact, they see so much trauma, and suppress their emotions so often that they may never experience the types of responses required by criterion A. They simply continue to use whatever coping strategies that work best for them, even the unhealthy ones. So in many cases, police and correctional officers simply do not fit the diagnostic criteria for PTSD.

In order to more effectively describe and diagnose the traumatic stress response of police officers, Dr. Beverley Anderson (2002), clinical director of the Metropolitan Police Employee Assistance Program in Washington, D.C., developed the diagnostic term, **Police Trauma Syndrome**. Although not found in the current DSM-IV-TR, the criteria established by Dr. Anderson for this syndrome is more relevant to police and correctional officers than the PTSD diagnosis. The benefit, of course, to establishing this new diagnostic category is that it allows criminal justice professionals suffering the effects of accumulated stress, but who do not meet the DSM-IV-TR criteria for PTSD, to get the services they need by applying a diagnosis, something quite necessary, unfortunately so, in the American system of mental health services.

This is not to suggest that police and correctional officers never experience acute PTSD, as described in the DSM-IV-TR. In fact, they oftentimes do. The correctional officer held hostage by inmates, the officer who survives being shot in the line of duty, or one who witnesses the death of a fellow officer, can all lead to acute PTSD. However that diagnosis does not lend itself well to the problem of accumulated stress. Many times the symptoms of PTSD present themselves years later after an event—not necessarily a traumatic one—causes the syndrome to become manifest. As formulated, the Police Trauma Syndrome diagnosis does cover this type of delayed onset.

According to Dr. Anderson, PTS oftentimes develops over time and follows a particular sequence of stages. These stages are as follows:

• *The Rookie stage:* During this stage the new officer tries to maintain an ideological view of the job. They are mission-oriented, and feel as though they can have a positive impact on the world around them. But very quickly they begin to see and experience things that tend to chip away at that ideology. They may begin to realize that the very public they risk their lives protecting has little appreciation for their efforts. Or they may find that their own supervisors have little appreciation for them. At the same time they see people at their very worst, and are forced to confront death and injury on a regular basis, sometimes in the most unspeakable ways. They are shocked by what they see, and suddenly they are adopting various defense mechanisms to avoid risking their reputation among their co-workers by showing any emotional response.

At this stage they simply repress the emotions. It is an ineffective long-term strategy, but it allows the officer the time to hopefully become desensitized to the sights and sounds of police work. It is during this stage when they also start to isolate themselves from non-police officers, whom they perceive as being incapable of truly understanding what they and their co-workers experience on a daily basis. This isolation justifies their emotional repression, but makes the problem ultimately worse by causing the repressed emotions to accumulate until they are externalized in the form of an acute stress reaction. It is also during this stage when the officer may even isolate from their own spouse and other family members.

• *The John Wayne stage:* During this stage the officer no longer simply represses their emotional response, but instead acts out just the opposite, a defense mechanism referred to as **reaction-formation**. For example, a new officer who is greatly troubled by the brutality they encounter at a particular homicide scene may simply remain quiet while they go about doing their job. They fight to avoid any emotional reaction that the other officers may potentially see. In contrast, an officer in the John Wayne stage may deal with the brutality by cracking jokes about the bodies. They divert an emotional response by externalizing an opposite response. This is quite common among veteran police officers. Their self-perceived emotional shortcomings are defended against by being tough and unemotional.

Like the Rookie stage, the danger with this coping strategy is that the lack of an emotional outlet will only facilitate the toxic accumulation of stress. In fact, the longer the officer is in this stage, the harder it becomes to continue to repress the emotional response. An officer who attempts to portray an image of toughness may become abusive. They may start drinking more often, and will likely have complaints filed against them at some point for their substandard performance on the job. During this stage they may also become abusive toward their spouse, as they project their own bad qualities onto them.

- ***The Professional stage:***   Eventually an officer will lose the need to conform tightly to the police identity. They no longer have anything to prove after years on the job, and may take on a very professional demeanor. Now nothing gets an emotional response from them. They remain calm and collected, even when confronting the most traumatic of circumstances. Rather than repress their emotions, or keep them hidden by acting out their opposite, they now simply deny them. During the professional stage the coping strategy is to dehumanize, depersonalize, and desensitize. Whereas an officer in the Rookie stage might just remain quiet or turn away from the body at a homicide scene, and the officer in the John Wayne stage might make light of the situation, an officer in the Professional stage does not even see a human being lying on the floor in their own dried blood. It is simply a body, and one to which they make no emotional connection.

- **THE ROOKIE STAGE**
Represses feelings in order to meet the expectations of the police culture.

- **THE JOHN WAYNE STAGE**
Reaction-formation used to portray strength and invincibility. Stress begins to accumulate with no viable outlet.

- **THE PROFESSIONAL STAGE**
Denial of emotions. Officer portrays mature and professional demeanor. For benefit of younger officers.

- **THE BURNOUT STAGE**
No longer able to effectively defend against effects of accumulated stress. Job performance begins to suffer, as well as personal life.

- **THE PTS STAGE**
Officer is no longer able to function in the job and is in need of intervention.

FIGURE 15.2 Stages of Police Trauma Syndrome.

In the Professional stage the officer begins to lose their ability to be sympathetically aroused, and they lose their connections to other people on any type of emotional level. They may become distant with their spouse, as even that emotional connection begins to diminish. They employ the denial strategy in any situation, professional or personal, that may elicit an emotional response. By the time they reach this stage it is likely they have repressed years of vicarious, professional, and occupational stress. Denial is their last ditched effort to fight off the delayed effects of accumulated stress. They may appear as healthy as those officers who have chosen healthy strategies for dealing with the stress of the job, but those officers passing through the Professional stage of PTS are not healthy in this same sense. In some ways they are ticking time bombs. They haven't chosen healthy strategies. To simply desensitize themselves to the trauma happening around them is entirely ineffective. Denying an emotional response from being externalized is like plugging a pressure valve. The pressure doesn't go away. Rather, it looks for another way out. And if it cannot find another escape route, it will create its own.

• **The Burnout stage**:   We all have a fairly good idea of what it means to be *burned out*. Regardless of what type of job a person is in, burnout is a possibility. For those officers progressing toward PTS, this stage represents a breakdown in the defense mechanisms that have been employed to deal with the stress of the job. Their self-image begins to suffer, and they lose all sense of mission and purpose. They may become contemptuous toward others, including their fellow officers. At this stage they are at risk of lashing out at people. Following the rules is no longer important, and they even become less concerned for their own personal safety.

The Burnout stage is when intervention is critically important. The police officer must be pulled off the street and the correctional officer out of the cell block when their supervisor recognizes the symptoms of this stage. It is even more critical if the officer has been involved in a traumatic incident in the past. When an officer enters this stage, the changes are usually quite noticeable. They isolate themselves and lose interest in practically everything, and not just things related to the job. They may become pessimistic to the extreme, or even nihilistic about their personal life circumstances. On the job they may start making critical mistakes, some of which may endanger them or their fellow officers.

• **Police Trauma Syndrome**:   The final stage, according to Dr. Anderson, is full-blown PTS. During this stage the officer is simply no longer able to function in their job. This stage represents a complete breakdown of the internal mechanisms used to maintain a state of psychological equilibrium. At this stage the officer is in crisis. Some of the symptoms may include:

- Sleep difficulties
- Anxiety attacks and depression
- Flashbacks and intrusive thoughts
- Extreme mood swings with periods of rage
- Social isolation
- Drug and alcohol abuse
- Suicidal ideation

At this point it becomes difficult for the officer to contain their internal crisis. It will impact nearly every aspect of their life. Their marriage will suffer, as will their relationship with their children and close friends. They may even act out in ways that will justify their lowered self-image, such as engaging in criminal activity or abruptly quitting their job. It is during this stage when so many officers choose to take their own lives rather than face their troubles head-on. For many it becomes an uncontained crisis. Their internal emotional problems only magnify and exacerbate any other personal problems they may be experiencing, and they find themselves in an emotional free-fall they cannot pull themselves out of no matter how hard they try.

PROACTIVE INTERVENTION

There was a time when the only thing an officer could count on following a traumatic event was a supervisor telling them to take a day off and then get back to work. There were no services provided to head off the effects of traumatic stress, nor was it recognized that the effects of accumulated stress can be devastating for an officer. Oftentimes it is a traumatic event, stressful in its own right, which unleashes the negative effects of years of accumulated stress and repressed emotional response.

The Critical Incident Stress Debriefing

In 1974, Jeff Mitchell, a training coordinator for keep Maryland, recognized the problem of traumatic stress among medical first-responders and developed the **Critical Incident Stress Debriefing** (McEvoy, 2010). This method is now one of the most popular proactive stress intervention programs currently being used with criminal justice professionals following a traumatic event. The debriefing is intended to allow a safe forum for those exposed to a traumatic event to describe and externalize their emotions before they rely on unhealthy defense mechanisms to cope with the stress. The debriefing is peer-driven, meaning the debriefing team is composed in part of other criminal justice professionals who have been through similar circumstances, and who share their own experiences during the session. The other members of the team are mental health professionals who are specially trained to deal with police and correctional officer stress, and who can make an immediate referral if they believe any person participating in the group is a danger to themselves or others. Typically the debriefing team attempts to meet with all officers involved in the incident in a group setting within 72 hours following the event. This gives them time to disengage from the event by writing reports, talking to supervisors, or finishing their investigation. It also gives officers time to re-engage their families, which is so critically important.

The debriefing consists of seven important steps (Mitchell, 1983). First is the *introduction phase*. This is the time when the team members attempt to create a safe atmosphere for the officers. They introduce themselves, and share with the group how they became part of the team. This is especially important for the peer members of the team. It immediately sends the message to the participating officers that they are not alone, and that it is safe to discuss the event and their personal experiences in the group.

Another very important duty of the team members during the introduction phase is to assure officers of the confidential nature of the debriefing. Most importantly, the officers are told that no notes are taken, and that anything said in the group stays in the group. Officers need to be assured that their words will not be shared with a supervisor who might want to discipline them, or with a defense attorney who might use their words against them in court. Others in the group are also reminded to keep what is said in the group completely confidential.

The second stage of the debriefing is the *fact phase*. During this phase, each officer in turn discusses the facts of their involvement in the event. Initially they avoid discussing how they felt, but rather the details of their involvement on a cognitive level. This stage serves two important functions. First, it allows the participants to begin talking about the event, and by keeping it on a cognitive level, to do so in a non-threatening way. Additionally, it is not uncommon after a traumatic event for the responders to that event to question and second guess themselves. They may feel they somehow failed to perform up to standards, or perhaps that they could have done things differently to create a better outcome. By having each person share the facts of their involvement, it can provide reassurance that things were done properly. It may even provide factual information that one or more of the participants were not previously aware of. For example, a veteran officer involved in a police shooting may be harboring negative thoughts toward a rookie officer

- **THE INTRODUCTION PHASE**
- **THE FACT PHASE**
- **THE THOUGHT PHASE**
- **THE REACTION PHASE**
- **THE SYMPTOM PHASE**
- **THE TEACHING PHASE**
- **THE RE-ENTRY PHASE**

FIGURE 15.3 Stages of the Debriefing.

for not shooting a suspect when he felt the rookie had the opportunity to do so, only to find out during the fact phase of the debriefing that the rookie had other officers in his line of fire at the time and could not safely make the shot. Another example is the officer who second-guesses his performance after unsuccessfully doing CPR on the victim of a terrible traffic accident. Perhaps he questions whether he performed the procedure correctly. During the debriefing, another officer, trained in CPR, describes how he assisted with the procedures, and how the first officer did everything correctly.

So the fact stage is a way to get everyone on the same page by bringing some clarity to the event. It serves to jog each participant's memory, and also helps to fill in the gaps to provide the participants a bigger picture of what actually happened, allowing them to better evaluate their own performance. Finally, by doing this factual sharing, when it comes time to discuss the emotional impact of the event, truly at the heart of any critical incident debriefing, the participants can focus entirely on their emotions without being distracted by trying to recall certain aspects of the event.

The third phase of the debriefing is the *thought phase*. Now the participants begin to explore their own internal processes during the event. They are asked to describe what went through their minds as the event was unfolding. This sets the stage for a discussion of the emotional aftermath of the event. It personalizes the event for each of the participants, and allows them to begin reacting in other than a professional, non-personal way, as when they are simply reciting factual details. Criminal justice professionals are quite adept at not allowing their personal feelings and emotions to creep into their professional persona. But those feelings and emotions are certainly there. By addressing their internal experience of the event first on a cognitive level ("what went through your mind?"), this opens a doorway into the all-important emotional dimension ("how did you feel?").

During the *reaction phase* the participants now address their emotions during and after the event. This oftentimes is the most threatening part of the debriefing for a lot of criminal justice professionals. Consequently, participants are not asked to share their feelings unless they choose to do so. The group is asked to discuss the aspects of the event that were most troubling or traumatic for them. This phase is a time of self-exploration, and a time for participants to confront some of the emotional aspects of the event they may have successfully repressed or dealt with in some other dysfunctional way. It also provides the group leader an opportunity to see who in the group may be having more difficulty with the event than the others. A participant who sits in silence, unresponsive to what the others are saying, may be suffering the early effects of a stress reaction, or even the onset of PTSD. By noticing this type of behavior, the group leader can approach the individual at a later time to discuss their emotional reaction to the event away from the other participants.

During the *symptom phase* participants discuss any changes that have taken place as a result of the event. They may be experiencing headaches, or perhaps they are unable to sleep, or maybe the event keeps replaying over and over in their mind. The briefing has shifted from the cognitive to the emotional, and now it shifts back to the cognitive, as participants describe in a rational way what they have experienced. During this time the group leaders take the opportunity to educate the group on the immediate and delayed effects of stress. This gives the participants the opportunity to learn that what they may be experiencing is normal in such situations. Many times, especially with criminal justice professionals, people try to keep hidden the effects of stress out of fear of being seen by their peers as weak. By having the group leaders explain to the participants what to expect, and that such things are normal, will allow the participants to better process and externalize the energy connected to the stress in healthy and productive ways.

The next phase of the debriefing is the *teaching phase*. It is during this phase when the participants learn about coping strategies, the telltale signs of stress-related illness, and community resources that are available if and when they are needed. During the previous phases the goal is to get the participants talking. During this phase the debriefing team does most of the talking, and they attempt to relate their discussion as much as possible to the various emotions and symptoms expressed during the meeting. Oftentimes during this stage the debriefing team will provide the participants handouts to facilitate learning, and also the names, numbers, and locations of the various community resources where they can seek assistance if needed. These resources may include counseling centers, Alcoholics Anonymous groups, chaplains, and private practitioners specializing in stress-related illness.

The final phase of the debriefing is the *re-entry phase*. This is a way to gain closure before ending the meeting. During this phase any final questions are answered, and the session is summarized by team members. It is also important that the team members advise the participants that they will stick around after the meeting in case any of them wish to talk alone. The participants are thanked for their attendance, and their willingness to talk openly about their thoughts and emotions is reinforced with positive strokes. Finally, the participants are encouraged to continue processing the traumatic event in healthy ways, and the meeting is concluded.

This seven-step debriefing is now used widely throughout the American criminal justice system. It is not without its detractors however. Critics have suggested that the critical incident stress debriefing (CISD) has never been shown to demonstrate efficacy as a strategy for reducing or preventing post-traumatic stress (Van Emmerik et al., 2002). Mayou, Ehleers, and Hobbs (2000) evaluated the three-year outcome of traffic accident victims who underwent a CISD during their hospitalization by comparing their progress to a control group who did not participate in the debriefing process. They actually found that the intervention group had a significantly worse outcome. They had more psychiatric, physical, and social problems than the control group. Both groups were randomly selected at the outset. Everly (2000) has suggested that the CISD process actually impedes the natural recovery mechanisms that most people develop over their lifetime, and that the debriefing could potentially worsen the effects of stress in high-risk individuals.

Litz, Gray, Bryant, and Adler (2002) have suggested that mandatory attendance at a CISD is inappropriate, and that a better approach is to pre-screen individuals to determine which among those exposed to the trauma are at risk for developing PTSD. Those not at risk are better served by allowing them to employ their own natural resilience to deal with any latent stress from the event. Mayou, Ehleers, and Hobbs (2000) are in agreement, and suggest that the CISD may "pathologize" what are otherwise normal reactions, and thus undermine a person's natural resilience.

Psychological First Aid

In response to the lack of research supporting the use of the CISD, another intervention model, **Psychological First Aid (PFA)**, has evolved to become for many agencies the desired strategy for intervening in the immediate aftermath of trauma. Although primarily geared toward disaster response, it is now being employed in many other types of situations, including throughout the criminal justice system in the aftermath of critical incidents. Uhernik and Husson (2009) have outlined four basic standards that the principles and techniques of PFA meet:

- PFA is consistent with research evidence on risk and resilience following trauma.
- PFA is applicable and practical in field settings.
- PFA is appropriate for all developmental levels across the lifespan.
- PFA is culturally informed and adaptable.

Unlike the CISD, PFA is not about having participants verbalize their feelings and emotions in the hope that it will serve a cathartic purpose and buffer the individual against the onset of PTSD. Rather, PFA is more about providing the individual various types of support while they process the trauma-related stress in ways they normally would do. The process has three main goals: 1) re-create a sense of safety, 2) reestablish meaningful social connections, and 3) reestablish a sense of efficacy, or a belief in oneself that they performed appropriately, and that they are capable of returning to their jobs and conducting themselves in a professional manner in spite of the trauma they were exposed to.

For criminal justice professionals in the aftermath of a critical incident, re-creating a sense of safety may involve a number of things. It may involve the engagement of a mental health professional to assess in a non-intrusive way the immediate need, if any, for psychological or medical assistance. It may involve simply comforting the individual, and being there to listen if they need to talk. It is a supportive engagement on the part of the person conducting the PFA in the immediate aftermath of the event to help stabilize the individual emotionally, and to assist in meeting any basic needs that may have been created by the event. There is nothing mandatory about it, as is often the case with the CISD, nor is it scripted. Rather, it is tailored to the individual or group for whom the PFA is being carried out. It may be something as serious as facilitating an officer's admission to a mental health facility, or as practical as providing an officer's spouse a ride to the police station or some other location. Again, the goal is to create a sense of safety by meeting the immediate needs of the officers following the traumatic event.

The second goal of PFA is to help the participants reestablish meaningful social connections. One of the things the CISD typically does not do is involve the family members of the participants. Family can be one of the most powerful factors in an officer's recovery from traumatic stress. They provide the necessary support and comfort to allow the individual's natural resilience to channel the stress into healthier behaviors that will have a healing effect. People who have experienced trauma, perhaps even more so criminal justice professionals, are at risk of isolating themselves, even from their families. This only speeds up and magnifies the effects of the stress, especially when their isolation then causes new tensions to arise within the individual's family. PFA engages the family immediately after the event. Once the participants are reconnected with their loved ones, group leaders may then schedule joint sessions to discuss the effects of traumatic stress, and the signs to look for when latent stress is impacting the participant in a negative way.

The final goal is to reestablish in the participant a sense of personal and professional efficacy, or, stated another way, a sense of worthiness. Many criminal justice professionals question themselves following their involvement in a critical incident. Stress can very easily distort their perception of the event. They may think they failed to perform as expected, when in fact they may have done things properly and to the best of their ability under the circumstances. During PFA, group leaders recognize the participants' efforts, and provide positive reinforcing messages that they performed their duties properly and commendably. They also encourage the participants to return to a normal duty schedule, and to continue to support and assist one another. Finally, participants are provided information about community resources that are available in the event they are needed, and a three-month follow-up meeting is scheduled.

The research on psychological first aid has been more promising. Litz, Gray, Bryant, and Adler (2002) argue that although PFA is not to be considered a therapeutic approach, it is an appropriate initial intervention to bolster the participants own resiliency. They argue that PFA must be used in conjunction with a screening process to identify those who are at risk of developing PTSD, and that a more extensive therapeutic approach must be employed for those individuals. Additionally, a number of studies support the benefits of reconnecting with family immediately after a traumatic event (Durkin and Bekerian, 2000; Orner and King, 1999; Ormerod, 2000). And according to Phillips and Kane (2006), PFA should be considered "best practice" for intervention with first responders following a traumatic event.

Chapter Summary

Crisis comes in many forms, but in essentially every case someone responds who is charged with containing and de-escalating the matter. Those who do respond tend to see people at their very worst. They see people in deep despair who want only to end their lives. Some intend to make a final statement of their anger by taking as many innocent people with them as possible. Crisis responders routinely take on the impossible task of convincing the mentally drained and the mentally ill that things will get better when in all likelihood they will not. When others run away from floods, hurricanes, and large-scale terrorist attacks, those who respond to crisis run toward them. And sometimes in their efforts to save lives they may even be forced to take a life.

Those who respond to crisis are oftentimes the last in line to get the help they need. Many never ask for it. Others do their very best to hide the fact that they need it. Humans are simply not biologically programmed to experience great amounts of trauma. It

has a cumulative effect on the physical and psychological systems that allow us to process the resulting stress. It truly is a bit of a paradox that the more those systems are activated, the less effective they become. Eventually people may find themselves in a hole from which they simply cannot free themselves. It is then when they are in danger of employing unhealthy coping strategies. Some may turn to drugs and alcohol to deaden the pain. Others may become abusive or engage in criminal conduct. And sadly, after spending perhaps years endeavoring to save the lives of others, some may simply choose to end their own.

The good news through all of this is that the criminal justice system is becoming more adept at preparing young professionals for the inevitable stress that will come once they are done with their training and are on the job. And once they are, they will find that in essentially every corner of the criminal justice system in America, whether in its largest cities or its remotest rural areas, there are dedicated intervention specialists standing by to mobilize when those who spend their days and nights helping others find themselves in need of help. America's criminal justice system is the finest in the world. It attracts the best that America has to offer to fill its ranks. It is critical that those ranks remain psychologically strong and healthy as society continues to evolve to become ever more complex in its problems, ever more astray in its quest for macro solutions, and ever more susceptible to the deleterious effects of trauma in its many forms.

Key Terms

Vicarious stress
Occupational stress
Professional stress
Post-Traumatic Stress
   Disorder

Re-experiencing
   symptoms
Avoidant symptoms
Hyperarousal symptoms
Officer burnout

Police Trauma Syndrome
Reaction-formation
Critical Incident Stress Debriefing
Psychological First Aid
   (PFA)

Discussion Questions

1. Discuss our cultural view of police officers, and how this has contributed to the development of the modern police culture.
2. Discuss the importance of a correctional officer's demeanor to their personal safety on the job, and how their demeanor may impact their ability to deal with stress in a healthy manner.
3. Discuss the suicide rates among police officers as outlined in the chapter, and give some reasons why you believe those rates are as high as they are.

GLOSSARY

acquaintance rapes Sexual assaults committed by persons who have had previous contact with their victims, and who are known to their victims

active listening A method of communicating with someone in crisis that focuses the dialogue on the person in crisis, and communicates to them the responder's empathic awareness of their situation

active shooter An uncontained crisis in which a perpetrator has already used deadly force against innocent victims and continues to have unrestricted access to additional victims

active victim Assaults in which the victim is a participant in the situation that led to their assault

active waiting A strategy for de-escalating a prison riot by waiting out the rioters while refusing to negotiate and significantly increasing their discomfort

acute violence phase After a period of rising tensions, when the abuser again becomes violent toward their victim

adapted child The part of our personality that seeks attention and acceptance from others as a child does from their parents

adrenal glands Endocrine glands located on top of the kidneys that secrete hormones in response to stress

adult ego state The part of our personality that is rational and engaged in problem solving. It operates on a cognitive level rather than on an emotional one.

alarm stage The initial response of the human body to the introduction of a stressor. Its purpose is to increase the level of energy in order to confront the stressor.

altruistic suicide Suicide resulting from excessive social integration

Amber alert A regional alert carried out through various media sources and communication devices notifying the general public of a child abduction, and any available descriptive information about the child, the abductor, and the vehicle used

American Red Cross The nation's premier emergency response organization

amygdala Sub-component of the Limbic system in the brain responsible for processing memory and emotional reactions

anger suicide Suicide resulting either from self-contempt or a desire to use their final act to exact revenge on another person

anger-driven panic Mass panic caused by the collective anger of a particular group over some event or circumstance, and oftentimes intensified by opportunists who join in as the crisis unfolds

anomic suicide Suicide resulting from an imbalance of social means and needs

anxiety disorders A grouping of psychological disorders marked by extreme and debilitating fear or worry, and a general and persistent uneasiness about life

apocalyptic belief A belief that the world will meet a violent and unavoidable end

arraignment A short hearing during which the judge advises a defendant of the charges against them

autonomic nervous system (ANS) The internal physiological system that controls the body's visceral functions, such as heart rate, breathing, and digestion

avoidance symptoms Behaviors related to isolating oneself from family, friends, and activities following the experience of a traumatic event

battered spouse syndrome Pattern of behavior typically demonstrated by victims of spousal abuse, to include feelings of helplessness, social isolation, high levels of anxiety, and self-blame

bipolar disorder Psychological disorder marked by extreme mood fluctuations from manic to depressive, with periods of normal functioning in between

blind entry A tactic in which the tactical entry team breaches an opening and immediately enters the location

breach Creating an opening in a structure to allow entry by the tactical team

breach and hold When an entry team breaches an entry point in an armed suspect's location, but then maintains their position rather than entering immediately

briefing phase The third phase of a tactical operation during which all team members and supporting personnel are fully briefed on the plan and any contingencies

buttonhook entry A tactical entry in which team members stack on both sides of the doorway and enter simultaneously, each moving to a point of domination on the same side of the room in which they entered

child ego state The part of our personality that includes the array of emotional responses developed during childhood primarily through parent-child interactions

Clara Barton Civil War nurse who founded the American Red Cross

cognitive dissonance A state of psychological tension created by two concurrent and competing thoughts or beliefs

collective mind The character, attitudes, and norms of a particular group that develop when the participants in that group no longer act as individuals

combination entry A tactical entry in which team members stack on the same side of the doorway and then enter, alternating between half of the team moving to a point of domination on the same side of the room in which they entered through the doorway, and the other half moving across the entry point to the opposite side of the room

communications officer The member of the hostage response team responsible for establishing and maintaining a method of communication with the hostage-taker

contact team The first team to enter an active shooter situation. Their objective is to make immediate contact with the shooter and de-escalate the crisis through the use of force if necessary.

contagion When the collective emotions and attitudes of a group spread rapidly to influence and propagate the process of deindividuation among individual participants

contagious shooting When one police officer firing their weapon induces other officers to fire even before they are consciously aware of the reasons for their use of deadly force

containment Preventing a crisis from worsening or spreading to other people, entities, or systems

contamination When a person's ability to think rationally and mediate internal conflict is disproportionately influenced either by their parent or child ego state

CRH (corticotrophin-releasing hormone) A neurotransmitter responsible for stimulating the pituitary gland in response to stress

crisis Any event in which our systems of control, both internal and external, become stressed to the point of dysfunction, requiring third-party intervention to regain control and return those systems to a state of equilibrium

crisis intervention team (CIT) Specially trained police and correctional officers who respond to crises involving the mentally ill, and who endeavor to de-escalate such matters without the use of force if possible and to connect those in crisis with needed mental health resources

crisis responders Those tasked with containing and de-escalating crisis in its earliest stages

crisscross entry A type of tactical entry in which officers stack on both sides of the doorway, and then enter by crossing each other's path and moving to the opposite side of the room

Critical Incident Stress Debriefing A structured proactive intervention following a traumatic event during which the participants are encouraged to share and discuss with a group of peers and mental health professionals their thoughts and emotions as the event was unfolding

critical parent That part of our personality that demands, directs, orders, and seeks compliance

crossed transaction A unit of communication in which the exchange is neither predictable nor anticipated because one or more of the participants is communicating from an ego state other than the one to whom the other participants are directing their words

cult A group of like-minded individuals who abandon their participation in the dominant culture and adopt an alternative belief system and a separatist worldview

custody-related hostage-taker A hostage-taker who takes their own children hostage after being ordered to relinquish custody to the other parent or a guardian

cutting the crowd Strategic placement of police and security personnel to channel a large group of people into smaller groups in order to lessen the probability of adverse or panicked group behavior

cycle of violence Repeated acts of violence followed by periods of relative calm often present in an abusive relationship

date rape Forced sexual contact by one party on a date when the victim is either non-consenting or incapacitated by drugs or alcohol and unable to consent

date rape drug A type of drug commonly used to incapacitate another person for the purpose of sexually exploiting them

death immersion The feeling of being unable to escape death after long-term exposure to violence and its aftermath

debriefing phase The final phase of a tactical operation during which the team members discuss the operation and ways to improve their methods and tactics

de-escalate Bringing a crisis to an end and returning those involved to a state of equilibrium

defense mode A pattern of behavior typically demonstrated by an offender who perceives themselves in control, but sees certain variables as being unpredictable

defensive-criminal hostage-taker A hostage-taker who does not intend to take a hostage at the outset of their crime, but who does so when unexpected circumstances cause a panicked situation

deindividuation When an individual is so influenced by the actions of a group that they lose their sense of self-identity and adopt the character of the group, thus diminishing personal responsibility for their actions as members of the group

deliberate entry A high-risk entry in which the entry team searches and secures each individual room or area of the target location before moving on to the next

delusions Irrational or unrealistic beliefs

depression Psychological disorder marked by a persistent and debilitating loss of interest in everyday activities, feelings of worthlessness, and a negative view of the future

despair suicide Suicide resulting either from chronic emotional or physical suffering

desperation-driven panic Mass panic caused by a collective sense of desperation over a loss of resources and sustenance

determinism A belief held by a cult that they are on the side of good, and thus predestined to survived the world's apocalyptic end as victors

direct negotiations Negotiations that take place directly between prison staff and those inmates designated by the rioters to speak on their behalf

disabling techniques A level of force in which an officer employs techniques designed to physically incapacitate a suspect, rendering them incapable of resisting further the officer's commands

disconfirmed expectancy The psychological state experienced by members of a cult following a failed prophecy by its leader

disordered Those whose motivation for joining a cult is directly influenced by mental illness or a history of social isolation

domestic abuse Abuse occurring between family members or intimate partners that can include physical violence, psychological abuse, sexual assault, social isolation, deprivation, intimidation, or economic coercion

domestic-defensive hostage-taker A hostage-taker who prevents family members from departing the premises when the police arrive for reasons unrelated to the hostage crisis

dualism A belief that the world is a battle ground between good and evil forces

dynamic entry A high-risk entry in which the entry team moves rapidly toward its target, leaving a containment team the task of securing rooms and any unarmed persons they pass along the way

egoistic suicide (Durkheim) Suicide resulting from too little social integration

egoistic suicide Suicide resulting from a depreciation of the person's self-concept

endocrine system Internal physiological system that is composed of a series of glands that secrete the hormones responsible for regulating bodily functions

enforcer Cult members whose duties include protecting the group's leader and ideology from both internal and external threats

engagement The initial approach to a person in crisis by a responding officer

epinephrine and norepinephrine Neurotransmitters released in response to stress that prepare the body for "fight or flight"

equilibrium A balance of opposing forces within a system

eros The part of our personality that instinctively compels us to seek pleasure

escape mode A pattern of behavior typically demonstrated by an offender who sees their situation as predictable, and themselves as having no control over the outcome

evacuation team Responsible for assisting those attempting to escape an active shooter scene

excitement-driven panic Mass panic caused by a contagious excitement following a particular event or circumstance that has the capacity to turn violent if not contained

execution phase The fourth phase of a tactical operation during which actual entry is made to the target location

exhaustion stage When the human body becomes unable to adapt to an ongoing stressor, and the energy needed to mediate the stressor becomes depleted

exocrisis A crisis event that has, and will continue to, spread by indirect influence to other previously unaffected people and systems unless contained

exosystem Influences beyond a child's immediate environment that impact their development indirectly

experiential-thinking mode Thinking that is automatic, rapid, and effortless. Information is processed below the level of conscious awareness

external systems of control Systems external to the individual that are tasked with maintaining public order

fatalistic suicide Suicide resulting from oppressive social conditions

fear-driven panic Mass panic caused by a fear-eliciting event or circumstance that intensifies when those affected perceive a lack or loss of control by the police and other relief agencies

Federal Emergency Management Agency (FEMA) The federal agency responsible for providing domestic disaster relief

fight, flight, or freeze response The three potential outcomes of a person's psychophysiological response to stress

final statement hostage-taker A hostage-taker who takes a hostage out of frustration over a matter in their personal lives, and who intends to use the event to express their frustration with the intention of bringing the crisis to a violent end if the matter is not resolved to their benefit

fleeing felon rule A now disallowed rule that identified specific crimes for which a police officer could shoot to kill a suspect attempting to flee custody

force continuum The continuum of force used by police and correctional officers in response to an increasing threat level

forensic hypnosis A type of hypnosis employed by the police to assist victims and witnesses in their efforts to recall details of a crime

General Adaptation Syndrome A three-stage model, proposed by Dr. Hans Selye, illustrating the body's reaction to stress

grievance riot A riot that erupts in protest to the lifestyle and living conditions forced upon the inmates

hallucinations False perceptions that lack any corresponding sensory input, or a failure to perceive things that are in the person's sensory experience

homeostasis A state of internal psychophysiological stability maintained by the coordinated efforts of the body's regulating systems

honeymoon phase Following an abusive episode, when the abuser attempts to convince their victim that things are better

hooking An effort by one person in a transaction to lead the other into a desired ego state in order to effect a parallel transaction

hyperarousal symptoms An agitated and stressed pattern of behavior demonstrated by a person following the experience of a trauma event

hyper-individuation When extreme fear or desperation leads an individual to develop a singular focus on their own needs and expectations, even to the detriment of other people

hypothalamus The part of the brain that links the nervous system to the endocrine system via the pituitary gland

hypothalamus-pituitary-adrenal axis The complex interaction of physiological systems that prepares the body for "fight or flight" in response to stress

identification The process by which we form a positive connection to those we perceive to be like us in some way

identity-formation The process an adolescent goes through to figure out the type of person they want to be

ideologue Those whose primary motivation for joining a cult is a belief in the message being offered by the cult and its leader

imminence A belief that the end of the world is near

impasse The point at which negotiations in general, or on a specific issue, are no longer possible due to one side or the other not being willing to change their position

intelligence officer The member of the hostage response team responsible for uncovering as much information as possible about a hostage-taker and their hostage(s) as the crisis unfolds

internal systems of control Cognitive and emotional coping mechanisms employed by the individual to alleviate stress and return to a state of equilibrium

intervention Actions taken to restore a system to a state of equilibrium

involuntary commitment The commitment of a suicidal person by police, family members, or the courts, to a psychiatric facility for a period of observation and evaluation

isolation or dehumanization of hostages When a hostage-taker takes steps to avoid any personal connection to their hostage

issue ultimatum When the negotiating team announces to the inmates that a particular issue will no longer be discussed

lethal force A level of force in which an officer intends to kill the suspect, or they take an action that could reasonably be expected to result in death

level of optimal performance The point at which a person's ability to meet the psychophysiological demands of a situation is at its maximum strength

locus of control The extent to which an individual feels they are in control of the events that affect them

macrocrisis A crisis event that has the capacity to initiate a chain reaction of new crisis events, and to spread to other previously unaffected people and systems even in geographic regions far removed from the original crisis

macrosystem The broader cultural and social values and norms that impact a child's development

mediator An objective third-party negotiator with no vested interest in anything but the peaceful resolution of the crisis

Memphis Model A program implemented by the Memphis Police Department in which specially trained police officers and community mental health professionals work together to respond to, de-escalate, and remediate crises involving the mentally ill

mesocrisis A crisis event that has, and will continue to, spread by direct contact to other previously unaffected people and systems unless contained

mesosystem A confluence of microsystems that interact to shape a child's psychosocial development

microcrisis A crisis event that is limited to a single individual or family and their immediate environment

microsystem People and institutions that directly influence a child's psychosocial development

mission-oriented hostage-taker A hostage-taker who takes a hostage out of the delusional belief that their actions will disrupt a perceived danger facing society or any subcomponent of it

mood disorders Grouping of psychological disorders marked by abnormal and debilitating emotions

moral regulation The rules and norms established by society that sets limits on what are otherwise limitless and destructive desires

multifactor ecological theory A theory that suggests that no single factor can explain why victims of abuse remain in their abusive relationships, and that they do so for a combination of personal, situational, social, political, and cultural reasons

natural child The part of our personality that is spontaneous and selfish, and concerned primarily with seeking gratification with little concern for rules or boundaries

negative critical parent The part of our personality that is authoritarian, inconsistent, overly harsh, and critical

New World Order cults Cultic groups that endeavor to reorder society in a way that is more consistent with their beliefs and practices

non-lethal compliance techniques A level of force in which an officer attempts to gain physical control of a suspect without causing disabling injury

nurturing parent That part of our personality that is empowered by the positive values we learn as children

occupational stress Stress resulting from the demands, risks, and dangers experienced while on the job

offender-centered Response by police in which the primary concern is the identification and arrest of the offender

offense mode A pattern of behavior typically demonstrated by an offender who perceives themselves in control and their circumstances predictable

one-on-one-plus-one detail A courtroom security protocol that requires that a detained defendant be escorted by a security officer, with a second security officer assigned to secure the courtroom

order of protection A court order that prevents an individual from having any contact with the petitioner of the order, typically a spouse or significant other

panic mode A pattern of behavior typically demonstrated by an offender who perceives themselves as having no control over their situation, and the circumstances as being unpredictable

parallel transaction A unit of communication in which the parties involved clearly understand the other's meaning and intention

paranoid hostage-taker A hostage-taker who suffers from the delusional belief that they are in some type of danger, and who takes a hostage as a way of bargaining their way out of this perceived danger

parasympathetic nervous system The sub-component of the ANS that inhibits the body's internal mechanisms to return it to a homeostatic state

parent ego state That part of our personality that serves as a storehouse for the rules, imperatives, and values we were taught as children, primarily by our parents

passive victim Assaults in which the victim has no prior connection to their attacker

passive waiting A strategy for de-escalating a prison riot by simply waiting out the rioters while continuing to be responsive to their daily needs and necessities

passive-apocalyptic cult Cultic groups that believe the end of the world is imminent, and whose activities, which are mostly passive in nature, are carried out in preparation for this final event

passive-frustration hostage-taker A hostage-taker who takes a hostage out of frustration over a matter in their personal lives, and who has no intentions of harming their hostage or bringing the crisis to a violent end

passive-ideological hostage-taker A hostage-taker who takes a hostage in order to draw attention to a political issue or cause, and who has no intention of harming their hostage or ending the crisis violently

perception The process by which we interpret and understand stimuli in our sensory field

perimeter team Responsible for securing a perimeter around an active shooter scene to cut off escape routes and prevent innocent people from entering the shooter's field of fire

persecuted chosen The belief held by a cult that they are persecuted by evil forces due to their chosen status before God of some other divine entity

pituitary glands Endocrine glands located in the base of brain that secrete the necessary hormones to maintain the body's homeostatic state

planning phase The second phase of a tactical operation during which the team members develop an approach and entry plan based on available intelligence

Police Trauma Syndrome A cluster of symptoms demonstrated by police and correctional officers suffering the effects of accumulated stress

positive critical parent The part of our personality that is authoritative, demanding, fair, and consistent

Post-Traumatic Stress Disorder (PTSD) A psychological diagnosis given to those whose lives have been significantly disrupted by some traumatic event or series of events, rendering them incapable of leading a normal and productive life

power riot A riot resulting from one group attempting to gain power and control over another group, or a faction within the same group

pragmatist Those whose primary motivation for joining a cult is the lifestyle it offers rather than the message it espouses

predictability The degree to which the variables and events associated with a crisis can be anticipated

prediction error A signal emitted by the brain when an expected outcome is in conflict with the actual outcome

prejudicial Circumstances that could potentially taint a jury's perception of any aspect of a trial or defendant

pretrial inmate An offender who remains in custody awaiting trial

prevention Steps taken to prevent a similar crisis from occurring under similar conditions in the future

primary negotiator The member of the hostage response team designated to negotiate with a hostage-taker once contact is made

proactive suicide Suicide resulting from the person's desire to benefit in some manner themselves, others, or society as a whole

probable cause evidence A reasonable amount of suspicion, supported by circumstances strong enough to justify a belief that certain facts must be true

professional stress Stress resulting from the organizational-logistical demands of the job

psychological entrapment theory The theory that suggests victims of domestic abuse remain in their abusive relationships because they believe they have too much invested to leave

Psychological First Aid (PFA) A proactive intervention following a traumatic event during which emotional and material support is provided to those exposed to the trauma while they process the event and allow their own resilience to mediate the resulting stress

public circulation system The area of a courthouse in which the general public can move about freely and unescorted once they have passed through a security checkpoint

public information officer The member of the hostage response team responsible for the dissemination of information about the crisis to the public and press

purposeful-criminal hostage-taker A hostage-taker who takes a hostage as a planned element of their crime

rape A word traditionally used to describe the act of sexual assault

rape kit A prepackaged and sealed set of instruments used specifically for the collection of evidence in a rape case

rape shield laws Laws designed to protect the privacy of a rape victim, and to prevent past sexual conduct from being a factor in the trial of her attacker

rape trauma syndrome A set of both short- and long-term symptoms commonly seen in rape victims

rapport A relationship of trust established by a responding officer with a person in crisis

rational-thinking mode The manner in which we normally process information when not under stress; conscious, deliberate, and analytical

reaction-formation When an individual attempts to repress an unwanted emotion by acting out and externalizing its opposite

reasonableness The legal standard for determining when the use of deadly force against a suspect is reasonable under the Constitution

re-experiencing symptoms The experience of reliving a traumatic event and having intrusive thoughts related to that event that seem beyond the person's ability to control

relationship-related hostage-taker A hostage-taker who holds a spouse or significant other hostage following a breakup or divorce

remediation Returning people, entities, and systems to their pre-crisis condition once de-escalation has been achieved

rescue team The second team to enter an active shooter scene. Their objective is to rescue the wounded as the contact team moves forward toward the shooter.

resistance stage The human body's attempt to adapt to an ongoing stressor by resisting its negative effects and returning to a state of homeostasis

response modes Distinct patterns of behavior in response to stress

restricted circulation system The area of a courthouse that is off-limits to the general public unless allowed admittance through additional security checkpoints

retaliation riot A riot that erupts in response to the actions of prison staff or other inmates during which retaliation is a goal

riot squad maneuver An announced unhurried, but assertive entry by a tactical team into the area of a prison riot with the goal of de-escalating the crisis by dividing, isolating, and intimidating the rioters

risk assessment profiles An effort to anticipate the risk of violence occurring during a court proceeding based on various factors related to that hearing

rules of engagement Guidelines that determine the collective demeanor the police will take toward the citizenry, and the level of force they are willing to use or threaten to use in response to the actions of the group

ruse The use of pretense to entice an armed suspect to move to a location that will allow either for an arrest or an appropriate level of force against the suspect to de-escalate the crisis

sally port A secure garage which serves as the entry point for bringing prisoners into a courthouse

salvation through conflict/enemy eradication A belief held by a cult that their perseverance in the face of conflict and persecution is preparatory for salvation

Schilling incident Any occurrence that has the capacity to set off panic-driven behavior once a crowd has gathered

scouting phase The first phase of a tactical operation during which team members conduct surveillance of the target location to gather important information about the physical structure

secondary negotiator The member of the hostage response team designated to negotiate with a hostage-taker if the primary negotiator is not able to continue

secure circulation system The area of a courthouse that is reserved for the movement of prisoners, and is off-limits to all but security personnel

self-efficacy The belief in oneself that they are capable of succeeding and achieving a desired goal

sentenced inmate An offender who has been convicted and sentenced to prison

Sir Robert Peel The father of modern policing who established the London Metropolitan Police Department, the world's first modern police force

slicing the pie A tactic used by tactical entry teams that allows them to scan the inside of a room from a safer location outside the entry point

social integration The extent to which an individual or group of individuals feels accepted as full members of the larger society

social-isolationist cults Cultic groups that isolate themselves from mainstream society in order to live some type of alternative lifestyle free of interference

speciocentric Concerned with, specific to, or in the interest of a single species

spiral of amplification When the apocalyptic beliefs of a cult are confirmed and reinforced by the confrontational actions of the police and other authorities

spontaneous riot A riot with no particular objective or pre-planning that breaks out following an action by prison staff or inmates that provokes aggressive behavior among the larger inmate population

statutory rape Non-violent and consenting sexual contact between an adult and an adolescent under the age of 18

Stockholm syndrome A psychological change that takes place in a hostage during the period of their captivity that can lead to the formation of a positive emotional bond with their captor

stranger rapes Sexual assaults committed by persons unknown to their victims

stress A person's felt response to psychophysiological disequilibrium

suicide by cop When an individual forces the police to use deadly force against them rather than taking their own life

surrender ritual The manner in which a hostage-taker desires to end the crisis peacefully

surround and call out Setting up a tight perimeter around the location of an armed suspect and demanding that they exit the location with their hands in plain view

symbolic riot A riot resulting from the inmates' desire to demonstrate symbolically either their protest against, or their support of some cause or individual

sympathetic nervous system The sub-component of the ANS that excites and stimulates the body's internal mechanisms to produce energy in response to a stressor and prepare the body for "fight or flight"

tactical intelligence Information obtained during the course of a crisis that has value to those planning containment and de-escalation measures

tactical strike An unannounced rapid entry by a tactical team into the area of a prison riot with the intent of de-escalating the crisis through the use of force

tactical team A specially trained team of police officers armed with military-style weapons and tactics who respond primarily to high-risk situations where the use of force is anticipated to contain and de-escalate the crisis

team leader A police officer with sufficient rank who commands the crisis negotiation team during a hostage crisis

team psychologist The member of the hostage response team responsible for providing other team members expert opinion during the crisis about the behavior of the hostage-taker, as well as the hostages

tension-building phase Following a period of relative calm, when a stressor causes the abuser to again become agitated toward their victim

Thanatos The part of our personality that instinctively compels us to seek calm and emotional equilibrium

third-party negotiations Negotiations in which a neutral third party acts as a go-between for all demands and counter-demands made by either inmates or prison administrators

thought disorders A grouping of psychological disorders marked by disordered and incoherent thought patterns

threat of force Level of force in which a police officer attempts to gain the compliance of a suspect by overtly threatening the use of physical force or a weapon against them in response to continued non-compliance

throw phone A telephone with a dedicated line the communications officer attempts to get in the hands of the hostage-taker in order for the primary negotiator to begin negotiations

tonic immobility A state of physical or psychological paralysis caused by the person's inability to mediate extreme stress

trance-state A state of heightened relaxation during hypnosis

transaction A verbal or nonverbal communicative exchange occurring between two or more people

Transactional Analysis A theory of communication first introduced by Dr. Eric Berne in 1958

traumatic bonding theory The theory that suggests an abused woman is attracted to, and remains in a dysfunctional relationship as a result of forming an insecure attachment to abusive or neglectful parents as a child

ulterior transaction A unit of communication between two or more people with an apparent message on one level, but a hidden message on another

Urie Bronfenbrenner Author of Ecological Systems Theory, one of the most important theories in developmental psychology

use of force A police officer's use of weapons and techniques designed to control, incapacitate, or kill a suspect threatening or perpetrating violence against the officer or other people

use-of-force ultimatum A demand that rioting inmates surrender control immediately or else be subjected to an overwhelming amount of force as the riot squad moves in

verbal commands Commands used by the police in an effort to gain the compliance of a suspect

verbal will When a hostage-taker begins discussing final arrangements and the disposition of their personal belongings during the course of a hostage crisis

vicarious stress Stress resulting indirectly from the interaction with or observation of others in crisis

victim A person subjected to injurious circumstances beyond their control or provocation

victim-centered Response by police in which the primary concern is the welfare of the victim

violent-apocalyptic cults Cultic groups that believe the end of the world is imminent, and that they have the ability to help usher in the end through some violent action

violent-ideological hostage-taker A hostage-taker who takes a hostage in order to draw attention to a political cause or issue, and who fully intends to bring the event to a violent end if their demands are not met

waiting solution A strategy for de-escalating a prison riot by simply waiting out the inmates until they grow tired, hungry, or lose interest

zoning A type of courthouse design in which points of entry and routes of movement throughout the building are kept separate for the general public, judges, and any detained prisoners

REFERENCES

"3 Die in Chicago Courthouse Shooting," *L.A. Times*, July 21, 1992.

"Seven Inmates Hospitalized after Riot at Folsom Prison," msnbc.com, August 27, 2010. Retrieved March 7, 2011, from http://www.msnbc.msn.com/id/38890984/ns/us_news-crime_and_courts/t/seven-inmates-hospitalized-after-riot-folsom-prison/

Aamodt, M. G., & Werlick, N. A. (1999). "Police Officer Suicide: Frequency and Officer Profiles," *FBI Conference on Suicide and Law Enforcement*. Quantico, VA.

AMBER Alert. (n.d.). "Frequently Asked Questions," U.S. Department of Justice, *Office of Justice Programs*. Retrieved August 25, 2011, from www.amberalert.gov/faqs.htm

Anderson, B. J. (2002). "The Echoes of Violence in the Police Family," *Gift From Within*. Retrieved October 2, 2010, from http://www.giftfromwithin.org/html/Police-Stress-Management.html

Artwohl, A. (2002). "Perceptual and Memory Distortions during Officer-Involved Shootings," *FBI Law Enforcement Bulletin*, 18–23.

Asken, M. J. (2005). *Mindsighting: Mental Toughness Skills for Police Officers in High Stress Situations*. Camp Hill, PA: Dr. Michael Asken.

"Aum Shinrikyo Cult and the Tokyo Subway Sarin Gas Attack." (2009). *Facts and Details*. Retrieved March 1, 2011, from www.factsanddetails.com/japan.php?itemid=596&catid=16&subcatid=183

Aveni, T. J. (2006, December). "Contagious Fire: Fact & Fiction," *The Police Policy Studies Council*. Retrieved November 23, 2009, from www.theppsc.org/staffviews/aveni/contagious.fire.htm

Bandura, A. (1977). "Self-efficacy: Toward a Unifying Theory of Behavioral Change," *Psychological Review*, 84(2), 191–215. doi: 10.1037//0033-295X.84.2.191

Barchers, W. (2010, April 19). "Active Shooter Research," *Hard Tactics*. Retrieved November 5, 2010, from www.hardtactics.com

Barnett, O. W. (2000). "Why Battered Women Do Not Leave, Part 1: External Inhibiting Factors within Society," *Trauma, Violence, & Abuse*, 1(4), 343–372. doi: 10.1177/1524838000001004003

Barrick, C., Taylor, D., & Correa, E. (2002). "Color Sensitivity and Mood Disorders: Biology or Metaphor?" *Journal of Affective Disorders*, 68(1), 67–71. doi: 10.1016/S0165-0327(00)00358-X

Berne, E. (1964). *Games People Play: The Psychology of Human Relationships*. New York: Grove Press.

Black, D. (1980). *The Manner and Customs of the Police*. New York: Academic Press.

Bonner, R. (1992). "Isolation, Seclusion, and Psychological Vulnerability as Risk Factors for Suicide Behind Bars." In *Assessment and Prediction of Suicide* (pp. 398–419). New York: Guilford Press.

Bonnie, R. J., & Wallace, R. B. (2003). *Elder Mistreatment: Abuse, Neglect, and Exploitation in an Aging America*. Washington, DC: National Academies Press.

Boudreau, A. (2008, February 18). "University Shooter's Girlfriend: 'I Couldn't Believe It,'" *CNN*. Retrieved November 4, 2010, from www.cnn.com

Bracha, H. S. (2004). "Does 'Fight or Flight' Need Updating?" *Psychosomatics*, 45(5), 448–449. doi: 10.1176/appi.psy.45.5.448

Brian Nichols. (n.d.). *Wikipedia*. Retrieved March 10, 2011, from www.wikipedia.com

Brockner, J., & Rubin, J. Z. (1985). *Entrapment in Escalating Conflicts: A Social Psychological Analysis*. New York: Springer-Verlag.

Bronfenbrenner, U. (1979). *The Ecology of Human Development: Experiments by Nature and Design*. Cambridge, Mass.: Harvard University Press.

Brown, J. M., & Langan, P. A. (2001). *Policing and Homicide, 1976–98: Justifiable Homicide by Police, Police Officers Murdered by Felons*. Washington, DC: U.S. Department of Justice, Office of Justice Programs, Bureau of Justice Statistics.

Brymer, M. (2005). *Psychological First Aid Field Operations Guide*. Los Angeles: National Child Traumatic Stress Network.

Bugliosi, V., & Gentry, C. (1992). *Helter Skelter: The True Story of the Manson Murders*. London: Arrow Books.

Calhoun, F. S. (2000). *Hunters and Howlers: Threats and Violence against Federal Judicial Officials in the United States, 1789–1993*. Darby, PA: Diane Publishing.

Cannon, L. (1999). *Official Negligence: How Rodney King and the Riots Changed Los Angeles and the LAPD*. Boulder, CO: Westview Press.

Cannon, W. B. (1915). *Bodily Changes in Pain, Hunger, Fear and Rage*. New York: D. Appleton and Company.

Cassavetes, N. (Director). (2002). *John Q* [Motion picture].

Cattabriga, G., Deprez, R., Kinner, A., Louie, M., & Lumb, R. (2007). *Crisis Intervention Team (CIT) Training for Correctional Officers: An Evaluation of NAMI Maine's 2005–2007 Expansion Program* (Rep.). Biddeford, ME: Center for Health Policy, Planning, and Research, University of New England.

Charles Whitfield, Robert Anda, Shanta Dube, and Vincent Felitti. (2003). "Violent Childhood Experiences and the Risk of Intimate Partner Violence in Adults," *Journal of Interpersonal Violence, 18*, 166–185.

Cherkis, C. (2008, November 28). "A Troubled Man Needed Help. He Got Shot Instead. How Did It Happen?" *Washington City Paper*.

Children, Law, and Disasters: What We Have Learned from Katrina and the Hurricanes of 2005. (2009). Chicago: ABA Pub.

Cohen, L. D. (Ed.). (1997). *Courtroom Security Manual* (State of Minnesota, Conference of Chief Judges).

Cohn, D. A., Cowan, P. A., Cowan, C. P., & Pearson, J. (1992). "Mothers' and Fathers' Working Models of Childhood Attachment Relationships, Parenting Styles, and Child Behavior," *Development and Psychopathology, 4*, 417–431.

Compton, M. T., Neubert, B., Broussard, B., McGriff, J. A., Morgan, R., & Oliva, J. R. (2009). "Use of Force Preferences and Perceived Effectiveness of Actions among Crisis Intervention Team (CIT) Police Officers and Non-CIT Officers in an Escalating Psychiatric Crisis Involving a Subject with Schizophrenia," *Schizophrenia Bulletin*.

Conrad, M., & Jahn, T. M. (1985). "The Family Stress Team Approach in Curbing Domestic Violence," *Police Chief, 52*(6), 66–67.

Cooper, M. (1999, February 5). "Officers in Bronx Fire 41 Shots, and an Unarmed Man Is Killed," *NY Times*.

Cop Tasers 10-Year-Old Girl [Television broadcast]. (2009, November 19). In *ABC News*.

Cordner, G. W. (2006). *People with Mental Illness*. Washington, DC: U.S. Department of Justice, Office of Community Oriented Policing Services.

Correll, J., Park, B., Judd, C. M., & Wittenbrink, B. (2002). "The Police Officer's Dilemma: Using Ethnicity to Disambiguate Potentially Threatening Individuals," *Journal of Personality and Social Psychology, 83*(6), 1314–1329. doi: 10.1037//0022-3514.83.6.1314

Correll, J., Park, B., Judd, C. M., Wittenbrink, B., Sadler, M. S., & Keesee, T. (2007). "Across the Thin Blue Line: Police Officers and Racial Bias in the Decision to Shoot," *Journal of Personality and Social Psychology, 92*(6), 1006–1023. doi: 10.1037/0022-3514.92.6.1006

Court Security and the Transportation of Prisoners: A National Study: Executive Summary. (1997). Alexandria, VA: National Sheriffs' Association.

Cox, T. (1979). *Stress*. Baltimore: University Park Press.

Cox, T., & Mackay, C. (1976). *A Psychological Model of Occupational Stress*. A paper presented to the Medical Research Council. Mental Health in Industry, London, November.

"Crime Victim Compensation Program." (2011). *Office of the Illinois Attorney General*. Retrieved June 3, 2011, from www.ag.state.il.us/victims/cvc.html

"Crisis Intervention Team." (n.d.). *Memphis Police Department*. Retrieved July 13, 2010, from www .memphispolice.org

"Criticisms of Government Response to Hurricane Katrina." (n.d.). *Wikipedia*. Retrieved March 1, 2011, from www.wikipedia.com

Crowell, N. A., & Burgess, A. W. (1996). *Understanding Violence against Women*. Washington, DC: National Academy Press.

Cullen, D. (2004, April 20). "The Depressive and the Psychopath: At Last We Know Why the Columbine Killers Did It," *Slate*.

"Cult of Death." (1993, March 15). *TIME Magazine*. Retrieved January 3, 2010, from www.time.com/time/daily/newsfiles/waco/031593.html

Curran, C. (2004). "Stimulant Psychosis: Systematic Review," *British Journal of Psychiatry, 185*(3), 196–204. doi: 10.1192/bjp.185.3.196

Day of the Gun [Television broadcast]. (2002). San Francisco: KRON-4.

Delattre, E. J. (2002). *Character and Cops: Ethics in Policing.* Washington, DC: AEI Press.

Diagnostic and Statistical Manual of Mental Disorders. (1952). Washington: American Psychiatric Association, Mental Hospital Service.

Diagnostic and Statistical Manual of Mental Disorders, 2nd ed. (1968). Washington, DC: American Psychiatric Association.

Diagnostic and Statistical Manual of Mental Disorders, 3rd ed. (1980). Washington, DC: American Psychiatric Association.

Diagnostic and Statistical Manual of Mental Disorders: DSM-IV, 4th ed. (1994). Washington, DC: American Psychiatric Association.

DiPetro, S. (1999). *Fairbanks Video Arraignment Assessment* (Rep.). Anchorage: Alaska Judicial Council.

Doctor, R. M., & Shiromoto, F. N. (2009). *The Encyclopedia of Trauma and Traumatic Stress Disorders.* New York: Facts on File.

Domestic Violence: Best Practices for Law Enforcement Response (Rep.). (1998). Raleigh: North Carolina Governor's Crime Commission, Violence Against Women Committee.

"Domestic Violence Counts 2008: A 24-hour Census of Domestic Violence Shelters and Services." (2009). *The National Network to End Domestic Violence.*

Doomsday Religious Movements. (1999). Ottawa: CSIS, Requirements, Analysis and Production Branch.

Drew, C. (1999, April 1). "The Diallo Shooting: The Charges; Prosecution Opts to Bring Top Counts for Shooting," *NY Times.*

Dunford, F. W. (1992). "The Measurement of Recidivism in Cases of Spouse Assault," *Journal of Criminal Law & Criminology, 83,* 120–136.

Dunlop, J. B. (2006). "The 2002 Dubrovka and 2004 Beslan Hostage Crises: A Critique of Russian Counter-terrorism," *Soviet and Post-Soviet Politics and Society, 26.*

Durkheim, E. (1951). *Suicide, a Study in Sociology.* Glencoe, IL: Free Press.

Durkin, J., & Bekerian, D. A. (2000). *Psychological Resilience to Stress in Firefighters* (Rep.). England, UK: University of London.

Durose, M. R. (2005). *Family Violence Statistics: Including Statistics on Strangers and Acquaintances.* Washington, DC: U.S. Department of Justice, Office of Justice programs, Bureau of Justice Statistics.

Dutton, D. G., & Painter, S. L. (1981). "Traumatic Bonding: The Development of Emotional Attachments in Battered Women and Other Relationships of Intermittent Abuse," *Victimology: An International Journal, 7*(4), 139–155.

Eberhardt, J. L., Davies, P. G., Purdie-Vaughns, V. J., & Johnson, S. L. (2006). "Looking Deathworthy. Perceived Stereotypicality of Black Defendants Predicts Capital-Sentencing Outcomes," *Psychological Science, 17*(5), 383–386. doi: 10.1111/j.1467-9280.2006.01716.x

El Paso County Sheriff's Department. (2004). *Policy and Procedure Manual: Active Shooter* (Chapter 7, no. 731).

El Paso County Sheriff's Department. (2004). *Sheriff's Office Police and Procedure Manual* (Chapter 7). Colorado Springs, CO.

Eltman, F. (1997, November 18). "Student Plans Own Shooting by Officers," *Associated Press.*

Epstein, S. (1994). "Integration of the Cognitive and the Psychodynamic Unconscious," *American Psychologist, 49*(8), 709–724. doi: 10.1037//0003-066X.49.8.709

Erikson, E. H. (1968). *Identity, Youth, and Crisis.* New York: W. W. Norton.

Erikson, W. H. (Ed.). (2001). *Report of Governor Bill Owens.* Denver, CO: Columbine Review Commission.

Estrich, S. (1993, October 25). "Balancing Act," *Newsweek, 64.*

Everly, G. S. (2000). "Five Principles of Crisis Intervention: Reducing the Risk of Premature Crisis Intervention," *International Journal of Emergency Mental Health, 2*(1), 1–4.

"Ex-Postal Employee Kills Six." (2006, January 31). *BBC News.* Retrieved January 4, 2010, from www.news.bbc.co.uk/1/hi/world/americas/4665790.stm

"FAQ: Rape Shield Laws." (n.d.). *National Center for Victims of Crime.* Retrieved July 2, 2011, from www.ncvc.org/FAQ

"Federal Bureau of Investigation, Uniform Crime Reports." (n.d.). *Crime in the United States, by Volume and Rate per 100,000 Inhabitants, 1990–2009.*

Festinger, L., Pepitone, A., & Newcomb, T. (1952). "Some Consequences of De-Individuation in a Group," *Journal of Abnormal and Social Psychology, 47*(2, Suppl), 382–389. doi: 10.1037/h0057906

Festinger, L., Riecken, H. W., & Schachter, S. (1956). *When Prophecy Fails.* Minneapolis: University of Minnesota Press.

Final Report of the U.S. House of Representatives Select Bipartisan Committee to Investigate the Preparation for and Response to Hurricane Katrina (Rep.). (2006). Washington, DC: U.S. House of Representatives.

Fischbach, R. L., & Herbert, B. (1997). "Domestic Violence and Mental Health: Correlates and Conundrums within and across Cultures," *Social Science & Medicine, 45*(8), 1161–1176. doi: 10.1016/S0277-9536(97)00022-1

"Five Years Later, Katrina Deemed 'Costliest Disaster' for Insurers." (2010, September 30). *Westlaw News & Insight.* Retrieved March 1, 2011, from www.westlawnews.thomson.com

Ford, D. A. (1991). "Preventing and Provoking Wife Battery through Criminal Sanctioning: A Look at the Risks." In D. D. Knudsen & J. L. Miller (Eds.), *Abused and Battered: Social and Legal Responses to Family Violence* (pp. 191–209). New York: A. de Gruyter.

"Fort Hood Suspect Charged with Murder." (2009, November 12). *CNN.* Retrieved November 5, 2010, from www.cnn.com

Fowler, J. C., Hilsenroth, M. J., & Piers, C. (2001). "An Empirical Study of Seriously Disturbed Suicidal Patients," *Journal of the American Psychoanalytic Association, 49*(1), 161–186. doi: 10.1177/00030651010490010901

Freud, S. (1995). *The Ego and the Id: And Other Works: (1923–1925).* London: Hogarth Press.

Freud, S., & Strachey, J. (1964). *Beyond the Pleasure Principle Group Psychology: And Other Works: (1920–1922).* London: Hogarth Press.

Fuchs, C. (Producer). (2003, June 1). "44 Minutes: The North Hollywood Shootout" [Television series episode].

Geller, W. A., & Scott, M. S. (1992). *Deadly Force: What We Know: A Practitioner's Desk Reference on Police-Involved Shootings.* Washington, DC: Police Executive Research Forum.

Greene, J. R. (2006). *Encyclopedia of Police Science,* 3rd ed., Vol. 1. London: Routledge.

Guinto, J., & Batino, C. (2010, August 24). "Manila Bus Siege 'Mishandled,' Philippines Tourism Chief Says," *Bloomberg Business Week.*

Haddock, D. D., & Polsby, D. (1994). "Understanding Riots," *Cato Journal, 14*(1), spring/summer.

Hammond, S. K., & Emmons, K. M. (2004). "Inmate Exposure to Secondhand Smoke in Correctional Facilities and the Impact of Smoking Restrictions," *Journal of Exposure Analysis and Environmental Epidemiology, 15*(3), 205–211. doi: 10.1038/sj.jea.7500387

Harmening, W. (1992). *Development of a Discrimination Scale for Police Officer Cadets Using the 16PF* (Unpublished master's thesis). University of Illinois at Springfield.

Harmening, W. M. (2009, May 15). *Police Trauma Syndrome.* Address presented at Chicago Police Academy, Chicago, IL.

Harmening, W. M. (2010). *The Criminal Triad: Psychosocial Development of the Criminal Personality Type.* Springfield, IL: Charles C Thomas.

Harris, A., & Lurigio, A. (2007). "Mental Illness and Violence: A Brief Review of Research and Assessment Strategies," *Aggression and Violent Behavior, 12*(5), 542–551. doi: 10.1016/j.avb.2007.02.008

Hauser, C., & O'Connor, A. (2007, April 16). "Virginia Tech Shooting Leaves 33 Dead," *NY Times.*

Heymann, P. B. (1993). *Lessons of Waco: Proposed Changes in Federal Law Enforcement.* Washington, DC: U.S. Department of Justice.

Hoenig, A. L., & Roland, J. E. (1998). "Shots Fired: Officer Involved," *Police Chief, October, 1998.*

Holtzworth-Munroe, A., and Stuart, G. (1994). "Typologies of Male Batterers: Three Subtypes and the Differences among Them," *Psychological Bulletin, 116*(3), 476–497.

Hutson, H., Anglin, D., Yarbrough, J., Hardaway, K., Russell, M., Strote, J., Blum, B. (1998). "Suicide by Cop," *Annals of Emergency Medicine, 32*(6), 665–669. doi: 10.1016/S0196-0644(98)70064-2

Illinois Compiled Statutes, 2006. (2007). St. Paul, MN.: Thomson/West.

Intimate Partner Violence, 1993–2001. (2003). Washington, DC: U.S. Department of Justice, Office of Justice Programs, Bureau of Justice Statistics.

Janik, J. (1991). "What Value Are Cognitive Defenses in Critical Incident Stress." In J. Reese, J. M. Horn, & C. Dunning (Eds.), *Critical Incidents in Policing* (pp. 142–148). Washington DC: U.S. Department of Justice.

Judicial Council of California. (2006). *California Trial Court Facilities Standards.* San Francisco, CA.

Karmen, A. (2010). *Crime Victims: An Introduction to Victimology.* Australia: Wadsworth Cengage Learning.

Kassin, S., Markus, H. R., & Fein, S. (2007). *Social Psychology.* Boston: Houghton Mifflin.

Kelson, S. (2001). "An Increasingly Violent Profession," *Utah State Bar Journal, 14*(8).

Klineman, G., Butler, S., & Conn, D. (1980). *The Cult That Died: The Tragedy of Jim Jones and the Peoples Temple.* New York: Putnam.

Klucharev, V. (2009). "Reinforcement Learning Signal Predicts Social Conformity," *Neuron, 61*(1), 140–151.

Kohn, R. H. (1972). "The Washington Administration's Decision to Crush the Whiskey Rebellion," *Journal of American History, 59*(December), 567–584.

Krebs, Lindquist, Warner, Fisher, & Martin. (2007). *Campus Sexual Assault (CSA) Study* (Rep. No. NCJ 221153). National Institute of Justice.

Kulka, R. A. (1990). *Trauma and the Vietnam War Generation: Report of Findings from the National Vietnam Veterans Readjustment Study.* New York: Brunner/Mazel.

Kurtz, D. L., & Williams, L. S. (2008, November 12). *Work Stress and Doing Police Masculinity: Stress and Emotional Responses in the Highly Gendered Police Culture.* Address presented at Annual Meeting of the ASC in Adam's Mark Hotel, St. Louis, MO.

Kushner, H. I., & Sterk, C. E. (2005). "The Limits of Social Capital: Durkheim, Suicide, and Social Cohesion," *American Journal of Public Health, 95*(7), 1139–1143. doi: 10.2105/AJPH.2004.053314

Lang, D. (1974, November). "A Reporter at Large," *New Yorker,* 56.

Lazarus, R. S., & Folkman, S. (1984). *Stress, Appraisal, and Coping.* New York: Springer Pub.

Le Bon, G. (1895). *The Crowd: A Study of the Popular Mind,* 2nd ed. USA: Norman S. Berg.

Ledgerwood, D. M. (1999). "Suicide and Attachment: Fear of Abandonment and Isolation from a Developmental Perspective," *Journal of Contemporary Psychotherapy, 29*(1), 65–73.

Lee, S. (Director). (1999). *Summer of Sam* [Motion picture]. U.S.

Lisa McCann, I., & Pearlman, L. A. (1990). "Vicarious Traumatization: A Framework for Understanding the Psychological Effects of Working with Victims," *Journal of Traumatic Stress, 3*(1), 131–149. doi: 10.1002/jts.2490030110

Litz, B. T., Gray, M. J., Bryant, R. A., & Adler, A. B. (2002). "Early Intervention for Trauma: Current Status and Future Directions," *Clinical Psychology: Science and Practice, 9*(2), 112–134. doi: 10.1093/clipsy.9.2.112

"Man Burns Self to Death at Pentagon, Baby in His Arms Saved from Fire before Hundreds." (1965, November 3). *Washington Post.*

Marcia, J. E. (1966). "Development and Validation of Ego-Identity Status," *Journal of Personality and Social Psychology, 3*(5), 551–558. doi: 10.1037/h0023281

Martin, R., & Zimmerman, S. (1990). "A Typology of the Causes of Prison Riots and an Analytical Extension to the 1986 West Virginia Riot," *Justice Quarterly, 7*(4), 711–737. doi: 10.1080/07418829000090831

"Mass Suicides Involved Sedatives, Vodka and Careful Planning." (1997, March 27). *CNN.* Retrieved March 4, 2011, from www.cnn.com/us/9703/27/suicide/index.html

Mayou, R., Ehleers, A., & Hobbs, M. (2000). "Psychological Briefing for Road Traffic Accident Victims: Three-Year Follow-up of a Randomized Controlled Trial," *British Journal of Psychiatry, 176,* 589–593.

McEvoy, M. (n.d.). "Psychological First Aid: Replacement for Critical Incident Stress Debriefing?" *Fire Engineering.* Retrieved October 11, 2010, from www.fireengineering.com

McEwen, B. S. (2006). "Protection and Damage from Acute and Chronic Stress: Allostasis and Allostatic Overload and Relevance to the Pathophysiology of Psychiatric Disorders," *Annals of the New York Academy of Sciences, 1032*(1), 1–7. doi: 10.1196/annals.1314.001

McGaha, & Stiles. (2001). "The Florida Mental Health Act (the Baker Act): 2000 Annual Report."

McMains, M. J., & Mullins, W. C. (2006). *Crisis Negotiations: Managing Critical Incidents and Hostage Situations in Law Enforcement and Corrections.* Newark, NJ: Matthew Bender.

McVeight, K. (2010, February 19). "Police Rape Response Officers Will Be Trained in Psychology," *The Guardian.*

"Memphis Police Are under Fire after a Bloody Siege." (1983, January 31). *TIME Magazine.*

Mertin, P., & Mohr, P. B. (2000). "Incidence and Correlates of Posttraumatic Stress Disorder in Australian Victims of Domestic Violence," *Journal of Family Violence, 15,* 411–422.

Milgram, S. (1974). *Obedience to Authority: An Experimental View.* New York: Harper & Row.

"Military Psychiatry: Preparing in Peace for War." (2000). In F. D. Jones, M.D. (Ed.), *Textbooks of Military Medicine* (1st ed., pp. 271–277). Department of the Army.

Miller, L. (2005). "Hostage Negotiation: Psychological Principles and Practices," *International Journal of Emergency Mental Health, 7*(4), 277–298.

Miller, L. (2006). *Practical Police Psychology: Stress Management and Crisis Intervention for Law Enforcement.* Springfield, IL: Charles C Thomas.

Miller, L. (2007, May 22). "Hostage Negotiations: Psychological Strategies for Resolving Crises," *Policeone.com.* Retrieved December 15, 2010, from www.policeone.com

Mills, K. C. (2005). *Disciplined Attention: How to Improve Your Visual Attention When You Drive.* Chapel Hill, NC: Profile Press.

Mitchell, J. T. (1983). "When Disaster Strikes: The Critical Incident Stress Debriefing Process," *Journal of Emergency Medical Services, 8*(1), 36–39.

Moose, C. A. (2003). *Three Weeks in October: The Manhunt for the Serial Sniper.* New York: Signet.

"Morrison's Sacrifice Remembered." (2005, January 5). *Vietnam News.* Retrieved October 5, 2011, from vietnamnews.vnagency.com.vn/showarticle.php?num=06WAR010505

Mullins, W. (2003). "The Effects of Caffeine and Caffeine Withdrawal/Deprivation on Hostage Negotiator Performance," *Journal of Police Crisis Negotiations, 3*(2), 39–60. doi: 10.1300/J173v03n02_06

Nally, J. (Producer). (2007). *The North Hollywood Shootout* [Television broadcast]. In *National Geographic.*

Nark, J. (2010, May 8). "Incident Shows Cops Need Training to Deal with the Mentally Ill," *Philadelphia Daily News.*

"Nation: What Happened to Our Men?" (1980, February 18). *TIME Magazine.*

National Elder Abuse Incidence Study: Final Report. (1998). Washington, DC: National Center on Elder Abuse.

Neil Weiner, Donald Harris, Frederick Calhoun, Victor Flango, Donald Hardenbergh, Charlotte Kirschner, Thomas O'Reilly, Robert Sobolevitch, and Bryan Vossekuil, N. A. (2000). "Safe and Secure: Protecting Judicial Officials," *Court Review, 36*(4), 26th ser.

New Jersey Police Suicide Task Force Report. (2009). Trenton, NJ: New Jersey Office of the Attorney General.

Noesner, G. W., & Webster, M. (1997). "Intervention: Using Active Listening Skills in Negotiations," *Law Enforcement Bulletin.*

Ochberg, F. (1978). "The Victim of Terrorism: Psychiatric Considerations," *Studies in Conflict & Terrorism, 1*(2), 147–168. doi: 10.1080/10576107808435404

Ochberg, F. (2005, April 8). "The Ties That Bind Captive to Captor," *L.A. Times.*

Oldham, K. (2009). "WTO Meeting and Protests in Seattle (1999)—Part 2." *HistoryLink.org.* Retrieved March 1, 2011, from www.historylink.org

Ormerod, J. (2000). *Exposure to Occupational Violence in the Emergency Services: An Investigation into Psychological Factors* (Unpublished master's thesis). University of Hull.

Orner, R. J., & King, S. (2000). "The Search for a New Evidence Base for Early Intervention after Trauma." In *Third World Congress of Psychotraumatology.* Melbourne, AU.

Osofsky, J. (1999). "The Impact of Violence on Children," *The Future of Children: Domestic Violence and Children, 9*(3), 33–49.

Parson, E. A. (1994). "Inner City Children of Trauma: Urban Violence Traumatic Stress Response Syndrome (U-VTS) and Therapists' Responses." In J. P. Wilson & J. D. Lindy (Eds.), *Countertransference in the Treatment of PTSD.* New York: Guilford Publications.

"Patrolman Robert Hester." (n.d.). *Officer Down Memorial Page*. Retrieved October 14, 2010, from www.odmp.org/officer/6450-patrolman-robert-s.-hester

Payne, B. K. (2001). "Prejudice and Perception: The Role of Automatic and Controlled Processes in Misperceiving a Weapon," *Journal of Personality and Social Psychology*, 81(2), 181–192. doi: 10.1037//0022-3514.81.2.181

Perrou, B. (2001). "Crisis Intervention: Suicide in Progress," *FBI National Academy Associates Magazine*, 3(4).

Petroski, W. (2009). "FBI Infiltrated Iowa Anti-War Group before GOP Convention," *Des Moines Register*. Retrieved September 23, 2010, from www.desmoinesregister.com/article/20090517/news/905170341

Phillips, S. B., & Kane, D. (2006). "Guidelines for Working with First Responders (Firefighters, Police, Emergency Medical Service and Military) in the Aftermath of Disaster," *American Group Psychotherapy Association*. Retrieved June 4, 2010, from www.agpa.org/events/index.html

Pina, A., Ortiz, C. D., Gottschall, A. C., Costa, N. M., & Weems, C. (2008). "Social Support, Discrimination, and Coping as Predictors of Posttraumatic Stress Reactions in Youth Survivors of Hurricane Katrina," *Journal of Clinical Child & Adolescent Psychology*, 37(3), 564–574.

"Prison Gangs." (n.d.). *U.S. Department of Justice: Organized Crime and Gang Unit*. Retrieved November 19, 2010, from www.justice.gov/criminal/gamgunit/gangs/prison.html

Reavis, D. J. (1995). *The Ashes of Waco: An Investigation*. New York: Simon & Schuster.

Reiterman, T., & Jacobs, J. (1982). *Raven: The Untold Story of the Rev. Jim Jones and His People*. New York: Dutton.

Remsberg, C. (1986). *The Tactical Edge: Surviving High-Risk Patrol*. Northbrook, IL: Calibre Press.

Reuland, M., Schwarzfeld, M., & Draper, L. (2009). *Law Enforcement Response to Mental Illness: A Guide to Research-Informed Policy and Practice* (Council of State Governments Justice Center). New York.

Romano, A. T. (1981). *Transactional Analysis for Police Personnel*. Springfield, IL: Charles C. Thomas.

Rosegrant, S., & Falkenrath, R. (2000). *The Flawed Emergency Response to the 1992 Los Angeles Riots*. Cambridge, MA: John F. Kennedy School of Government.

Rotter, J. B. (1954). *Social Learning and Clinical Psychology*. New York: Prentice-Hall.

Rotter, J. B. (1990). "Internal Versus External Control of Reinforcement: A Case History of a Variable," *American Psychologist*, 45(4), 489–493. doi: 10.1037//0003-066X.45.4.489

San Jose Police Shoot, Kill Knife-Wielding Man [Television broadcast]. (2009, May 11). In *CBS News*.

Sapolsky, R. M. (2004). *Why Zebras Don't Get Ulcers/Robert M. Sapolsky*. New York: Times Books.

Saunders, D. G. (1992). "A Typology of Men Who Batter: Three Types Derived from Cluster Analysis," *Journal of Orthopsychiatry*, 62(2).

Scanlon, J. (2001). "Active Shooter Situations: What Do We Do Now?" *The Police Marksman*, XXVI (4).

Scanlon, J. J. (2005). "Dynamic Entries: Lessons Learned," *Tactical Response, March-April, 2005*.

Schelling, T. C. (1960). *The Role of Theory in the Study of Conflict*. Santa Monica, CA: Rand.

Seattle Police Department. (n.d.). *The Seattle Police Department after Action Report: World Trade Organization Ministerial Conference, Seattle Washington November 29-December 3, 1999* (p. 41).

Seligman, M. E. (1975). *Helplessness*. San Francisco, CA: W.H. Freeman.

Seligman, M. E., & Maier, S. F. (1967). "Failure to Escape Traumatic Shock," *Journal of Experimental Psychology*, 74(1), 1–9. doi: 10.1037/h0024514

Selye, H. (1956). *The Stress of Life*. New York: McGraw-Hill.

Shaffer, D., Scott, M., Wilcox, H., Maslow, C., Hicks, R., Lucas, C. P., Greenwald, S. (2004). "The Columbia Suicide Screen: Validity and Reliability of a Screen for Youth Suicide and Depression," *Journal of the American Academy of Child & Adolescent Psychiatry*, 43(1), 71–79. doi: 10.1097/00004583-200401000-00016

Shastri, K., & Wald, H. (2004). *An Evaluation of Video Preliminary Arraignment Systems in Pennsylvania* (Rep.). Pittsburg, PA: Pennsylvania Commission on Crime and Delinquency.

Shenon, P. (1996, May 17). "His Medals Questioned, Top Admiral Kills Himself," *NY Times*.

Sherman, L. W., & Berk, R. A. (1984). *The Minneapolis Domestic Violence Experiment*. Washington, DC: Police Foundation.

Sherman, L. W., & Cohn, E. G. (1987). *Police Policy on Domestic Violence, 1986: A National Survey*. Washington, DC: Crime Control Institute.

Siegel, J. A., & Williams, L. M. (2001). *Risk Factors for Violent Victimization of Women: A Prospective Study: Final Report*. Washington DC: National Institute of Justice.

Siegel, L. J. (1998). *Criminology*, 6th ed. Belmont, CA: Thomson/Wadsworth.

Solomon, R. M., & Horn, J. M. (1986). "Post-Shooting Traumatic Reaction: A Pilot Study." In J. T. Reese & H. A. Goldstein (Eds.), *Psychological Services for Law Enforcement*. Washington DC: U.S. Government Printing Office.

Sparger, J. R., & Giacopassi, D. J. (1992). "Memphis Revisited: A Reexamination of Police Shootings after the Decision," *Justice Quarterly*, 9(2), 211–225. doi: 10.1080/07418829200091341

Staff writer. (2005, September 2). "Military Due to Move into New Orleans," *CNN*. Retrieved February 1, 2011, from www.cnn.com/2005/weather/09/02/katrina.impact.html

Staff writer. (2005, September 3). "Police Chief: Urban Warfare Slowed New Orleans Rescue," *Newsmax Media*. Retrieved February 1, 2011, from www.newsmax.com/archives/ic/2005/9/3/102146.html

Staff writer. (2005, September 10). "Police in Suburbs Blocked Evacuees, Witness Report," *NY Times*.

Stamm, B. H. (2002). "Measuring Compassion Satisfaction as Well as Fatigue: Developmental History of the Compassion Satisfaction and Fatigue Test." In C. R. Figley (Ed.), *Treating Compassion Fatigue*. New York: Brunner-Rutledge.

Stone, G. (2001). *Suicide and Attempted Suicide*. New York: Carroll & Graf.

Stonewalled, Still Demanding Respect: Police Abuses against Lesbian, Gay, Bisexual and Transgender People in the USA. (2006). London: Amnesty International.

Strentz, T. (1991, September). "13 Indicators of Volatile Negotiations," *Law and Order*, 39(9), 135–139.

"Suicide: Facts at a Glance." (n.d.). *Centers for Disease Control*. Retrieved January 1, 2011, from www.cdc.gov/violenceprevention/pdf/suicide_datasheet-a.pdf

Temple, S. (1999). "Functional Fluency for Educational Transactional Analysts," *Transactional Analysis Journal*, 29(3), 164–174.

"The 1973 McAlester Prison Riot and Fire." (n.d.). *Oktrooper.com*. Retrieved October 21, 2010, from www.oktrooper.com/bigmac.html

"The Duluth Model on Public Intervention." (n.d.). *Duluth Domestic Abuse Intervention Project*. Retrieved April 8, 2011, from www.theduluthmodel.org

The Task Force on Court Security Report to the Chief Judge and Chief Administrative Judge. (2005). Albany, NY: New York State Unified Court System.

Tobias, M. L., & Lalich, J. (1994). *Captive Hearts, Captive Minds: Freedom and Recovery from Cults and Abusive Relationships*. Alameda, CA: Hunter House.

Tomaka, J., Blascovich, J., Kelsey, R. M., & Leitten, C. L. (1993). "Subjective, Physiological, and Behavioral Effects of Threat and Challenge Appraisal," *Journal of Personality and Social Psychology*, 65(2), 248–260. doi: 10.1037//0022-3514.65.2.248

"Tracking the Katrina Diaspora." (2006). *NPR*. Retrieved September 12, 2011, from www.npr.org/news/specials/katrina/oneyearlater/diaspora

Tyuse, S. (2006). *Year 1 Evaluation of the Crisis Intervention Team (CIT) Program of Greater St. Louis* (Rep.). St. Louis: Saint Louis University School of Social Work.

Uhernik, J. A., & Husson, M. A. (2009). "Psychological First Aid: An Evidence Informed Approach for Acute Disaster Behavioural Health Response." In G. R. Walz, J. C. Bleuer, & R. K. Yep (Eds.), *Compelling Counseling Interventions*. Alexandria, VA: American Counseling Association.

Ursin, H., Baade, E., & Levine, S. (1978). *Psychobiology of Stress: A Study of Coping Men*. New York: Academic Press.

U.S. Department of Justice, Federal Bureau of Investigation. (2007). *Law Enforcement Officers Killed and Assaulted, 2006*.

"U.S. House, Bipartisan Committee to Investigate the Preparation for and Response to Hurricane Katrina." (2006). *A Failure of Initiative* [H.R. Rept. 377 from 109 Cong.].

Useem, B. (1995). *Resolution of Prison Riots.* Washington, DC: U.S. Department of Justice, Office of Justice Programs, National Institute of Justice.

Useem, B., & Kimball, P. (1989). *States of Siege: U.S. Prison Riots, 1971–1986.* New York: Oxford University Press.

Utah State Courts. (1987). *Utah Judicial System Master Plan for Capital Facilities.*

Van Poppel, F., & Day, L. H. (1996). "A Test of Durkheim's Theory of Suicide—Without Committing the 'Ecological Fallacy,'" *American Sociological Review, 61*(3), 500–507.

Vanemmerik, A., Kamphuis, J., Hulsbosch, A., & Emmelkamp, P. (2002). "Single Session Debriefing after Psychological Trauma: A Meta-analysis," *The Lancet, 360*(9335), 766–771. doi: 10.1016/S0140-6736(02)09897-5

Vetter, S. M., & Kosinski, Jr., F. A. (2000). "Work-Stress Burnout in Emergency Medical Technicians and the Use of Recollections," *Journal of Employment Counseling, 27,* 216.

Violence and the Family: Report of the American Psychological Association Presidential Task Force on Violence and the Family. (1996). Washington, DC: American Psychological Association.

Violence in the Workplace, Risk Factors and Prevention Strategies (1996). National Institute for Occupational Safety and Health (Bulletin 57).

"Virginia Dept. of Criminal Justice Services." (1999). *Sample Procedures: Prisoner Transport.*

Vitanza, S., Vogel, L. C., & Marshall, L. L. (1995). "Distress and Symptoms of Posttraumatic Stress Disorder in Abused Women," *Violence and Victims, 10,* 23–34.

Vonk, K. (2004). "Heart Rate as It Relates to Police Performance under Stress," *Ann Arbor Police Department.*

Walker, L. E. (1984). *The Battered Woman Syndrome.* New York: Springer Pub.

Walker, L. E. (1991). "Post Traumatic Stress Disorder in Women: Diagnosis and Treatment of Battered Woman Syndrome," *Psychotherapy, 28*(1), 21–29.

Walker, L. E. (1995). "Understanding Battered Woman Syndrome," *Trial, 31*(2), 30–37.

Wambaugh, J. (1973). *The Onion Field.* New York: Delacorte Press.

Wambaugh, J. (1987). *The Choirboys.* New York: Dell Pub.

Weiner, N. A., Harris, D. J., Calhoun, F. S., Flango, V. E., Hardenbergh, D., Kirschner, C., O'Reilly, T., Sobolevitch, R., & Vossekuil, B. (2000). "Safe and Secure: Protecting Judicial Officials," *Court Review, 36*(4), 26th ser.

Weiss, J. M. (1972). "Psychological Factors in Stress and Disease," *Scientific American, 226*(6), 104–113. doi: 10.1038/scientificamerican0672-104

White, R. J. (2000). "Implications of Personality Profiles for Batterer Treatment," *Journal of Interpersonal Violence, 15.*

Whitfield, C., Anda, R., Dube, S., & Felitti, V. (2003). "Violent Childhood Experiences and the Risk of Intimate Partner Violence in Adults," *Journal of Interpersonal Violence, 18,* 166–185.

Williams, C. (2010, March 16). "Racial Tensions Cited in Report of Prison Riot in Chino: Changes Underway at Facility," *L.A. Times.*

Wilson, M. (2006, November 27). "50 Shots Fired, and Experts Offer a Theory," *NY Times.*

"Witnessing Domestic Violence: The Effect on Children." (2002). *American Academy of Family Physicians.* Retrieved August 20, 2011, from www.aafp.org/afp/2002/1201/p2052.html

Zimbardo, P. G. (2007). *The Lucifer Effect: Understanding How Good People Turn Evil.* New York: Random House.

Zoris, Rim, Rad, & Tsuang. (2007). *Overview of Methamphetamine-Induced Psychotic Syndromes.* UCLA Semel Institute for Neurosciences and Human Development.

INDEX

Page numbers followed by "*f*" indicate figure.

1. True

2. adult = adult - transaction

3. X wrong de-escaluation

4. X wrong True Correct answer false

5. True

6. X wrong true Correct answer false

7. Motives

8. true

9. X wrong true Correct answer false

10. 1 message

11. long pauses

12. Megative Nurturing Parent wrong X

13. X wrong True correct false

14. Comtamination

15 false

16 true

17 Parnel transaction wrong

18. wrong & Manipulative transation

19. true

20. wrong false correct true

21. adult contaminates parent wrong

22 Nuturing Parent wrong

23. false wrong it's true

24. Crossed transaction

25 true wrong false right